100 YEARS of BRODIES WITH HAL ROACH

100 YEARS OF BRODIES WITH HAL ROACH:

The Jaunty Journeys of a Hollywood Motion Picture and Television Pioneer

by Craig Calman

BearManor Media

2014

100 Years of Brodies with Hal Roach:
The Jaunty Journeys of a Hollywood Motion
Picture and Television Pioneer

For information, address:

BearManor Media
P. O. Box 71426
Albany, GA 31708

bearmanormedia.com

Typesetting and layout by John Teehan

Published in the USA by BearManor Media

ISBN—1-59393-577-3
978-1-59393-577-1

Table of Contents

Acknowledgments

THANKS TO: Richard W. Bann, Randy Skretvedt, Dave 'Lord' Heath, Ned Comstock & Staff, including Tony Casanova Rettenmaier, Gavin Fink, Emily Kulaga, Stephen Helstad, Matthew Ivan and Giulia Corda, USC Cinematic Arts Library; Lynn Nashorn & Staff, National Archives at Riverside; Jim Jarvis, Jason Rosenberg, Eleanor Demmler, Rick and Michael Mitchell, Jeffrey McGivern, Annette D'Agostino Lloyd, Anthony Tringali, Mrs. Dorothy Sprungman, René Riva, Jean Darling, Harry Hoppe, Craig Raguse, Ron Hutchinson, Lloyd Chaffin & Richard Freer. And special thanks to Rick Greene for his assistance in quality control, and to Jan Lyons, my favorite hillbilly whose incessant nagging got me to finish this book in record time. [She told me to write that. Actually, Jan's not a nag at all. I'd call her an inspiration in a hillbilly sort of way.]

Last but not least, let us remember Mark Twain, another great American humorist who, like Hal Roach, had a strong connection to the town of Elmira, New York. Samuel Clemens summered near Roach's hometown for nearly twenty years at Quarry Farm, which he called "the home of *Huckleberry Finn* and other books of mine, for they were written here." Mark Twain made a lasting personal impression on Roach when he was a guest speaker at the Elmira grade school when Roach was a boy. The final resting places of both Samuel Clemens and Hal Roach are in Elmira's Woodlawn Cemetery.

Prologue

MY RELATIONSHIP WITH HAL ROACH was one of creative curiosity and sharing. When I first met him in 1973, I was a budding 20-year-old filmmaker, a newly-arrived undergraduate at UCLA's Motion Picture/Television Department, who was fascinated by all phases of movie making, and was especially enamored of the kind of movies produced by Hal Roach in the 1920s and '30s, movies that I had begun to study and emulate as a teenager.

In my hometown of San Diego, California, my tenth-grade English teacher, Mrs. Dorothy Sprungman, saw that I was bored with the study of our current subject, Greek mythology, and knowing that I enjoyed filming with my father's 8mm movie camera, suggested I write a script and make a movie as my class project. What a wonderful suggestion! I had loved the TV show *Fractured Flickers*, that marvelous series produced by the infamous "Ponsonby Britt" (actually Jay Ward and Bill Scott) and narrated by Hans Conried, which utilized scenes from the silent comedies of the custard pie slapstick era. I never tired of watching the marvelous energy, the zany inventiveness and the wild physicality of it all. And I had recently seen another comedy—a talkie—slower paced, less hysterical, with sound—yet it reminding me in some odd way of those earlier films. After having just experienced the tragic images from television in recent months—the assassinations of Dr. Martin Luther King Jr. and Robert F. Kennedy—what a great relief it was to laugh at the innocent nonsense of *Saps at Sea* which happened to have been the last classic comedy film made by Laurel & Hardy at the Hal Roach Studios, released in 1940.

So with the encouragement of my tenth grade teacher, in December 1968 I wrote a comedy script, *Is There a Gardener in the House?* as a sort of homage to those two funny men drifting on a boat, only this time they were hoboes hired as gardeners of a wealthy estate. There were two kids in my class, one large, the other slender, who were always goofing around with each other and seemed a natural comedy team. They agreed to "star" in my movie. I cast the rest from among my eager classmates and off we went to make a comedy. There was a hilarious scene in *Saps At Sea* where the boys are visited by a doctor—that was the first time I had seen Dr. Finlayson—and I HAD to play him myself. Long story short, the 20-minute (two-reeler) *Is There a Gardener in the House?* was a BIG hit when I showed it at class in the spring of 1969; I was even asked to screen it again in the auditorium for even more classes, and I was praised for my film-making skills. This led me to make more and more movies, graduating to Super 8mm with synchronized sound, and eventually to be admitted to the UCLA Motion Picture/Television Department in the fall of 1973. (Alas, my "Laurel & Hardy" style comedy disappeared in 1979. It is my *Hats Off*.)

The year following making that movie, in 1970, I had a simple yet VIVID dream. I was peacefully watering the garden, and out of the blue in sauntered those two comical gentlemen, Mr. Laurel and Mr. Hardy. They smiled warmly at me, lifted their derbies in greeting, and were gone as quickly as they had arrived. I woke up with a start. It seemed so REAL. That day I made a drawing of the two; I reproduce it here. How could I have known then that some three and a half years later I would be meeting their boss—the man responsible for making their immortal and unforgettable comedies some three and four decades earlier—and know him for nearly twenty years?

I was eager to learn the fundamentals of filmmaking—telling stories via image and acting—and become a faithful practitioner, and this must have been what Mr. Roach picked up on when he first met me. I was also an actor who was a natural comedian; without knowing it, I was emulating the process by which Stan Laurel created—seamlessly integrating acting, writing and directing into the creation of motion pictures.

Decades later, during my research for this book, I was startled to discover some uncanny "coincidences." For example, my birthday of June 11 is significant as being the date (1) Stan Laurel began production on his very first film for Roach, *Do You Love Your Wife?* in 1918 and (2) this date marked the first day of filming *The Second Hundred Years* in 1927, considered to be the first "true" Laurel & Hardy comedy. Also, the first mailing address I obtained when I moved to New York City in 1979 happened to be the address of Roach's first New York office on West 45th Street. And when I returned to Los Angeles some eight years later, one of my first long term "temp" assignments was to work as an executive assistant at Mitchell, Silberberg & Knupp, which I later learned was Hal Roach's law firm in the 1940s and '50s. I also worked for a time at MGM/UA. They had merged in the 1980s; separately both studios were significant to Roach from the 1920s on. Ironically, I obtained that job while I was staying at Mr. Roach's home.

I am eternally grateful that Hal Roach so wholeheartedly shared his time and thoughts with me throughout the years, right up to his final 100th, and never tired of tackling creative challenges, exploring the nuts and bolts of translating story ideas into motion pictures, appreciating development and production fundamentals, respecting the flexibility needed for dealing with ever-changing circumstance and sharing that indefinable spirit of generosity and healthy enjoyment of life.

Most prominent and all-encompassing, and the reason I believe this man should be considered one of our National Treasures is that in addition to his many great and good contributions, especially the spreading of joy and laughter all over the world, is that he acknowledged his inspiration from the writings and humor of Mark Twain while keeping alive (in scandalous Hollywood of the Golden Age) the sense of family and friendship, the camaraderie and mutual enterprise shared by people of all classes and diversities, those potent values that were lived and breathed by those of goodwill and humor, that good and healthy legacy of 19th century America.

The details are related in the following chapters, but here I'd like to say that when I first met Mr. Roach that October day in 1973 there was no Internet, no Google, no way a 20-year-old (who had just returned from months in Mexico) could know the history of the great man I was about to meet. I had read the three prominent books on Laurel & Hardy, by John McCabe, William Everson and Charles Barr, and that was it. Mr. Roach shared as much of his history as time and circumstances permitted in our two long meetings together that year. From that I fashioned my term paper which earned me an A+. I stayed in touch with Mr. Roach over the years and learned more, eventually creating a long article in 1982. This article kept growing as I kept in contact with Mr. Roach, visiting him at his Bel Air home on occasion, discussing the developments of movies and TV.

My long Hal Roach article had been accepted for publication by *American Film* magazine in the mid '80s; the contract was negotiated by Mitch Douglas of ICM New York. However, it was never published. In 1988 Hal Roach invited me to move into his home to help him write what he was calling his "comeback comedy." He was 96-years-young. That experience, as well as descriptions of the phone conversations I had with Mr. Roach during the following four years, were added to my article.

The last time I saw Mr. Roach was in May 1992, when he was several months past his 100th birthday. And my article kept getting longer.

I attended Hal Roach's funeral in November 1992. Spanky was there, and Joe Cobb. And Anita Garvin. I added some final paragraphs to my article in the months following his passing, then put my completed article away in the proverbial drawer, where it remained undisturbed for the next twenty years.

Introduction

WHY DID IT TAKE UNTIL 2013 for me to write this book? It was quite out of the blue when a Sandy Grabman emailed me in October 2012 regarding a photo she had seen on my website of George Clayton Johnson, the writer. I had a handsome photo of him taken at a Hollywood celebrity convention a number of years ago and had posted it on my website. Ms. Grabman told me she wanted to use it as the cover of a book she was in the process of assisting to have published. BearManor Media? Oh, I noticed, they publish books about old Hollywood. "I've written a long article about Hal Roach," I mentioned. "And I have photos taken when I knew him. Do you think there might be a book in that?"

No matter that they decided to use another photo of Mr. Johnson for their cover. The rest is history. My slim volume was accepted. It was suggested by my BearManor Media production manager Michelle Morgan to fill it out since I had the opportunity. "Didn't I know there was a Hal Roach Collection at the University of Southern California which housed many of his papers?" someone asked. Good heavens—and I live only two miles from campus!

Soon, with the grateful assistance of Archivist Edward "Ned" Comstock, I was plunging into box after box of documents, contracts, letters and telegrams that had been rescued at the 11th hour from the doomed and bankrupt Hal Roach Studios' offices in August 1963, just before an M4 army tank demolished the buildings. It was apparently the generosity and foresight of the head auctioneer, Milton J. Wershow, who handed the material over to USC. Or did he merely permit a brave university librarian to rush in, as walls were tumbling, and dump every scrap of paper into boxes, thus rescuing that precious material from destruction and oblivion? Some of this material had originally found its way to an abandoned jail where it was stored for a planned Hollywood Museum that was never built. Roach associate Richard W. Bann also donated materials in the early 1980s.

1

However the rescue of these documents was accomplished, those heroes deserve a medal, nay, a statue of honor! From the earliest days of 1914 to the very end, the rich legacy of the Hal Roach Studios exists in that simple yet powerful medium of print and paper, there for all to study and explore, thanks to these valiant rescuers.

And what a legacy is contained in the Hal Roach Collection! How vividly it all comes to life—the young men eager to succeed in the brave new world of Hollywood movie making, the desperate attempts to create saleable product, the relentless determination to find that invaluable distributor, to figuring out how to satisfy the public and make them want more of these films!

The technology was continuously evolving and improving and the challenges were enormous. The personalities, the creative talents, the desire to make better movies and to refine the crudities of production and performance—all was there to be discerned, embedded in the ink of those decades-old documents.

Looming over me as I toiled, often wearing a heavy winter coat to protect me from the Arctic chill of that reading room, hung the huge portrait of Cecil B. DeMille. I was, after all, in the Cecil B. DeMille Reading Room of the USC Cinematic Arts Library.

Cecil B. DeMille, legendary figure of Hollywood, that prominent and powerful director who had arrived in Hollywood shortly after Hal Roach did—in fact, it was DeMille who nixed 21-year-old Roach from appearing as an extra in that very first of all Hollywood feature pictures *The Squaw Man* in 1913. "Too much" scrawled DeMille over Roach's name, for the upstart dared to request the sum of $5.00 a day salary because he would supply his own cowboy outfit.

WHAT'S A "BRODIE"?
100 YEARS OF BRODIES WITH HAL ROACH
The Jaunty Journeys of Hollywood's Movie and Television Pioneer

"100 Years of Brodies?" I can hear the reader ask. I wondered what a "Brodie" meant myself when Mr. Roach used the phrase "taking a Brodie" the first time I interviewed him over forty years ago. He also used the phrase in 1984 when he won his Honorary Oscar, saying "a comedian for Mack Sennett did a Brodie." I didn't know what it meant then and I didn't have an opportunity to ask him, but as it sounded quaint, I jotted it down, spelling it "brody." Years later—despite what the Internet's *Dictionary of Slang* or the *Urban Dictionary* may say (which has so many wildly varying descriptions for "Brodie" as to defy common sense)—I have discovered that it originally referred to a certain brave (or foolhardy) American from New York named Steve Brodie (1861-1901), who on a dare, or a bet, on July 23, 1886 jumped off the Brooklyn Bridge and survived. "Doing a Brodie," "taking a Brodie" or "making a Brodie" became a slang expression in the years following to mean surviving great stunts, surmounting catastrophes and taking pratfalls. Metaphorically as well as physically (he was a football player, wrestler, polo player, flyer and world traveler) taking Brodies was something Hal Roach did his entire life.

My book may not be the definitive biography of the life and career of Hal Roach. That would be a gargantuan task, considering the many decades the man lived through, the myriad personalities he worked and played with, the talents he hired, fired and befriended, the projects, plans, accomplishments, adapting to and surviving all the incredible changes that occurred in Hollywood and the world from 1892 to 1992. But I do attempt to present a complete picture and give an idea of the scope and breadth and complexity of the tasks Hal Roach dedicated himself to as well as the new technological trails he blazed. I wish to present the man and his times in both long shot and close up, and introduce and reintroduce some of the remarkable personalities with whom he was associated from my perspective as a faithful and regrettably minor latecomer to the adventure. Late I came to the game, indeed, yet I was still able to personally experience the fading echoes of that grand parade as it passed by, for the man remained vibrant, alive and enthusiastic to his last days, and he left behind enduring entertainments and vivid replicas of lives well lived.

HAL'S GANG

In the course of my research I discovered five motion picture executives of the early years whose extensive correspondence fills the Hal Roach Collection. These five emerge as great personalities possessed of enormous dedication and energy, and all were eager to assist Mr. Roach in the first decades of his Hollywood career in the creation of quality motion pictures. They especially valued good comedy. They are: **Dwight Whiting, Warren Doane, Fred Quimby, Henry Ginsberg and David Loew**. These are the unsung heroes of the formative years of the Hal Roach Studios. While his directors, stars, supporting players and even composers and editors are quite well known to aficionados, and deservedly so, the executives, those often forgotten souls left to brood and ponder, to dictate letters and make telephone calls and wheel and deal behind the scenes in the privacy of their offices, deserve to be acknowledged and remembered.

Their distinct voices come to life while reading their letters and telegrams; I want to do them honor and reproduce quite simply their down to earth conversations and communications in their own words. Sometimes they are heated, opinionated, at other times confused, delighted, frustrated. I let them speak for themselves without editorializing (much). I do so throughout the following narrative simply by including these communications where appropriate, indicating the date of the communication, the writer, the recipient, the method (either via letter, Western Union telegram, or night letter). I have edited out extraneous matters.

DWIGHT WHITING (1891–1974) Hal Roach's very first creative partner, who worked with him from 1914-1918. Roach was directing comedies for Essanay when business partner Dwight Whiting succeeded in getting Pathé Exchange interested in distributing the Rolin product beginning with the Harold Lloyd Willie Work short, *Just Nuts*.

WARREN DOANE (1890–1964) Doane was an assistant to Dwight Whiting when the latter worked in the automobile business. He joined the board of directors of the Rolin Film Company on Aug. 17, 1914. Doane began as an assistant manager and became Vice President from 1920 to 1931. He was also a production supervisor, location supervisor and director of Charley Chase shorts.

FRED QUIMBY (1886–1965) In the early 1920s he was a Pathé executive in New York City. In 1926 Quimby began to work with Roach directly and continued to do so when he joined the MGM payroll. He greatly assisted Roach in improving his shorts and was instrumental in having them successfully distributed via MGM. From 1937-55 Quimby was head of MGM's Animation Department, home of the Tom and Jerry cartoons. He won eight Academy Awards for his cartoon shorts between 1940 and 1952.

HENRY GINSBERG (1897–1979) General Manager of Hal Roach Studios from 1931-36. Although often seen as a figure of controversy, whose tightfisted methods put a damper on the "fun loving" atmosphere of comedy making, he is revealed through this correspondence to have been a dedicated and faithful executive faced with tackling the economic challenges of the Great Depression. Hal Roach trusted him enough to leave him completely in charge of the Studio in 1932 while he was off on a South American tour. Ginsberg was directly responsible for suggesting the Academy of Motion Picture Arts & Sciences create a category for Short Subjects in 1932 (which led to a win for Laurel & Hardy) and he also singlehandedly saved Our Gang from extinction when some MGM higher ups wanted to axe the series in 1933!

DAVID LOEW (1897–1973) Son of Marcus Loew, the man who helped create MGM in 1924. David Loew was Vice President of Loew's, Inc. in New York City from circa 1920-35. From the mid-1920s Loew had been very encouraging to Roach and was an invaluable advisor during the transition to the talkies. In 1929 Roach offered to make him his Hollywood partner, but Loew, although flattered, had to decline due to prior business arrangements. He eventually did replace Henry Ginsberg in January 1936 as general manager of the studio, but stayed for only three months after which he formed his own company through which he produced a series of Joe E. Brown comedies. David Loew was a good friend, as was his twin brother **Arthur Loew** (1897-1977) who was in charge of MGM's overseas market and who traveled with Roach during his flying tour throughout South America in 1932.

SPECIAL MENTION must be given to the following individuals who, although they have little or no personal correspondence in the Archive files, their names and influence are strongly felt:

J.A. BERST (1875–?), Pathé New York City's Vice President and General Manager through whom the young Roach strived to distribute his earliest films. Berst was often described as 'autocratic' and difficult to get along with. But he was the one who accepted *Just Nuts* in 1915 and then ordered more comedies from Roach. He signed the long term contract with Roach in February 1917 for the two-reel Harold Lloyd Lonesome Luke comedies which lead to Hal Roach's success as a movie producer. Berst resigned from Pathé in April 1918 when he accepted the presidency of United Picture Theatres of America, Inc., a company which apparently went bankrupt two years later.

PAUL BRUNET (1873–?), head of Pathé in New York City from 1918. Brunet worked with Roach more congenially than his predecessor did.

Brunet resigned from Pathé in 1922 and returned to France where that year he received the Légion d'honneur. Roach become dissatisfied with his Pathé set up; in 1926 he secured a new distribution deal with Metro-Goldwyn-Mayer. By 1936 Brunet was once more head of the Board of Directors while Pathé was filing for bankruptcy.

NICHOLAS SCHENCK (1881–1969) Negotiated the MGM Distribution deal with Roach 1926 and was the man Roach reported to directly while associated with MGM to 1938. Schenck was Marcus Loew's right hand man in the early days and along with Louis B. Mayer they created MGM in 1924. When Marcus Loew died in 1927, Schenck took over. He was located in New York City, his brother Joseph in Hollywood. Nicholas Schenck was said to be the eighth richest individual in the United States during the 1930s. In 1955 Arthur Loew, David's brother, succeeded Schenck as President. Schenck remained Chairman of the Board and retired 1956.

H.M. WALKER (1878–1937) A sports writer and cartoonist for the *Los Angeles Examiner*, Walker was a freelance title writer for Roach from 1916. He began to work full-time for Roach in 1920 and by 1927 was Vice President and Production Manager of the Hal Roach Studios until 1932. He attended previews of each film and wrote the critiques that would be used as a basis for improving the films. Walker also became head of the editorial department. *Film Daily* of April 1927 reported that Walker had by that time "titled 1,300 pictures, two-thirds two-reelers and between 40 and 50 multiple reel productions." He also wrote dialogue for the early talkies, 1929-32.

RICHARD CURRIER (1892–1984) Head of the Editing Department 1920-32. Mastered the transition to sound and was made a Director in 1931, but was ousted following a dispute with Henry Ginsberg. His policy to make two fine grain master positive prints of every Laurel and Hardy film helped preserve their work for posterity.

F. RICHARD JONES (1893–1930) Worked for Roach from 1924-27. F. Richard Jones became director-general of the studio in July 1925 and has been credited, along with Leo McCarey, Richard Currier, and others as being among the first to recognize the star power in the teaming of Laurel & Hardy. He resigned from the Roach lot in March 1927 to launch his own (what turned out to be short lived) feature directing career.

CHARLES H. ("DAD") ROACH (1860–1936) Hal's father was born in Alexandria, Virginia and moved to Elmira, New York at age twenty-one. He was the Secretary-Treasurer of Hal's company from 1918 to his death. "Dad" was well loved by all.

BENJAMIN SHIPMAN (1892–1975) Business manager for Roach in the 1920s who eventually worked solely for Laurel and Hardy as their manager and lawyer. He negotiated their contracts and represented the team in various court cases, usually involving their former wives.

LEO MCCAREY (1898–1969) Former script clerk and second assistant director for Mack Sennett, then at Universal, he joined Roach in the early 1920s as a gag writer and became a director for the Charley Chase series in the mid-1920s. McCarey became supervising director and Vice President in 1927. Many consider him responsible for the teaming of Laurel & Hardy. He certainly guided them in their first shorts together. He left Roach around 1930 to become a world famous Hollywood director and returned to the Studio in 1955 as writer-director for the TV series *Screen Directors Playhouse*.

FRANK BUTLER (1890–1967) actor, *The Spat Family, King of Wild Horses, Our Gang*, etc.; writer: *No Man's Law* (1927), Laurel & Hardy's *Babes In Toyland, Bonnie Scotland, Bohemian Girl, Vagabond Lady*. After his years with Roach he wrote *Strike Me Pink* (Eddie Cantor), *The Milky Way* for Harold Lloyd, several of the great *Road* movies with Hope & Crosby, and individual screenplays for both including *Going My Way* and *Fancy Pants*. Also *The Perils of Pauline* (1947), a look back at old time slapstick Hollywood.

CHARLES PARROTT (1893–1940) Hired in 1920, the next year he was made supervising director of all comedies except Lloyd's. By 1924 he was performing in his own series of supremely successful shorts as comedian Charley Chase. He was responsible for bringing Robert McGowan and Oliver Hardy to the Hal Roach Studios, and he guided newcomer Leo McCarey in the art of comedy directing. Chase triumphed with the arrival of talkies and remained on the Roach payroll until 1936.

JAMES PARROTT (1897–1939) Brother of Charles, was hired as a gag writer for Harold Lloyd in 1917. Became an actor known as Paul Parrott 1920-23 and then became one of the studios best directors: Laurel & Hardy shorts from 1928-33 and director for Charley Chase, the Todd-Kelly and the *Boy Friends* series.

SIDNEY S. VAN KEUREN (1901–1971) Hal Roach's cousin, whose mother lived on the Studio Lot with Hal's mother Mabel after "Dad" Roach passed away. After receiving an Engineering degree back East, Van Keuren joined the Studio in 1931 and worked in every department on the lot. He became the associate producer of the last twenty-two Our Gang shorts, as well as for many features and was made Vice President by 1937. After World War II he assisted with the studio's conversion to television production, handled the first continuing television series and developed the commercial division. He was production supervisor on some thirty-five television shows and remained at the Studio until the very end.

And let us acknowledge those elusive gentlemen whose financial, legal and business acumen helped Mr. Roach get his start at the very beginning:

DAN LINTHICUM (1878–1952) Roach's first partner who lent part of his last name to the RO-LIN Company in 1914. He was a former bank president and businessman from Arkansas.

IRA H. NANCE (1888–1978) Rolin's first Vice President, 1914. A California born attorney. Nance resigned less than a month after the date of the film company's incorporation. From the 1930s to the '50s he was Deputy Los Angeles County Coroner.

EARL WISDOM (1883–1944), Rolin's second Vice President 1914 to 1920. Born in Iowa, Wisdom moved to California in 1910 and became an attorney the year he met Roach, and served in that capacity for Rolin during those first few years.

W.B. (WILLIAM BOZARTH) FRANK (1884-1963) Roach's New York rep from 1923 to 1927. He had been Pathé's sales manager since 1917 and would become Mack Sennett's New York rep from 1927 to 1933. In 1935 he worked for producer Walter Wanger and by 1938 Frank was with Associated Features, distributors of such all-Black Westerns as *Harlem on the Prairie* starring Herb Jeffries, who celebrated his 100th birthday in September 2013 and who passed away in May 2014.

RUTH BURCH (1901–2000) Hal Roach's longtime personal secretary who later became a casting director and worked on such television series as *The Andy Griffith Show, I Spy and The Dick Van Dyke Show*. She lived to virtually the same venerable age as her boss.

GRACE ROSENFIELD (ca.1902–1986) Hal Roach's longtime New York City sales rep, the only female in that position in motion pictures. She began working as a stenographer for Henry Ginsberg in 1925 and was brought on board by him to work at the Hal Roach Studios New York City office in 1932 and remained until 1950.

SPECIAL MENTION TO:

CAPTAIN JAMES DICKSON (1900–1932) Roach's faithful pilot and friend, who flew his boss cross country from California to New York and back on many business trips starting in 1930. He piloted Roach and MGM executive Arthur Loew on the extensive South American trip in 1932 wherein they broke several world flying records. His tragic death in a plane crash in South Africa while piloting Arthur Loew and his attorney friend in November 1932 ended a grand association.

I did not see any correspondence from the great directors Leo McCarey, James Horne, James Parrott, Charles Parrott, very little from Robert McGowan nor H.M. Walker (though he and director Fred Jackman provide interesting testimony in the *Rex the Wonder Horse* copyright infringement case of 1926). Nothing either from the composers T. Marvin Hatley and LeRoy Shield, nor anything from Nicholas Schenck or director Charley Rogers. Undoubtedly these gentlemen would have added enormously to the complex tales of that fabulous enterprise. Fortunately there have been interviews with some of them already published, some quotes in newspaper articles, as well as the correspondence from that marvelous website *Letters From Stan* (Laurel) from which to explore.

There are so many others associated with the Hal Roach Studios, valiant loyal employees and talents too numerous to mention. But I'll name a few here out of respect and with the knowledge that I can't include everyone who contributed over the decades to the Hal Roach Studios. Each one deserves their own separate biography! In no particular order: **Milton H. Bren** (Producer), **Edith Udell** (Hal Roach's personal secretary in the 1940s and 1950s following Ruth Burch), **T.J. Crizer** (film editor who later became an Executive), **L.A.** French (production manager), **Lloyd French** (writer/director), **Herbert Gelbspan** (New York rep), **Fred Guiol** (longtime director), **Hugh Huber** (executive who ended up in a legal battle with Roach), executives **Mat D. O'Brien** (Hal's boyhood friend who joined him in 1924) and **Joe Rivkin, Fred Jackman** (one of his first directors), **Bert Jordan** (editor), **Art Lloyd** (cinematographer), **Lew Maren** (publicity director), **George Marshall** (director), **Fred Newmeyer** (director), **Elmer Raguse** (sound technician), **LeRoy Shield** (background music composer), **T. Marvin Hatley** (film composer and musical director), **Charley Rogers** (director), **Roy Seawright** (special effects), **George Stevens** (cinematographer and director), **Clyde Bruckman** (writer and director), **Hal Yates** (writer, director), etcetera.

And to all the great cast of characters, **"Snub" Pollard, "Sunshine Sammy" Morrison, the Our Gang kids, The Parrott Brothers, James Finlayson, Charlie Hall, Mae Busch, Anita Garvin, Stanley "Tiny" Sandford, Dorothy Coburn, Kay Deslys, Harry Bernard, Leo Willis, Thelma Todd, Patsy Kelly, Edgar Kennedy, Walter Long, Charles Middleton, Arthur Housman, Billy Gilbert** and on and on...I tip my derby.

For an extensive exploration of hundreds of the actors who appeared in Hal Roach movies, including even those who had itty bitty parts and mere extras who somehow stood out, be sure to visit Dave 'Lord' Heath's website Another Nice Mess at www.lordheath.com. 'Lord' Heath deserves a medal or maybe a plaque for his fantastic, thorough and accurate research. Mr. Roach might think he's "Just Nuts" for his meticulous attention to detail, but the rest of us loonies, fanatics and Sons applaud him.

1

Tall Oaks From Little Acorns Grow
The Journey Begins

IN THE FALL OF 1973 I enrolled in UCLA's Motion Picture/Television Department. One of my first courses was The History of American Film Comedy taught by Professor Robert Rosen. We were, of course, required to write "a paper." Now what could I write about American Film Comedy? There were already hundreds of books on the subject. Even then, one could easily find three or four biographies each on Charlie Chaplin, Buster Keaton, Harold Lloyd, Laurel & Hardy, W.C. Fields... there were books devoted to silent comedy, to talkie comedy, to British, French, and black comedy. There were volumes devoted to comedy teams, comedy shorts, and musical comedies.

I felt a bit dissatisfied even amidst this literary abundance. I wanted first-hand information, first-hand impressions; I was not content merely to accept and digest the scholarly opinions of screening room aficionados. Since I lived so close to Hollywood and Beverly Hills, I knew I should be able to find some Golden Age veteran of movie humor who would be willing—nay, eager—to talk about those special days. And not just any veteran, I said to myself, no two-bit supporting player or anything of the sort, but someone of authority who was involved in a significant way in the creation, on a day-to-day basis, of those classic comedies made between 1910 and 1940. Alas, most of those old-timers were dead and gone by 1973. Mack Sennett, the first King of American film comedy and the originator of the Keystone Kops, received his big custard pie back in 1960. Buster Keaton took his last tumble in 1966. Harold Lloyd, the great skyscraper climber, made his final ascent in 1971. As for Oliver Hardy, Stan Laurel, W.C. Fields, Harry Langdon—they'd all taken that celestial ride to the cosmic laugh house. The only one extant, as far as I could figure it, was the

11

Grand Old Comedian himself, Charlie Chaplin. Indeed, early in that year of 1973, Charles Chaplin, at the age of eighty-four, returned to Hollywood after some twenty years "in exile" to receive an honorary Academy Award. He quickly departed, commenting that Los Angeles now looked like "a city of banks," and returned to his secluded home in Switzerland.

I had a hunch, however, that there was one other great figure from the world of film comedy who might still be alive and living within the shadow of the Hollywood sign: a man who had been involved with the movies for just as long a time as Chaplin; one indeed (though it is unfashionable to say so) who must be ranked along with Chaplin—and Keaton—as a primary creator of the best comedy on film. His name: Hal Roach.

During his heyday, which spanned from the earliest days of slapstick through to the 1950s, Hal Roach had the pre-eminent ability to spot and develop comic talent. Unlike Sennett he held on to his comedians, and a free and creative atmosphere existed at his studio. Through his efforts, the world's screens would shine with the celluloid antics of Harold Lloyd, Laurel & Hardy, Charley Chase, the Our Gang kids, and some of the funniest supporting characters ever to grace the screen: James Finlayson, Edgar Kennedy, Snub Pollard, Patsy Kelly, ZaSu Pitts, and Billy Gilbert. The Hal Roach comedy shorts were especially noted for the plentiful supply of lovely flappers displaying their charms, and one could enjoy such enchanting creatures as Anita Garvin, Dorothy Coburn, Thelma Todd, Kay Deslys, and Edna Marion, to name but a few. Hal Roach was also responsible for the screen debut of Jean Harlow—who is stripped to her black lingerie in a Laurel & Hardy short called *Double Whoopee* (1929). Yes, he was the man I had to meet.

But where was this bringer of joy, and how could I find him? On a whim I looked in the most obvious place: the West Los Angeles telephone book. Sure enough, there was his name.

I dialed the number, and a girl answered.

"Is this the home of Hal Roach, who used to be a movie producer?" I asked a bit uncertainly.

"Yes, it is," came the pert reply. "Would you like to speak with him?"

Within five seconds I was talking with Hal Roach.

I told him that I was a UCLA film school student and had made my own comedy shorts, inspired not a little by Mr. Roach's own creations. He seemed cheerful and cordial over the phone, and as I was just bursting with questions and curiosity, I took the plunge and asked him if we could meet and talk about his career and about comedy in general.

He said "Sure! Meet me at the Bel-Air Country Club tomorrow afternoon. Just ask for me when you get there."

The next day, October 30, 1973, a sunny, smog-free day, I drove over to the Bel-Air Country Club. What followed could have occurred in one of Mr. Roach's own two-reelers.

The uniformed doorman eyed me suspiciously and asked me my business. I cockily informed him that I had a date to see "Mr. Hal Roach."

"Well, he hasn't arrived yet. Why don't you wait inside till he comes."

I entered the plushly carpeted room, walked under the glimmering chandeliers, and passed the gaudy oil paintings and the even gaudier Bel Air matrons who were sipping their afternoon cocktails. Feeling a bit out of place, I sank into the nearest sofa.

From this vantage point I could see out the double glass entrance doors. Every time the inevitable Caddie or Rolls would pull up the doorman would perform his duty and the inevitable white-haired gentleman would step out and enter the club. This event repeated itself several times, and each time I would wonder: "Is THAT Hal Roach?" for I had no idea what he looked like. I HAD seen a photo of a middle-aged Mr. Roach taken with Stan and Ollie in 1933, but one never knows what alterations the passage of forty years can bring to the human organism. Somehow, though, I knew that none of the old gents stepping from their cars was he.

While waiting, I reviewed the many questions I had prepared for Mr. Roach. I had no idea what to expect. Would he turn out to be gruff old codger who'd snap snarling monosyllables to my impertinent queries? Or was he a senile old goat whose past was as dim to him as his eyesight? ("'Laurel'? Isn't that some kind of tree?") Or was he an alert, friendly, outgoing gent who had plenty to say and a good memory to boot? Luckily, Hal Roach turned out to be the latter, and definitely so. But it took me another half hour to find this out.

I finally decided to inquire for myself at the front desk.

"Yes. Mr. Roach has been here all day. You'll find him in the card room."

Opening the door to the card room, I saw table after table of old men smoking cigars and playing poker or pinochle, or whatever it is old men play in large, smoky card rooms. Now, how the hell was I to find the old guy I sought? I didn't have to think long. At the far end of the room a bald and portly gent in a bright pink sports shirt and wire-rimmed glasses stood up and motioned me over.

"You must be the young fellah that wanted to see me. Deal me out, boys," he said as he threw down his hand, and we went to a quiet room to talk.

Eighty-one year old Hal Roach was a jolly man who looked a good deal like a beardless Santa Claus. His lively, mischievous eyes were fringed with bushy salt-and-pepper brows. He had a gravelly voice with a pinch of what seemed to be Brooklynese, and when he laughed it was hearty and genuine. Had I not known his age, I would have guessed him to be in his late fifties.

We spoke for nearly three hours that first time, and we met again a month later for another stimulating and informative talk. For the sake of convenience, I have combined the contents of those two occasions into the following narrative. I urged Mr. Roach to talk about his movie career in chronological order, and he was most happy to comply. He mixed fact, opinion, anecdote, asides, and quips very freely. Our meetings were most enjoyable.

2

Just Nuts
The Creation of Rolin
1914-1923

MR. ROACH BEGAN by telling me of his youth. He was born in Elmira, New York on January 14, 1892. He didn't mention what an all around athlete he had been, star of his football team, wrestler, a boy generally beloved by his community. According to Charles Champlin in a 1992 *Los Angeles Times* article, Hal's father sold jewelry and his mother ran a boarding house.

"I wasn't a very good student," Roach said during a videotaped interview in the early 1980s, "so after working as a blacksmith's helper when I was seventeen I left there quickly. From there to Alaska...." where he worked as a prospector. He also reportedly lived for a time in Seattle, Washington where he worked for an ice cream company as well as in a gambling hall.

"The White Company sold sixteen trucks to haul pipe and supplies across the Mojave Desert and he hired me to come down as foreman to Los Angeles... But in those days the trucks weren't ready for the desert or the desert wasn't ready for the trucks and they busted up all of the trucks in about two weeks...."

Once in Los Angeles, in 1912, twenty-year-old Hal Roach "...saw an ad in the newspaper, a dollar, car fare and lunch to work in motion pictures in Western costume... Well, any kid from Elmira, New York who rode horses out on the desert as I did, you had a pair of cowboy boots, a Stetson hat and a bandana handkerchief. So I put them all on and went and stood in front of the post office at six o'clock in the morning and they hired me...."

At the Bison Studio he was brought to a western saloon set and when he informed the director that they were spinning the roulette wheel the wrong way (something he had learned while working in the Seattle gambling hall), he was cast as the croupier and was then told to return the next morning and would be paid the salary of five dollars a day.

"Well, five dollars a day in 1912 was a lot of money. I was superintendent of freighting and I was only getting $65 a month... out in the desert... and so I became an actor."

Roach worked as an extra in a few more films: he and his new friend Harold Lloyd played eunuchs in *The Birth of Sampson* and Hottentots in *The Patchwork Girl of Oz* (1914). When Roach and Lloyd were asked to take a pay cut and work for three dollars a day, they both quit.

One day an attorney called on the studio to talk to the boss. Since the boss (who was also the leading man) was busy shooting scenes, Roach met with the attorney himself. Realizing that this was a man of considerable means, (was it Earl Wisdom or I.H. Nance?) Roach convinced him that "I was the greatest unfound director in the business, and he financed me to make pictures." Three investors joined Roach to form a new film company: attorneys Earl Wisdom and Ira H. Nance and businessman Dan Linthicum.

Wealthy energetic young real estate agent and automobile dealership executive Dwight Whiting replaced Nance at the first board of directors meeting. As simple as that, Hal Roach began his career as a motion picture producer and director.

A *Los Angeles Times* article dated January 10, 1937 stated that Hal Roach started production on January 8, 1914 with $850. Other reports have stated that he inherited $3,000, which enabled him to start his own company. Frick, Martin & Co., an Investment Securities firm, affirmed in an October 1, 1928 document that Rolin "was started with a paid up capital of $7,500." *The Moving Picture World* of June 1915 gives the sum with which they incorporated as $10,000.

Businessman Dan Linthicum also contributed to the creation of the Rolin Film Company, but he quickly faded from the scene after providing a lasting legacy by supplying part of his name to form the company's name, RO[ach]-LIN[thicum] . Rolin was incorporated on July 23, 1914. (Which happened to have been the date Steve Brodie jumped off the Brooklyn Bridge in 1886.)

Virtually nothing has been written about Hal Roach's early partner. Daniel Anthony Linthicum (1878-1952) was born in Arkansas. In the early 1900s he was a bank president in New Mexico and Texas, and by 1913 he was living in Los Angeles with his wife and son where he was listed in the City Directory as President of the Linthicum Chemical Company. How he met Roach is unknown but he actually appeared as an actor in an early unreleased Rolin comedy *Two Bum Heroes*. Dan Linthicum left in mid February 1915 because it was said he failed to come up with the funds to buy additional shares in Rolin that he had subscribed to. The parting seems to have been amicable. "I bought out the man who financed it," Roach told author Anthony Slide many years later, "and owned the whole company myself."

What happened to Roach's partner after his early departure? Linthicum's 1918 draft card has him listed as being a distributor for the Nilson Tractor Company in Stockton, California. In 1920 he was back in Arkansas as the general manager of a store. In 1925 he had moved to Mississippi, where he was a Captain in the National Guard. By 1930 he had returned to California, and lived in Long Beach apparently for the remainder of his life. He became President of the Red Anchor Dock and Steamship Company and died on July 2, 1952 at the age of seventy-three.

Dwight H. Whiting (1891-1974) became Rolin's Secretary & Treasurer. His job was to search for distributors for the Rolin films in those earliest days. He advised Roach on the reactions to their product and also handled the actors' payroll. Whiting was instrumental in eventually helping Roach to secure a distribution contract with Pathé Exchange whose committee in New York City reviewed and critiqued the Rolin films. Whiting even steered Roach toward comedy, though the young director wanted to make dramatic films as well.

"They seem to like the wrong party getting hit," Whiting wrote to Roach in March 1915, "so stick in a lot of it. Say you work up to climax then fall down. Take more time and figure it out better at first and we will show them." A few days later he wrote, "Graham [a Pathé executive] says your work amateurish in all ways but we better stick at comedies and make good ones. I have faith in your ability. Go to it." They did, producing several more one-reelers.

"The first person I engaged was Harold Lloyd, "Roach told me in 1973, "for the simple reason that he was the best hard-working actor I ever saw."

"Roach paid me seven dollars a day and we began grinding out hobo farces," said Lloyd in the February 1920 issue of *Motion Picture* magazine. "The lure of high salaries hit me just about that time and I decided that I was underpaid. So I went over to Mack Sennett as a juvenile."

Roach had quite the competition in the slapstick comedy field. Mack Sennett had begun his own studio in 1912 and his Keystone Kops were all the craze.

"Mack Sennett was an Irish blacksmith before he was an actor," said Roach in the acclaimed British Thames Television mini-series *Hollywood*, which aired in 1980, "and Roach was a truck driver before he was an actor so we had a little something in common. We were both Irish and we were despite what the press said we were friendly. Sennett had a broad sense of the visual ridiculous and he played that to the hilt."

"Sennett established a formula, and never deviated from it," wrote film historian William K. Everson. "As the years went by, his films because slicker, funnier, faster, but the basic pattern of sight gag and chase never changed.... From the beginning, with his first Harold Lloyd films, Roach had aimed at adding sophistication and 'prestige' to his films....His comedies were more carefully planned than Sennett's, and the care showed....Roach certainly made his quota of slapstick, and good slapstick it was too. But violence, sight gags and chases were usually more solidly integrated into good story material and situational comedy than was the case with Sennett. Some of the best Roaches eschewed slapstick entirely in favor of wit and farce...."

"Lloyd's association with Sennett was not to be a long one," wrote Richard Schickel in his 1974 biography of Harold Lloyd, "but if nothing else, it taught Lloyd mastery of an important element in the comic's trade, the 'Brodie' (named after the celebrated Brooklyn Bridge jumper)."

"Sennett seemed to like me," said Lloyd, "but Roach came back with an offer of fifty dollars a week. [That was in June 1915.]

"Fifty looked mighty big to me and I told Sennett I was leaving. 'All right, young fellow,' said Sennett, 'come back when you get to it—I can use you.'"

"In those days all comedians were clowns who wore funny clothes," Roach told me in 1973. "Harold Lloyd was not a comedian but he was the best actor to act the part of a comedian of any person I ever saw. Audiences loved to watch a regular American guy take pratfalls and act like a clown. Harold worked like hell at being a good actor. He wasn't a funny man. He played his comedy as seriously as drama. It was his energy that gave him appeal."

Before Lloyd came up with his iconic Glass Character as he called it, he and Roach began with a series of one-reel comedies with Roach directing and Harold Lloyd playing a brash, Chaplin-style comic called Willie Work.

1914 RELEASES:

CA. FOURTEEN HAROLD LLOYD/WILLIE WORK ONE-REEL COMEDIES
TWO ONE-REEL NEWS FILMS

"We filmed in the park, at the beach, and in someone's backyard. The whole downtown of Los Angeles became my property room," recalled Roach.

Back in 1914-15, one-reelers were made one a week, for about $350.

"In those days, we had no scripts. I'd come in with the gags, the premise—the type of comedy we were going to make. I'd call in the cast and they'd improvise. Then we'd go out to the park and shoot.

"If we could only concoct stories now like Hal and I did in the old days!" reminisced Harold Lloyd in the February 1927 issue of *Motion Picture* magazine. "We used to take a cameraman and the cast to Westlake Park [now MacArthur Park]. We would sit on a bench and start talking story. 'What'll we do this time, Hal?' I would say. Hal would start the story. 'Well, a pretty girl and an old man are sitting here on the bench and you come along and eye the girl and she gets up and walks away with you. The old man protests and you push him in the lake.' We would take this scene and think up another to follow, and in four days we would have a picture made entirely around Westlake Park."

"Here's how we went about filming those early comedies," Roach explained to *Boston Globe* reporter John A. Jerome for his 1935 article "From Custard Pie to Polo."

"First we assembled our bankroll, what there was of it. This was the most important feature of our program but it was surprising how little money was needed to turn out films in those days... After we had taken care of the financial arrangements, we gave our undivided attention to the production itself. Someone offered an idea that he thought would make a funny picture. We discussed it for a while and if no one could think of a funnier idea, that was our story and we stuck to it, or were stuck with it, however it happened to turn out.

"Next, we assembled a variety of soft pies, custard if the price was right. Then we gathered up what costumes we could beg, borrow or steal. Naturally, our story idea had to be flexible enough to permit changes to match up with the wardrobe we assembled.

"If we were lucky enough to get a hold of a cop's uniform, a policeman would be in the picture. Or if we had a French maid's costume, we would write in a part for a petite girl. However, cast-off and misfit suits of clothes, battered derbies and silk hats made up the greater part of our wardrobe. Often our close friends would recognize their once-prized personal wardrobes adorning the figures of our screen clowns.

"During this particular period we had not acquired a studio; we couldn't even afford to rent space at another producer's lot. So we met this situation by shooting our entire picture on location, on public streets, parks, vacant lots and even the lawns of homes whose owners were not home at the time.

"Early in the morning I would start out in a big seven-passenger car which I had bought fourth-hand, and within an hour would pick up the various actors and others who were working that day. Often our location would be at or near the boarding house, hotel or home of one of our employees. This maneuver saved time, money and gasoline. It was an unwritten law that the actors had to have their make-up on and be ready for shooting immediately upon arrival on location. To meet this condition they used to put on grease paint while we were driving along to the scene of the day's work."

These early comedies were made on speculation, and the new movie company was often destitute. According to the *Watertown* (New York) *Herald* of September 23, 1916, "With capital down to the zero point, Roach decided to risk all on one last attempt. He put his company 'over the jumps' by putting them through every funny scene he could think of. There was no story and no rhyme or reason to it. He called it *Just Nuts* and sent it to Pathé."

Pathé Exchange was quite literally the oldest motion picture company in the world, having been started in Paris in 1896 by four brothers, the driving force being Charles Pathé (1863-1957). In 1904 Charles sent J.A. Berst to open an office in New York City, and Berst was the executive in charge when Rolin offered their cinematic wares.

Miraculously, Pathé bought this little comedy *Just Nuts* "and asked for more," reported the *Watertown Herald*. "In the meanwhile before the good news came Roach had got starved out and had secured a job as director with Essanay when the good news came."

"I made six pictures with Lloyd," Roach told me, "and then went over to work at Essanay [in June 1915]. I made one-reelers using the comedians Chaplin didn't need. All the sets were right next to each other, so while I'd be shooting one picture, Chaplin would be shooting another right next door. All the time he'd come over to our set and ask a comic, 'What was that gag so-and-so did in vaudeville?' And he'd put that gag into his picture. Chaplin had a fund of visual gags from all the comedians from the

Karno Company. When he wore out his repertoire he went down. But he was a genius. He used all that vast experience he had learned at Karno's. [Fred Karno (1866-1941) was an English impresario who toured United States theaters in 1910-12 with his pantomime comedy shows starring Charles Chaplin—Stan Laurel was the understudy. Roach actually hired Karno in 1929 as a writer and director under a five year contract. However, Roach soon realized that Karno was merely a businessman who had no comic talents himself and his contract was canceled after only four months.]

"Chaplin and I were intimate friends when I worked at Essanay," said Roach. "We'd have at least one meal a day together and also spend the evenings together. Chaplin was a student of comedy, but he was an ignorant man. What I mean by that is that he couldn't have had more than three or four years of schooling.

"He was constantly working. He'd go down to Main Street and just watch people, looking for funny events he could put in his pictures. Even at night, over dinner, he'd discuss his pictures. Chaplin was a perfectionist. I remember he went into a hole six times so it would look right. And the funny thing is, he never drank. I can't remember ever seeing him intoxicated. We'd go down to Levi's Cafe on Spring Street or the Alexandria Bar at the Alexandria Hotel, and Chaplin never drank. Laurel drank a lot, and that makes a big difference. And liquor killed a top comedian I had, Charley Chase.

"Anyway, I didn't have any studio in those days until we sold three dramatic pictures to Universal at a profit." Roach's first studio was located in the Bradbury Mansion, a former Victorian era Queen Anne home located near downtown Los Angeles in an area called 'Bunker Hill,' close to where the Dorothy Chandler Pavilion now stands. It is said Harold Lloyd called the mansion "Pneumonia Hall" because of its excessive draftiness. The thirty-five room structure, complete with five chimneys and five turrets, was eventually demolished in 1929.

Roach's special effects man Roy Seawright recalled years later, "My father was construction boss and architect for all the sets at Rolin Film Company which consisted of one little open-air stage...." Though most exteriors were shot on location around Los Angeles.

Pathé offered Roach a contract on condition that he sign the three leads of *Just Nuts*, Roy Stewart (1883-1933), Jane Novak (1896-1990) and Harold Lloyd (1893-1971). Stewart and Novak were contracted elsewhere, but Roach was able to get permission to produce comedies with just Lloyd. That's when he signed him for $50 per week. Just a few months later, on October 14, 1915 Whiting was able to send Roach a triumphant telegram: "SUCCESS PATHÉ ACCEPTED ALL PICTURES." Thus Pathé Exchange became Roach's sole distributor of films for the next twelve years.

1915 RELEASES:
16 HAROLD LLOYD/LONESOME LUKE ONE-REELERS

"But I have been with Roach ever since," said Lloyd in 1920. "We created the 'Lonesome Luke' series for Pathé." This character, in contrast to Willie Work who mimicked Chaplin to a great degree, wore tight fighting clothes and gave Lloyd a lanky loose look.

In 1974 author Richard Schickel wrote, in his biography of Harold Lloyd, "Roach has flatly claimed that 'Lonesome Luke was my idea,' but Lloyd long ago disputed that notion. It was his father, according to Lloyd, who created the figure's costume, and since no one ever talks about Luke except in terms of apparel, Foxy deserves at least some of the credit for his creation."

Harold Lloyd has been quoted in Suzanne D'Agostino Lloyd's book, *Harold Lloyd: Magic in Horn-Rimmed Glasses*:

"I told Roach that I had something that was an improvement on Willie Work, at least. When he saw it he approved. Later it was tagged with the name of Lonesome Luke. For it my father had found a worn pair of Number 12AA last shoes in a repair shop on Los Angeles Street... In a haberdashery dad found a black-and-white vertical-striped shirt and bought out the stock. The coat of a woman's tailored suit, a pair of very tight and short trousers, a vest too short, a cut-down collar, a cut-down hat and two dots of a mustache completed the original version of Lonesome Luke. The cunning behind all this, you will observe, was to reverse the Chaplin outfit. All his clothes were too large, mine all too small. My shoes were funny, but different; my mustache funny, but different."

A family friend of Dwight Whiting, Dorothy Tree, enjoyed these Lonesome Luke comedies so much so that she sent in her own story ideas which Whiting found to be excellent. "Be careful or you will be famous overnight," Whiting wrote to her in July 1915. He offered her $20 per scenario and eagerly awaited her next efforts. "We are... still in the market for good slapstick ideas," he wrote to her late October, "and can now freelance and buy out right without delay." In December he wrote, "*Rag*

Time Snapshots is really a very good comedy and I am sure you will laugh at seeing your work on the screen."

The Harold Lloyd Lonesome Luke comedies became extremely popular, even rivaling Chaplin's, though Lloyd grew to "loathe" doing them. On November 16, 1915 an executive from the Canadian office of Pathé Exchange sent a congratulatory telegram to the Rolin Film Company. "…YOUR LAST RELEASE BUGHOUSE BELL-HOPS WAS CERTAINLY A VERY GOOD COMEDY AND IF ALL YOUR FILMS WILL BE AS GOOD AS THAT ONE, THEY WILL CERTAINLY MAKE A NAME FOR YOUR MAKE."

A year later came this letter from a Mr. I.D. Stanford, manager of The Lyric Theatre, Chicago: "[Lonesome] Luke is as popular as Chaplin here, if not more so, and his comedies are better by far in every way than those of the Chaplin kind."

Roach and his gang began sending amusing true event anecdotes pertaining to their zany filmmaking adventures to the movie magazines. In November 1915 two humorous incidents occurred, as described by the Rolin Film Company's publicity department:

"A scandal was narrowly averted last week during the production of the latest Phunphilm when the company was on location at one of the fashionable millionaire's palaces of this city. Ten members of a company of skilled Oriental dancers were secured to take part and were given directions to be at the location at a certain time. The owner of the mansion together with his family and friends were interested spectators of the operations when a call for the dancing girls was sent out. Imagine the surprise and horror of Director Roach and the balance of the company when the dancing girls appeared on the lawn in gee-strings and breast plates. Some of the more artistically inclined had even left their breast plates at home. As the board of censors would never pass such films as this would have made, two precious hours were lost while the girls were sent downtown to don bloomers and uppers. Happily the scandal ended without trouble before it started."

And, to emphasize the unpredictable nature of early day filmmaking, another amusing happenstance that year was also dutifully noted: "Last week it was necessary to employ a billy goat in the current picture. Among other amusing incidents which Billy pulled off was the confiscation and swallowing of three scenarios direct from Director Roach's hip pocket. When Mr. Roach discovered his loss, the only part of the scenario in sight was a portion of one of the final pages on which was written 'finis.'"

Less amusing was the day a blast in Edendale "rocked the ground like a miniature earthquake," reported the *Moving Picture World* in December

1915 "and shattered many windows in the neighboring houses" when a keg of blasting powder was set off in a Phunphilm comedy scene at the Rolin studios.

"The property man evidently got the wrong kind of keg," explained the *Moving Picture World*, "and when the explosion came off the whole company was covered with dirt and debris. The assistant director had to be sent to the hospital with a piece of the barrel embedded in his leg and the Rolin Company is now busy paying for all those broken windows. Fortunately Director Roach was safely hidden behind the camera man."

Rolin was not completely happy with their arrangement with Pathé as evidenced by the December 23, 1915 letter Dwight Whiting sent to William Fox of the Fox Film Corporation in New York: "We have at present one company only making Phunphilms for weekly release by Pathé. These comedies, while fair and above average, are not the best we could do, reason for same is that Pathé is not willing to spend the necessary money to get elaborate pictures. As you know, Pathé are shrewd and close buyers and unless our comedies were better than any others they could get for a like price, we would not be under contract with them. Should we enter into negotiations with you on a suitable basis, we could put on a first class company, turning you out any style of comedies you would like. Would not care to go into the deal at all with you unless you wanted comedies of the very highest class, and would be willing to spend the money necessary to obtain the best results." Apparently Fox was unwilling to spend any money on Rolin, and thus Pathé remained their distributor for the next twelve years.

The early one-reelers were made in one week for $1200-$1500 each and usually included Australian comic Harold H. Fraser, aka "Snub" Pollard (1889-1962) and Texan-born teenager Bebe Daniels (1901-1971) who from 1915 to 1919 made about 143 shorts with Lloyd and became his sweetheart. Most of Hollywood thought they would marry.

1916 RELEASES:
THIRTY-FOUR HAROLD LLOYD/LONESOME LUKE ONE-REELERS

In early 1916 it was determined that the Bradbury Mansion required the electrical wiring to be improved; it was decided that a new enclosed stage needed to be built as well, so the Rolin Film Company temporarily moved to a plant in Edendale, the same Los Angeles neighborhood where Mack Sennett was producing his comedies. In April they moved to a well-appointed studio in Hollywood and remained there until their original mansion studio near downtown Los Angeles was ready in September.

To gauge where the Rolin Film Company fitted into the scheme of things Hollywood in that year, it is interesting to note that *Moving Picture World* in their August 1916 issue proclaimed Universal Studios to be "the biggest film company in the world" with a weekly payroll of $50,000 and a weekly overhead of $40,000. Mack Sennett's Keystone Studio had a $30,000 weekly payroll and an equal amount of overhead; little Rolin Film Company in contrast had a weekly payroll of $2,000 with the same amount in weekly expenses.

In late 1916 they began producing two-reel Lonesome Luke comedies, the first being *Lonesome Luke's Lively Life*, released in March 1917. No better endorsement for this comedy was needed than that given by S.L. "Roxy" Rothapfel, the famous showman who later built Radio City Music Hall, who was quoted in *Moving Picture World* stating this was "the funniest comedy I have ever seen." After viewing a series of "Lonesome Lukes" Mr. Berst of Pathé stated, "I saw the whole seven in one morning recently. Fourteen reels of comedies at one sitting is a pretty severe test. I found myself laughing just as heartily at the last one as I did at the first." In addition, by June 1917 *Just Nuts*, the first Willie Work bought by Pathé "made such a hit" said *Moving Picture World* that it was still playing two years later.

Harold Lloyd eventually purchased the rights to all prints of Lonesome Luke from Pathé Exchange but in August 1943 a vault fire at his home Greenacres destroyed negatives and prints and only twelve of nearly seventy Lonesome Lukes are known to have survived. After the vault fire Lloyd built two concrete vaults and made dupe negatives from the best surviving prints.

At this time Roach expanded his repertoire, not content to only make Harold Lloyd comedies. In August 1916 he began producing one-reel comedies starring 18-year-old fat boy Dee "Skinny" Lampton who was five feet tall and weighed 285 pounds, billed as "the fattest fat boy west of the Rocky Mountains," but the few shorts that resulted were considered quite poor. According to Richard Lewis Ward in his 2005 study *A History of the Hal Roach Studios*, "When the films finally reached the theater screens in early 1917, five had been cut to seven minutes, half of the normal running time of a single reel comedy... Rolin accepted a flat payment of five hundred dollars for each of the Skinny comedies without argument, despite the fact that the films had cost one thousand dollars apiece to produce." The Skinny series died, and so did poor Dee Lampton, of a ruptured appendix, just a couple of years later in 1919.

Other Roach employees who began to become prominent in the shorts included Fred Newmeyer (1888-1967) a one-time minor league ball player who became a director and would helm more than half a dozen of Harold Lloyd's classic features of the 1920s; little Sammy Brooks (1891-1951), who chalked up over 200 credits until 1938; the matronly Evelyn Thatcher (1862-1942), who had been on the stage since 1877; Harry Todd (1863-1935), whose film career started way back in 1909 and continued until 1935 where he appeared as a crabby clerk in Hal Roach's feature *Vagabond Lady*; Bud Jamison (1895-1944), who later became well known as a foil for The Three Stooges; Earl Mohan (1889-1928), who would appear with Stan Laurel, Will Rogers and Charley Chase in the 1920s; and Noah Young (1887-1958), a circus weightlifter who became a popular "heavy" for Hal Roach through 1927 and also appeared in several of Harold Lloyd's early talkies. His last credit for Hal Roach was as a member of the Highland Quartet in Laurel & Hardy's *Bonnie Scotland* (1935).

1917 RELEASES:
THIRTEEN HAROLD LLOYD/LONESOME LUKE TWO-REELERS
TEN HAROLD LLOYD/GLASS CHARACTER ONE-REELERS
SIX SKINNY HALF REELERS
FIVE HAROLD LLOYD/LONESOME LUKE ONE-REELERS
TWO SKINNY ONE-REELERS

A performer whom Roach expected to reach the same cinematic heights as Harold Lloyd was the Italian clown Armando "Toto" Novello (1889-1938), who had been a successful star at the Hippodrome Theatre in New York City for the past two years and was called "the most celebrated clown of the day." Roach signed Novello to a two-year contract for a series of two-reel shorts in February 1917 and set to begin June 15th.

Special clause: Toto does not have to jump into water. Salary: $200 per week the first six months, $250 per week the second six months and $300 per week the second one year. Roach would say that Toto was the result of a two-year search "to find a true comedian who would be absolutely different from any working in pictures." The first Toto two-reeler would be released in January 1918.

In May 1917 a new two-year contract was signed with Pathé stipulating the production of three comedies made for $8,000 each with a bonus of $6,000 on acceptance of the third comedy and $10,000 for the fourth and each ensuing comedy. "Pathé agrees to submit to its Film Reviewing Committee... all sample positives delivered by Rolin... Said Film Reviewing Committee is composed of not less than fourteen (14) members selected by Pathé among its prominent employees... Each of the members present at any session makes an individual report in writing stating whether the films submitted can be classified as GOOD, NEARLY GOOD, FAIR or POOR with a prief [sic] criticism to justify the classification adopted." Pathé has the right to reject "any comedy which shall not be considered either GOOD or NEARLY GOOD by the *majority* of the members...."

The contract also stated in Exhibit C "...Harold C. Lloyd shall play the leading part in same in a make-up different from the one heretofore used by him." Hence Lloyd modified his character, becoming an energetic, all-American boy-next-door, and acquired his famous trademarks—round, wire-rimmed glasses and a straw hat." Actually, the glasses Lloyd was to use were horn-rimmed.

"They [the Lonesome Lukes films] proved popular," said Lloyd in 1920, "but I was always dissatisfied. I felt that every one believed I was a mere imitator and I wanted to do something absolutely original. I hit upon the idea of my present bespectacled character, but it was no easy matter to persuade anyone to let me drop the more or less popular Luke for an untried idea. But I finally got it over."

Sixty years later, Hal Roach presented a different version of the appearance of the "Glass Character." For the Thames Television miniseries *Hollywood* in 1980 he said, "We had a guy that did a great drunk [Earl Mohan] and one day he came out on the set with a pair of glasses, rims that didn't have any glass in them, and he looked very funny with these things on and that's where I got the original idea of the glasses for Lloyd. Much to the disappointment of Pathé, we changed the character from Lonesome Luke to a straight character and the only identification were the glasses. That character was almost an immediate success."

The "Glass Character," as Lloyd called him—in distinction to the "Glasses Character" which many authors inaccurately write, alternated as one-reelers, with two-reel Lonesome Lukes. The first Glass Character comedy was *Over The Fence* released in September 1917, with the last Lonesome Luke was *We Never Sleep* being released in December. There were about ten Lonesome Luke one-reelers released in 1915; thirty-four in 1916 (the entire Roach output for that year); in 1917 Harold Lloyd made five Lonesome Luke one-reelers and twelve two-reelers, and ten "glass" character one-reelers.

Beginning in 1917 Alfred J. "Alf" Goulding (1884-1972) began sharing the directing duties with Roach. A former vaudevillian from Australia, Goulding would became great friends with Stan Laurel and stay involved with the Studio for decades.

Roach would do less and less actual directing as the years progressed, though he always kept his hand in. Richard Schickel reported that Harold Lloyd "would later recall that Roach, as a director, seemed insecure. 'Hal had an excellent mind, a very fertile mind for thinking of comedy ideas... But because he hadn't had the experience, he wasn't quite as good at setting up a scene. There were many times, even in the very early days, Hal would say, 'How would you do *this*, Harold?' Now he was the boss, and it was his company and I was working for him.'"

Years later, the great veteran director George Marshall (1891-1975) would state that he felt Roach got bored by the day-to-day mechanics of directing; in 1972 Victor Mature, who had been directed by Roach in the early 1940s, stated that Roach would "willingly hand the directorial reins to his assistant, with little concern, if the mood took him, particularly if there was a race meeting that he didn't want to miss."

These observations were confirmed by historian William K. Everson: "[Roach] seemed unsure of himself as a director," he wrote in his booklet *The Films of Hal Roach* prepared for a New York Museum of Modern Art retrospective and published in 1971, "and frequently—even though the film might be developing quite smoothly—would throw up his hands, exclaim, 'This is going badly!' and assign someone else to finish it. It is far more likely that Roach was merely bored....Clearly for Roach...the real work of movie making took place before the cameras rolled, at the typewriter and at the story conferences. Once the script was finished, what followed was largely mechanical, or so dependent on a player's personality, that the directorial contribution was theoretically minimal."

Roach as a director would even be disrespected, as in a December 1939 *Photoplay* article wherein stars Joan Bennett and Adolphe Menjou described the filming of *The Housekeeper's Daughter* as "horrible," even though the movie itself received excellent notices. But that negative attitude may have been due more to what the players considered to be an inferior script.

Another Roach actress was far from critical of her boss. A petite and pretty young performer who appeared in the four half-reel Skinny comedies released in 1917 by the name of Marguerite Nichols consented to become Mrs. Hal Roach on September 29, 1916.

In October 1917 a young gag writer was hired for the Harold Lloyd series. His name was Jimmy Parrott and the 20-year-old also worked as a guaranteed extra, paid $5 a day five days a week regardless of how many days he actually worked.

Harold Lloyd created the first of his skyscraper "thrill" pictures, *Look out Below* in 1918 and he became world famous for his skyscraper antics.

"We always gave Harold a 'good opening' in his pictures," Roach told me in 1973. "For example, at the beginning of *Doctor Jack*, Lloyd comes across a little girl crying over a broken doll. Lloyd fixes it, mends it like a doctor, and makes the girl happy. Then, in *Bumping into Broadway*, he has a hole in his sock, so he paints the bare spot on his leg black. This was always done to make him sympathetic, a nice guy."

In September 1917 *Moving Picture World* reported that the second Toto comedy produced was shown to the Pathé screening committee and the verdict was that it "easily ranks as one of the best laugh producer that has ever been made... Toto is destined to be a great favorite."

The following month lovely brunette 19-year-old Clarine Seymour was signed as Toto's leading lady. "That Mr. Roach, who is admittedly one of the very greatest comedy directors in the country," stated *Moving Picture World*, "should have selected little Miss Seymour for such an important role speaks volumes for her beauty and talent."

But just as Rolin was getting a new lease on life, Uncle Sam came calling. They wanted 25-year-old Hal Roach to go "over there" and fight in World War I. Several Rolin employees wrote letters to the U.S. military explaining why Roach should be exempt from military duty. H.M. Walker, the Sporting Editor of the *Los Angeles Examiner*, who was Rolin's freelance title writer at $40 per picture, wrote "...Rolin Film Company would be obliged to suspend business if said Harry E. Roach should leave or be removed from the personal direction of the production of said company." W.H. Doane, Assistant Manager, wrote "Both parents are advanced in age. Father Charles H. 58 is crippled in one leg from hip disease. Mother 52. Their son contributes $95 per month for both parents." Earl L. Wisdom, Vice President, wrote "The contract with Pathé requires Roach's personal direction. About 70 employees would be affected."

Whiting wrote, "The success of Rolin Film Company has been entirely due to the peculiar talents of said Harry E. Roach in the assembling of actors and the direction of the making of the pictures themselves."

Roach received his military exemption from active participation in World War I, but the U.S. military would not forget about him. In September of 1917 another branch of the U.S. government contacted Mr. Roach. This time it was a certain Herbert Hoover of the U.S. Food Administration in Washington, D.C. who prevailed upon Mr. Roach "to help us in all possible manner to preserve our Country's food stuffs by eliminating the use of actual food in the production of your pictures so far as possible." So much for pie fights and such. Mr. Roach patiently waited ten years to have fun with food again when he produced one of the greatest of all pie fights in cinema history in Laurel & Hardy's *The Battle of the Century*.

1918 Releases:
Thirty-four Harold Lloyd "glass" one-reelers.
Eight Toto one-reelers
Six Toto two-reelers
Two Stan Laurel one-reelers

In 1918 Dwight Whiting sold his Rolin stock to Roach and left the company. According to journalist and author Joe Moore, "Roach, himself, always said that it was Pathé who was eager to get rid of Whiting. As to why they wanted Whiting gone we don't know for sure. Maybe they thought that Roach alone would be easier to manipulate than the shrewder Whiting. At the time of Whiting's departure Rolin had only just recently gotten the upper hand on Pathé with the surprise success of the new Harold Lloyd glasses films that had been launched the previous fall.

"Prior to that it looked like there was a very good chance that Pathé might be dumping Rolin over the costly Toto fiasco and the abandonment of the successful 'Lonesome Luke' series. With the new Lloyd series such a big hit (apparently surprising everyone but Lloyd) maybe Pathé felt that by eliminating businessman Whiting they could negotiate things more to their benefit."

It is not clear why Moore called the Toto series a "costly fiasco." Perhaps, as indicated by author Richard Lewis Ward, Toto was experiencing health problems and could not perform at that time. Novello was to die some twenty years later, at the age of forty-nine. The two-reelers released in early 1918 received excellent reviews and in April, Pathé Vice President and General Manager J.A. Berst publicly announced that two Toto two-reelers would be released per month instead of just one because of the great success and greater demand for the clown's comedies. Yet only a few months later the two-reelers were reduced to one reel in length; and on July 20, 1918 the trades announced that Toto had left Rolin-Pathé and was returning to the stage. His leading lady Clarine Seymour, "the cutie Beautiful" as she was dubbed, was immediately signed by D.W. Griffith and after appearing in two of his pictures became an overnight star. One reviewer noted that Clarine "...seems brimming over with electrical fascination. She seems to be fashioned of a thousand magnets." Her last picture was *The Idol Dancer* with Richard Barthelmess, wherein she played a half-caste tropical island nymphet. Tragically, Clarine Seymour died in a New York hospital on April 25, 1920 after a four day abdominal illness at the age of twenty-one.

Not long before his departure Whiting had written the following to members of the British Consulate in Los Angeles who were inquiring as to the nature of the U.S. film industry:

"Making pictures that are worthwhile and which will be successful is an art, just as fully as is the creation of anything else which is the product of the intellect... it is unlikely that as long as a finished picture must be the blending of the artistic abilities of a number of specially gifted people that it will ever be possible to put the production upon an efficient factory manufacturing basis in a successful manner."

Of course, the "factory system" is indeed what Hollywood was later to adopt, and the quality of the work of "specially gifted" individual artists (such as Roach stars Laurel & Hardy) were to suffer as a result of that "efficient factory manufacturing basis" that is modern mainstream movie making.

After Whiting left Roach he became an executive with the Union Oil Company. His position as Rolin's Secretary & Treasurer was then taken up by Hal Roach's own father, C.H. "Dad" Roach (1860-1936) who had, along with his wife Mabel (1868-1962) and Hal's older brother John B. "Jack" Roach (1889-1979), moved to California from Elmira, New York. Warren Doane (1890-1964), who had trained under Whiting, ended up taking over much of Whiting's duties and Roach himself had also become more business savvy after having worked with Whiting for nearly four years. Roach and Whiting continued to maintain an association. In 1925 Whiting was instrumental in selling Roach's yacht and in the 1930s became a partner in the creation of the Santa Anita Racetrack.

According to Ted Okuda and James L. Neibaur in *Stan Without Ollie* (2012) Alf Goulding recommended Stan Laurel to Hal Roach after Toto had left.

"The replacement was contingent on Pathé's approval, so on or about May 25, 1918 a short film was made featuring Stan (as a slapstick waiter) and Roach contract comedian Harry 'Snub' Pollard. Pathé liked what they saw and on June 11 Stan Laurel began working on his first Hal Roach production *Do You Love Your Wife?* a one-reeler released January 5, 1919 with Marie Mosquini, William Gillespie, Bud Jamison, Charles Stevenson, Noah Young, James Parrot and Lois Neilson, who became Stan's first wife from 1926 to 1933. This short was released after *Just Rambling Along*, Stan's second film for Roach.

Stan Laurel made five shorts for Roach, then left to work elsewhere for the next four years. For comedian Larry Semon at Vitagraph Laurel appeared in three two-reelers and then appeared in eight shorts for 'Bronco' Billy Anderson including *The Lucky Dog* made in 1921 and notable as Stan's first screen appearance with Oliver Hardy.

On June 15, 1918 Hal and Marguerite Roach became parents for the first time with the birth of Hal Roach Jr. who would play such an important role in later years.

1919 RELEASES:
THIRTY-SEVEN HAROLD LLOYD ONE-REELERS
TEN SNUB POLLARD ONE-REELERS
THREE HAROLD LLOYD TWO-REELERS
THREE STAN LAUREL ONE-REELERS
ONE TOTO ONE-REELER

On April 12, 1919 a new contract between Rolin & Pathé was signed. Nine two-reel comedies were to be made within the next eighteen months, with Harold Lloyd to get half of Rolin's profits. Greater care was now taken in making the comedies, with as many as ten takes per scene. The practice of presenting audience previews was introduced at this time. But the following month Roach faced a dilemma: Bebe Daniels who was Harold Lloyd's leading lady, left Roach to become a dramatic actress with Cecil B. DeMille.

Roach sent a telegram to Paul Brunet, the Vice President and General Manager of Pathé in New York: "BEBE DANIELS SIGNED WITH LASKY CO. TO BE FEATURED BY C.B. DEMILLE IN BIG PRODUC-

TIONS. IMPOSSIBLE TO KEEP HER WITH US. HAVE YOU ANY SUGGESTIONS TO ADVISE FOR LEADING LADY WITH LLOYD?"

Brunet's reply: "REGARDING BEBE DANIELS WE HAVE NO SUGGESTIONS TO MAKE TO HER SUCCESSOR. AS YOU ARE MORE FAMILIAR WITH COMEDY SITUATION SUGGEST YOU ATTEMPT TO FIND SOMEONE IN L.A. IF YOU LEARN OF A PROSPECT WORKING IN NY WE WILL BE PLEASED TO INTERVIEW HER IN YOUR BEHALF."

On May 22, 1919 Roach wrote to Brunet: "I am trying to get Mildred Davis who played lead in Bryant Washburn picture 'All Wrong' to play leads with Lloyd. Kindly ask the opinion of people there regarding this girl." Brunet responded, "Mildred Davis is very satisfactory. We suggest that you get her."

Mildred Davis indeed became Harold Lloyd's new leading lady. The first short Mildred made with Harold was called *From Hand To Mouth* released in December 1919. They made fourteen more films together, including Lloyd's early features. She signed a new contract on February 1, 1921 for six months at $250.00 per week. After the famous skyscraper thrill feature *Safety Last* Mildred became Harold's leading lady in real life. They married in 1923 and she bore him three children. Mildred Davis retired from the screen to manage their home, the 44-room Beverly Hills mansion Greenacres, until her death in 1968.

Bebe Daniels, meanwhile, the leading lady Harold Lloyd didn't marry, went on to a successful dramatic career with DeMille and Lasky throughout the '20s. She appeared in some comedies too and triumphed in the early talkie musical *Rio Rita* (1929). She married actor Ben Lyon in 1930. After her memorable performance in *42nd Street* (1933) as the temperamental Broadway diva who sprains her ankle enabling Ruby Keeler to become the new sensation of the Great White Way, the Lyons found success in London on stage and radio. After World War II Bebe returned to Hollywood and to the Hal Roach Studios in 1946 as a producer, and is credited with Roach's streamliner film *The Fabulous Joe* about a talking dog which was part of *The Hal Roach Comedy Carnival*. She then returned to England and starred with her husband in the television series *Life With the Lyons* from 1955 to 1960. Ironically, she passed away eight days after Harold Lloyd did, on March 16, 1971.

Mildred Davis proved to be a worthy replacement. Great success came with *Bumping Into Broadway* (1919). On June 5th Roach wrote to Paul Brunet at Pathé: "I have just finished reviewing our first two-reel picture, which I hope Pathé will be pleased with. We have placed all our efforts in making it not only funny, but trying to put a consistent heart interest and story in the picture, and I think it has brought it up to a very high standard." Some criticized the film as having a slow start, but Roach disagreed. "There is nothing worse in comedy than to start off with a bang and then slow up at the finish."

Roach's enthusiastic opinion in June about Lloyd's first "glass" comedy was borne out when he received a telegram from H.M. Walker who was in New York City that fall. "SAW 'BUMPING INTO BROADWAY' BEFORE TWO PACKED SUNDAY HOUSES. IT WENT OVER LIKE A MILLION DOLLARS. HAVE TAKEN WHOLE PAGE IN CALIFORNIA THEATER PROGRAM FOR YOUR NAME IN BIG TYPE WITH STUDIO ANNOUNCEMENT."

Bumping Into Broadway had cost $17,274 to produce. Rolin's net profits in the first three years of distribution amounted to $63,987. It wasn't long before Harold Lloyd was one of the wealthiest actors in Hollywood.

"All the subsequent Lloyd shorts were released to the type of fanfare and exhibitor excitement usually reserved for special features," wrote Richard Lewis Ward in his *A History of the Hal Roach Studios*. "Thus, after five years of marginal success, Rolin ended 1919 with two significant gains: Lloyd was now a first-rank comedy star, and the new series of Rolin one-reelers was a popular production-line replacement for the Lloyd one-reelers."

Ask Father (1919) directed by Hal Roach is considered "perhaps the finest of the one-reel comedies for its construction and clever gags" according to author Jeffrey Vance and Suzanne Lloyd, Harold's granddaughter in their book *Harold Lloyd, Master Comedian*. He followed that excellent film with more and more of consistent quality, including his first "thrill" comedy *Look Out Below.*

In addition to Roach, Harold Lloyd's directors were Gilbert Pratt (1892-1954) who stayed for over twenty years, and was one of the screenwriters for Laurel & Hardy's last film at Roach, *Saps At Sea* (1940) and Alf Goulding, who also worked long for Roach, directing L&H's penultimate Roach film, *A Chump At Oxford* (1940). Englishman Frank Terry (1870-1948) joined Rolin in 1919 as a gag man. He later worked with Laurel & Hardy as writer and bit actor. Terry became notorious as the man who inadvertently handed Lloyd the NOT-fake bomb, which exploded at a photo session in August 1919, disfiguring poor Harold's hand. It was feared Harold Lloyd might have become blind by the bomb explosion; fortunately he made a full recovery, although his right hand was disfigured.

Critic and author Richard Schickel, ever suspicious of Roach's claims, wrote in his book on Harold Lloyd, "It is Roach, to be sure, who claims to have designed the device to disguise the deformed hand. He says he found a firm in New York to manufacture it, and that 'by the time [Lloyd] was well and out of the hospital we had the whole thing ready for him.' About this point, the truth will probably never be known."

Well, thanks to the documents in the Hal Roach Collection at USC the truth is now known. Letters reveal that Roach personally spent months in an effort to find the exact prosthetic glove that would be not only comfortable for Lloyd to wear but that would also give the best illusion of a real hand that had five fingers. It was finally on April 24, 1920 that the Rubber Limb Company of New York sent the most satisfactory rubber hand for Mr. Lloyd. The accompanying letter stated "[This glove] is the result of many experiments, and we believe that you will agree with us that it is just what you desire."

Before *Bumping Into Broadway* could be released and Lloyd resume movie making, Roach realized he needed to add more comedies to his roster. Two days after Lloyd's accident production began on Snub Pollard's first one-reeler.

In September 1919 Roach hired a little boy named Ernest "Sunshine Sammy" Morrison to act with Lloyd; Morrison (1912-1989) was the first African-American actor to sign a long term contract in Hollywood. "Sunshine Sammy" Morrison signed (rather, his father signed for him) a two-year contract as Hal Roach was planning to feature him in his own starring series. But Pathé's Paul Brunet vetoed that idea, so Roach cast him in support of Snub Pollard's comedies, and this series became Rolin's staple product. I met Mr. Morrison in 1987 at a Way Out West meeting in North Hollywood, California and mentioned to him that I also was working for Mr. Roach. He broke out into a literal sunshine of a smile. "What a fine man he was!" he beamed.

By the end of 1919 Harold Lloyd had produced eighty one-reelers and Roach was ready to expand. But a fire ordinance prevented him from adding on to his Bunker Hill facilities. He looked west, to a place called Culver City, which at that time was, according to writers Anthony and Edmonds, "little more than soy bean fields and orange groves. The area was considered too far a commute from downtown Los Angeles, and commerce was reluctant to settle there." Real estate developer Henry Culver had convinced film pioneer Thomas Ince to build a studio there in 1915. The Ince-Triangle Studio, run by Ince, D.W. Griffith and Mack Sennett was taken over by Samuel Goldwyn in 1918; it became M-G-M in 1924. Ince built a second studio on Washington Boulevard in 1918 which later was taken over by Cecil B. DeMille and then RKO. It became Selznick International Studios in 1935 and later, as a television production center, by Desilu in 1956.

According to the Culver City website, Hal Roach purchased his initial ten acres from his friend Harry Culver for $1,000 an acre on land located not far from the Ince Studio. Construction began in November 1919. The studio was later expanded to fourteen acres and ultimately to a reported eighteen acres by the 1950s.

The Hal Roach Studios became known as the Lot of Fun, but it opened under tragic circumstances.

"After they finished the administration building," recalled Roy Seawright according to Anthony and Edmonds, "during construction of the big stage my father was up in the scaffold with his assistant, and this big wind came up and it tore the scaffold down, and he fell and was killed. So that was, dare I say, my entrée as an office boy to the Hal Roach Studios in 1920."

Once the main facilities were completed, production commenced in March 1920 with the filming of Harold Lloyd's *An Eastern Westerner* although the official completion date for the Culver City studio was listed as April 20, 1920.

1920 RELEASES:
FORTY SNUB POLLARD ONE-REELERS
SIX HAROLD LLOYD TWO-REELERS
SIX VANITY FAIR GIRLS ONE-REELERS

On August 12, 1920 the Rolin Film Company officially became the Hal E. Roach Studios. There were now 150 employees on the payroll, including H.M. Walker, who had been working freelance as title writer since 1916 and was now offered a contract. He remained with Roach until 1932, remembered today for the amusing titles and later dialogue he contributed to the films of Laurel & Hardy.

However, real life communications at the new location became a nightmare. Being so far flung from Los Angeles, the studio simply was unable to secure adequate phone service. Roy Seawright recalled that there was one telephone on the whole lot and he was "running back and forth giving messages and taking messages from people all over the studio...."

By September 1920 there was still no exchange service or trunk lines; they had to share a party line with another subscriber. It took many heated and frustrating communications to finally obtain a hearing by the Railroad Commission of the State of California and then many more months of waiting before the Railroad Commission was finally able to state "Your installation should be readied between June 1 and 8, 1921." But the following year there were still problems. "We are having a great deal of difficulty in hearing people who are calling in," a Rolin letter to the Southern California Telephone Company complained. "This condition has continued ever since the switchboard was installed... reporting a telephone out of order is a farce as absolutely no attention appears to be made to these reports...."

But bad telephone service in Los Angeles was apparently a well known joke even before Hal Roach moved to Culver City. *The Morning Oregonian* (Portland, Oregon) newspaper of July 21, 1919 had run this anecdote:

"Harold Lloyd came out of his office recently with a broad smile on his face.

'I just called on the telephone and got the r-i-g-h-t number,' he announced. 'Whaddaya know about that?'

'How did it happen?' asked General Director Hal E. Roach.

'I called the wrong one,' said Mr. Lloyd, proudly."

Apparently the telephone situation was at last resolved by that June 1922 complaint. In any event, the comedies kept being churned out in spite of it.

By 1920 gag writer Jimmy Parrott was placed in front of the cameras to co-star with Snub Pollard in the short *Cut Your Cards*. The following year he starred in his own series, playing a comedian by the name of Paul Parrott. He was paid $65 a week for these one-reelers.

"He was a nice guy," said Roach, "but he was not a well guy... I never tried to make him a big comedian because I was afraid the epilepsy would show up." That's not the only thing that would show up with Paul Parrott. He brought his older brother Charley Parrott, a former vaudeville performer, over to the Roach lot. A song and dance man from the age of fourteen in 1912, Charles Parrott, who would best be known by his screen name, Charley Chase, appeared in his first picture at Universal Studios.

Then he joined Mack Sennett's at $5.00 a day as a film extra and later became a permanent member of the stock company. Roach immediately assessed Charley's talent, adding him to the studio payroll in the summer of 1920 at the rate of $200 per week. His salary was raised to $300 per week shortly thereafter.

Roach began expanding his comedy repertoire. In the fall of 1920 he produced five one-reel comedies starring Beatrice La Plante (1891-1973) whose entire movie career lasted only about three years.

1921 RELEASES:
THIRTY-SIX SNUB POLLARDS ONE-REELERS
NINETEEN ONE-REEL HAROLD LLOYD RERELEASES
EIGHT EDDIE BOLAND ONE-REELERS
SEVEN VANITY FAIR GIRLS ONE-REELERS
FIVE GAYLORD LLOYD ONE-REELERS
FOUR HAROLD LLOYDS SHORTS (ASSOCIATED PRODUCERS:
THREE THREE-REELERS, ONE TWO-REELER)
ONE SUNSHINE SAMMY TWO-REELER
ONE HAROLD LLOYD FOUR-REELER: *A SAILOR-MADE MAN*

In February 1921, twenty-six-year-old Charles Parrott began directing the Snub Pollard one-reelers, alternating with Alf Goulding.

Hal Roach began producing one-reelers with actor Eddie Boland and the Vanity Fair girls in a series that lasted until the fall of 1921. Edmund L. Boland (1883-1935) had been in the movies since 1912. His most famous role after he left Roach would be as "The Obliging Gentleman" in F.W. Murnau's classic *Sunrise* (1927). Boland was apparently not very obliging when he worked at the Hal Roach Studios, as indicated in a 1925 note from Warren Doane to Ben Shipman: "He suffered from acute drunkenness and became seriously ill and unable to work, causing us considerable inconvenience and expense."

During 1921 Roach also produced five one-reelers starring Harold's older brother, Gaylord Lloyd (1888-1943) who performed, often uncredited, in over fifty shorts with Harold beginning in 1916. While his brother was recuperating from his bomb accident in 1919, Gaylord appeared in twenty-one Snub Pollard comedies. After Harold left Roach's employ in 1923, Gaylord became Harold's assistant director and business manager until the late '30s.

A union strike affected several Hollywood studios in the summer of 1921 when the carpenters and painters protested wages being cut by the Motion Picture Producers' Association from one dollar a day to less than five dollars a week and time and a half overtime being discontinued unless the overtime ran over two hours. Roach shut his studio down for a week before the issue was resolved.

Harold Lloyd's final short for Roach was *Never Weaken*, released in October 1921. That year Lloyd and Roach produced their first four-reel comedy, *Sailor Made Man*.

"Long ago were the days when Hal Roach could dock Harold Lloyd's salary if he showed up late for work," wrote Richard Lewis Ward. His new contract in November 1921 gave him eighty percent of the net profits of his films versus twenty percent for Roach. "Lloyd was virtually an independent producer using Hal Roach Studios as his production facility." Lloyd's unit consisted of a twelve-member team: writers, directors and camera operators who turned out four smash hits in 1922-23: *Grandma's Boy*, *Dr. Jack*, *Safety Last* and *Why Worry?* By 1927 Lloyd would become one of Hollywood's top major stars with an estimated net worth of $15 million a year.

In August 1921, the Hal Roach Comedies started to feature Paul Parrott (actually Charles' brother, James), who replaced the departing Eddie Boland. In December 1921, Charles Parrott was appointed director-general of the studio, "a position he had held unofficially almost since his arrival," according to Anthony and Edmonds. This gave him supervisory status over all of the non-Lloyd films.

"Roach had a 'hands off' policy with his newly appointed director," wrote Anthony and Edmonds. "He must have sensed a kindred spirit and therefore allowed Charley a free rein in shaping the various production units. Much of the distinctive, whimsical style associated with the Hal Roach comedies are contributed by Charley Parrott. He was responsible for bringing the best directors and the most endearing actors into the Roach fold."

Charley Parrott brought scenario writer Robert McGowan, with whom he had worked at Paramount in 1920 in the child comedy *Kids Is Kids*, to Roach as a gag writer in 1921. This move proved prophetic, as McGowan would become THE director of the Our Gang series for over a decade.

1922 RELEASES:
FORTY-FIVE HAROLD LLOYD ONE-REEL RE-RELEASES
TWENTY-NINE PAUL PARROTT ONE-REELERS
TWENTY-SEVEN SNUB POLLARD ONE-REELERS
SIX OUR GANG TWO-REELERS
FOUR SNUB POLLARD TWO-REELERS
TWO SERIALS: *WHITE EAGLE, THE TIMBER QUEEN*
HAROLD LLOYD'S *GRANDMA'S BOY* FIVE-REELS
HAROLD LLOYD'S *DR. JACK* FIVE-REELS

The year 1922 began with the release of Roach's first dramatic serial, *White Eagle*, starring Ruth Roland (1892-1937) in fifteen two-reelers. Another serial with Miss Roland followed later that year, *The Timber Queen*. The next year Roach produced another serial *Her Dangerous Path* in ten two-reel chapters starring Edna Murphy (1899-1974).

Snub Pollard graduated to two-reel comedies, some of which were real gems, directed by Charley Parrott.

Lloyd's *Sailor-Made Man* had been released at Christmastime 1921 and by April 1922 it had broken box-office records in thirty cities across the United States. Roach and Lloyd followed this success with a five-reel feature and another box-office hit, *Grandma's Boy*, in September 1922. This feature was distributed by Associated Exhibitors.

"We didn't intend for it to be a feature," said Lloyd in *Harold Lloyd, Master Comedian* by Jeffrey Vance & Suzanne Lloyd. "We had started it as a two-reeler. In fact, our group—Hal and myself, our staff—we were thoroughly entrenched in making two-reel pictures and doing pretty well with them. But this had such a nice theme that it just kept growing, and we let it grow. But when it came to getting more money for it the exhibitors were a little loath to pay us more than they had been paying for two-reelers… So we took a third-run house that was showing newsreels and we put the picture in there. They thought we were off our rocker, but the picture ran nineteen weeks. It established a tremendous record and from then on we had no trouble." After fourteen weeks, *Grandma's Boy* broke both the Los Angeles and the New York records for the longest running film. It finally closed during the nineteenth week.

Dr. Jack later that year also brought profits, and *Safety Last* (1923) became Lloyd's most famous skyscraper caper and one of Hollywood's greatest successes, both financially and critically.

Meanwhile, another great success was being created: the Our Gang Comedies. Buckwheat, Spanky, Alfalfa, and Farina are still household names decades later: the Our Gang comedies, first reaching the screen in 1922, lasted an incredible twenty-two years in motion picture theaters and they continue their phenomenal success with four decades (and counting) on television. A total of about fifty children headlined the cast in this series throughout the years; Roach sold the series in 1938 to MGM.

Generally there were six children under contract, with a complete turn over every four years. There were a few exceptions to the four-year rule: Allen "Farina" Hoskins (1920-1980) wins the prize has having appeared in the most shorts—105—from 1922 to 1931. George "Spanky" McFarland (1928-1993) is second with ninety-five shorts from 1932-1942; Billie "Buckwheat" Thomas (1931-1980) appeared in ninety-three shorts from 1934-1944; Fat boy Joe Cobb (1916-2002) was in eighty-six shorts from 1923-1929; Jackie Condon (1918-1977) performed in seventy-eight shorts from 1922-1928. Carl 'Alfalfa' Switzer (1927-1959) appeared in about sixty-one shorts from 1935-1940.

The first Our Gang picture was helmed by Fred Newmeyer but was "previewed with disastrous results," according to Anthony and Edmonds. Charles Parrott then requested that the talented Robert McGowan, who had proven his affinity with children, reshoot the picture, and this time the results were encouraging.

Robert F. McGowan (1882-1955) helmed the Little Rascals series (soon to be known as Our Gang, based on the title of the first short) from its inception into 1933.

Years later, Jackie Cooper, an Our Gang member from 1929 to 1931, recalled "Without asking for it, [Robert F. McGowan] commanded respect. We wanted to please him, because we loved him."

Bob F. McGowan's nephew Robert A. McGowan (1901-1955), known as Anthony Mack, also directed the Gang; from 1934-1936 it was Gus Meins (1893-1940) who also directed the Thelma Todd/ZaSu Pitts/Patsy Kelly shorts in the mid-1930s; and Gordon Douglas (1907-1993) directed the Gang from 1936 until they left Roach to go to MGM in 1938.

For the complete story and filmography of Our Gang and its 221 shorts, the book *The Little Rascals: The Life and Times of Our Gang* by Leonard Maltin and Richard W. Bann is essential reading. It was first published in 1977; an updated version became available in 1992.

In 1973 I asked Mr. Roach how the conception of this kids series came about.

"I had spent the whole day auditioning children for one of my pictures. Every audition was the same: one of these stage mothers making their kid tap dance or whatever for me. There was something very phony about the whole process; these phony kids smiling at me and trying to 'act.' Well, after I had had enough of this, I shut the door to my office and just stared out the window. I noticed some kids playing in the street. Just ordinary kids building moats and drawbridges and things like that with a few pieces of wood. Playing in the gutter. And I was utterly fascinated. I must have watched them for half an hour. And suddenly, I thought: 'If I could become so engrossed in watching every-day kids playing with nothing but a few sticks—imagine what a success a comedy would be with just such kids.'"

Hal Roach had discovered his great inspiration and model for making comedies: children.

"Charlie Chaplin's running around the corner on one leg—that's the child in him. Charlie walking down the street and swinging his cane, hitting himself in the back of the head with it and turning around to see who did it—that's the little kid in the high chair with a spoon, swinging it around and hitting himself. I mean, Laurel & Hardy, Charlie Chaplin, Buster Keaton, Fatty Arbuckle—they were all children."

In a recorded interview with Anthony Slide for a 1970 publication *The Silent Picture*, Roach explained the immediate commercial success of his kids' series. "The name of the thing was THE LITTLE RASCALS, but the first picture was called OUR GANG. It had previewed very well, and I took it to Sid Grauman, who at that time had the biggest theater in Los Angeles, and I said, 'Sid, I'm going to show you a picture before I send it to New York.' He put the picture on his theater immediately; it went great and he said this is great entertainment. Then there was a lot of publicity about it but they didn't pick up the name LITTLE RASCALS, they picked up the name OUR GANG comedies. So the theaters began asking for OUR GANG comedies, so we changed the name, and we then called them OUR GANG. If the country hadn't gone double feature, they'd probably still be going."

Christmas 1922: A Hal Roach Studios tradition began which would last for eight riotous seasons. "The Follies of Culver City" was an extravagant live show performed by the studio company. Some of the members of the all-male cast wore dresses. The central skit was "The King of Honolulu" in which the "ladies" danced in hula skirts. Even Our Gang members Jackie Davis and Mickey Daniels were flower girls. The three hour combo of raw burlesque and vaudeville was seen by producers, exhibitors and stars from all over Hollywood. The event would get wilder and wilder as the twenties roared on.

"The guests and cast got so drunk each year," wrote Anthony and Edwards, "that Culver City police would be on special alert just for the show. Eventually eight to 900 people were coming to the yearly Roach Christmas shows. But the whole thing was called off after the Christmas show of 1930 when several people died in auto accidents caused by drunken guests leaving the studio after the show.

Harold Lloyd made *Why Worry?* in 1923, his final film with Hal Roach. With Roach engrossed in the production of his new Our Gang series, they amicably agreed to part company, and in July 1923 Lloyd went on to produce his own films.

"It was the nicest separation it could possibly have been," Lloyd said in later years. "The relationship was splendid."

Yet according to Anthony and Edmond, "Relations were so strained [between Roach and Lloyd] that Lloyd's final contract with the studio stipulated Roach's name would not even appear in the main credits of Lloyd's films." This situation would lead to a legal challenge by Roach some forty years later.

Nevertheless, "the two men decided to end their nearly ten-year partnership on a high note," wrote Vance and Lloyd, "by lavishing the picture with the best production values money could buy (making it the most expensive Lloyd film up until that time) and incorporating the highest number of gags of any Lloyd picture...." Seven months in the making (December 1922—June 1923) and costing $220,626, it was released on September 16, 1923 and grossed $1,476,254, making it one of the biggest box office attractions of 1923.

At a screening at the American Film Institute in 1969 Lloyd told the audience, "Hal Roach came to me and said, 'Harold, you don't need me anymore. I got so many pictures of my own to do, we might as well go our own way.' Which we did, in the most amicable way that any two people could have done."

"The truth was that the parting was inevitable," concluded Anthony and Edmonds. "Lloyd had an ego as voracious as Roach's, and there was room for only one boss at the studio." After Lloyd left Roach he eventually built his own studio on forty acres of land in Westwood.

In 1932 Harold Lloyd bought Pathé's remaining interest in all of his films from *Bumping Into Broadway* (1919) to *The Freshman* (1925). He then released through Paramount Pictures. Roach retained his producer's percentage to all the films through *Why Worry?* Why, indeed.

3

The All Stars
Consolidating a Legacy
1923-1926

1923 RELEASES:
TWENTY-EIGHT PAUL PARROTT ONE-REELERS
FOURTEEN OUR GANG TWO-REELERS
THIRTEEN STAN LAUREL ONE-REELERS
TEN SNUB POLLARD TWO-REELERS
SEVEN DIPPY DOO DADS ONE-REELERS
FIVE SNUB POLLARD ONE-REELERS
FOUR STAN LAUREL TWO-REELERS
FOUR SPAT FAMILY TWO-REELERS
THREE WILL ROGERS TWO-REELERS
TWO HAROLD LLOYD FEATURES: *SAFETY LAST* AND *WHY WORRY?*
ONE SERIAL: *HER DANGEROUS PATH* (TEN CHAPTERS)
ONE DRAMATIC FEATURE: *CALL OF THE WILD*

"In 1923," wrote Anthony and Edmonds, "[Roach] pumped several hundred thousand dollars more into his films than he had the previous year."

"SEES GREAT FILM ACTIVITY" ran the *Los Angeles Times* headline. "Hal Roach, After Eastern Survey, Predicts Unprecedented Era and Plans to Enlarge." The April 1923 article went on to state that Hal Roach had been on the East Coast making an "exhaustive study" of the general conditions of the distribution and exhibition of motion pictures .

"There seems to be no questioning that we are in for one of the biggest years in our business," Roach wrote to his general manager Warren Doane. "Everything points that way. Theaters in the East are back to the

45

days when overflowing crowds were the rule and not the exception. Good pictures seem to be the answer to the situation...

"Throughout New England conditions are now at their best. Cotton mills, and other industries are increasing their wages, which is having its influence on theater attendance. There seems to be an ever increasing demand for comedies. I would not be surprised if we have to increase our output in the very near future... We better get busy immediately on our new ranch, for I have made plans while here that will necessitate enlarging our facilities right away. I would not be surprised if we will have to add another dark stage, for it is almost a certainty that we will need three stages this summer."

"[Roach] used to be a truck driver," reminisced long-time employee Roy Seawright decades later, "and he ran his business the way he did a truck. He saw a road to take, and he was going to go down that road come hell or high water."

At the beginning of 1923 Stan Laurel came down that road once again, returning to the Hal Roach Studios after several years of performing in vaudeville and making shorts for other studios. His new contract called for $300 a week for the first year, $400 the second year and $500 a week the third year. Laurel actually only stayed one year because of problems caused by his common-law wife, Mae Laurel, as she was insisting she star with Stan even when the directors had other ideas. For producer Joe Rock (1893-1984), Laurel appeared in twelve two-reelers in 1924-25. Rock had thought Mae Laurel "would have done very well as a character woman... but she wouldn't have it. I guess she never looked in a mirror."

Stan would return to Roach soon enough—without his would-be Australian ingénue.

In the Spring of 1923 a new series debuted, the one-reel all-animal *Dippy Doo Dads* starring trained monkeys dressed in people clothes and enacting a variety of melodramas. It lasted only one season. In May Pathé Exchange signed a distribution deal with Mack Sennett, of all people, and this angered Roach because by 1924-25 the Sennett shorts were outselling all of Roach's product except for the Our Gangs. As late as November 1925 Roach's executives were trying to convince Pathé to drop Sennett. W.B. Frank, in a letter to Warren Doane, that month wrote: "I have not had much success with Mr. Pearson [a Pathé director] as far as trying to sell him the idea to get Sennett off the program is concerned."

That same month Roach signed several directors to long term contracts: Charles Parrott (1893-1940), soon to be known as Charley Chase,

George Jeske (1891-1951), an original Mack Sennett Keystone Kop as well as a writer and director, and Jay A. Howe (1889-1962), a prolific silent era writer-director. Robert McGowan and Tom MacNamara (1886-1964) were also signed to long term contracts for the *Our Gang* series. Roy Clements (1877-1948), formerly of Essanay, and who directed the first four episodes of *Her Dangerous Path*, was hired to alternate with Bob McGowan on the Our Gang comedies. Val Paul (1886-1962), who had worked on *The Timber Queen* returned to do more serial directing. Robin Williamson (1889-1935), who had directed Ben Turpin and Stan Laurel was brought on board to work on the Paul Parrott one-reelers.

Fred Jackman (1881-1959) was signed to a long-term contract at $425 per week to direct more outdoor features, beginning with *Rex the Wonder Horse*. Jackman was an accomplished cinematographer who had started with Sennett in 1916. He had co-directed the Ruth Roland serial *White Eagle* with W.S. Van Dyke and was solo director for the second Ruth Roland serial *Timber Queen*, both released in 1922; hence he had found his niche directing outdoor action adventures . At the time of signing his new contract he was in the midst of producing *Call of the Wild*.

The *Los Angeles Times* noted, "Chick Morrison, one of the best known horsemen on the west coast, has been engaged by Mr. Roach to co-operate with Jackman in the selection of the stock which will appear in the new feature. Morrison left yesterday for Arizona with a commission to purchase twelve of the finest stallions obtainable. It will take him about a month to round up the type of animals the story will require."

The *Times* went on to note that "Roach's entrance into the field of feature production will in no way minimize his efforts in the comedy realm. The noted comedy producer will continue to make comedy paramount in the Culver City lot. Just now he is preparing for the Will Rogers comedies...."

In addition to hiring new writers and preparing new comedy series, including *The Spat Family*, a situational comedy about a dysfunctional family starring Frank Butler (1890-1967), and new shorts as well as new dramatic features, Roach elevated three of his team to partnership level and turned over active direction to them. They were Warren Doane, who had started with Roach in 1914 and for the past three years had been the studio's general manager, Harley M. ("Beanie") Walker (1878-1937), the sole title writer for the past seven years, and Tom J. Crizer (1888-1963), who had been an actor at Essanay with Bronco Billy Anderson 1913-16 and had been Roach's film editor since 1918. He also was a writer for several of Harold Lloyd's feature films.

"In relinquishing the active direction of his various production units," said The *Los Angeles Times* in a May 22, 1923 article entitled HAL ROACH REORGANIZES, "it is Mr. Roach's intention to devote all his energies to the other problems of the producer. He will give much of his time to solving the questions that perplex exhibitors, in so far as they are affected by production. He will also give part of his time to the development of new talent for comedies...

"With the ever-increasing calls on his plant for comedy production, Mr. Roach has found it difficult to attend to some of the details which are most important to a producer. He feels that a tighter bond should be cemented between producer and exhibitor, and this is one of the jobs he has now outlined for himself."

The great Will Rogers began his series of shorts for Roach in 1923, but as his humor relied so much on his unique homespun talk, this was lost in the silent medium. What did succeed was Rogers' great and ongoing friendship with Hal Roach, who became a superb polo player as a result. In 1932 Roach purchased forty Chilean polo ponies and had them shipped to California. His favorite pony was Alfonz, which he rode for more than three years. Alfonz died of heart failure following a fast game.

In July 1923 Roach was made chairman of the welcoming committee for President Warren G. Harding's tour of Hollywood motion picture studios. As reported in the *Los Angeles Times* on July 28, "Prominent producers will be placed in each car of the President's party to act as guides for announcing the studios and stars as the trip proceeds... The trip [to take place Friday, August 3rd] will take in the principal studios, United, Niblo, F.B.O., Fox, Warner Brothers, Century, Christie, Famous Players-Lasky, Metro, Hollywood, Principal Pictures, and conclude at the Fairbanks-Pickford studio on Santa Monica Boulevard, where one of the big scenes from *The Thief of Bagdad* will be taken, with the President and party as audience."

Alas, this grand event was not to be. The day before his scheduled tour of Hollywood, the 29th President of the United States, Warren G. Harding, died suddenly in San Francisco.

In September 1923 Roach's first feature-length motion picture was released, *Call of the Wild*, based on the Jack London novel about a St. Bernard stolen from his home and sold as an Alaskan sled dog. This was the first of Hal Roach's animal adventures, adapted for the screen and directed by Fred Jackman. Fred's brother Floyd Jackman (1885-1962) was the cinematographer, and worked for Roach until 1928.

Variety noted that the action in *Call of the Wild* tended to drag, and that the film "is minus any human love interest, although the finish reveals 'Buck,' the dog, with his wolf mate and a new-born brood of pups... it looked as if 'Buck' pleased, while at the same time the patrons didn't think so much of the picture."

The *Variety* reviewer might have changed his tune had he been witness to the enthusiastic audience reaction to the film when it was shown a couple of years later in a Chicago school auditorium. On May 4, 1925 thirty-two-year old teacher Miss Alice M. Arneson felt compelled to write to Hal Roach:

"*The Call of the Wild* was shown in our auditorium last Friday. A more fitting title would have been 'The Call *to Be* Wild,' judging from the actions and blood-curdling yells of the children...."

She then offered her services, to come to Hal Roach Studios in July and August for $175 a month plus a round trip ticket to help create pictures that have "a well defined moral, depicting truthfulness, honesty, bravery, etc.' 'These pictures wouldn't necessarily have to be 'goody-goody' or lacking in comedy to be effective... In so far as I can see this project would cause no damage to the regular industry, as the bad effects of 'movies' on children: overstimulation of emotions, late hours, views of suggestive situations, etc. would be eliminated and a great many children who have been denied the 'movies' would be permitted to enjoy them. I am writing your studio first because of your lovable 'Gang.'"

Of historical note, the heavy of *Call of the Wild* was played by tough guy Walter Long, later to become a memorable foe to Laurel & Hardy. He was hardly the teacher's pet.

That same month the *Baltimore Sun* reported that Hal Roach was opening a school for directors. "Good directors are needed as badly as good actors."

"While some directors may be 'born' that way, we've reached a point in the growing pressing public demand for first-class comedies where we can't afford to rely on such accidents of birth; we've got to get to work and 'make' directors."

"Mr. Roach himself started as an 'extra,' and assistant director," states the article, "He wants to give every man in his organization an opportunity to advance. Classes are now meeting every Monday night, with the Roach staff of directors acting as 'professors.'... Among the directors who form the 'faculty' of the Roach School are Bob McGowan, Charles Parrott, Ralph Cedar, George Jeske, J.A. Howe, Percy Pembroke, Fred Jackman, Len Powers, Robin Williamson, Roy Clements and Val Paul.

"'I do not look for the development of a director under our new plan for at least six months,' said Mr. Roach, who gives much of his own time to the school, 'but I feel that we have the right idea and the right instructors. It's up to the boys.'

"The Roach innovation is reported to be an absorbing topic throughout the Coast film colony. Many applications from outside the Roach organization are reported, and these, it is said, will have favorable considerations when the school is seen to have fully justified its existence and is ready to expand beyond the limits of the Roach organization."

Apparently the school did not "expand beyond the limits of the Roach organization." In fact, the whole idea simply faded away before long. There was too much work to do supplying the growing public desire for more comedies. And Roach already had plenty of directors quite capable of making them without further schooling.

1924 RELEASES:
TWENTY-SIX CHARLEY CHASE ONE-REELERS; ONE CHARLEY CHASE TWO-REELER
THIRTEEN OUR GANG TWO-REELERS
THIRTEEN SPAT FAMILY TWO-REELERS
TEN WILL ROGERS TWO-REELERS
EIGHT STAN LAUREL TWO-REELERS
FIVE ARTHUR STONE TWO-REELERS
FIVE DIPPY DOO DADS ONE-REELERS
THREE EARL MOHAN ONE-REELERS
THREE GLENN TRYON TWO-REELERS
TWO GLENN TRYON FEATURES: *THE BATTLING ORIOLES, WHITE SHEEP*
ONE DRAMATIC FEATURE: *THE KING OF WILD HORSES*

In August 1923, another breezy comedian began what became a thirteen-year series of shorts for Roach. It appears that Charles Parrott (aka Chase) resigned as director-general in December 1922 to concentrate on acting. The Paul Parrott series was retired in August 1923 as Parrott (whose first name was actually James) was moved behind the camera. Charley Chase (aka Parrott) started a series of one-reelers as "Jimmy Jump," and in December 1924, Charley Chase graduated to two-reelers.

Although he starred in only two- or sometimes three-reelers throughout his career, which lasted until his early death in 1940, Charley

Chase became one of Roach's most popular stars. Charley Chase was the same attractive, breezy, dapper, all-American young man that Lloyd came to portray, though his pencil-thin moustache and jet black hair did give him the added touch of the cosmopolitan.

By 1923 Charley Parrott was prematurely gray. Roach insisted he dye his hair to maintain a youthful appearance. "Charley asked for and received complete creative control over his films," wrote Anthony and Edmond, "from story conception to final cutting... Roach believed he had little to worry about with Charley, who rarely displayed any of Lloyd's ego or temperament. Also, if Charley Parrott could successfully supervise the entire Studio output, Roach felt he could be trusted to competently handle his own series."

"Charley [Chase] was terrific," wrote former Roach child actor Tommy "Butch" Bond in his 1994 autobiography, "but so high strung that he reminded me of a thoroughbred race horse. He was hyper, and worked best under pressure. And...he was great! He was very professional, loads of fun, and kind to all the cast and crew."

The Charley Chase comedies went into production in the fall of 1923. *At First Glance* was completed in October and released in January 1924 to excellent reviews.

Chase's two-reelers were characterized by their lack of spectacular physical gags and their reliance on subtler, though quite hilarious, commentaries on the absurdities of modern life. His films were definitely forerunners of television sit-coms.

"Charley Chase was a most delightful person," Roach told me in 1973. "And he was a very good actor. He had a good comic sense and a good sense of story construction. He was just as good as his writers. The two-reelers in those days took a month to make. Chase would be shooting one while the writers were working on the next. When he'd finish, he would come up to me and ask, 'All right, boss, what's next?'"

"Those Chase pictures had some of our best stories. In one, Charley has over-grown teeth and his wife has a huge nose. They both go to the doctor's to get their problems fixed, unbeknownst to each other. They both meet after their improvement, and thinking they're meeting a stranger, flirt with each other."

Mr. Roach gave one of his hearty belly laughs. "Charley Chase was very, very popular."

Although three serials and a feature had been produced by 1924 the Hal Roach Studios was primarily a two-reel comedy factory. Charley

Chase made twenty-six one-reelers that year, as well as a two-reeler; Will Rogers completed his contract with ten additional two-reelers; there were five final one-reel *Dippy Doo Dads* to complete that series; five two-reelers starring comic Arthur Stone; three one-reelers with comic Earl Mohan; eight Stan Laurel two-reelers and thirteen two-reel *Our Gangs*.

His old rival Mack Sennett was still churning them out, but Hal Roach was now considered the King of Comedy. Although Hollywood publicity had pictured Sennett and Roach as bitter enemies, Roach told me, "We were the best of friends." He believed that Sennett's comic abilities declined with the introduction of the "Bathing Beauties."

"They weren't very funny. But you see, every newspaper and magazine was clamoring for more pictures, so Mack felt he had to keep boosting them. These gals just slowed his comedies down to a walk: it was tough to pick up the momentum again, and audiences stopped laughing." (Had Roach forgotten about his own Vanity Fair Girls?)

Another contributing factor to Mack Sennett's decline was that he allowed his top talents to be lured away by the enticements of higher salaries and greater creative freedom offered by other studios.

Fred and Floyd Jackman teamed up once more for their second animal adventure, this time starring Rex "King of Wild Horses." The reviews were ecstatic. *Variety*'s review in May 1924: "A black horse of unusual intelligence is the actual star of the picture and he's some actor… but the equine actor leaves the human actors out in the cold when it comes to holding the spectators' interest… There are numerous scenes showing the 'King' and his herd of wild horses roaming their native haunts and they're all engrossingly entertaining. These scenes have been beautifully photographed and possess high class educational values… The Circle audience voted it a wow."

Charley Chase had his only dramatic role in that feature, which was mostly filmed before Charley began acting in his own comedy series.

Meanwhile, on July 7, 1924 a fire broke out at the Hal Roach Studios that caused $100,000 in damage when a gas generator from a wind machine exploded. The blaze destroyed one entire stage and several costly sets in less than twenty minutes.

"Only a stiff sea breeze, coming from the beach towards Los Angeles that blew the flames onto a vacant lot east of the studio, kept the entire place from being burned to the ground," stated a report. The company had just left for the day.

Work was resumed at the studio within two days, but rebuilding didn't take place until a month later when Hal Roach returned from his Alaska vacation.

August 1924: *Motion Picture* magazine noted: "Hal Roach, the comedy magnate, has just finished a six-thousand-mile voyage in his yacht, the Gypsy. Most of his travel was along the Alaskan coast."

Variety September 1924: "The Association of Motion Picture Producers held their annual meeting and re-elected Joseph M. Schenck as President, Hal E. Roach as First Vice President, Thomas H. Ince, Second Vice President, Fred Beetson, Secretary and Treasurer. Will Hays is the 'power behind the throne.'"

On October 19, 1924 a five year contract was signed between the Hal Roach Studios and F. Richard Jones, who had been a Supervising Director for Mack Sennett, having worked at that studio since around 1914. The five year contract with Roach was for $1,000 per week plus five percent of the net profits. According to Wikipedia, "In 1926, Jones was responsible for signing Mabel Normand to a contract with Roach Studios after health and drug addiction problems had kept the star actress out of films for three years. He would direct or produce Normand in all five of her films made at Roach Studios until her permanent retirement in 1927. As well, during his time with Roach, Jones worked on nineteen different film projects with Stan Laurel. In later years, Laurel would state that it was Dick Jones who taught him everything about comedy filmmaking."

Jones would leave Roach after just three years when he joined United Artists to direct Douglas Fairbanks in the acclaimed feature *The Gaucho* (1927) and then for Samuel Goldwyn he directed the excellent early talkie, *Bulldog Drummond* (1929) starring Ronald Colman. Ironically, like his leading lady Mabel Normand, Jones died of tuberculosis at the age of thirty-seven. Normand died in February of 1930; Jones in December of that year.

Another director began his career at the Hal Roach Studios in 1924. Leo McCarey had been working for Mack Sennett when he met Roach at the Los Angeles Athletic Club playing handball. Some time later McCarey visited Roach at the lot and was offered a job as a gag man for the Our Gang comedies. Soon McCarey was directing the Charley Chase series.

"We worked together in fifty pictures at the Hal Roach studios," McCarey later recalled. "I received credit as director but it was really Chase who did most of the directing. Whatever success I have had or may have, I owe to his help because he taught me all I know."

McCarey was instrumental in the formation of the immortal team of Laurel & Hardy and would later go on to greater Hollywood glory in the 1930s and '40s writing and directing some of the best comedies to be produced during those decades, becoming a three time Academy Award winner.

Remarkably, Chase was also responsible for bringing Oliver "Babe" Hardy to the Roach lot that same year. Charley and "Babe" had worked together at the King Bee Studio when Parrott was directing and co-starring in the Billy West series there in 1918. And according to Charlie Hall in his 1938 London newspaper article, "It was Charley Chase that brought Stan Laurel back to films... During Charley's reign as studio manager he saw Stan Laurel at the old Pantages Theater in Los Angeles. He thought him extremely funny and brought him straight-away to the studios."

Hal Roach was the boss, the leader; he trusted his top-notch team, and together combined their talents to created immortal comedy.

In addition to his superb recruiting and supervising skills, Charley Chase was a delightful companion. Hal Roach brought him to his meetings with Pathé executives in New York because of his winning personality and his ability to liven up the boring business meetings. "They were New York executives," Roach recalled. "I used Charley to soften them up."

This was truly the age of unique and eccentric character actors and comics. When James Finlayson got his U.S. naturalization papers he needed two U.S. citizens of five years acquaintance to "vouch for his moral character." Into the courtroom came Ben Turpin and Charles Parrott. What a comedy short THAT would have made!

In November 1924 another Roach feature was released, this time a comedy, *The Battling Orioles* starring Roach's new find, the young Glenn Tryon (1898-1970). The movie was given a good review by *Variety* with a special commendation to Tryon, which ensured his employment at the Hal Roach Studios for the next several years:

"This five-reeler from Hal Roach's plant is a slam-bang slapstick farce furnished with a good story, a capable light comedian and support and general detail that is of a quality to make all the directorial efforts successful. The Battling Orioles are the members of the famous old baseball team... who have grown old and are, at the time the picture begins, in their dotage... Glenn Tryon, as Tommy, is a corking little comedian whose bag of tricks is seemingly inexhaustible. Maybe Pathé means to use him as a No. 2 Harold Lloyd, and if they do they're not far wrong, for their separate lines bear resemblance." The cinematographer of *The Battling Orioles* was 20-year-old California-born George Stevens (1904-1975). He was Roach's chief cinematographer throughout the rest of the 1920s, filming the Rex the Wonder Horse features and Laurel & Hardy's shorts. Stevens began directing the *Boy Friends* series in 1930 but soon thereafter left Roach to ultimately become a freelance Academy Award-winning director.

1925 RELEASES:
TWELVE OUR GANG TWO-REELERS
ELEVEN GLENN TRYON TWO-REELERS
TEN CHARLEY CHASE TWO-REELERS
SEVEN CHARLEY CHASE ONE-REELERS
SIX SPAT FAMILY TWO-REELERS
FIVE JAMES FINLAYSON ONE-REELERS
THREE ONE-REELERS AND TWO TWO-REELERS DIRECTED BY STAN
LAUREL
THREE ARTHUR STONE TWO-REELERS
ONE DRAMATIC FEATURE: *THE BLACK CYCLONE*

By 1925 Roach was spending more than one million dollars each year on his comedies. Charley Chase was his top money maker. In February 1925 Roach sent a survey to exhibitors: "What comedies do you think enough of to advertise? Do audiences object to slapstick if it is funny? How important are leading ladies in comedies? Does the name 'Hal Roach' mean anything to your audiences? Does a comedy need a story or will a bunch of gags which follow in sequence be more entertaining?"

March 15, 1925: *Hard Boiled*, the first Charley Chase two-reeler is released.

March 30, 1925: Egyptian and Aztec Theatres, San Francisco run Hal Roach Comedy Week for first time. "Our business is beyond expectations," wrote the exhibitor. "Everyone pleased and I will run more Hal Roach weeks with full comedy bill."

Variety April 8, 1925: "'Sunshine Sammy' [Morrison] en route to New York with his daddy, nurse and tutors to play a number of picture house engagements."

April 16, 1925 Hal Roach letter to Joseph M. Schenck, United Studios, 5341 Melrose Ave regarding his brother Jack: "several years experience as a cameraman and I can recommend him as a sober, conscientious worker."

May 13, 1925 Mission Beach Amusement Center letter from Claus Spreckels: "invitation at Hotel Del Coronado for dedication of Mission Beach Amusement Center May 29, 1925 To Hal Roach & wife."

In a videotaped interview in the early 1980s the ninety-something Hal Roach was asked what he would like to be remembered for. "I think that I would most like to be remembered for the laughter that I gave the people of the world more than anything else," Roach responded. "The drama and serials and those things I did, they were just the run of the mill."

A man of so many accomplishments, he must have completely forgotten the accolades one of his early dramatic features had received some sixty years earlier:

On April 20, 1925 a Special Report from the National Board of Review of Motion Pictures in New York City rated *The Black Cyclone*. "Entertainment Value: Exceptional. Educational Value: Unusual. Artistic Value: Dramatic Interest of Story: Very Strong. Coherence of Narrative: Gripping. Acting: Remarkable For Animals. Photography: Excellent. Technical handling: Skillful and imaginative. "This is a remarkably interesting photoplay, with horses in a wild state on the range for its principal actors. It has thrill, love, adventure—all the qualities of intense dramatic action."

The *Christian Science Monitor* of May 20, 1925 had an equally laudatory review. "Here is one of the screen's triumphs... Here is a tale that no mere words could so tell, a tale that gives the screen one more undisputable claim to being a medium of expression apparently without limits. Mr. Roach's name goes into the group of selected contributors to screen history."

And this from *Variety*: "An astounding film... full of laughs, thrills, drama and suspense. They don't come much nearer to filling the entertainment order... The way these horses perform is little short of miraculous... *Black Cyclone* is a film to make movie history... They couldn't be much better than this...."

But despite such laudatory reviews for *Black Cyclone* and the previous *King of Wild Horses*, one individual was not at all happy with those horse pictures. Her name was Vingie E. Roe-Lawton, an author who had achieved some success as the writer of wild horse stories. Early in 1925 she learned that the Hal Roach Studios had produced a wild horse picture and was in the midst of creating a second one temporarily being called "*Black Thunder*"—which just happened to be the very title of one of Ms. Roe's stories. As her short story was apparently being filmed without her permission, she became infuriated, journeyed to Culver City from her home in northern California and made a fuss. She eventually filed a copyright infringement lawsuit against the Hal Roach Studios; the trial finally took place in October 1926. I have found the transcripts for that trial and share the pertinent details below, where chronologically appropriate.

May 6, 1925: Tryon's *Hold My Baby* "is wonderful entertainment. Frankly it ranks with the very best comedies we have ever shown."—Harry W. Crull, [Exhibitor] Providence, Rhode Island.

May 17, 1925: Spat Family two-reeler *Wild Papa* released, historically significant because Oliver Hardy appears in a Hal Roach comedy for the first time.

June 11, 1925: Average employees 230 average weekly payroll $19,000.

July 5, 1925: *Chasing the Chaser* is released, a one-reeler starring James Finlayson directed by Stan Laurel with Fay Wray and Helen Gilmore. This was an historic combination.

July 7, 1925 a five page single space typed letter from Frank Howard Clark of Glendale, California to Hal Roach: "What are 2 Reel Comedies Coming To?" "If the comedy situation is to be bettered you are the man to do it. Comedies aren't funny anymore. The movie theater is now a tomb where formerly it was a volcano of laughter. Comedies lack SINCERITY. Harold Lloyd is so absolutely SINCERE in everything he does. Comedies need less buffoonery and more sincerity. The silliest comic I ever saw is Larry Semon. He never was funny and never will be. He is just a mugging, burlesquing buffoon, a clown. Don't leave it all up to the director. Let the writers write the story and the director direct it. *Seven Chances* is just a chase picture with one funny gag in it. Hated the spoof of Fairbank's Arabian Knights."

Maybe Mr. Clark of Glendale, California was somewhat appeased when Stan Laurel returned to the Hal Roach Studios in 1925, this time as a director and writer. Laurel directed James Finlayson (1887-1953) a bald-headed comic from Scotland who had worked for Mack Sennett for four years and later to become Laurel & Hardy's perennial nemesis, in *Chasing The Chaser* with 18-year-old Fay Wray among the cast. Then *Unfriendly Enemies, Yes, Yes Nanette* with Oliver Hardy in the cast, recently hired by Roach. Released on July 19, 1925 *Yes, Yes Nanette* was also noteworthy in that it was the last silent one-reeler produced at the Hal Roach Studios (although previously unreleased one-reelers were presented through 1926). This was also the first time Stan Laurel and Oliver Hardy had worked together at the Hal Roach Studios.

Laurel's subsequent 1925 shorts were *Moonlight and Noses* with Clyde Cook, *Starvation Blues* and *Wandering Papas* with Cook and Hardy released in February 1926.

In 1980 Cook, who starred in five two-reelers of his own in 1926 stated, "Stan Laurel was the most creative person I worked with. Of all the pictures

I did for Mr. Roach, the ones with Laurel are the funniest." Stan co-wrote *Madam Mystery*, a comeback for vamp Theda Bara (1885-1955), who had started in the movies in 1914, quickly became a star, but hadn't filmed since 1921. Finlayson and Hardy were in the cast. Stan co-wrote *Wife Tamers* starring Lionel Barrymore, as well as several other shorts in 1926. He co-directed Mabel Normand's three-reel comeback *Raggedy Rose* and co-wrote *The Nickel Hopper* featuring Oliver Hardy.

The Hal Roach Studios was a very busy place in 1925. That year he bought ten acres of land a couple of miles away, on Robertson Boulevard between Pico and National, in what was then a rural section of Los Angeles. It was dubbed The Hal Roach Ranch and it eventually became the home to a variety of animals and fowl. Farm buildings were constructed, there were more than fifty "antiquated motor cars" kept there, and the land had rotating crops.

Glenn Tryon produced eleven two-reelers that year, Charley Chase eight one-reelers and six two-reelers, The Spat Family produced their final six two-reelers before the series was cancelled; James Finlayson, signed in January, starred in five one-reelers before he began his memorable association with Laurel & Hardy. Arthur Stone completed two two-reelers and then left the Roach lot. Earl Mohan, whose specialty was playing drunks, starred in three one-reelers, Clyde Cook in three two-reelers, Lucien Littlefield, Katherine Grant and Gertrude Astor appeared in *Laughing Ladies*, a two-reeler, and Frank Butler, the father of the Spat Family, appeared in one final one-reeler *Tol'able Romeo* before turning his attention to the script department.

A new comedienne appeared at the Hal Roach Studios in 1925, fourteen-year-old Martha Sleeper, who the *Los Angeles Times* called "an eye-shocking mixture of youth and maturity."

"Oh, yes, I've been learning the things that help me make pictures ever since I was a baby," declared Miss Sleeper during one of her first newspaper interviews. "My very first years were spent on a sheep ranch in Wyoming. And every day my daddy used to take me horseback riding all over the ranch... I lived outdoors most of the time and learned to ride and swim almost as soon as I could walk. That's why I'm not afraid of anything... Oh, it's glorious to be here [at the Hal Roach Studios]. Nothing seems like work—even the slapstick and the ugly clothes—I love every bit of it and everybody around this studio."

Leo McCarey was enjoying himself as well; his working relationship with Charley Chase "slowly evolved into a personal friendship," wrote Anthony and Edmonds, "and they often harmonized Irish ballads on the Chase set. Hal Roach must have been delighted—as he played the saxophone in his office... By 1925... Charley considered McCarey his full equal and a collaborator rather than an underling." As a matter of fact, Roach and Chase saw to it that there was no caste system at the studio.

That year Charley Chase was sent on a promotional tour to New York, Chicago, Philadelphia and Detroit to promote his two-reelers.

In July Roach was in Colorado Springs, Colorado as a member of the Midwick polo team, which promptly carried away the western open polo championship in the tournament there.

August 1, 1925 Hal Roach Studios loan Lucien Littlefield to William S. Hart Productions for $600 per week on August 8 to 10.

On October 18, 1925 The Los Angeles Times announced "Hal Roach comedies recently received a great impetus in eastern sales, due to the revolutionary change in policy of the Keith-Albee circuit of vaudeville houses, which have booked Hal Roach comedies, the entire output of the one studio, the first booking of the kind they have ever made. Since the first announcement of this deal, covering fifty-six houses, including the Hippodrome, Palace and Keith-Albee, the largest of the circuit, fifteen more associated theaters have signed the contract."

"They have taken our comedies, not as 'fillers,'" Roach reflected proudly, "but as an act, giving them box office rating of a high-class act, capable of bringing in the same money."

"There is every indication, according to the producer," concluded the Times article, "that a second large vaudeville circuit will follow the Keith movement in signing for the comedies as a definite and permanent part of their program."

November 9, 1925: Hal Roach was invited to join The 400 Club of Hollywood $1,000 membership. One hundred and fifty founding members include Paul Bern, Tod Browning, Warner Baxter. C.B. DeMille, John Gilbert, Buster Keaton, Joseph Schenck, Hunt Stromberg, Irving Thalberg, King Vidor: at the Bernheimer Mansion, Hollywood with Japanese Gardens.

November 11th the Los Angeles Times carried the headline "VAMP COMES BACK. THEDA BARA SIGNS WITH HAL ROACH FILMS."

"'I'm glad to return to the screen before the class of audiences which this contract offers,' Miss Bara said. 'Any actress loves to reappear before the best possible audiences, the sort which a combination of the Keith circuit and the country's leading key-city theaters offers. It is an opportunity highly satisfactory to any actress, providing the elements of production quality are assured, which in this case is settled.'

"Signing Theda Bara is a further step in the somewhat revolutionary policy of Hal Roach," continued the article, "who is attempting to make comedies to compete with features and is securing feature standard players for the roles. Eileen Percy, Mildred Harris (formerly Mrs. Charlie Chaplin,) George Siegman, Stuart Holmes, Cesare Gravina, and other artists of note, usually associated with features only, have been in the Roach organization recently or are working now. The announcement of many new players of the same character is a development expected daily."

On December 8, Charley Chase's leading lady, the young and vivacious 21-year-old Katherine Grant, was struck by a hit and run vehicle while crossing the street from the Studio. She was deemed to be uninjured at the time, and she returned to work. But on May 22, 1926 a handwritten letter was sent to Hal Roach from Iris G. Worth of Pasadena regarding Katherine Grant: "taken to a sanitarium—not on location."

The accident had resulted in a shock so severe that five months later her entire nervous system was so affected she became unable to care for herself. The Hal Roach Studios paid for her treatment as well as board and lodging at the sanitarium.

On June 23, 1926 A.E.W. Yale, M.D. of Burbank wrote to Roach, "Miss Katherine Grant's physical condition is very much improved. She is now eating very well and her mental condition also shows marked improvement. In fact I am seeing her only every third day instead of every second." On June 30th Katherine's mother, Mrs. Kerr, "spoke of great improvement in Katherine's condition."

However, Katherine Grant was to remain institutionalized for the rest of her short life. She passed away in 1937 at the age of thirty-two. Yet another young and beautiful Hollywood actress had met with a tragic end.

December 21, 1925: Mike Jolson, brother of Al, "Riot as comedian. Weighs 265 lbs and has wonderful personality."—Harry Berman (agent?)

December 26, 1925: Johnny Downs, an Our Gang kid from 1923-26 was a great hit at the Spreckels Theatre, San Diego with Our Gang in a live presentation. "The applause was the greatest ever heard at any picture showing in this city."

December 28, 1925: $7,475 (minus $25 cash advanced) to Theda Bara for services rendered.

1926 RELEASES:
TWELVE ALL-STAR TWO-REELERS
ELEVEN CHARLEY CHASE TWO-REELERS
TEN OUR GANG TWO-REELERS
EIGHT PAUL PARROTT ONE-REELERS (PRODUCED 1921-23)
SIX GLENN TRYON TWO-REELERS
FIVE CLYDE COOK TWO-REELERS
FIVE SNUB POLLARD ONE-REELERS (PRODUCED 1922-23)
THREE FEATURES: *THE DEVIL HORSE; THE VALLEY OF HELL; THE DESERT'S TOLL*
TWO MABEL NORMAND THREE-REELERS
ONE SUNSHINE SAMMY ONE-REELER (PRODUCED 1921)

January 2, 1926: Surplus account of studio slightly in excess of $373,000.

Hal E. Roach Studios name legally changed to Hal Roach Studios in 1926.

In 1926 Charley Chase made ten two-reelers; he was now considered the most popular comedian in short comedies. That year Leo McCarey left the Charley Chase series to work as supervising director of all the Hal Roach comedies, which, according to Anthony and Edmonds, "left a serious void in the Chase creative team... and Charley began to imbibe heavily, possibly to ease the strain of his hectic schedule."

Roach had two real Hollywood stars in his next two shorts: *Wife Tamer* starred Lionel Barrymore, released on March 28; and *Madame Mystery* with Theda Bara, the original Vamp, premiered on April 18; then three features were released: *The Devil Horse* (Rex) September 12; *The Valley of Hell* and *The Desert's Toll*, five and six reel Westerns which were distributed by MGM.

January 1926: *Photoplay's* review of *Madame Mystery*: "See it and howl! It's Theda Bara's first comedy and not once is her face garnished with custard pie. *Madame Mystery* is one long scream from start to finish with Theda furnishing the charm, and Jimmy Finlayson funnier than he or anyone else ever hoped to be... Hal Roach should be proud of Richard Wallace for the direction and H.M. Walker for the titles." Stan Laurel co-wrote this. Oliver Hardy was in cast too. Released as a two-reeler in the United States, *Madame Mystery* was shown on foreign screens in five-reels.

But all was not well between Pathé Exchange in New York and the Hal Roach Studios in Culver City by early 1926.

January 26, 1926: Warren Doane to W.B. Frank: "...the print is bad, and one would imagine that as frequently as this has been brought to the attention of the management of the Pathé Organization that some steps would have been taken to correct the condition. Instead of this what presumably happens is that we are given an argument that the prints are not bad, or are not very bad, or are not always bad, and the matter appears to stop there.

"...It is my private opinion that Pathé are starving their print factory in the same method they are starving their whole business, including their producers. I believe we are just wasting our time and energy in quarrelling with them over the quality of our prints and that we should rather devote ourselves to some other means of correcting this situation."

And correct the situation they did. In March Roach signed a distribution agreement with Metro-Goldwyn-Mayer and would begin releasing their product through the Hollywood giant later the following year. As early as January 1926 *Variety* was reporting Roach's "dissatisfaction" with Pathé and on February 9th published this item: "According to reports, anticipating the withdrawal of Hal Roach, Pathé has arranged with Mack Sennett to add three new units to his organization. These units will make 12 pictures a year. Hal Roach says his contract with Pathé has still 18 months to run and that he is to turn over 40 pictures to that organization for lease during that time."

January 20, 1926 telegram to Hal Roach from Mazatlan: "LEAVING BY TRAIN TODAY HAD WONDERFUL TIME THANKS TO YOUR GREAT KINDNESS WILL TELEPHONE ON ARRIVAL JACK (Barrymore). Perhaps it was during that trip that Roach persuaded Jack to invite his brother Lionel to star in one of his shorts, *Wife Tamers*, released in March of that year.

When it was announced that Mabel Normand, the former Mack Sennett comedienne who had been involved in a variety of scandals in the early 1920s was returning to the screen via the Roach Studios, there was a strongly mixed public response.

March 4, 1926: Letter from Ward B. Sawyer, Attorney & Counselor, Chicago: "I desire to enter a strong protest in the name of public decency against [Mabel Normand] appearing in pictures."

Mrs. F.H. Tallman and family, Omaha, Nebraska: "The screen is robbed of some of its brightness without her. No one can fill her place. The screen needs Mabel Normand. The public needs the smiles she gave us. What if a few 'catty' women's clubs put up a howl? Let them howl. Perhaps Miss Normand has her faults, but she is good as most of them, and no doubt better than some."

Letter from Robert Greaves, London: "Some of my friends and myself want to thank you for 'signing up' a dear favorite of other days, Mabel Normand. Nothing I am sure will please the English public more than to see her romping her way 'thro' the films as she used to do."

And just at the time Mabel signed with Roach, the newspapers headlines exploded with new clues as to who the possible murderer of director William Desmond Taylor might be. That mystery had remained unsolved since 1922. Even though Mabel was reported as being the last person to have seen Taylor alive, she was cleared as a suspect, but only by the officials; many others had serious doubts. Especially when only two years later Mabel's chauffeur shot and wounded a prominent millionaire oil broker with her very own pistol.

March 25, 1926: W.B. Frank to Warren Doane: "It is certainly too bad that all this had to come up again just at the time Miss Normand came on our lot to make a picture. As to what damage it will do, I am unable to say. However, nobody in the motion picture field has said a word to me about it."

March 1926: Hal Roach makes it clear he is not interested in making comedies of newspaper comic strip characters Orphan Annie, Moon Mullins and Smitty—*Chicago Tribune Syndicate*

March 16, 1926: Distributing contract signed between Hal Roach Studios and MGM Distribution Corporation. The news of this association was not made public until early in 1927 and would not take effect until September of that year.

The *Baltimore Sun* had an interesting article in their March 28, 1926 edition. Under the headline "THEY USE QUEER THINGS MAKING COMEDY FILMS" they describe the items assistant general manager and purchasing agent L.A. French has requested for the comedy series in the last few weeks:

"One rooster which would crow without looking at the camera. One dog trained to run away when called and come when ordered away. Seven tons of corn foddy, a by-product very popular with bakers who fear the high cost of shredded coconut, but possessing also a remarkable photographic likeness to snow. Three big apes, one trained to do the Charleston and one trained to walk sideways, facing the camera... One parrot with a fondness for riding on steering wheels. One brand-new, nifty-looking roadster, equipped for a romantic driver, with all dashboard fixtures and the hand-brake, gearshift, etc., on the left side of the steering wheel."

April 10, 1926 Letter to Ted Healy: $200 per week May 12-July 3 as comedian and then "if both parties agreeable, to negotiate a term contract." Healy appeared in *Wise Guys Prefer Brunettes*, which was released in October 1926. It was the first solo directing assignment for Stan Laurel, who was also directing *Get 'Em Young* with Oliver Hardy when Ollie accidently burned himself while cooking a leg of lamb forcing Stan to play his role, thus returning to acting once again.

By April the contract with Mabel Normand was finalized. "Normand contract satisfactory," wrote Roach on April 24th. "$25,000 arrangement made with bank." Normand would receive $6,000 per picture for eight pictures of two reels in length to be made within forty-eight weeks; then she would sign a two-year contract to make features at $1,000 per week for the first year, $3,000 per week the next year.

April 28, 1926 Telegram Warren Doane to Hal Roach: "NORMAND-FINLAYSON PICTURE LAUREL IS DIRECTING LOOKING GOOD AND FUNNY."

H.M. Walker attended a preview of *Raggedy Rose* and informed Roach via telegram that he thought it should be released in the U.S. as a five reeler as "FIRST INTRODUCTORY SHOT [of Mabel] RECEIVED AN OVATION STOP IT WAS IN FOUR REELS AND IS MIXTURE OF LAUGHTER AND TEARS CLICKED 109 LAUGHS… CONGRATULATIONS."

For some reason it was decided that *Raggedy Rose* should be released in three reels, which is how audiences finally saw it when it premiered that November.

May 3, 1926: W.B. Frank to Warren Doane regarding a new Charley Chase two-reeler being reviewed: "The twelve member reviewing committee gave twelve good votes. Practically all of them said that they think it is one of the best two reel comedies they have ever seen, and the majority think it is better than anything Lloyd had ever done in the two reel line… I have unbounded faith in Charlie [sic] and sincerely believe that he will eventually become one of the greatest comedians in the business."

On June 9, 1926 *Variety* reviewed a new feature film starring Rex King of Wild Horses: "This is the third of the horse pictures made by Hal Roach… Now comes *The Devil Horse*, best of the lot… The plot here is better than that of the other two… *The Devil Horse*, reel for reel, is as filled with thrilling situations and incidents as possible… That it is better than *Black Cyclone* is the most succinct way to praise *The Devil Horse*. And that is praise enough."

June 9, 1926: L.B. Mayer to Hal Roach: "I hereby approve for our company your selection of Francis McDonald to appear in three western pictures which you are to produce for us."

June 16, 1926 Warren Doane telegram to Hal Roach: "...At present time plans call for thirty people making trip includes four bandits three Indians drunk miner and one extra member Bucks gang. Will it be feasible secure these characters Moapa?"

June 25, 1926: "Troupe poisoned caused by drinking lemon water from galvanized canteen. Cliff Smith, Anita Garvin, Jack Roach, Harry Black seriously ill but improving. The rest of troupe out of danger. Hal Roach not sick. Have doctor here and doing everything possible."

July 24, 1926: Ollie burned himself on leg of lamb so Stan had to play butler role in *Get 'Em Young*, the short he was directing, thus returning Stan to acting.

"HAL ROACH SIGNS FIVE FOR COMEDY" was the headline of The *Los Angeles Times* on August 22, 1926. "Five players of radically different types and training are under contract at the Hal Roach Studios to insure the success of the 'star comedy' series inaugurated by Roach, a series based on the 'all-star' idea.

"This group is composed of Jimmy Finlayson, who will play part of the time in comedies featuring himself alone; Vivien Oakland, former vaudeville favorite; Tyler Brooke, well known on the legitimate stage; Oliver Hardy, veteran 'heavyweight' comedian of the screen, and Martha Sleeper, 16-year-old eccentric comedienne.

"Although it is Roach's policy to secure the best names from feature picture ranks for leading roles in the 'star comedy' series, the group of five players forms the basis of casting....

"The fact that Mr. Roach believes in stage training as a background for screen work is well evidenced by this list of players. He has not picked them simply as types but partly because of the variety of experiences which they have obtained. Yet they are five distinct personalities, each with its own indications of genius, offering as a group possibly the most flexible human 'material' for pictures yet gathered by one producer.

"Jimmy Finlayson already has been given several featured roles and the others will be given their opportunities as individual stars when the combination of story material and experience warrants it.

"The general trend of comedies upward in the scale of quality has been a conspicuous development in the past year and the steps each producer is taking to boost his own standards are being watched closely by critics and exhibitors, who influence, to a great extent, the molding of public opinion."

August 24, 1926 Warren Doane's suggestions for *Swift Eagle*: "Foreword to suggest days when disputes were settled with a six-shooter and life was rough and ready. I believe that it would be more convincing if the idea were gotten over that Brady's gang consisted of four or six desperadoes instead of implying that the whole town is more or less in his gang."

August 28, 1926: Five-reel *Swift Eagle* featuring Francis McDonald. Hal Roach requests Louis B. Mayer to review film for his views.

From October 27 to 28, 1926 a trial was held in the U.S. District Court in Los Angeles. Mrs. Vingie E. Roe-Lawton (1879-1958), a writer of "horse stories" had filed suit against Hal Roach Studios in November 1925 for infringement of copyright regarding *Rex King of Wild Horses* and *Black Cyclone* and the testimony recorded during that trial gives a vivid picture of the inner workings of the Hal Roach Studios at that time.

Between 1915 and 1918 five of Ms. Roe's horse stories were published in *Collier's* magazine and she felt these stories were utilized without her knowledge or consent in the creation of Roach's movies. She had seen *King of Wild Horses* at a movie theater, and then had read in the newspaper about the making of the second horse movie, which at that time was tentatively entitled *Black Thunder*—the exact name of one of Ms. Roe's own horse stories. She became incensed and immediately traveled by herself to Culver City from her home in Napa, California, north of San Francisco, a journey of some 400 miles, with a package of her stories. She arrived at the Hal Roach Studios and demanded to see the man in charge. She was sent to the office of Vice President Warren Doane.

"I was introduced to him and he asked me what my business was," testified Ms. Roe on the witness stand. "I asked him if he was making a new picture called *Black Thunder* and he said he was. I asked him where he got the story for *Black Thunder*, and he told me it was his story; that he had given the plot of the story to Mr. Jackman, who was making the film. Then I told Mr. Doane about my own stories. I started to unroll the package, but he didn't want to see them; he wouldn't look at them. And he told me they never made a picture but what someone came up to claim it, some author. And a few heated words ensued, and he used the word 'blackmail.' I told him I was not a blackmailer, but a reputable writer, with a market on both sides of the ocean, and I wasn't after blackmail because I didn't need it, but I was after a recognition of authorship. I told him that if he was using my stories, or had used them, I wanted recognition, and if he was not I wanted nothing. Well, Mr. Doane said, of course, he wasn't using them... And finally Mr. Doane arose and told me he didn't need to listen to me; that if I wouldn't leave the room, he could. And I rose also, and I think we pounded the table between us. And I said, 'If you won't listen to me, you will listen to the Author's League of America, perhaps.' And then Mr. Doane said, 'Blackmailers, a bunch of blackmailers, organized for blackmail.' And I said no, we weren't."

Ms. Roe testified that Mr. Doane's attitude calmed down and that he virtually apologized for having used her title and that he knew she "had written some wonderful animal stories. Then Mr. Doane said that perhaps I could write for them in the future, and told me about this wonderful horse that they had, and I said I could not write for him because I was under contract now to *McCall's*... Then Mr. Doane asked me if I wouldn't like to see the studio, to look the studio over, and I said I would. And he very graciously had someone dismiss my taxi, and had somebody take me through the studio, and then sent me home in his private car over to Hollywood, which was very nice of him. And, by the way, he told the driver to stop at the stable and show me the beautiful black horse, which the driver did, and showed me a lovely black horse, and drove me back to Hollywood. Then Mr. Doane agreed to keep this roll of stories and look them over and see if he thought there was any infringement. So I left them with him and went to Hollywood, the anger seemed to have all disappeared, and we seemed to be on comfortable terms. I told him I would be at the Christie Hotel for several days, and if he had anything to say to me he could call me there."

Mr. Doane returned her stories, claiming there was no infringement. Ms. Roe asked if she could view the yet to be completed movie *Black Thunder* and Mr. Doane consented, and invited her back to the Studio for a private screening.

"He introduced me to Mr. Jackman and several other gentlemen, and we went into the projecting room, and I was shown the greater part, I think, of the film, which was *Black Thunder* then but later called *Black Cyclone*. When we came out of the projection room we were standing talking on the walk, and Mr. Jackman said to me, 'Now Miss Roe, since you have seen the picture you don't think it is an infringement of your stories, do you?' And I said, 'Yes, sir, I do.' And he said he was sorry to hear that, because he had always admired my work, had read my stories and admired them, and was sorry I would feel that way."

She returned to Mr. Doane's office for a private discussion with him.

"...and the last words of this interview with Mr. Doane, or about the last words, as I recall them, were in connection with this title, would I sell him the title, and I said, 'Yes, for $5,000.' And he said, 'You don't want to sell.' And I said, 'You are right, I don't.' And that is the end of the interview, as I recall it from memory."

"Q: You have never had any further conversation with them?

"A: No, sir; I have never seen any of them since.

Fred Jackman, the director of these films, took the stand. He denied ever having read any of Ms. Roe's, stories, but then remembered he had read one about "a buck deer and a hunter. I thought it was a very beautiful story…

"Q: Did you know of her as a writer of wild horse stories?

"A: No, sir…

"Q: Now, who originated the idea of taking this first film of *The King of Wild Horses*?

"A: The originality was with Mr. Roach. We had finished *The Call of the Wild*, and our dog was taken ill with distemper, I think, and died. I have photographed animals in films. It has been practically half the work that I have done in my twelve or fifteen years' experience in the business. And my natural thought was if I were to make any pictures for him, it would be of some animal…

"Q: Now, *The King of Wild Horses*, who contributed to the ideas that went into the story on which the film was based?

"A: Well, Mr. Roach contributed all of the basic ideas. My principal business on the story was, we had experienced writers who knew dramatic construction, arranging them, and my principal business was to see that things that were written into the story were things that were possible to do, especially where it was with a horse.

"Q: Well, who was the writer of the story of *Rex, the King of Wild Horses*?

"A: Hal Conklin…

"Q: And did Mr. Doane contribute anything to the story?

"A: Not that I recollect of…

"Q: And who contributed to the story of *Black Cyclone*?

"A: Well, *Black Cyclone* was developed in a similar manner. Mr. Roach had the original ideas—the basic ideas, as I would call them, for the film…

"Q: Prior to making your own films, had you ever read any horse stories?

"A: Yes, sir.

"Q: You don't remember reading horse stories in *Collier's* magazine?

"A: I am positive that I didn't, because I would have remembered it if I had read them…."

Direct Examination by Hal Roach:

"Q: What is your business, Mr. Roach?

"A: Moving picture manufacturer.

"Q: What company are you connected with?

"A: Hal Roach Studios.

"Q: What is your official position with that company?

"A: President.

"Q: Did you have anything to do with this film of *Rex, the King of Wild Horses*?

"A: Yes, sir.

"Q: State what, if anything, you had to do with the production of that film, the making of the story, and so on.

"A: I supervised the construction of the story, and supervised the production of the picture, and supervised the cutting of the finished picture…

"Q: Who made the original story on which the film plans were started?

"A: Well, I think I conceived the basic ideas. I never write anything. Any thought I have I give to someone else and they put it in writing. Then if it is written, I correct it afterwards. [This is precisely the way Mr. Roach worked with me when I stayed at his home to help create his come back comedy more than sixty years later!]

…."Q: Did you ever read any of these Vingie E. Roe stories?

"A: I have read some of them.

"Q: You have read them now, haven't you?

"A: I have read parts of them.

"Q: Did you know that she had written a story called 'Black Thunder'?

"A: No, I did not.

"Q: Have you ever read it up until recently?

"A: No; not until recently…

"Q: What stories had you read of hers?

"A: Of hers?

"Q: Yes.

"A: Oh, I can't tell. I may have read some stories of hers without knowing them. Unless it is an outstanding story I don't as a rule pay much attention to the author's name…

…."Q: What were Mr. Jackman's duties with respect to the production of this film?

"A: He was the director.

"Q: Did he make any contributions toward the development of the story?

"A: Oh, yes, a great deal.

"Q: Will you go into that a little more fully, so far as your knowledge is concerned?

"A: All we wanted to give Fred was a skeleton to go on, something to go out and get started on, because in making a picture with those horses, after you see the finished product it looks like they went ahead and did the things you told them to do, but what you really did is make thousands of feet of film and cut out of that film action which you could use in the pictures. And many things we would write into a story or try to get the horses to do would be impossible, while many things the horses did do, that they just did naturally, were things that brought out fine points in our story, and that we have been commended on has having marvelous action when really the horses did them themselves. Fred was a man who knew when the horses did something that was good, or when they did something that was bad, and when he got the shot he wanted, that is the one he kept and threw the rest away."

Mr. Roach was asked about the titling of his films.

"A: Mr. [H.M.] Walker approves the titles... I never title any picture personally... You see, a title is quite an important thing to a picture, and as a rule Mr. Walker writes out a sheet with a lot of titles on it and submits it around to everybody, that is, all of the officials or anybody that has anything to do with the picture, and lets them mark out which one they think would be the most appropriate title for the picture, or have the most appeal to the eye...

"Q: When was the first time that you heard about these stories that are involved in this action?

"A: When Mr. Doane came in my office and told me that Miss Roe had called on him...

"Q: What have you to say as to the value of plaintiff's stories for scenarios after the production of *Black Cyclone*, that is, with respect to whether that value would be enhanced or diminished by the production of the two films, *The King of Wild Horses* and *Black Cyclone*?

"A: My thought would be that it certainly could not decrease their value, because we had popularized a type of picture that had never been made on the screen before, and if anyone else had the material, that is, the horses and trainers, to make horse pictures with, presumably if their pictures were picture material they would have increased in value rather than have diminished.

"Q: Did you consider after the production of *Black Cyclone* that the market had been exhausted for such a class of pictures?

"A: No. We have made a picture called *The Devil Horse*, and are now starting production on another picture ourselves, and I believe Universal and Famous Players are also making horse pictures now...."

Mr. Roach was then cross-examined.

"Q: You said that you suggested the basic idea. What did you mean by that? What do you regard as the basic idea of that first story?

"A: You build a story for pictures out of a series of visual incidents that must be grouped together to make screen entertainment. Grouping those visual incidents together was my work. To put that on paper so it could be in turn submitted to a director or assistant director and the staff was somebody else's work.

"Q: Isn't the story the first thing written, or prepared, rather?

"A: Surely.

"Q: The story is prepared first and then from it you make these visual pictures, don't you?

"A: Why certainly not. If you had an idea to write a story you would have to have the idea before you wrote it. Wouldn't you?...

"Q: Who was it that had actual charge of the actual detail of the story and the scenario?

"A: In starting out any new series, I always give that my personal attention, and strange as it may seem to you, I did give this my personal attention.

"Q: To the extent of writing the scenario?

"A: I never write.

"Q: You just simply dictate the form?

"A: I simply tell it to somebody, and they write it and bring it back to me to see what it looks like . If I write, it looks terrible...."

Warren Doane takes the stand.

"Q: Do you recollect the conversation that took place between you and Miss Roe in January, 1925, at the Studio?

"A: Why, in general I remember about it. I don't remember it in exact words.

"Q: Where did this conversation take place?

"A: In my office.

"Q: Was anybody else present?

"A: No.

"Q: Will you state that conversation, so far as you remember the substance of it? ...

"A: One of the girls in the office, either my secretary or one of the girls in the front office, came in and said there was a lady in the front office claiming we had stolen something, and creating a disturbance, and they were rather excited about it. So I said to have her come in, and Miss Roe came in... But she seemed to be very greatly excited , and the first thing she said was, 'You have stolen my story.' I was rather surprised, and said that I was surprised to hear her make that statement; that I didn't know what story she referred to or how she knew we had stolen her story. And all this time she was apparently very much wrought up, and she threw down on my desk a clipping, I think, from a San Francisco paper, possibly, and had reference to our production of the picture called *Black Thunder*. And she said, 'There is the proof.' I then explained to her that that happened to be a title that we had chanced on, feeling it was an appropriate title, but that it would have to be changed when we presented the film for copyright; that it was not an infrequent thing for us to present films with titles that had previously been used, and to change them... She persisted, however, in the statement that we had stolen her story, and that she was there to collect for it; that she was going to make us pay. I told her that I felt she was very unfair in continuing to make that statement prior to having seen the picture. She had, in my opinion, no way of knowing what the story was or what the picture was. The conversation got rather bitter, I imagine, and I told her that I refused to continue it; that I had no other recourse, if she continued such remarks, than to walk out of the office, and I started to do that and she quieted down, and I went back and we had quite a long talk after that, and I arranged to show her the picture and show her the studio...

"Q: Did you discuss with her whether or not you knew of her stories or knew what her stories were?

"A: No...

"Q: Did you tell her you were familiar with her stories?

"A: No...

"Q: What did you do about the title 'Black Thunder'?

"A: ... The picture was referred to as *Black Thunder*, in press stories, and I notified our publicity man that we shouldn't use that story any longer, and I believe they next used the name *Black Fury*.

"Q: You say you notified him that you shouldn't use that story any more?

"A: No; that title I meant to say...

"Q: Do you personally know who originally conceived of the idea of *The King of Wild Horses*?

"A: I know positively.

"Q: Who was it?

"A: Mr. Roach.

"Q: How do you know that?

"A: That was the first horse picture, and he presented the idea of making a horse picture and at the same time a general intimation of what kind of a story could be used."

Mr. H.M. Walker takes the stand.

"Q: Mr. Walker, what is your business or occupation?

"A: Title writer.

"Q: For what company?

"A: Hal E. Roach Studios.

"Q: How long have you been employed by them?

"A: Since 1916.

"Q: Did you write the titles for the films, *The King of Wild Horses* and *Black Cyclone*?

"A: Yes, sir.

… "Q: Now, will you give the process by which you prepare titles and sub-titles for a film?

"A: The purpose of a sub-title is that the story of the film may be more easily and more enjoyably understood by the audience. The film is run for me to look at, and then I work along those lines.

"Q: Did you find that titling and sub-titling the film *Rex, the King of Wild Horses* was similar or did it differ in any respect from titling and sub-titling other films?

"A: It was the first horse picture that I had titled, and it was more difficult.

"Q: Why was that?

"A: Well, you had to say in titles—you almost had to explain what a horse was thinking about…

"Q: Did you ever read any of Miss Roe's stories?

"A: I never had that privilege."

It wasn't until March 7, 1927, over four months later, that the Honorable Judge William P. James (1870-1940) rendered his Opinion:

"It is intimated in some decisions that the appropriation of a theme violates an author's copyright. In its ordinary meaning a theme is understood to be the underlying thought which impresses the reader of a literary production, or the text of a discourse. Using the word 'theme' in such a sense will draw within the circle of its meaning age-old plots, the property of everyone, and not possible of legal appropriation by an individual.

"It is the theme presented in an original way—with novelty of treatment or embellishment—which becomes the property of an author, in the exclusive use of which a copyright will protect him...

"It was shown in evidence that the existence of bands of wild horses within rugged and unoccupied sections of the western portion of the United States had been well known long before they were used to form the basis for the stories written by the plaintiff... However, comparing the picture stories, as told by the films and their explanatory legends, with the written stories of the plaintiff, I have been unable to conclude that there is substantial identity of scenes, incidents depicted, or treatment of theme in whole or in substantial part.

"If it could be said in this case that the Roach Studios, using the underlying theme of plaintiff's stories, had adapted characters and incidents closely resembling those used by the plaintiff in the exposition thereof, infringement would be shown. There are a few incidents in the film which are quite strikingly similar to those which the stories describe, but they all belong to the character of the natural and expected happenings, considering the normal action of animals and persons placed as the characters are in the environment which we find them. It is not a test of infringement that such similarities exist...

"Unless the public is deceived by the pictures and led to believe that the films are a picturization of the plaintiff's literary work (the standard of the ordinary observer being applied) then no infringement is shown.

"Having read with much care the stories written by plaintiff, and having witnessed an exhibition of the film pictures, I am not of the opinion that the latter do more than show to the viewer that the common and open field used by plaintiff has been selected by the picture producers within which to build their stories.

"Decree is ordered for defendants...."

That same month, Jackman was on location in Nevada filming the western *No Man's Law*. This time there was conflict, but it came from no outside source—this time it was domestic.

November 11, 1926 Fred Jackman letter to Warren Doane, Moapa, Nevada: "Dear Sir: I burned your telegram after the first reading... I am very much perterbed [*sic*] at the extravagant manner in which expenses can mount up on this picture through hasty and un-businesslike decisions... Mr. [F. Richard] Jones is a clever writer and director but he himself knows he is such a rotten businessman that he puts his personal finances in the hand of a competent businessman and has his pinn [sic] money doled out to him like a schoolboy."

Warren Doane to Jackman: "Mr. Jones is supervising director and we approve without reservation his doing what in his judgment is best. Economy of production will be best served by your giving us complete cooperation."

Mabel Normand's *Raggedy Rose* three-reeler co-directed by Stan Laurel was released November 7 followed by another three-reeler, *The Nickel Hopper* on December 5. Stan Laurel co-wrote this one, and Oliver Hardy was in the cast.

The last Hal Roach Studios release for 1926 was *45 Minutes From Hollywood,* which reached the nation's screens the day after Christmas. Production for this comedy starring Glenn Tryon had begun nearly a year earlier and was then abandoned. When it was resumed, a totally new second half was created. This two-reeler included appearances by virtually all of the regular "stars" of the Hal Roach Studios: Stan Laurel, Oliver Hardy (appearing separately—they weren't an official team yet), the Our Gang kids, Charlotte Mineau, Edna Murphy, Rube Clifford, Stanley "Tiny" Sandford, and even two REAL stars past and future—Theda Bara and Janet Gaynor. *45 Minutes From Hollywood* was a harbinger of things to come—the triumph of Hal Roach and his "All Stars." Within a year this Irish-American adventurer from Elmira, New York would become Hollywood's uncrowned King of Comedy.

4

The Battle of the Century
Achieving Success with Short Features
1926-1928

THE YEAR 1926 was the year Hal Roach made his aggressive bid to enter the big time in Hollywood by aligning his Studio with that of Hollywood's greatest, Metro-Goldwyn-Mayer, whose own facilities were located not far from Roach's in Culver City, California.

Fred Quimby (1886-1965) was the executive who really helped Roach launch his brand during the transition from Pathé to MGM. He had been Paul Brunet's sales manager in 1918. Years later Quimby was in charge of the MGM Animation Department and eventually won seven Academy Awards for the "Tom & Jerry" cartoons. He has been quoted as having said, "I suppose that the Hal Roach trademark on a reel of a completed film is as good a guarantee as one could want."

January 4, 1926 Fred Quimby Short Subject Sales Mgr for Fox Film Corp. , New York City letter to Hal Roach: "My daughter Elizabeth... has asked me several times to get her some autographed pictures of your 'OUR GANG' cast... you have no idea how wild Betty is about 'OUR GANG' comedies. Every time I see her all she talks about is Harold Lloyd, Tom Mix and 'OUR GANG.'

May 29, 1926 Fred Quimby to Hal Roach: "Someone over at Famous Players told Elmer Pearson you had signed a contract to release your product through Metro-Goldwyn, and yesterday Ed Hatrick was telling me about the deal you are consummating with Mr. Hearst in connection with the comedy production. The whole plan is a marvelous line-up and cannot help but be very successful."

June 12, 1926 Telegram Fred Quimby to Hal Roach: "Today when I was closing with Dave Loew for all Fox short subjects for entire New York Loew circuit Nick Schenck learned I was in Dave's office and sent for me. We talk-ed for about one hour he telling me all about the new short subject program how he thought it should be handled, etc. He spoke very highly of you how he admired you as a producer STOP from the way he talked he understands that you and I have made definite arrangements for me to go to work for you as outlined by you STOP I will be in Los Angeles about July Tenth."

July 6, 1926 Hal Roach Studios letter to Dr. A.H. Giannini, President East River National Bank, New York City: "As you know, we have been financed by Pathé Exchange in the past for the major portion of our needs but in contemplation of the change to Metro production we must arrange to finance the production ourselves. To do this will require roughly one million dollars... Our earnings for the past seven years have average(d) $166,000.00 per year and upon entering into the Metro contract will be at least $100,000.00 per year greater on account of the more equitable method of charging for prints."

July 20, 1926 Hal Roach telegram to Public Theatres, NY: "Chas. Chase... is making best two reelers we ever made... Our Gang comedies have increased 30 percent in negative cost from last year for we must keep putting more and more in these comedies to lead the field."

September 18, 1926: Agreement between Hal Roach and Quimby to transfer Quimby's contract to MGM effective February 17, 1927.

September 19, 1926 *Film Daily*: "Hearst Plans Tie-Up with Hal Roach.

"Negotiations are in progress between the producer and publisher and Roach, calling for the financing of a comedy unit by Hearst, as a first step. Comedy unit Hearst would finance would make a series of pictures based on one of the cartoon strips featured in the Hearst newspapers." Roach later decided to nix that project.

October 10, 1926 *Film Daily*: "Hal Roach announced yesterday that he will build a first run theater, to be devoted exclusively to short subjects, in the downtown district." Another dream that was not realized.

October 11, 1926 Warren Doane letter to Fred Quimby: "I was very gratified when Mr. Frank wired me during Mr. Roach's visit in New York that a contract had been made with you... I have had the idea for a number of years that if we could have the benefit of your ability in charge of the sales of our product, there would be very little left to desire, and you can be assured that every possible effort will be made to furnish your product with which to sweep the Industry. I only hope it will be possible for you to spend a little while here at the studio before you assume your new duties."

October 14, 1926 *Film Daily*: "Hal Roach continues to sign important featured players for two-reel comedies. In the past few days he has placed under contract Priscilla Dean, Matt Moore, Mae Busch and Agnes Ayres."

November 2, 1926 Telegram from Doane to Frank: "Due to cost of Normand Pictures which average $45,000 plus difficulty of getting proper cooperation from her to enable us to work cheaper and better we believe advisable discontinue Normand Pictures upon completion of number five for 60 days and substitute Star pictures… which are cheaper to produce and will give us better quality."

November 17, 1926 Warren Doane to W.B. Frank, New York City Pathé: "With regard to [Stan] Laurel, we may eventually make a comedy star of him. He shows a good deal of promise…."

November 18, 1926: Comparing Sennett's and Our Gang. Number of theatres booked: Sennett: 1484 Our Gang: 1198.

November 1926: Warren H. Doane letter to W.B. Frank: "Because some of the larger companies make arrangements with employees of the Western Union Company we have prepared a list of names and phrases for code words. MGM: Marconi; Hal Roach Studios: Rector; Hal Roach: Renfrew; Louis B. Mayer: Jerome; Irving Thalberg: Wilkes; Mack Sennett: Grant; Harold Lloyd: Wilson; Charley Chase Comedy: Nelson; Our Gang Comedy: Swift. Take time to truly investigate: TRULY."

November 27, 1926: Net profits thirty-four weeks ending this date: $106,365.12

December 20, 1926 Hal Roach Studios, Inc. @ Pathé Bldg. 35 West 45th Street, New York City. Hal E. Roach, President, Warren Doane, General Manager, C.H. Roach, Secretary & Treasurer; W.B. Frank, V.P.; H.M. Walker, Production Manager; F. Richard Jones, Vice President-Director General; M.D. O'Brian, Assistant Secretary & Treasurer.

Christmas 1926: Hal Roach Studios sends boxes of nuts to Loews executives.

1927 RELEASES:
SEVENTEEN ALL-STAR TWO-REELERS (INCLUDING THIRTEEN WITH STAN LAUREL AND OLIVER HARDY)
FOURTEEN CHARLEY CHASE TWO-REELERS
THIRTEEN OUR GANG TWO-REELERS
SIX MAX DAVIDSON TWO-REELERS

ONE CLYDE COOK TWO-REELER
ONE GLENN TRYON TWO-REELER

On January 16, 1927 the Our Gang short *Bring Home the Turkey* featured a new little cast member, a girl by the name of Jean Darling. Cute and blonde, barely four and a half, this was the first of thirty-four shorts in which Jean would appear, including the first five talkies the Rascals would make in 1929.

In November 2013 Miss Darling shared with the author some memories she still has of her days at the Hal Roach Studios more than eighty-five years ago:

"Hal Roach was very good to me. When I was four he was delighted to find out I could write in joined up letters. So he had fan photos sent to my dressing room for me to sign, which I did: FROM YOUR LITTLE FIEND, JEAN DARLING. Yes I left out the R in 'friend' on about fifty stills. On seeing them he said I was a very good girl and gave me a Hershey bar. Then we went to the photo studio where I signed a negative while he spelled 'FRIEND.' And I don't know what happened to the photos I signed."

"[Roach] did his best trying to make my mother change her mind about putting me in Vaudeville, as touring was a hard grind and he thought, at my age, it would be best for me to stay with the GANG. When I was eleven he cast me as Peg in the upcoming film *Peg o' My Heart*, which was scrapped in favor of *Babes in Toyland* and I became Curly Locks."

February 2, 1927: Hal Roach loans James Finlayson to Warner Bros. for *The First Auto* feature for $750 per week (six days) and furnish first class transportation when required to go on location and pay meals and lodgings on such locations. *The First Auto* was a Vitaphone feature that mixed music, sound effects and some talking sequences and was released three weeks before *The Jazz Singer*.

February 21, 1927 Telegram Fred Quimby to Warren Doane: "Effective week ending February 19th will receive my salary from MGM."

February: Rex the Wonder Horse was sold to Universal Studios where he continued to appear in Westerns into 1933.

February 1927 *Motion Picture* magazine, "Hollywood Notes" by Eugene V. Brewster: "Mabel Normand and Hal Roach have severed relations. Mabel has been making a series of feature comedies for Roach. Somebody said that Mabel was told to go home one day when she arrived for work.

Knowing Mabel, I don't believe this. More than likely it was Mabel who told Hal to go home...

"Billy Joy, brother of Leatrice Joy, who has just severed his long connection with the Hal Roach studio, said 'One thing about the Roach lot is that it is clean and above reproach in every respect. Any child or young girl would be just as safe there as at home and Hal Roach has always insisted on keeping everything on a high plane mentally, morally and physically.'

Which reminds me of a conversation I had in the late 1990s with one of the producers of the television documentary series *E! Mysteries and Scandals*, all about sordid tales of Hollywood's dark side. When I mentioned to him that I had worked for Hal Roach he scoffed and muttered under his breath, "Hal Roach? We'll never do a show about HIM. He was Hollywood's Poster Child for Mental Health."

March 3, 1927 Letter Hal Roach to Fred Quimby: "...I am counting on you to be a big success with the new organization... and rest assured that we are going to do our darndest to make our product stand up to the very best compliments you may pay it."

Fred Quimby contract with Hal Roach Studios is transferred to MGM effective March 17, 1927.

March 10, 1927 Letter Hal Roach to Fred Quimby: "...we are most proud of our association with Metro-Goldwyn-Mayer... we are to produce not fillers to take up time in theatres, but short features to have box office value, plus entertainment value equal to the same amount of minutes that the best features on the market can give for the amount of time they are on the screen. That will be the future policy of our company. That the Heads of Metro-Goldwyn-Mayer are allowing us to engage the cast, build sets, engage directors and writers that will equal the best in the feature field, and with these facilities available for ourselves we pledge to the Metro Sales Force our best efforts to rank second to none as comedy producers regardless of length."

March 14, 1927 Hal Roach letter to Fred Quimby: "I like the spirit in which you are attacking your new job. We will try our damndest to give you quality, with the hope that some day we will be on an equal with features."

March 17, 1927 Hal Roach letter to Fred Quimby: "The biggest sales talk a comedy can possibly have to the subsequent run buyer is the fact that the picture ran in a downtown first-run theatre. Now, if a picture runs in a downtown theatre and they give it no advertising or no recognition, it will just go as an also ran, the audience caring little for it. Whereas, if this comedy is advertised as a definite part of the program, and the management of the theatre boosts it to their patrons as they would boost a high-class vaudeville act, jazz band, or any other act or innovation that they would be putting in their features, the audience will look at the comedy, not as a filler but as a definite part of that show's entertainment.

"As soon as the big theatres in the downtown districts advertise two reel comedies and give them some prestige, just that quickly will the subsequent-run theatre follow suit and I believe a very little energy used at the start by the Loew houses in plugging our comedies will reap an enormous profit to them from the balance of the Industry... I am serious in my belief that if the time can come when we can spend as much per reel on our comedies as Metro-Goldwyn spend per reel on their features, we will have drawing power—although a shorter picture in length—equal to that of the average feature; and when that time arrives, comedy output for Metro-Goldwyn will be as provitable [*sic*] to them as their feature output."

March 18, 1927 Fred Quimby letter to Hal Roach: "...Harry Langdon's features are not selling nearly as well as they expected... In two reelers he would be the most outstanding comedy star on the market and his pictures would gross not less than $300,000 in the U.S. and Canada—and my guess would be about $75,000 on the foreign market... Many big exhibitors will tell you that he is not good enough for feature comedies and that they would be willing to pay almost as much for a good two or three reeler as for a feature length comedy."

March 23, 1927 Hal Roach letter to Fred Quimby: "Our quality is improving rapidly but it is costing us more to get this quality. From the previews and comments we are getting here I think the cost is justified in the product. I believe by the time we start releasing for Metro-Goldwyn-Mayer we are going to have a class of short comedy that will stand up well in quality with the features released today... If we can gross $100,000 in the United States and $25,000. Abroad and in Canada we can all make a great profit even at a greater cost than we are now spending."

March 24, 1927 Hal Roach letter to Fred Quimby: "Now, Fred, you know perfectly well that you can sell two reel Chaplins, Lloyds, Arbuckles and Keatons to the first-run theatres and they would certainly find place for them and figure they were box office value; therefore, it comes right back to a question of quality of production... We have got to prove the worth of high-class comedies in the big first-run theatres... The average theatre runs a two reel comedy off in eighteen minutes, and if the quality is there they will certainly find room for that eighteen minutes—and—we are certainly going to put that quality into the pictures if we have to go broke doing it.

"The reason that men like Lloyd, Chaplin and Keaton go into feature length pictures is because they figure there is no prestige in shorter-length pictures, and when the theatres give short comedies the proper prestige, these comedians will be perfectly contented to make two reel pictures instead of features."

March 25, 1927 Fred Quimby letter: Pathé Sales of Our Gang 1925-26 $4,528: MGM Sales 1927-28 (projected) $9,475.

March 25, 1927: Telegram to Chief of Police, Louisville, Kentucky: Sam Fox making Our Gang comedy in Louisville? Eldorado Arkansas *News* of March 4 said they were! Fox not connected with Roach Organization now nor at any time and any representation by him to this effect obviously false. Imposter calling himself former assistant director stated Hal Roach Studios buys all his Gang negatives at fifty cents a foot and uses local kids. (Sam Fox is NOT with Fox Pictures either.)

Another Our Gang imposter, March 1927: Mrs. Maizie Kilner of Los Angeles wrote to Hal Roach that "Carl 'Tubby' Hayes says he is on the Hal Roach payroll doing comedy bits for $300 per week. Plays opposite Mabel Normand and Marceline Day. Says you owe him $700 and Snub Pollard owes him $86.00 and that you'll pay him on December 31st."

June 28, 1927: Mr. I.D. Spidle of Schuyler, Nebraska says gentleman associated with Hal Roach Studios stopped his ten-year-old freckle faced son and said he'd be good for Our Gang. Warren Doane's reply: we start kids at two to four years of age. Oldest is now ten. Could it be Sam Fox? Cannot locate him or another person falsely claiming to be Hal Roach associate."

April 1927: Irving Green, Manager, Fellsway Theatre, Medford, Massachusetts suggests Jimmy Finlayson in a series of Scotch comedies. Warren H. Doane replied: "Jimmy is very Scotch himself and the idea has been thought of a number of times. However, when it comes to playing with it everyone starts thinking of things which are possibly offensive to those of Scotch descent, and we have not yet been able to figure out any way of making them funny and not offensive."

Interesting that Mr. Doane was worried about possibly offending the Scotch, as the Roach lot was producing a series of funny Jewish comedies at that very time. Max Davidson, born in Germany in 1875, played a comical little stereotypically Old World Jewish immigrant living in America, unassimilated and VERY ethnic. Hal Roach saw him in some comedies with Jackie Coogan and liked him so much he hired Davidson to appear in the Mabel Normand comeback *Raggedy Rose* in 1926. After several more successful shorts Roach signed Davidson to a five year contract in January 1927. His salary was to begin at $400 per week, rising to $1,250 in the final year.

Though the series was popular, Davidson's persona was a very uncomfortable one for MGM's Louis B. Mayer, who was, after all was a Russian Jew from the lower rungs of society who had emigrated to America and, unlike the Davidson character, was now a wealthy and assimilated tycoon who wanted to completely erase his past and thoroughly embrace the ideals of Americana. The little rag picker Max was a painful reminder of that past. Mayer alone could not have pressured Roach into squashing the series, as he had no power over him. Roach answered only to Nicholas Schenck of Loew's Inc., MGM's parent company, in New York. Well, it so happened that Nicholas Schenck was a Russian Jew himself who, like Mayer, had made it big in America. And when Schenck put pressure on Roach to end the Davidson series, that was that.

"Any evaluation of behavior or ethics during the 1920s needs to be conducted in the context of contemporary morality at that time, and not vis-à-vis evolving standards and social change nearly a century later," wrote Richard W. Bann.

"Unless a stereotype was malicious or immoral, this attitude of celebrating diversity was much healthier than what we have now. Today, one or a few are endlessly taking offense at something, at *everything,* and then insisting that the rest of the world should change to accommodate their narcissism. We need to recognize that everyone, everywhere, each of us, is a member of *some* kind of minority; we should be able to laugh at ourselves, and not be so sensitive… A politically correct society achieves behavior that is polite at the cost of being real. It leads directly to censorship and the diminution of what America has traditionally cherished as the First Amendment right of freedom of expression. If we cannot see, study, and most importantly enjoy experimental films like the ones Hal Roach courageously tried making with Max Davidson and others, we will wind up censoring not only films, but books, all through history. You lose a sense of who you are, if you do not know who you were."

The Davidson series was terminated in September 1928. The comedian appeared in several early Roach talkies in 1929 and went on to appear in many films in mostly uncredited bit parts until 1945. He died in 1950 "almost forgotten," says the blurb on IMDb, "in a retirement home."

April 5, 1927: "Mr. Royal Baker, Censor will not pass 'No Man's Law' the way it is. Merely seven reels of brutality without any point or without any redeeming feature of any kind... We believe that it can be remedied at the home office by setting in new titles and cutting out parts mention[ed] so as to get by all right." – Oscar Hanson, Pathé, Detroit.

April 7, 1927: "Smith & Allen, Inc. announce a Panchromatic of Higher Speed, Better Color Separation and Finer Grain giving a higher resolving power than has heretofore been offered to the discriminating producer and artistic cinematographer." It was this film which enabled Stan Laurel to return before the movie cameras, as his pale blue eyes did not photograph well when the older film stock was used.

"On the screen he looked almost blind," said Roach, "so we couldn't use him in pictures. But I'd already put him under contract. So he was a writer at the studio for the first several months. Then Panchromatic film came in which photographed blue better than the old film did."

April 7, 1927: H.M. Walker telegram to Warren Doane: "PAPRIKA PETE APPROVED BY MGM FOR WESTERN COMEDY"

April 8, 1927: Eugene A. Tucker, Attorney at Law, Los Angeles to Warren Doane regarding 'Farina' Hoskins: "Clayton H. Hoskins 'against her will' forced Mrs. Florence Hoskins to purchase a house and lot for $4,000 and induced his wife to sign a note for $2,000... Hoskins left, and she paid on it for a time, but was unable to keep up payments on this and also her house."

April 9, 1927: Telegram: "Pleased to inform you that you have been appointed member Civic Reception Committee Italian Fascista Commander De Pienedo Four Continents Flyer STOP Please be at City Hall Sunday one PM—Italian Vice Consul Gradenigo" This is interesting in light of the Roach-Mussolini incident that occurred ten years later.

April 11, 1927 Warren Doane letter to H.M. Walker, Hotel Astor, New York City: "Charley's Big Bear picture was one of his best... Leo's picture 'Don't Tell Everything' [a Max Davidson short released July 2] was considerably improved by the retake scenes he made, but doesn't rank better than 'nearly good.'... It would be a good picture for anybody else to make but it is below the standard of what we hope to do... Fred Guiol's boat picture was previewed in every house in Southern California and worked over here at the studio and a new finish made, so it is now I would say a 'nearly good' rough comedy. Hal's picture is proceeding satisfactorily... He is taking his time and it is the consensus of opinion that it is a good picture."

April 11, 1927: Letter from Warren Doane to H.M. Walker: "At present time Babe Hardy seems logical comedian for Western Series. Mr.

Roach feels and I concur that PAPRIKA PETE more suitable for little character than for Babe. Expect these comedies to be rather melodramatic and spectacular therefore believe can find better name for series. The selection of series name if possible should be delayed until we can get better line on nature of series."

April 14, 1927: Doane telegram to Walker: "...we consider they [Pathé] have breached the contract on many instances as regards selling our pictures by themselves and that if their present attitude continues we have in mind using the fact they have breached the contract to justify terminating production for them immediately...."

April 19, 1927: Doane telegram to Walker: "...we do not agree we require Pathé permission make Metro pictures prior September first. Also do not agree must go to Pathé for release of Our Gang trademark... The conception of the Our Gang idea was and has been at all times our own and privilege of copyrighting titles of various pictures this series was given Pathé in order facilitate distribution of pictures and for no other purpose...."

April 19, 1927: Walker telegram to Doane: "Rammed home every point contained in your letter and telegrams STOP Believe favorable effect will be felt immediately giving us easier sailing from now on."

April 19 1927: Warren H. Doane letter to "Mr. Grasnier" at Victorville: Holmes, Pallette, Finlayson cow ranch. "...warn Pallette not to strain to be funny—to hold himself down and play with repression. Corrals too empty—hire horses and cattle. I thought the interior film of Finlayson was very good indeed and we all think that Holmes is okay as the other partner."

April 21, 1927: Hal Roach telegram to Fred Quimby: "I like the name M-G-M Short Features very much."

April 25, 1927: Walker to Doane: "Disappointed and disgusted with today's conference STOP Pathé brought up all petty arguments of the past and tried to make them stick... Think thing to do is go right ahead with our production according to your schedule and let them cool off for awhile... Had lunch today with Feist and MGM sales heads everything lovely on this side of fence."

April 28, 1927: Doane to Walker: "Everything going fine... Believe quality of pictures showing consistent improvement. Cost well in hand and general progress excellent."

April 26, 1927: Comedies previewed: highest 104 laughs—but you've got one now having 107!—Howard Dietz, Director of Advertising & Publicity, MGM

April 27, 1927: Lupe Velez loaned to Douglas Fairbanks Productions for *The Gaucho* for $600 per week.

September 7, 1927: Ralph W. Smith, Attorney at Law writes Lupe Velez "disaffirms her contract with Hal Roach as she was only 17 when she signed 3/18/27 contract for three years." [Virtually all records indicate Ms. Velez was born on July 18, 1908. Thus on March 18, 1927 she would have actually been exactly eighteen years and eight months of age.]

Lupe Velez Expense Trip to Mexico City:

"Registration Lupe 80 pesos, $40; Bribe $1500, $750, Expense Crossing Border 50, $25; Railroad Fare to Mexico City $540; Telephone and telegrams $174.63"

May 25, 1927 Warren Doane telegram to Fred Quimby: "Understand from Mr. Roach Charley Chase has apparently offended your Sales Force or at least certain numbers. Please investigate and advise what they took exception to and what if anything we can do to remedy situation."

May 26, 1927 Fred Quimby telegram to Warren Doane: "Unable to find anyone who was offended by Chase and quite to contrary Chase very popular with the boys and held in very high regards… Do not let Chase episode cause you any concern because there is nothing to worry about."

May 10, 1927: Fred Quimby letter to Hal Roach: "To date we have engaged 43 short feature salesmen and two special short feature representatives… To complete our short feature sales personnel we have 11 men more to hire. I expect this to be completed by convention time. Our short feature salesmen have been carefully selected—they are seasoned men, well grounded in the selling of short features and as a whole, represent the cream of short feature salesmen."

May 21, 1927: The MGM Short Convention was held in Los Angeles to inaugurate the new MGM-Hal Roach alliance.

May 1927: All Hal Roach Studios employees offered chance to deduct one-sixth of their regular weekly rate to go to the American Red Cross for the Mississippi Valley Flood Relief. $1 million will provide each flood victim $3.00.

June 1, 1927 Fred Quimby letter to Hal Roach: "You sold yourself, personally, to the M-G-M Sales Force 100 percent. Every man in the train returning to New York had the highest regard for you as a man and honestly believes that your product is far superior to any other comedies on the market; and that they are going to be able to secure the increases we have asked. As for the entertainment you provided—it far surpassed anything that has ever been done before in this, or any other industry. Many of the boys said they thought you were too generous and that you spent too much money. However, the main thing is that I want you to know that every one fully appreciates what you did to entertain them and that it will be returned to you in dividends."

June 1, 1927 Fred Quimby letter to Warren Doane: "Firstly in connection with your wire about Charley Chase—…It is true in fun Charley threw some ginger ale or beer around promiscuously but the boys all understood it was in fun and they were having equally as much fun. The tremendous reception and entertainment prepared by you and Mr. Roach far over-shadowed any little incident that could have been caused by one person. All of our men were loud in their praise of what you did for them and I can assure you that they will never forget it."

Chase was more than likely just being a fun-loving party boy. True, he enjoyed hitting the bottle more often than was good for him; perhaps he was celebrating the fact that a fan club had been formed in his honor.

June 1927: "For Mr. Roach from Ray Coffin: Opinion of Charley Chase comedy "Fluttering Hearts" "A good average Chase comedy, not absolutely convincing, but with plenty of laughs…Story seemed a bit disconnected and rambling to me. Titles were very good. Chase did his usual good individual work. Thought Martha Sleeper better than ever before; she looked very pretty, was well-dressed and displayed plenty of animation and ability. Chase's pantomime with the model a riot. Should grade quite highly and please most audiences."

June 8, 1927 Fred Quimby letter to Warren Doane: "We have cleared our decks for action and have started to sell. The first contract being closed for your comedies has just reached my desk, and although it is for a small theatre in the neighborhood section in Baltimore, I want to tell you about the increases we secured over last year. On the Roach All Stars, Pathé got $6.00 Chase $7.50 and $10.00 for Our Gang. We closed for $10 on Davidsons, Roach All Stars and Charley Chase.—and $15.00 on the Gangs. I can assure you that these increases are good indications of what you may expect generally."

June 29, 1927 *Variety* reviewed *No Man's Law* (identified as *No Man's Land*): "Excellent western production suffered from padding. Too long, but otherwise okay. It's one of the very few western pictures with real laughs… [James] Finlayson shows up strongly as a character at which many actors in westerns have aimed but have never achieved. The easy, almost supercilious attitude masking polished strength has been so often portrayed with ridiculous results that Finlayson should prove a treat. The story is simple but carries tremendous appeal. Had the producers wanted to make a higher grade production they could easily have done so... Miss Kent looks and acts well. A couple of the almost nude scenes will not stand much chance with the censors out of town."

Censorship was quite a concern in Hollywood, especially since the Fatty Arbuckle scandal of 1921 which led to the creation of the Will Hays Office. Narrator James Mason explained, in the Thames Television mini-series *Hollywood* in 1980, "Local censor boards were springing up all over the country. Each had its own degree of prudery, its own sensitive spot. In some states you couldn't flash an ankle."

Alan Dwan, famous feature director of the '20s explained. "Well, there was so much censorship it's hard to tell where it begins, because every political group in the country had a censor board, every police department had a censor. There was a national censor. There was a state censor. I think that more people earned salaries as censors than all the combined motion picture people that ever worked in pictures ever picked up. Just everybody was a censor."

June 14, 1927 Hunter, Duline Company Investment Securities: Seven million daily patrons to picture theatres compared to a few thousand who attended the early 'nickelodeons.' $2 million daily admissions; $650 million yearly in U.S. and Canada. 20,500 theatres in U.S. over 18,550,000 seats. There were 9,000 theatres in 1910.

In 1927, 300,000 people employed in production, distribution and exhibition of motion pictures, 750 features produced yearly, sixty motion picture publications.

June 16, 1927 Hal Roach letter to Fred Quimby: "As you know we are now at work on the M-G-M pictures, and everything is breezing along fine here—looks like we will have some excellent product for you. Would it be possible for you to have some kind of a committee there to review our comedies as they come in? So that we will have something to go by as an assurance that our quality will be kept at a high standard."

June 22, 1927: Mrs. Helen Gilmore, sixty-eight years of age, a stage and screen actress for fifty years "now finds herself in destitute circumstances and poor health. Ask Alex Pantages to use his theatre for midnight matinee July 13. Request to Fred Niblo, Tom Mix, Harold Lloyd. Others interested are Joe Keaton, Francis Powers and several high-grade vaudeville acts, the press and the writer (K.P. Walton In Charge of Publicity). Ms. Gilmore (1862-1936) aside from her stage work appeared in over 130 movies between 1914 and 1930. She had been practically a fixture at the Hal Roach Studios since 1918.

June 1927: George Sully & Co. Publishers New York City propose a children's book based on Our Gang. Hal Roach Studios sends synopsis for *Love My Dog* and requests flat fee, author to view the picture and acquire stills from Pathé.

June 28, 1927: The Erosian Club, A Colored Screen Talent Association, 1948 Central Avenue, Los Angeles affiliated with Unit 112, United Veterans of the Republic "places us in position to furnish any number of orderly and well disciplined Colored Extras as needed."

June 30, 1927: Hal Roach Studios inquires of the Eastman Kodak Company if it would be interested in making 16mm of Our Gang, Clyde Cook, Charley Chase, All Star Series, Glenn Tryon, Mabel Normand. They offer $10,000 for exclusive rights. But Pathé hasn't given consent as of September 8, 1927 when Hal Roach arrives in New York City.

July 1, 1927 Fred Quimby letter to Hal Roach: "Boston Our Gang price from $12.50 to $20. Charlotte, North Carolina, Our Gang from $10 to $17.50 Chicago from $10 to $20. In Wisconsin (Sheboyan) a 30% increase over the previous top. Omaha 25% increase on Our Gang. 50% increase Chase, All Stars, Davidsons."

Film Daily reported that the Hal Roach Studios "earnings show the three months ended July 2, 1927 to have been one of the most profitable periods in the studio's history."

July 1927: "For Mr. Roach from Ray Coffin: Opinion of Charley Chase comedy "What Women Did For Me." "This comedy should prove very popular. Chase does some of his best work, and I think Lupe screened very well and displayed a fascinating personality. The girls were very effective and the story well done. Photography was mighty fine. Titles are good. The snow sequences were a pleasant relief in comedy... Well directed. Think it one of the best audience comedies to leave the lot in months. I mean by that, it will have a distinct appeal for all classes of people. A few shots will undoubtedly be censored, such as Chase shaking out of his drawers, the girl tickling him rather low down, and possibly the episode where he steps on the hot water bottle and it springs a leak. Would call this a knock-out."

July 27, 1927: William W. Cohill letter to Warren Doane: Ben Turpin is now freelancing after eleven years with Mack Sennett. "If I might suggest, Mr. Turpin would be valuable as the comefy [*sic*] relief in a feature picture, as it would not be necessary to star him."

August 15 and 20, 1927 Helen Gilmore sends handwritten notes to Hal Roach requesting work. She was hurt while working on the set of Cecil B. DeMille's *King of Kings* "I haven't worked but a couple of weeks in months."

August 4, 1927 Preview presentation in New York City of representative short subjects to be released by M-G-M for the Season 1927-28. This is indeed the birthday of M-G-M Short Features."

Film Daily August 5, 1927: "MGM Makes Debut in Short Subject Field at Embassy Theatre in New York City. 'Sugar Daddies' featuring Stan Laurel, Oliver Hardy, Edna Marion and Jimmy Finlayson and four other shorts of the series, a one-reel Ufa travelogue, Charlie [*sic*] Chase short 'Soaring Wings', a two-reel Technicolor production 'The Flag' and 'Yale Vs. Harvard', a two-reel Our Gang comedy."

August 8, 1927: Hal Roach letter to Howard Dietz: "...without decreasing the popularity of the M-G-M feature players you could add the better known players that are appearing in our short comedies, such as Chase, Davidson, Our Gang, Glorie [*sic*] Richards and Edna Marion, which would greatly help to popularize these people who may some day be appearing in M-G-M features as well."

August 17, 1927: Famous Players wanted Hal Roach Studios to loan Leo McCarey but Warren Doane wrote: "...it would be impossible for us to spare Mr. McCarey as he is supervising production for us, but I would be glad to loan out Clyde Bruckman for any reasonable length of time...."

Clyde Bruckman (1894-1955) an extremely talented writer and director, helmed Laurel and Hardy's first teamed efforts in 1927-28 while having a successful career writing some of the best features for Buster Keaton and Harold Lloyd, both silents and talkies. He directed W.C. Fields in two of his best, *The Fatal Glass of Beer* (a 1933 short) and the 1935 feature *Man on the Flying Trapeze*. Bruckman returned to the Roach lot as a writer for fifteen episodes of Abbott & Costello's television series that were filmed there in 1953.

Variety August 24, 1927: *The Valley of Hell* "Undiluted western melodrama, lightning paced and sure to have the kids whistling and stamping and adults interested despite a superior snicker every now and then when the hero's exploits seem just a bit too miraculous. There's a sweep to the yarn that brushes aside needless plot detail and rushes forward in a mounting crescendo of sheer action. Nobody pauses to do any meditating in this busy opera. It's bang-bang from the main title to the clinch."

August 30, 1927: Bobby Dean Morton, fat boy, offered six week engagement by Hal Roach Studios.

August 30, 1927: Doane night letter to Hal Roach, Ambassador Hotel, New York City: "Finlayson prefers freelancing to contract at any figure we can afford. His freelancing salary to be seven fifty. He was not interested in four hundred on contract. Believe we can use him as much as necessary on freelance basis at no increase of cost. If satisfactory to you will drop negotiations with him."

September 3, 1927 Released one a week: Charley Chase, All Stars, Max Davidsons, Our Gang.

September 24, 1927: Doane to Hal Roach on Santa Fe Chief westbound "Chase suggesting placing himself in McCarey's hands as to story and direction. Therefore look for great improvement in this series."

September 26, 1927 The *New York Sun* article by Eileen Creelman:

"Hal Roach looks like a prizefighter, walks like a prizefighter, even on occasion, talks like a prizefighter. A stocky, determined young man, he clings tenaciously to his own idea of comedy producing and polo playing. Last week his conferences with Metro-Goldwyn-Mayer were completed and Mr. Roach, about to leave for his Hollywood studios, was ready to discuss his plans for next year. Chin thrust forward, eyes fixed ahead of him on a remote spot beyond the window, he talked of two-reelers and their future. 'They haven't been good enough. That's been the whole trouble lately. We just haven't made them good enough. The theaters, the public, even the comedians have got the idea that they're unimportant. They've lost prestige. Now we've got to work and get it back....'

"'We're not competing just with Mack Sennett and Educational and other short subject producers. We're competing with Harold Lloyd and Charlie Chaplin and any one else who makes comedies, short or long. Our films appear on the same program with a feature. It is natural for a spectator to compare them in quality. They must be able to stand that comparison in every way. A short comedy is usually much funnier in proportion than a long one. We need not spend so much footage building toward a climax or introducing characters. And the public likes them, misses them when they're not shown. Should Chaplin make a two-reeler that picture would be advertised over nearly any feature film. The public would consider it quite as important. That's what we have to do now, make the short subject what it used to be, an essential and recognized part of the show.' And Mr. Roach, without ever telling whether Farina was a boy or a girl, departed for Hollywood." [Farina played both boy and girl in the Our Gang comedies, thus confusing moviegoers as to his true gender.]

October 5, 1927: Thomas W. Gerety of MGM, New York City: "Let me congratulate you on your best Max Davidson production *Love 'Em and Feed 'Em*. This is a perfect scream and everyone who has seen it is exceedingly enthusiastic about it." [Today, unfortunately, only about two minutes remain of this short, which co-starred Oliver Hardy, Martha Sleeper and Viola Richard, as the negative had deteriorated over the years.]

October 6, 1927: Hal Roach letter to Felix Feist, M-G-M, New York City: "Dear Felix:—I want you and your organization and the whole cock-eyed world to know that my visit in New York convinced me that my affiliation with Metro-Goldwyn-Mayer was the smartest business move I ever made. I feel that I am one of the family with my duty to make funny pictures with assurance that you and your gang will do the rest. With kindest regards, I am sincerely yours."

October 1927 Press release: More than 4,000 children registered with Central Casting but Bob McGowan wants only natural kids with no prior stage or picture experience.

October 10, 1927: Hal Roach letter to an Exhibitor: "We are no longer competing against other short subject companies, but with feature comedies, using the same class of players, directors and sets that the features use; and the feature-length comedies released immediately after production are going right into the first run theatres and then into the subsequent-run theatres, and in nine times out of ten are using the same material that we are using but beating us to the market and making our pictures look second rate.

"Every picture made by us so far for Metro-Goldwyn-Mayer has had a first-run in a downtown house in Los Angeles and has been very well received, and has given us a marvelous boost here because the comedies are new and fresh... if our release dates are to be backed up like they were with Pathé, where our pictures do not get on the market until four or five months after release date, it puts us back in the class of 'just a filler.'"

October 14, 1927: Doane telegram to Hal Roach Eastbound Chief Train #20—Santa Fe Drawing Room D—Car 206: "Velez contract agreed upon and signed by mother. Expect girl's signature tonight or in morning. Believe deal closed."

October 30, 1927: Doane letter to Mrs. Richard Daniels: Mickey Daniels "left because of our inability to agree as to the terms of a proposed new contract with him. At the time he left we would have been glad to have kept him had you seen fit to accept the contract offered you."

October 31, 1927 Hal Roach letter to Fred Quimby: "Our product looks better this year than it has ever looked before and in my estimation the only thing interfering with most excellent business for us is the lack of first run cooperation. If the Loew theatres will advertise our comedies this year I am sure the quality of the product will justify what they say about them. Whereas, if the Loew theatres fail to advertise our comedies it is difficult for us to expect independent theatres or other chains to do it for us. It will not cost them five cents more to devote a portion of their advertising to the comedies and more than ever do I feel that when the theatres once start this they will always continue because our comedy production is certainly on a standard now with feature comedy production."

November 14, 1927 Telegram to Thomas Hitchcock Jr. Racquet Club, New York City: "My plan is to have approximately thirty houses [theatres] in big key cities and change vaudeville to that of review increasing price to two dollars top cooperation with producers of reviews in New York City and sending unit shows out... headed by names of celebrated players, orchestras and novelty acts but each show a unit in itself STOP There would be little difficulty in tying Ziegfield [*sic*] George White, and other review producers into this idea."

November 15, 1927 Tommy Hitchcock Jr. Telegram: "NO LUCK"

November 18, 1927: Norbert Lusk, Editor *Picture-Play* magazine to Hal Roach: Regarding the story "So Long, Slapstick" by Carroll Graham, "to which you take exception." "...I cannot agree with you that it is a slam at you as well as other producers of short comedies, because the present development of short subjects is so obvious to everyone who attends motion pictures... Of course, discerning spectators know there is frequently more artistry displayed by players in two-reel pictures than in longer ones, but unfortunately the majority of picture goers do not possess this particular degree of discrimination." Glenn Tryon stated something about "inadequate material and unsympathetic handling." "It is quite possible that in the opinion of Mr. Graham, and also Mr. Tryon, these conditions existed without necessarily having been the opinion of everyone. What really constitutes inadequate material and unsympathetic handling is a question open to argument, as I have discovered in listening to the plaints of players who insisted on being unhappy at all costs."

Hal Roach's reply November 23, 1927: "Dear Mr. Lusk:—Thanks for your reply to my letter of November 10th—I guess I was just a little bit sore head anyway. Things look like they are breaking for the Short Comedy Product at last so I haven't a kick in the world for anybody, and I wish long life and prosperity to Mr. Graham, Mr. Tryon, yourself and myself! Kindest regards Sincerely yours."

November 22, 1927 Fred Quimby letter to Hal Roach: "...The Loew theatres in Washington [D.C.] did not run any of your comedies during the week that you were there [Roach was in the nation's capital training for his commission as Major in the Signal Corps Reserve.] and I can assure you that you need not be alarmed about the Loew theatres not properly advertising your product. Every time any of the Loew theatres in the State of New York and throughout the country run one of your comedies, they are properly publicized in their theatre program, in the lobby, and either your name or the brand name of the comedy is advertised on the marquee lights... We have no competition in the quality of comedies, but our competitors, especially Paramount and Educational, are selling their comedies at such a ridiculously low price that it does work a hardship on us in trying to maintain good prices. I am safe in saying that where Paramount gets One Dollar, we get Two or more. We are doing a great job of selling, and I am pretty sure of winning that suit of clothes from you."

November 1927: The proposal was made to give gratis to most important accounts a Technicolor Christmas film featuring the kids of Our Gang and Chase. But the plan was abandoned because the 500 prints needed "would make print cost prohibitive and excessive."

November 30, 1927 Fred Quimby letter to Hal Roach: "It would warm the cockles of your heart if you could see how big the OUR GANG comedy *Dog Heaven* is going over at the Capitol Theatre this week, and some day during the week I will clock the laughs and send you a report on it... I just finished visiting about half of our exchanges, and in every city where there is a unit house such as Publix Boston, Buffalo, Kunsky, Detroit, Chicago and Uptown Theatres, Chicago, etc., theatres that put on big presentation shows, I visited the house managers to feel them out and get their reaction as to what they thought about running an occasional good comedy, and to my amazement found that these house manager were not in favor of it... that a good two reel comedy is not worth a cent, and that the public want stage bands, dancers, singers, soloists, etc... However, fortunately, with the exception of Detroit, we have all your comedies sold 100% to first run theatres... Up to November 19th our sales averaged about $40,000 per picture...." He was amazed to find that Paramount's sales average is a little less than $17,000 per picture.

November 30, 1927: Letter from Roland Cummings, M.D., to Warren Doane: "I have just completed an examination of Mr. Robert McGowan and find his symptoms are due to a state of nervous exhaustion. Mr. McGowan is an overly cautious individual who tends to absorb the troubles of those around him. He 'works too hard at his job' and he takes his work home with him. I think it is very important that he get a rest at the present time and I am inclined to think it will take him a couple of months at least to get back his energy. Then, he must learn not to take the problems of life so seriously and to let other people assume their own responsibilities, and learn not to solve the problems that belong to others. He wanted me to write you regarding his condition."

December 1927: Our Gang as Boy Scouts? Hal Roach: "Educational put out three or four pictures closely tied in with the Boy Scouts in which they received the sanction of the National Organization; however, they were not very successful... Mr. McGowan has the idea in mind, however, and says if he ever gets a story that would work in suitably with the Boy Scout movement he will be glad to make it in this atmosphere."

December 2, 1927 Fred Quimby Confidential letter to Hal Roach: M-G-M selling shows increase of nearly $478,000 over Pathé's selling for the same period in 1926. "The way we are selling, and with the great number of accounts to be closed yet this season it is going to be a 'lead pipe cinch' to sell not less than 8000 accounts. However, the figure we are fighting for is 9000 accounts, and if we reach our goal, I know that you will be mighty happy as this will be by far the best circulation that your comedies have ever made."

December 5, 1927 Warren Doane letter to Fred Quimby: "We have just made a new contract with Leo McCarey whom I consider the outstanding comedy director of the entire business, whereby we will be assured of having his supervision for a period of years to come."

December 16, 1927 Fred Quimby letter to Hal Roach: Pathé contracts 1926-27: Gangs 2218, Chase 2345, All Star 2165, Normand 2335

MGM: Gangs 5486, Chase 5440, All Star 5335, Davidson 5295

December 17, 1927 Fred Quimby letter to Hal Roach: "What do you think of the idea of having a Hal Roach Broadcasting Company to broadcast Hal Roach Comedy Hour or Our Gang Hour, or any good title that would publicize your comedies [?] You could have singers, an orchestra, or any kind of good entertainment that the public would be glad to tune in on." Hand-written at the bottom of the typed letter: "I do not think it would be helpful."—W. Doane

December 1927: Hal Roach Studios drops the idea to create Our Gang boys' shirts.

December 1927: Hal Roach Studios nixes the idea to make an Our Gang feature remake of Mary Pickford's *Poor Little Rich Girl*. "While we agree that the picture would probably have good drawing ability, we believe that it would be harmful to the shorter product being made by the children, and therefore are not interested." Doane.

Hal Roach: "If a comedy I produce is funny to me it is usually funny to the audience." "A little bit of something good goes a lot better with the American public today than a lot of something that is mediocre."

He had, by this time, become known as a producer who could spot talent and nurture it to success. Roach then consolidated his success and earned his lasting place in movie history for the bringing together of two of the most glorious children ever—Stan Laurel and Oliver Hardy.

"They told me there was a good act down at the Main Street vaudeville house, so I went to see it. ["They" most likely being Roach director Alfred Goulding.] It was Stan Laurel, who had come over with one of Fred Karno's acts, and his wife. I hired him, but his light blue eyes wouldn't photograph. So he became a gag writer. When panchromatic film came out, he started acting again. Babe (Oliver Hardy's nickname) played heavies and was working at the studio at that time, and just happened to be in some of Laurel's pictures. They worked well together, and little by little they became a team."

By 1926 Harold Lloyd and Buster Keaton were making about one feature-length comedy a year. Chaplin released a film every three years or so and Mack Sennett's product was rather spotty. Roach, meanwhile, had a stable of gifted comedians, writers, directors, and gag men churning out two-reel gems weekly. They didn't call his studio "The Laugh Factory" for nothing. The time and circumstances were right for the emergence of the screen's greatest comedy team.

Stan Laurel, the slender, vaudeville comedian from the north of England, and Oliver Hardy, the rotund, comic, movie villain from Georgia, first appeared together in a Hal Roach comedy in 1926. After a brief period during which they were discovering and refining the characters of Stan and Ollie as we know them today, they hit their stride within a few months and by the spring of 1929 had made thirty-two silents that won the hearts of the public. Between 1929 and 1935 they made forty-two talkie shorts and from 1930 to 1940, eighteen feature-length films for Roach—a prolific output by any standard. These were to be years of incredible change, not merely within the motion picture industry, but in the society at large. It seems, in retrospect, that this was the only period during which such unique and universally-loved comedies could have been created, for there is a simple innocence coupled with a good-natured cynicism which weaves its way through all their comedies. It was a spirit at once anarchic and humanitarian: Laurel & Hardy as lovable outcasts in a cockeyed world which is forever putting cops and banana peels, garbage cans and battle-axe wives, nasty landlords and alluring ladies in Stan and Ollie's wayward paths. The honest naiveté of these comedies has been woefully lacking in movies made during and after the Second World War, and one can well ponder the implications. To consider the comedies of Laurel and Hardy as national treasures would not, in this light, seem untoward.

"They are the most universal of comics, in range as in appeal," wrote Charles Barr in his perceptive celebratory appreciation, *Laurel & Hardy* published in 1968. "They are supreme liberators from bourgeois inhibitions, yet essentially they are, or aspire to be, respectable bourgeois citizens. For all the appealing predictability in their films, their feelings and attitudes are not yet hardened to a crust but preserve the fluidity, the 'overlapping' quality, the moment-to-moment inconsistencies of childhood. This is why they can play so many different roles, householders and vagrants, criminals and policemen, without undergoing change."

"The first time I intentionally cast Stan Laurel and 'Babe' Hardy together," wrote Hal Roach in a 1972 affidavit, "was in a short subject in my 'All Star Series' entitled *Slipping Wives*. In the next six or seven silent shorts, I pitted these two actors against each other experimentally, and gradually and carefully built their relationship as a team.

"By trial and error, shooting and reshooting, story conferences, brain sessions, and other hard work, I, together with various of my other employee-associates, created, evolved and perfected the characteristics, mannerisms, dress, postures, gestures, grimaces, etc. that formed the whimsical atmosphere in which these two actors could frolic under my direction.

"They clicked with the public, as I knew and planned that they would. The atmosphere became familiar to the public, which anticipated with eagerness in every comedy the appearance and reappearance of the now familiar identifications...."

Slipping Wives was actually the SECOND Hal Roach short subject to team Laurel & Hardy. Perhaps Roach himself did not "intentionally cast" Stan and "Babe" in their first—the historical first—which was *Duck Soup*, based on a sketch by Stan's father Arthur Jefferson and filmed from September 20 to October 2, 1926 and released on March 13, 1927. *Slipping Wives* was filmed a month later and released April 3, 1927.

Film Daily, April 3, 1927 Review of *Duck Soup*: "Entertaining stuff. There is a lot of fun and no little drollery in the antics of two vagabonds of the gentlemanly school...." [There was no mention of the actors' names in this review.]

In the early 1980s Roach stated, "In the projection room I saw that there was an affinity between them. There was something that one guy sort of fit the other. So I told them to make, uh, Leo McCarey, a very fine director was working for us at the time. He became one of the tops of the business. And I told Leo, let's figure to put these two in a better, you know what I mean, and, and see if they, one won't compliment the other. Which they did. And the thing that made Laurel & Hardy so important as a team was exactly what I say: they fitted each other."

By the summer of 1927, Hal's Gang was becoming more and more aware of the unique potential of those two comics, Stan Laurel and Oliver Hardy:

July 1927: "For Mr. Roach from Ray Coffin: Opinion of Stan Laurel's *Why Girls Love Sailors*. "Saw this at original pre-view, and again today since it has been remade. It fails by far to measure up to your standard, and my own impression was that it is not as good as before. The story is poor, and it seems generally unfunny to me... Stan does some great work, individually... Miss Richard screened well, and believe after she reduces a bit, as I understand she is now doing, and has her teeth straightened, she will be a great bet."

August 3, 1927 Warren Doane letter to Fred Quimby: "...the entire second reel of the picture 'Sugar Daddies' was one continuous laugh. I am personally of the opinion that we have on the [West] Coast audiences that respond better than those in the eastern part of the country and we are sometimes misled by reason of this fact."

August 25, 1927 Fred Quimby letter to Warren Doane: "We all thought that this comedy [*The Second Hundred Years*] was much better than the previous subjects you have sent us. Personally, I like it very much and was laughing continuously throughout the entire two reels. In theatres it should go over very good."

August 31, 1927: Doane night letter to Hal Roach: "Walker says last Chase and last Roach Star with Laurel and Hardy well above average. Greatly pleased with McCarey supervision."

September 3, 1927: Benjamin W. Shipman to Hal Roach in New York City: "All pictures seem to have very unusual promise."

September 8, 1927: Doane to Hal Roach: "Laurel Hardy picture [*Putting Pants on Philip*] previewed last night near riot one of best laugh pictures for long time because picture is very good we feel justified working day or two longer make it still better."

September 14, 1927: Doane to Roach (still at Ambassador Hotel, New York City) "LAST LAUREL HARDY PICTURE EXCEPTIONALLY

GOOD BY REASON OF GREATLY IMPROVED PERFORMANCE BY PRINCIPALS. CURRENT PICTURE HAS GOOD CHANCE BEING AS GOOD OR BETTER. MCCAREY WALKER MYSELF WISH YOUR OPINION OF A LITTLE LATER ON SUGGESTING TO METRO FURNISHING TO THEM PICTURES WITH THIS COMEDY TEAM IN PLACE OF DAVIDSONS GOING INTO OPENED MARKET FOR TALENT FOR ROACH STAR PICTURES...WE ALL FEEL TIME IS HERE TO START INTENSIVE DEVELOPMENT OF LAUREL AND HARDY AT THE SAME TIME USING ROACH STAR SERIES TO DEVELOP NEW TALENT STOP WE FEEL THIS IDEA WOULD BE EASILY ACCEPTABLE TO METRO AFTER THEY RECEIVE LAST ROACH STAR AND ONE NEW IN PRODUCTION."

Film Daily September 15, 1927 announces "New Team For Roach. Hal Roach has decided to feature a new comedy starring team for M-G-M consisting of Stan Laurel and Olive [*sic*] Hardy."

September 17, 1927: Doane to Hal Roach: "Sample print of Gang comedy THE OLD WALLOP shipped to New York September twelfth. Sample print of Roach Star comedy HATS OFF will be shipped to New York September nineteenth. Consider these two of best comedies we ever made."

September 23, 1927: Doane to Hal Roach Ambassador Hotel New York City: "Have just completed picture with Laurel and Hardy [must be *Putting Pants on Philip*] which should be still better."

October 7, 1927: *Motion Picture News*: Laurel and Hardy New Roach Team for M-G-M During the coming year Hal Roach will feature Stan Laurel and Oliver Hardy as a new starring team in the comedies he is producing for release through Metro-Goldwyn-Mayer. Both comedians have been with Roach for several years and have appeared in the same productions as members of a comedy trio."

October 10, 1927 Fred Quimby letter to Hal Roach: "I screened HATS OFF, OLD WALLOP, LOVE 'EM AND FEED 'EM and WAY OF ALL PANTS...and I am almost safe in saying that we laughed continually from the start of the first subject up until the finish of the last reel of the last subject. It is our joint opinion that all four of these comedies are knock-outs...I think that Hardy and Laurel make a great comedy team, and hope that you keep them working together."

October 24, 1927: Doane telegram Roach c/o Pullman Conductor Santa Fe Chief westbound train #19 due Dodge City 3:55 P.M. Monday October 24th. "Previewed Laurel Hardy pie picture [*The Battle of the Century* was released on December 31st] Saturday very good everything fine."

Frank Butler, long time Roach gag man insisted "It was Leo McCarey, and no one else, who created the team of Laurel & Hardy... At the time Leo first thought of giving the boys the biggest roles... Roach was on an around-the-world tour." But he was mistaken about that part of it. Roach was away from the studio in New York City in August and September 1927 when senior staff member Warren Doane wrote to Roach stating that he as well as Leo McCarey and H.M. Walker "all feel time is here to start intensive development of L&H." (Doane to Hal Roach, September 14, 1927).

The very next day *Film Daily* published the announcement about "a new team." Roach didn't begin his five month around-the-world tour until January 1928 and by that time Laurel & Hardy had already appeared in eleven shorts, including "*With Love and Hisses*" filmed in March 1927 (released in August), *Do Detectives Think?* Laurel & Hardy's "quantum leap in the evolution of their partnership" [Okuda and Neibaur] and the first time they wore their trademark suits and derby hats, had been filmed in late April to May 1927 (released November 12); *The Second Hundred Years*, filmed in June, *Hats Off* filmed late July-early August (released November 5); and *The Battle of the Century* filmed late September—early October (released December 31, 1927) had therefore all been publicly screened PRIOR to Roach leaving on his round the world trip; the Laurel & Hardy team was by the end of 1927 firmly and incontrovertibly established. Roach himself had directed Stan and Ollie in *Sailors Beware!* and *Flying Elephants* in April and May 1927 though others were credited with the direction.

"I teamed them," stated Leo McCarey unequivocally in an interview with Peter Bogdanovich at the end of his life in 1969.

"One day I got this idea to have them act together in a film. We called Hardy and I told him I had a project for him that would bring in $10 a day, six days a week.... I said, 'What's more, if the movies are good you'll earn that much every week.' Laurel was already earning a hundred dollars a week, so for $160 a week I had the greatest of comedy teams. Of course they got a raise pretty soon."

The Second Hundred Years, filmed late June and released October 8, 1927 is considered "the first 'official' Laurel & Hardy comedy" according to Okuda and Neibaur, "the Stan-Ollie relationship is still rough around the edges, but the basic characters are in place and these personas would be developed and refined to perfection... Once teamed with Hardy, Laurel soon discovered that Ollie's character didn't compete with him, it completed him."

Randy Skretvedt concurs: "*The Second Hundred Years* is the first true Laurel & Hardy film." Yet it was, according to Hal Roach, *Putting Pants on Philip*, filmed in August and released December 3, 1927 which was "Hal Roach Studio's first film in which Stan and Babe were billed together as stars."

Film Daily, December 4, 1927 review of *Do Detectives Think?* "Droll Stuff. Stan Laurel and Oliver Hardy are a funny pair and in this picture their excellent comedy team-work garners a wagon-load of laughs."

December 10, 1927: *Sugar Daddies, The Second Hundred Years, Call of the Cuckoo* and *Hats Off* all produced by this date.

December 13, 1927: Frank L. Newman of Metropolitan Theatre letter: "Mr. Coffin called me to say our Organist was playing too loudly during the Comedy. I want to take this opportunity to thank you. I immediately got in touch with the Organist and told him to soften down a little bit, it seems the Organist has tendency when the audience is laughing to play louder. For your information, the Comedy has been very well received. I feel sure if this team make another Comedy or two as good as this one they will be made." [This must be referring to *Putting Pants on Philip*.]

December 21, 1927 Hal Roach letter to Fred Quimby: "...we must gross $60,000 average per picture to break even... Our product is rapidly improving; Laurel and Hardy will be box office attractions for the coming Season. We are getting marvelous reaction from the first-run showing at the Metropolitan here. Any Laurel-Hardy comedy is a first-run piece of merchandising! ... We at the studio are thinking and believing that we are making feature comedies; we want to get you thinking the same way... I want to see the day come when we are giving the M-G-M features a run for their money so far as popularity of the two types of amusement is concerned [features and shorts], and with the continued improvement of the quality of our pictures I feel that this is not far off."

December 27, 1927 Hal Roach letter to Fred Quimby: "Laurel and Hardy went over with a bang at the Metropolitan Theatre! Looks like we have a big bet in these two comedians... While figures on business look very good I still believe my winter suit will be at the expense of Mr. Fred Quimby!"

December 31, 1927 Fred Quimby telegram to Hal Roach: "JUST FINISHED SCREENING 'LEAVE 'EM LAUGHING' FOR COMMITTEE. STOP TO A MAN IT WAS A CONTINUOUS ROAR. I HAD A PAIN IN MY SIDE WHEN I LEFT THE PROJECTION ROOM IT IS A RIOT LAUREL & HARDY DOING MARVELOUS WORK WE SHOULD GET THOUSAND DOLLARS A DAY FOR THIS ONE REGARDS AND A HAPPY PROSPEROUS NEW YEAR."

February 11, 1928: Motion Picture Exhibitors Herald-World: Review of 'Battle of the Century': "Absolutely the best comedy I have ever played and I don't mean maybe. Hal Roach comedies are in a class by themselves." – Dayton Theatre Owner.

Nearly twenty years after *The Battle of the Century* had ceased to be screened in movie theaters, and was completely unseen during those long years before television, revival houses and the Internet, author Henry Miller, in the bleak depths of World War II, wrote movingly about that comedy in his book *The Cosmological Eye* published in 1945:

"And after thousands of slap-stick, pie throwing Mack Sennett films… came the chef d'oeuvre of all the slap-stick, pie-throwing festivals, a film the very title of which I forget, but it was among the very first films starring Laurel & Hardy. This, in my opinion, is the greatest comic film ever made—because it brought the pie-throwing to apotheosis. There was nothing but pie-throwing in it, nothing but pies, thousands and thousands of pies and everybody throwing them right and left. It was the ultimate in burlesque, and it is already forgotten."

Fortunately, the great pie-throwing sequence of *The Battle of the Century* was preserved and resurrected for the screen in 1957 for Robert Youngson's *The Golden of Comedy*; and it has been available for viewing, in one medium or another, ever since. The entire first reel which features Stan in a comic prize-fight, with a young Lou Costello recognizable among the crowd watching the pugilistic antics, was discovered in the 1970s, leaving only the majority of reel two as missing in action.

Photoplay, March 1928 "*Leave 'Em Laughing* review: "Another rib-tickler furnished by the famous pair—Stan Laurel and Oliver Hardy… A two reeler—but better than most feature length productions."

"The whole angle of Laurel and Hardy's comedy is based on children," Roach told me during our first meeting in 1973. "Babies are always falling down. If a grown man fell as many times as a baby, he'd break his spine. The babies don't cry when they fall. Their mother will point to them and laugh and say, 'Look at Johnny—isn't that funny!'

"For example, Hardy is on top of a forty foot mast, painting it, and Laurel saws off the bottom. So Babe falls forty feet and lands in a mud puddle. In real life it would kill him—but he just gets up and gives one of those stares into the camera."

Hal Roach rumbles with merriment at the image. Oliver Hardy would indeed step outside of the cinematic world by looking directly into the camera's lens, hence at the audience, and express any number of emotions: exasperation, impatience, horror, resignation. And one could never be sure whether these emotional appeals were coming from the *character* Oliver Hardy, or the man. The ambiguity is delicious.

"Laurel and Hardy were so popular for various reasons. First of all, teams up to that time consisted of a straight man and a comedian. Here, we had two funny guys. Something would happen, the audience would laugh. We cut to Stan, they would laugh at that. We'd cut to Ollie, they'd laugh at his reaction. They could get at least twice as many laughs as other comedians.

"Another reason is the childish traits they have, as I mentioned before. You'll notice that Stan never cries when he's hurt or scared—only when he's confused—like a child that is caught stealing cookies. He doesn't know how to react, so he cries.

"The third reason is the *anticipation* of comedy. Laurel and Hardy were first known through word of mouth. Then, when their names would appear on the screen, accompanied by their tune, the audience would laugh with anticipation. This is the height that a comedian can reach.

"Comedy is a very elusive thing. Fifty percent of what is written won't play for one reason or other. For example, one scene I wrote when they were making all those prison pictures has Laurel and Hardy in jail for making bootleg whiskey. The scene shows Laurel and Hardy escaping from jail, with a pack of bloodhounds on their trail. We fade out and in to a two-shot of Laurel and Hardy in blackface. They're disguised as cotton pickers in the South. Stan and Ollie have some dialogue and then start to leave. So Ollie calls, 'Come on, boys,' and two of the bloodhounds follow, wagging their tails. They're friends now, see? Well, the audience didn't even snicker at that one, so we cut it out.

"As an example of the reverse situation, we did a two-reeler once where there was a leaky fountain pen that squirted ink all over this guy's face. I said, 'Come on, we've done this gag a thousand times. Can't you come up with anything better than that?' But, as it turned out, the audience loved it."

"One of the most precious souvenirs I have," stated Leo McCarey in 1969, "is a fan letter Chaplin sent me in which he congratulates me on my work with Laurel & Hardy and predicts a beautiful future for me."

In March 1926 Hal Roach had signed up with the biggest studio in Hollywood, MGM, to distribute his comedy shorts, though the first releases did not begin until September of 1927. This was a very lucrative move, as he now had more and better theaters in which to show his films. Unfortunately, many of the Charley Chase silent shorts released by

MGM between 1927 and 1929 have been lost, as they were deposited in the vaults after their initial releases and allowed to deteriorate. Chase's earlier Pathé titles through mid 1927 do survive, mainly because copies were made in 16mm for the "sub standard" markets.

"[Louis B.] Mayer and I were good friends too. We got along well in business matters." Roach told historian Mike Steen in 1969. "For many years MGM distributed my pictures on a percentage basis through their parent company, Loew's Inc. There was a very close relationship between their lot and mine, which were also physically close in Culver City. Many times MGM used writers, directors, and performers whom they borrowed from me. I also borrowed talent from them. If some VIP was visiting MGM, I was usually invited there for lunch… the only person I answered to was Nicholas Schenck, at Loew's in New York. The MGM studio out here had absolutely nothing to do with anything I produced. If they wanted to use any of my talent, they almost always called Schenck and asked him to ask me."

By the end of that year Laurel & Hardy's comedies had become big hits with the public and by this time the apex of the production of silent pictures had been reached and the technical aspects mastered; a far cry from the early one-reel days of 1914.

I asked Mr. Roach to describe the typical development of a Laurel and Hardy silent two-reel comedy.

"I would bring in half a dozen writers and give them a particular situation and locale. All morning we'd kick around the story; adding ideas, taking off others. Then the writers would take over. They'd consult Laurel, too, and with his experience in pantomime he'd add gags. There was no better gagman than Laurel. So, after a week they'd have a treatment and submit it to me. If I approved of it, they'd begin shooting, or else revise it 'til I was satisfied.

"I would appoint the director, and then the casting director would select from our company for the lesser roles. I had at that time quite a few contract players: that great comic foil, Jimmy Finlayson (tight as a Scot); the 'slow burn' Edgar Kennedy; Noah Young; that gal from New York, Anita Garvin; and Mae Busch, a nice gal. And I had thousands of other actors.

"We'd have at least four or five other productions going at the same time: the Our Gang series, Charley Chase, and for a time we had an all-animal series, *The Dippidy Doo Dads*. Later there was the Thelma Todd-ZaSu Pitts or Patsy Kelly pictures, and *Taxi Boys* with Ben Blue that lasted only a season. We turned out, on the average, forty-five two-reelers a year."

Late December 1927 Leo McCarey was made a Hal Roach Corporation Vice President and given a new contract wherein he was to receive a percentage of the Laurel & Hardy profits. For the twenty-six weeks ended January 28, 1928 the studio earned $83,793.39, the most profitable Roach period to date.

In December 1927 Mr. and Mrs. Hal Roach were exchanging "Darling Wife, Darling Husband" telegrams while Hal Roach was away quail hunting. On January 7, 1928 The *New York Times* stated "HAL ROACH AND WIFE PART. Film Producer Expresses Hope the Separation Will Be Temporary. "The film producer said that the question of a divorce had not been discussed by them and that he was sure they could live happily together again 'when certain matters are settled.' The separation was said to have occurred shortly after Christmas."

One week after this news item, the couple sailed for Hong Kong on a round-the-world tour that was to last until the following May. During these five months, Vice President Warren Doane was in charge of the Studio; Leo McCarey had been made another Vice President in December. Within a year McCarey would leave Roach to become a renowned free-lance feature director.

April 7, 1928: *Motion Picture News*: "Charley Chase is to spend the five weeks' annual vacation of the Roach studios in a short vaudeville tour on the West Coast Theatre Circuit. 'Red' Daniels and Charles Hall, two other Roach players, are to work with him in the skit."

Undoubtedly refreshed and raring to go, Roach was back in New York discussing the movies later in 1928. "The short film," Roach told The *New York Times*, "requires just as careful planning, in its way as the long subject... The average person might be surprised to learn that the well-planned two-reel comedy takes more time, in proportion to its length, than the eight-reel feature...

"I have often wondered what would be the result of an experiment in which a big theatre could be turned over to the exclusive showing of short feature material. What would be the public reaction? Would there be enough patronage to insure a fair profit? I believe so... What reception would be given to a program made up, for example, of short features totaling eight or ten reels altogether; perhaps two-reel comedies, a news reel and a number of one-reel novelties? I'd certainly like to see."

Ever eager to experiment, it wasn't to be the all-shorts program that would consume his energies in the coming months, but another novelty, one Hal Roach quickly realized was to become a revolutionary success for his industry, and the reason he was in New York was to get into a new angle of the movies—The Talkies.

Hal Roach was star of his high
school football team in Elmira, NY
c. 1910

Twenty-two year old Hal Roach at
the start of his Hollywood producing
career, c. 1914

Built in 1887 the home of Rolin
Film Company 1914-19. Nicknamed
"Pneumonia Hall" by Harold Lloyd
due to the drafty corridors.

Motion Picture World April 1916 ad for
Lonesome Luke films

Motion Picture World 1916 ad for Rolin Film
Company's Phunphilms

Pathé Exchange, Inc. Executives, New York
City, Hal Roach's film distributors 1915-27.
Upper left is Paul Brunet who replaced J.A.
Berst in 1918.

The trademark name "Phunphilms" was
discontinued in 1916.

Beautiful female star Clarine Seymour of the Toto comedies died in 1920 at the tender age of twenty-one.

Motion Picture World ad announcing new Rolin comedy star Toto the clown, November 1917

Hal Roach in 1919, a success at twenty-seven, about to move into his new studio in Culver City.

Seven-year-old Ernest ("Sunshine Sammy") Morrison and his father sign with Hal Roach in 1919. Ernest was the first African-American actor to be offered a long term movie contract. Photo courtesy Laurel Hardy Archive.

Harold Lloyd's co-star Australian comic
Harry "Snub" Pollard was teamed with
"Sunshine Sammy" in 1919.

Hal Roach with his Jordan Playboy Roadster
in front of his Culver City studio c. 1923.
Photo courtesy Laurel Hardy Archive.

Hal Roach and Harold Lloyd sharing some laughs
at the studio c. 1923. Photo courtesy Laurel Hardy
Archive.

Hal Roach with two of his stars of the
Dippy Doo Dads series of one-reel all
animal comedies produced in 1923.
Photo courtesy Laurel Hardy Archive.

Photoplay in 1924 features the Our Gang kids studying their lessons during school time at the studio.

Katherine Grant in 1924. Delightful Charley Chase co-star suffered a hit and run car accident in 1926. Her injuries were more mental than physical, but she died in 1937 at the age of thirty-two.

Allen Clayton Hoskins was Our Gang star "Farina" from 1922 to 1931. At the beginning   he played boys or girls. With his mother Florence Hoskins in a 1925 issue of Photoplay.

Glenn Tryon, the young former vaudevillian who replaced Lloyd in 1924, lasted only a couple of years with Roach. He became a writer, producer and director in the 1930s and returned to Roach as a producer in the early '40s.

Hal Roach (sitting far left) knew he had really made it when he was invited to a swank party attended by the Hollywood elites of 1926. Among the MGM stars, directors and executives are Edmund Goulding, Greta Garbo, Nicholas Schenck, Harry Rapf, Norma Shearer, John Gilbert, Buster Keaton and Irving Thalberg. Photo courtesy Laurel Hardy Archive.

Hal Roach and his grown-up Gang of creatives c. 1926. Left to right: James Parrott, Charles ("Charley Chase") Parrott, F. Richard Jones, Hal Roach, Warren Doane and H.M. "Beanie" Walker. Photo courtesy Laurel Hardy Archive.

"The ever popular Mae Busch" as Jackie Gleason used to call her. This leading lady of the silent screen became a Laurel & Hardy regular well into the talkie era.

Scotsman James Finlayson in a 1927 trade ad. He became the perfect foil for Laurel & Hardy beginning that year and until the duo left Roach in 1940.

Fred C. Quimby, newly associated with Hal Roach studios, and W. B. Frank, vice-president and New York representative, arrive in Los Angeles and are met by Roach and Martha Sleeper, who promptly sells them tickets for the Wampas Frolic

Fred C. Quimby, who later became head of MGM's cartoon studio, joins Roach in 1927. With Roach star Martha Sleeper and Roach's New York representative W.B. Frank.

Hal Roach had been releasing via Pathé for a dozen years. His 1926 distribution deal with MGM was implemented in the fall of 1927 and lasted for eleven years.

Although exempted from serving in World War I because of his new business, Roach did not shirk his military duties. In November 1927 he was in Washington, D.C. training for his commission as Major with the U.S. Signal Corps Reserve. Photo courtesy Laurel Hardy Archive.

Hal Roach was the undisputed King of Short Film Comedy with the announcement of the 1927-28 season.

H.M. Walker; F. Richard Jones; Hal Roach; Warren Doane and W.B. Frank of the New York office confer on the studio lawn in the mid 1920s. Photo courtesy USC.

During a stage tour to New York City in 1928 the Our Gang kids met Mayor Jimmy Walker, whose fun-loving personality was popularized on stage and screen.

5

Unaccustomed As We Are
The Talkies
1928-1932

1928 RELEASES:
TWELVE OUR GANG TWO-REELERS
ELEVEN ALL-STAR TWO-REELERS (SIX WITH LAUREL & HARDY)
NINE CHARLEY CHASE TWO-REELERS
SIX MAX DAVIDSON TWO-REELERS
FIVE OFFICIAL LAUREL & HARDY SERIES (FIVE TWO-REELERS)
AND NINE SHORTS WITH SYNCHRONIZED MUSIC AND EFFECTS
SOUNDTRACKS

A new development in motion pictures had been taking place. On June 25, 1925 Warner Bros. and a Mr. Walter Rich set up The Vitaphone Corporation to engage in join experimentation with Western Electric to produce and exhibit sound motion pictures utilizing large records synched to the projector. On April 20, 1926 Rich, Warner Bros. and several AT&T officials signed a contract giving the Vitaphone Corporation exclusive license to produce sound pictures using the Western Electric system and to equip theatres with Western Electric Sound Systems for picture exhibitions. On August 6, 1926 Warner Bros. debuted the feature *Don Juan* starring John Barrymore in New York City complete with a synchronized music and sound effects soundtrack. Also shown were Vitaphone shorts and an address by Will B. Hays. The Vitaphone system were large 33 ⅓ discs synched to the projector.

Meanwhile the Fox film Corporation developed a sound on film method called Movietone and on April 20, 1927 released their first talking newsreel. Their product achieved worldwide acclaim when they screened an audible newsreel of Lindbergh taking off from Paris on May 21, 1927. By October there were weekly screenings of Movietone Newsreels. Some lucky theatres were equipped with new Western Electric dual equipment combining Fox newsreels and shorts with Vitaphone shorts and features, a combination of disc and sound on film projections.

The "talkie" revolution sparked by Warner Bros: *The Jazz Singer* in October 1927. At that time, according to *Okay For Sound How The Screen Found Its Voice* edited by Frederick Thrasher, there were only 100 theaters wired for sound in the United States; Warner Bros. owned 7,500 silent theaters. It was estimated that it would cost $8,500 to wire theaters of less than one thousand seats and $20,000 for theaters with more than 2,500 seats. Producers were reluctant to commit to such an expenditure, though another 120 movie theaters were wired for sound by June 1928. But when the first all-talkie feature, *Lights of New York* was released in July and grossed $1,200,000 in the U.S. alone, followed two months later by Al Jolson's second part-talkie (well, three-quarter talkie) *The Singing Fool* and became the movies' all star box office champ until *Gone With the Wind* eleven years later—the stampede for sound was on.

By the end of 1928 there were a thousand movie theatres that could show talkies. By the end of 1929 the number had jumped to nearly four thousand. And Hal Roach was right there at the front of the race. In fact, he had gone to New York in the spring of '28 to learn about the new medium. The *Film Daily & Weekly Film Digest* of June 26, 1928 reported: "Roach Maps Sound Plan. Comedy Producer Gets 15-year Western Electric License. Sound pictures were discussed at a dinner given by Hal Roach to 35 players, directors and departmental heads, with plans outlined for the comedies to be made utilizing sound. Roach has secured a 15-year license for production of sound pictures under Western Electric patents. Those who addressed the diners, in addition to Roach, were Benjamin Shipman, Warren Doane, H.M. Walker and Leo McCarey. Shipman recently returned from New York where he investigated angles of the sound film possibilities."

On September 6, 1928 Stan Laurel had written to a friend, "What do you think of the Talkies? Up to now I don't think so much of them—of course they are not perfected yet by a long way—I think will take quite a while before they are. It is a wonderful thing, but I like the silent ones better."

An editorial in *Photoplay* magazine for October 1928 stated "The whole world is talking talkies. The fans are listening to their favorites' voices like kids at their first Punch & Judy. The film makers are hysterical over plans for new audible movies, and the actors are practicing scales and having their voices renovated. The signs on Broadway now read—'Moonlight & Roses—A Talking Picture.' The talkies have swept the Main Stern. Seemingly, the silent drama has forgotten it was ever silent. Some of us are bitterly disappointed in the talkies so far. Some of us are going haywire and screaming that they have kicked all quiet films out of the back door. Neither is true or just. Right now talking pictures are getting fat on their novelty. They need a lot of development."

That same month it was announced that Roach signed a contract with the Victor Talking Machine Company for the purchase, installation, and utilization of sound equipment. Actually, on May 18, 1928 he had signed a contract with the Electric Research Products, Inc. (ERPI) a subsidiary of Western Electric formed to assume Western's sound-picture and other non-telephone business as of January 1, 1927. It was a twenty-six page document stating in part "Products has patents and inventions relating to methods, systems and equipment for recording and reproduction of sound... Whereas Licensee [Hal Roach Studios] is desirous in engaging in recording sound for reproduction for motion picture audience purposes and making the same available to exhibitors."

"I look forward to a very interesting season of talking and sound comedies from our studios for two reasons: one is the minuteness of detail with which the Victor Company is going about this special cooperation with us, and the second reason is traceable to the fact that practically all of the players under contract to me have had previous stage experience. Stan Laurel, Oliver Hardy, and Charley Chase in their experimental tests for spoken humor have lived up to the expectations, which their previous stage experience warranted.

"As for the Gang, the success of their recent nation-wide tour of the leading motion picture houses of the country has proven their stage presence and their ability to amuse the public not only with their antics but through the spoken word."

June 16, 1928 *Motion Picture News*: "Hal Roach Opens Eastern Office in New York...located in the Loew's State Building....Mrs. Helen Harris Jones has been made eastern representative and will be in charge of the New York branch."

July 28, 1928: Hal Roach Studios balance sheet showed total assets of $2,996, 519. "Earnings of the company for the fiscal year ending July 28, 1928, after making provision for Federal income taxes, were $321,439, or five times the preferred stock requirements… This increase is greater than the company's entire surplus as of January 29, 1927."

In August 1928 Hal Roach traveled to New York City to confer with Eastern executives about the changing industry.

"There may be some speculation as to the ultimate place of sound effects and dialogue for full-length pictures," Roach told The *New York Times*, "but I don't see any question about the value of sound in the one or two reel film. There you have a fine opportunity to try all kinds of novelties without getting the public tired. It's easy to imagine the variety of humorous and farcical effects possible for a sound comedy. And a good dialogue comedy might be compared to a vaudeville skit, with the extra action that the screen can give. The public has already shown unqualified approval of the short sound pictures, the Movietone news reel and the like."

Film Daily on October 28, 1928 reviewed one of the first synchronized shorts released by Roach: "The Hal Roach comedy *Imagine My Embarrassment*, featuring Charlie [*sic*] Chase, reviewed on July 29 as a silent two-reeler has now been synchronized, principally with comedy sound effects. There is very little talking, which only occurs in a few warbled lines of an amateur singer. The synchronization is indifferent, and seems to add little if any to the comedy values of what is a really unusual laugh number."

Memorandum to Mr. Roach from Mr. Doane November 27, 1928:

"There are some basic thoughts I wish to present with regard to the making of dialogue pictures.

"In the first place, a distinction should be made between picturized dialogue and dialogued moving pictures. In the first class I would place vaudeville acts, musical acts, picturized monologues and dialogue acts. The second class would consist of moving pictures, the spoken titles of which are audible rather than visible. It is the second class which represents our greatest opportunity inasmuch as we have a number of comedy stars under contract who enjoy a much greater national popularity than the average stage or musical star.

"It would be my idea that we should continue the making of silent pictures exactly as we have in the past up to the time when the picture has been previewed and finally accepted as ready for shipment. At that time I believe it will be possible in a very short space of time—not more than an hour or two—to photograph synchronized dialogue action, which when cut into one of the negatives will give us a dialogued motion picture. This dialogued motion picture can then be synchronized by the Victor Company as they are now doing…

"If possible, suggest that the camera be sound-proofed by enclosing in a quilted bag the camera mechanism, permitting the lense [sic] to project through, endeavoring to be relieved of the necessity of placing the cameras in a sound-proof structure and shooting through glass...

"I would like to strongly recommend that we immediately take steps to urge the Victor Company to furnish only a movietone outfit so that the cost of the studio installation may be kept at a minimum, thus we could avoid loading the picture costs unnecessarily and derive a substantial benefit as well by keeping their percentage at a more modest figure. It should be borne in mind that we have definite plans for a sharp reduction in picture costs and if their input is not carefully watched the percentage will be very detrimental."

A month later *Film Daily* reported "Metro Movietone Showing today. M-G-M is showing a program of Metro Movietone shorts at 11 A.M. today at the Astor, New York. A *Gus Edwards Musical Revue*, the screen's first Technicolor Movietone presentation; and the first Hal Roach sound comedies."

Roach and his team were very fortunate, and the feeling of optimism at The Lot of Fun at the dawn of the talkie era was not shared by all of Hollywood. Indeed, *Film Daily* observed in its December 21, 1928 edition, "Dismal Christmas For West Coast Colony"

"Christmas is not going to be so merry in Hollywood this year. The sound situation causing a letdown in production schedules from midsummer up to and including the present time have caused havoc with actors, directors, writers and studio mechanicians. Most of the studios in Hollywood, Culver City and environs have either been closed or shooting less pictures in the past six months than has ever been known since this locality has become a motion picture production center."

Roach liked to boast that his new sound productions were presented six months before the great MGM (his distributor since 1927) released *its* first talkie. *Film Daily*, December 19, 1928 stated "Only Month Needed For Construction Purposes. Production to be resumed January 28 [1929] at the Hal Roach Studios which previously had intended to remain dark until April. The studio is closed to permit reconstruction of a stage and installation of sound equipment."

Sound engineer Elmer Raguse (1901-1972) and a small crew from the Victor Recording Company in Camden, New Jersey came to Culver City to install the new Western Electric sound equipment. Sound and music flourished at the studio: Hal Roach was known to play his saxophone; for about a year (1929-30) Victor maintained a recording studio for commercial 78s; and radio station KFVD was set up inside the lot, where composer T. Marvin Hatley and his Happy-Go-Lucky Trio played popular tunes for a weekday morning program. Hatley composed the famous Laurel & Hardy "Coo Coo" song in 1930.

"Initially, it was Raguse who received the blanket credit on all of the Roach films as head of the sound department...." wrote Dave 'Lord' Heath on his website *Another Nice Mess*. "...he not only supervised every aspect of the sound process from start to finish, it was he who made the final mix." Raguse went to work at Fox Studios for a year and a half or so in the early thirties and then returned to Roach, "and once again supervised and provided the final mix (as well as editing the music cues and effects) on every film made at the studio through 1941...." Raguse returned to the Hal Roach Studios after World War II and resumed his duties as sound department chief right up to the very end, to 1959.

According to Ron Hutchinson, film historian and the founder of The Vitaphone Project, from the beginning, all film studios recorded optical tracks from which discs were made. The only exceptions were Warner Brothers/First National and the Hal Roach Studios which first recorded directly onto disc. Both Warners/First National and Roach abandoned that practice by early 1930 and would make disc dubs for theaters that required them until that practice was finally abandoned in the early thirties.

1929 RELEASES:
EIGHT OUR GANG SILENT TWO-REELERS
SIX OUR GANG TALKIE TWO-REELERS
SEVEN LAUREL & HARDY SILENT TWO-REELERS
SIX LAUREL & HARDY TALKIE TWO-REELERS
SIX CHARLEY CHASE TALKIE TWO-REELERS
SIX ALL-STAR SILENT TWO-REELERS
FIVE CHARLEY CHASE SILENT TWO-REELERS
FIVE ALL-STAR TALKIE TWO-REELERS (THREE WITH HARRY LANGDON)

On February 28, 1929 Hal Roach sent a letter to David Loew of MGM. "The confirmed report of the purchase by Fox of your family's interest in Loew's Inc. arrived yesterday. It brought back to my mind the conversation we had while you were here, regarding the possibility of your entering the production field with me. Of course, I have not the slightest idea of what the Fox purchase amounts to or how it will change the present Loew Organization, nor have I any idea of your future plans. However, if you have any thoughts of living in Los Angeles I think we could make a deal which would be satisfactory to us both, whereby you could purchase an interest in this company, assist in the business management and also the placing of our product and contacting with the distributor of same—which would leave me free to devote my entire time to picture production. With the excellent installation for sound pictures now being put in by Victor, and our very fine Victor contract, plus the new interest in sound shorts—these should make this business a very attractive one, and if Fox intend to maintain two organizations we undoubtedly could make all the shorts for both companies. Perhaps this thought is premature and probably your plans, if any, are already set. However, I would like to have you as a partner and believe we could have a very pleasant association. Please give my regards to your mother and Meta—Sincerely yours."

David Loew replied on March 8th: "I received your letter of February 28th and carried it around in my pocket for several days so that I could give it plenty of thought… For the present and for the future, it looks as tho' I will stay here… I certainly appreciate your offering the proposition to me. As you know, I would like to live out at the Coast, but it will be rather hard now on account of the investments I intend making… [My brother Arthur and I] intend buying a 'seat' on the Exchange… Therefore, while I feel I would derive a great deal of pleasure in associating with you, I am afraid, now more than ever, that it will be impossible… if at any time you think I can do anything for you in connection with your… business in New York, do not hesitate to call upon me."

The first all-talkie made at the Hal Roach Studios was Laurel and Hardy's two-reeler, *Unaccustomed As We Are* produced in March 1929 co-starring Mae Busch, Thelma Todd and Edgar Kennedy. Much of the filming took place at night because there was only one set of sound equipment, as Our Gang's first talkie, *Small Talk*, was filming during the day. The novelty of sound caused some problems. First of all, Kennedy had a high-pitched voice, but he quickly learned to lower it. Roach says that this was the only time any of his silent actors had any trouble adjusting to sound. The second problem was a little more difficult to solve, and it occurred during the production of *Hurdy Gurdy*, the third talkie short and directed by Roach himself.

"While I was watching the rushes with the cast and my assistants, I kept hearing at the end of each shot someone saying, 'That's good.' After hearing 'that's good' several more times, I turned around and yelled, 'Who the hell keeps saying that?' They were all kind of scared of me, so nobody spoke up. I turned around again and yelled, 'I said, who is the jerk on the soundtrack?' Finally the projectionist said, 'It's you, Mr. Roach.' That was the first time I ever heard my own voice."

Unaccustomed as We Are was previewed in April, 1929, and was highly praised by the critics. When it was released to the general public on May 4, 1929, a new era was well underway. As a matter of little known fact, Roach's rival Mack Sennett had actually released his first talkie *The Lion Roars* five months prior to Roach's first sound release, in December 1928. But the race as they say is not always to the swift. Mack Sennett was washed up in the movie business in 1933—in December of that year Hal Roach triumphantly celebrated his upcoming 20th anniversary as a comedy producer with a star-studded party.

April 30, 1929 Hal Roach to Dave Loew: "Please keep me posted on what you think of the quality of our all-dialogue comedies. We seem to be progressing pretty well out here and not much different than making silent pictures."

May 6, 1929 David Loew to Hal Roach: "...I saw your first all-dialogue comedy with LAUREL and HARDY. I think it is very good, and I expect it to go very well with the audiences. I think the standard that they have set in the past is kept right up with this one—though some around here do not agree with me! I saw it in the projection room, and I am positive that my experience in the past has proven that if I like a comedy in the projection room, it passes the acid test,—as I am a very poor judge of comedy in the projection room. You just keep on making a standard, and the other fellows will start petering out, as they usually do, and you will hold the same position with the dialogue comedies."

On May 17 David Loew wrote again: "I just saw the first OUR GANG talking comedy. There were quite a few of us in the Projection Room, and we all liked it very much. As I promised that I would let you hear from me, it gives me pleasure to write you this." David Loew proved to be a good early judge of the success of Roach's first talkies.

Film Daily reviewed the Our Gang's first all-talkie *Small Talk* on May 26, 1929: "All of the charm and delight of the Gang that reached out from their silent comedies, plus the brand new kick of hearing them speak. That should be enough-plus—for any theatre... To hear Wheezer and little Mary Ann Jackson talk is cunning beyond words. Nab this sure."

The new medium gave Laurel and Hardy world-wide fame. This was confirmed when they appeared in MGM's all-star, all-talking *Hollywood Review of 1929* which was premiered at Grauman's Chinese Theatre on June 20, 1929. On December 5, 1929 Laurel & Hardy's *Night Owls* was selected to screen alongside the Ronald Colman feature *Condemned* at Grauman's Chinese Theatre.

Stan and Ollie adjusted beautifully to the new medium; they did not allow the soundtrack to hamper their style in the least, and the fact that their early talkies were filmed in French, Spanish, German, and sometimes Italian language versions secured their international success. Translators were hired to teach the boys to speak the foreign languages phonetically, and the resultant mispronunciations and mangled grammar only added to their universal appeal.

The third Roach all-talkie, *Hurdy Gurdy*, was released on May 11. The cast included Max Davidson, Edgar Kennedy and Thelma Todd. Restored by the Vitaphone Project, the two-reeler is noted for its superior technical proficiency. There is variety of music, the blending of various ethnic accents and fluid camera movement.

Charley Chase also adapted smoothly to the talkies. He had been loaned out to Universal in March 1929 to appear in the six-reel part-talkie *Modern Love* starring Jean Hersholt, though his first Roach two-reel talkie, *The Big Squawk*, while filmed afterward, was released first, in May 1929.

In June 1929 Roach wanted to make talkies with Western star William S. Hart whose last film had been *Tumbleweeds* in 1925. Hart was eager to appear in sound films and apparently the two actually signed a contract to that effect. But MGM executives, when they learned of this deal, informed Roach to stick to comedies. They were, however, apparently willing to permit Roach to "release this one elsewhere, but we do not expect you to do this again." The contract with Hart was cancelled, which caused a couple of headlines, and Mr. Hart, who had first been a successful Shakespearean actor on Broadway and then a cowboy matinee idol during the silent era, faded into the sunset, never to have a career in the talkies.

In July 1929 the *Baltimore Sun* announced that Hal Roach would make silent versions of twenty of the thirty-two all-talking comedies scheduled for the coming season. "Because of the demand of the foreign distributors and of small-town exhibitors for comedies, Mr. Roach has changed his decision to make no silent pictures. The soundless two-reelers will be re-edited versions of the talkers.

"Each of his four production units, Laurel and Hardy, Harry Langdon, Charley Chase and Our Gang, will make eight talk films. In addition, the studio will release synchronized versions of four recently completed silent comedies, Laurel and Hardy's *Bacon Grabbers*, and *Angora Love*, and Our Gang's *Saturday's Lessons* and *Cat, Dog and Company*.

"The Roach Studio estimates a production cost of one million and a half dollars for the coming year's program. One hundred and fifty thousand dollars is the scheduled expenditures for improvement and additions to the sound stages and equipment.

"Each of the four production units will have made five all-talking pictures when the present fiscal year ends on July 27. The studio started production of sound pictures on March 25, Laurel and Hardy's *Unaccustomed As We Are* being the first talk film."

By September 1929, according to *Picture Play* magazine, Stan Laurel was receiving $2,000 per week. His contract provided $500 increase each six months until he achieved $3,000 for every six days' work. Charley Chase was paid $1,500 per week and Oliver Hardy $1,000+. Anita Garvin, Edna Marion and Thelma Todd earned $750 per week each. Thelma would co-star opposite Charley Chase in twelve of his talkie shorts; she also appeared in six of the eight Harry Langdon talkie shorts before Roach decided to team her with ZaSu Pitts and later Patsy Kelly.

Hal E. Roach, President, Letter to the Holders of Preferred Stock, November 25, 1929:

"As you know, the advent of talking pictures was a sudden one in the motion picture business and compelled on the part of all producing companies a large expenditure of money and occupied a considerable time in changing from the old method of making silent pictures to the new method of making talking pictures...

"The product at the present time is of a very high standard of excellence, and the future for the success of the company looks good. It is felt, however, that in view of the heavy cash payments that it has had to make as outlined, and the transition that has occurred in the business from silent to talking product, dividends should not be paid on preferred stock until the current earnings ascertained in a most conservative manner are adequate to make such payments.

"The company at the present time is producing four series of comedies: Our Gang comedies, Laurel and Hardy comedies, Charley Chase comedies, and Harry Langdon comedies; all of them known the world over and having a world wide market.

"The business on silent pictures of the company has been very satisfactory and is coming in in good volume, and the company will not have any loss on its silent pictures produced under the present release. The business on talking pictures is excellent. The first twelve talking pictures produced by the company have firm, non-cancellable business written on them of about $70,000.00 per picture, which is more than adequate to pay all costs, and the further business is coming in in very good volume. It must be remembered that the first talking picture was not released until May 4th of this year. A large part of the operating capital of the company has been tied up for some time past in the pictures produced for the Pathé Exchange, Inc., who were distributors of the company's product up to September 1st, 1927. At this time, court action is pending, brought by the company against Pathé, seeking reimbursement from Pathé for this company for what the company believes to be improper distribution of its product by Pathé. This action is being vigorously prosecuted.

"Installation of equipment in various theatres for the purpose of being able to reproduce sound is progressing more rapidly than was expected a short time ago, which will place more and more theatres in a position to use the talking pictures of the company. The rentals the company is getting for talking pictures are very good.

"In concluding, I would like to leave the thought with you that the outlook for the success and future of the company is very good. The product of the company is of recognized excellence, and the transition period apparently much easier than has been experienced by others. This was greatly due, no doubt, to the cooperation that the Company has received at all times from the Victor Talking Machine Company, with whom we have a working arrangement for the product of our talking pictures."

November 27, 1929 Hal Roach to David Loew: "We think we have made sufficient changes to bring the standard of OUR GANG back to where it was, and believe we can show a steady improvement with LANGDON. However, making funny comedies is not the easiest job in the world and I am sure sometime our efforts must look pretty sad to those that review them. Believe that if we can ever get into a short subject theatre where the comedies have to stand on their own, then and then only will we be able to judge the merits of two-reel comedies."

The Charley Chase talkie shorts were certainly not looked upon sadly by critics or the public. They were "both critical and box-office successes" according to Anthony and Edmonds. "But the strain had taken its toll on Charley's health. Chase had dangerously overextended himself and drank heavily throughout the anxious period...." In November 1929 he was admitted to the Mayo Clinic for an emergency operation that removed part of his stomach due to ulcers. Unfortunately, Chase did not heed this warning, and would continue to drink up until his untimely death eleven years later at the age of forty-six.

The Hal Roach Studios' profit for the forty-four weeks ended November 30, 1929: $29,245.15. It was a bit of a letdown from the previous year's profit, but considering the fact that so much had been invested in the transition to sound, it was still a good year. The Wall Street Crash of the previous month would not affect Hollywood for some time to come.

1929 Publicity Release: The services of a staff of three men are required to open, sort and answer the load of mail, which the Culver City Post-office department dumps on the Hal Roach Studios lot each morning. George Miller, chief of the fan mail department said, "I can almost sort the letters without looking at the addresses. The letters for the Gang are almost always addressed in a child's handwriting. The letters to Laurel and Hardy come in heavier envelopes, with masculine writing. And Charley Chase's fan mail is usually on feminine notepaper...

"The Gangsters are very proud of their mail. Joe Cobb and Farina are the only Rascals who can read, so they pore over their letters and treasure them with the joy of their grown-up brothers of the silver screen. The parents of the other four read the letters aloud to their starlets.

"Interspersed with the letters are gifts galore. From China, from India, from darkest Africa, from everywhere, come presents for the Gangsters. They have received everything from candy to Collie pups. Every day is almost like Christmas day to the six Roach Rascals. The main cry of the Gang's fans is, 'Please don't grow up.'

"Strange as it may seem, the greater part of Stan Laurel and Oliver Hardy's fan mail comes from business and professional men. Doctors, lawyers, merchants and professors write to the slapstick pair, to tell them how much they enjoy their fun making. There is an air of self consciousness about the letters, of guilt at joining the ranks of the fan writers. 'We don't want to seem silly, but we just had to tell you of our enjoyment of your pictures.' These letters Laurel and Hardy treasure as real applause. Requests for pictures, petitions for a chance in the movies and regular fan messages pour in upon the two Roach funsters. Most of them are from men and boys. College students, in hordes, write to tell of the hilarity caused by the antics of the comedy pair...."

According to Randy Skretvedt, by the end of the 1928-29 season, the eleven silent Laurel & Hardy comedies made a profit of over $35,000 and the five sound films made a profit of $43,000. A good sign for talkies, indeed.

And the particular difficulties and challenges of recording sound films were being swiftly met.

"Heretofore our films have been made with silent spaces between the dialogue," Roach explained to a reporter in January 1930, "but people have become so accustomed to hearing an orchestra in the theatre accompanying the film that we thought it best to weave music in as the picture is being made instead of synchronizing it later.

"The organ notes will also, as a musical background, kill all the irrelevant natural noises. There has been too much sound in pictures anyway. We at first injected everything we heard, but that is unnatural. Our ears are selective and we listen to only those things we want to. Of course, natural noises are well enough, but it detracts from the film.

"For example, when we are making the picture we sometimes must halt our operations because an airplane is overhead. This is a natural noise and there is no reason to believe that an airplane should not be flying at that moment, but in the theatre an audience will associate the sound as a significant part of the plot and will expect something to come of it.

"The noises we do add artificially, however, mean twice as much and are doubly effective. For example, in a Laurel and Hardy comedy one of the comedians hits the other over the head with an automobile jack. The sound version of this blow is a great 'Bong!' which some one offstage struck on a gong. This brought roars of merriment from the audiences and taught us the value of adapting the methods of sound cartoons to comedies."

The development of sound movies had a different time table in Europe and the rest of the world. While *The Jazz Singer* had premiered in October 1927 as a silent with talkie sequences in New York, it had originally been released as a silent in Europe. The part-talking version finally debuted at the Piccadilly Theatre, London in September 1928. In January 1929 there were only 11 Western Electric cinemas in the British Isles. In France, the first musical shorts were presented in October 1928 but by January 1929 Paris still had only two movie theatres wired for sound. ERPI spent the spring of 1929 'wiring theatres busily in Europe' according to Donald Crafton and Richard Koszarski in their *History of American Cinema*. By the summer of 1929 theatres throughout Asia were being fitted for sound by ERPI, RCA and Tobis Klangfilm. By the fall of 1929 Hal Roach realized that he could export his comedies to the international market by creating special foreign language versions, with his casts learning to speak phonetically.

In November 1964 Stan Laurel explained the process in a private letter to fan Ray Atherton: "The foreign language was NOT DUBBED IN—we first made the film in ENGLISH—after this was previewed & final editing was completed—we then called in four interpreters, FRENCH, SPANISH, GERMAN & ITALIAN who translated the script & engaged a different cast for each version, excluding of course L&H & principal characters such as Jimmy

Finlayson etc. The interpretor [*sic*] read each scene to us word by word & we wrote it on a blackboard as it sounded to us (Phonetic system) these boards were placed in back of each of us (out of camera range) so we had no difficulty in speaking the lines in every language...."

November 13, 1929: Western Union Night Letter Hal Roach to Arthur Loew, MGM New York City. Arthur Loew was the Head of the Culver Export Corporation, the Foreign Department for Metro-Goldwyn-Mayer which distributed MGM products throughout the entire world. "FIRST LAUREL & HARDY SPANISH VERSION WILL BE COMPLETED THIS WEEK STOP WILL PROBABLY SHIP LAUREL HARDY ABOUT TWENTY-SEVENTH NOVEMBER AND OUR GANG ABOUT DECEMBER SECOND. REGARDS"

November 23, 1929: Hal Roach letter to Arthur Loew: "Dear Arthur:— Am pleased to know from your letter that you still have enough money left to purchase refreshments. However, to send you a bill would be most embarrassing to me—recalling the large portions of 'joy water' I have consumed at your home and apartment, plus the fact that I am in New York about three times to your once in Los Angeles, and I certainly want to have further the same hospitality that I have had from you in the past. Therefore, please forget about it for I am very thankful that you didn't happen to be in the room when I made the bet on U.S.C. or I probably would have lost more money.

"Shipping soon the first Spanish version of Laurel and Hardy comedy and will anxiously await your opinion of same. Please keep me informed on how things are going in the foreign market and any changes we may make for better business."

November 29, 1929: Hal Roach letter to Arthur Loew: "We have not started any comedies in German as yet but at present are making them all in Spanish. It will cost me approximately $2500 in production to make the German version and our thought was it would be better to rush the Spanish version through and let you get it to the exchange as soon as possible and find out the reaction before we got too deep into the foreign idea... We also thought that as soon as the people get used to the Spanish version it would be easier for them to take up a German one than to have them doing both at the start, as it is quite difficult for them to remember their lines in the foreign language at present. However, if you think it is important that we should immediately start German versions we will do so. Kindly let me hear from you regarding this matter."

December 26, 1929 Hal Roach to David Loew: "Did they run the Laurel and Hardy picture NIGHT OWLS Spanish version in a NewYork [*sic*] theatre if so will you let me know how it was received."

1930 RELEASES:
NINE CHARLEY CHASE TWO-REELERS (PLUS SIX FRENCH VERSIONS,
FIVE SPANISH VERSIONS)
EIGHT OUR GANG TWO-REELERS (PLUS THREE SPANISH, ONE
FRENCH, ONE GERMAN)
FIVE LAUREL & HARDY TWO-REELERS AND TWO THREE-REELERS
(PLUS FIVE SPANISH, THREE FRENCH, ONE GERMAN, ONE ITALIAN)
FIVE HARRY LANGDON TWO-REELERS (PLUS TWO SPANISH, ONE
GERMAN)
THREE *BOY FRIENDS* (ENGLISH ONLY)
ONE FEATURE (*MEN OF THE NORTH*) (PLUS SPANISH, FRENCH, GER-
MAN AND ITALIAN VERSIONS RELEASED IN 1931)
(Note: The Foreign language versions of the shorts often ran three
reels plus and combined more than one original two-reeler)

In January 1930 as a sure sign that the Roach stars had conquered
sound, Charley Chase, Laurel & Hardy, Harry Langdon, Thelma Todd and
the Our Gang kids appeared on the network radio program "Voices of Film-
land" at KHJ Studio in Hollywood. However, Charley Chase got drunk and
wouldn't get off the air. "I was very angry about it," Roach said later. On future broadcasts he put his brother Jack in charge of keeping Charley sober. It
would prove to be an impossible task. Chase's brother, director Jimmy Parrott, meanwhile, was gaining weight and becoming addicted to pep pills, and
he would disappear from the Roach lot for unpredictable periods of time.

Western Union to Hal Roach January 8, 1930: "YOUR SPANISH
COMEDY SURE KNOCKED THEM DEAD YESTERDAY AT HUN-
DRED SIXTEENTH STREET THEATRE STOP BROKE ALL RECORDS
FAR SURPASSED HAROLD LLOYD PICTURE CONGRATULATIONS
KEEP IT UP REGARDS"

January 8, 1930 Postal Telegraph David Loew to Hal Roach: "FIRST
DAY OF SPANISH VERSION LAUREL AND HARDY COMEDY CA-
PACITY BUSINESS STOP TWO TO THREE TIMES AVERAGE BUSI-
NESS STOP LINE IN AFTERNOON FROM MIDDLE OF BLOCK TO
CORNER HANDLED FIVE THOUSAND SIXTY FIVE IN ONE DAY
STOP CAPACITY HOUSE ABOUT EIGHTEEN HUNDRED SEATS"

That month Hal Roach was visiting his New York City office and was
interviewed for The *New York Times*.

"Hal Roach, the well-known producer of comedies… himself seems
especially amenable to laugh-provoking situations. Heavy-set and Fal-

staffian in demeanor, his eyes seemed perennially twinkling with mirth. Half the things he talked about he concluded with a humorous anecdote. Most of his subject matter concerned the making of comedies—a matter, he gave one to understand, of great and serious moment...

"'When we were making our silent comedies,' Mr. Roach said, 'our foreign distribution amounted to twenty-five percent of our total production. Now that we have sound our foreign business has jumped to fifty percent of our product. This is accounted for by the fact that we have begun making our films in the languages of other countries.

"'If a star of the John Gilbert type, for example, was to make a feature-length picture in a foreign language his accent, unless he were fully acquainted with that language, would be deplorable, no matter how perfect his performance.

"'In comedies the shoe is on the other foot. The accent doesn't matter so much; it's the action. We teach our actors the few essentials of the language, and they are able to pronounce the 'sí' or 'oui' as perfectly as any Spaniard or Frenchman.

"'If there is any part of the story that should be interpreted to the audience—and there is hardly a plot and sub-plot in most slapstick affairs—we introduce a minor character who speaks the language like a native and who conveniently talks the plot into the film.

"'Nevertheless, we have two classes a week on the lot in both languages and most of our performers, including the youngsters of the Our Gang lot, attend and pick up the Latin fundamentals.

"'It is not very difficult to teach children phrases in unknown words because when they are instructed to repeat the same words in English it means just as little then. For example, when we ask a child to repeat 'How do you do, sir?' during the course of a picture it means as little to him as if he were to say 'Como está usted?' or "Comment allez-vous.' With the child it is simply a trick of memory. But too often that memory is liable to fail, and we have to start all over again.

"'It takes so long for the interlock—that is, for silence to settle and the cameras to turn to their required speed and the other measures that have to be taken before a scene can be shot in sound—that by the time the red light comes up signifying the start the children have forgotten their lines and we are forced to begin again.'"

"...According to Mr. Roach, it takes twenty percent longer to photograph a comedy in each language. This means five days more on each version than ordinary....'"

While the Spanish version was tremendously popular in New York, a word of warning had been communicated to Mr. Roach by Carl J. Sonin, Managing Director of M-G-M Argentina for South America: "Will you please allow me to caution you on one thing? Certainly, we don't want the Studio to think we are trying to run their business. You don't know that the Argentine Republic produces a great big part of the revenue of the Spanish speaking countries. Spanish is spoken slightly differently in all South American countries and also in Spain; these people here will not accept Spanish as spoken by Mexicans, Central Americans, Cubans, etc. I suppose the others will complain about using Argentines...

"The only feasible proposition is for you to secure native-born Spaniards to play with your Companies. Of course, the public will accept anything from your artists, kids, Chase, etc. themselves but if you can get away from using Mexicans it will be greatly appreciated here and the results will warrant the taking of this step."

In January 1930 Warren Doane wrote to Adolfo Ka, Manager of MGM Mexico City: "As you have no doubt already learned, we are making Spanish versions of our comedies for use in the wired theatres in Spanish-speaking countries. In this connection as you have an opportunity to listen to them we would certainly greatly appreciate any criticism you will be able to make for the improvement of these pictures. Charley Chase is making his first Spanish comedy and would be available in March or April to come to Mexico for personal appearances. He gets $1500 a week in the United States for personal appearances. We have, of course, no idea what it may be possible to secure in your city."

February 5, 1930: David Loew to Hal Roach: "Just wanted to let you know that yesterday we played the first Our Gang Spanish version comedy at our 116th Street Theatre and the receipts amounted to $650.00. It was quite disappointing and indicate that the novelty did not last very long."

February 13, 1930 Robert Lynch, MGM PA to Hal Roach: "I happened to be talking to Fred Quimby yesterday regarding the Gang comedies and I voiced the opinion to him what was wrong with them, and he said that was your opinion also, and so that you understand clearly what I mean, I think if the Gang comedies were just about 25% dialogue and 75% silent they would be a whole lot better, for it was the fast action that these kids could put over in a silent comedy that got the laughs. As matters now stand, it takes these kids too long to get their dialogue over to make the thing rapid fire enough, so why not try to make the next one along these lines. Please bear in mind I am not trying to tell you how to make comedies, but merely offering a suggestion, as nothing makes me so happy as to see the Hal Roach Comedies stand out above all others."

February 24, 1930 WESTERN UNION Hal Roach to Arthur Loew: "LAUREL HARDY COMEDY ENTITLED BRATS HAS GERMAN VERSION ONLY. WE CAN MAKE FRENCH AND SPANISH VERSIONS OF THIS PICTURE FOR FIVE THOUSAND A VERSION AS IT HAS SMALL AMOUNT OF TALK IN IT STOP THESE TWO VERSIONS WOULD BE IN ADDITION TO THOSE DISCUSSED IN NEW YORK WIRE IF IN YOUR OPINION WE SHOULD MAKE THESE OTHER VERSIONS REGARDS"

February 25, 1930 WESTERN UNION Arthur Loew to Hal Roach: "MAKE FRENCH AND SPANISH VERSION BRATS REGARDS"

February 27, 1930 WESTERN UNION Arthur Loew to Hal Roach: "SAW SPANISH BLOTTO THIS MORNING PHOTOGRAPHY VERY POOR STOP BAD DUPING THROUGHOUT STOP WHY DO YOU USE DUPE NEGATIVE ON SCENES SPECIALLY SHOT IN SPANISH AND WHY DON'T YOU MAKE BETTER DUPES STOP...."

Laudy Lawrence, MGM Paris, to Arthur Loew: "As far as Hal is concerned, I think that our primary endeavours have already far exceeded his wildest expectations... we grossed over Pes[etas] 70,000 the first week in Madrid. Do you know, Arthur, that this means a gross for Hal Roach of perhaps $10,000 for two weeks? I am wondering if he ever got that much out of any picture anywhere in the United States! However, at this point, I must tell you that I was rather disappointed with the first French Laurel and Hardy although I am sure we will do very big business with same. It appears very much drawn out, which naturally always harms a comedy of this character and the entertainment that Hal tried to offer with his cabaret turns, etc., were not tied in at all properly. As a matter of fact, it appeared rather poorly put together although the entertainment itself was fairly good. The dancers might have gone much better in a Spanish than in a French comedy! As a comedy, the Spanish 'LADRONES' was a far better picture for its purpose than the first French one. If, therefore, all the possibilities that we see can be obtained, it may be that Hal could afford to do even better, for undoubtedly whether he should like it or not, he will be obliged to do so by competition in the future, and, since we have the inner track already, I see no reason why Hal should relinguish [sic] the great reputation he has established for himself and his stars, in the future. I feel sure that Hal, as well as you, yourself, realizes the fact that everybody here is just as appreciative as I am of Hal's efforts...."

April 3, 1930 WESTERN UNION Warren Doane to Arthur Loew: "PRATT MANAGER ERPI MILLS MUSIC DIVISION ADVISES MUSICAL NUMBER LAMENTOSO IN OUR GANG COMEDY NOISY NOISES NOW AVAILABLE STANDARD TERMS ALL COUNTRIES EXCEPT ITALY FOR WHICH THREE HUNDRED DOLLARS DEMANDED NO REDUCTION POSSIBLE STOP IF SYNCHRONIZED VERSION NOT YET SHOWN IN ITALY THIS PENALTY CHARGE MAY POSSIBLY BE SAVED."

April 1, 1930 WESTERN UNION Night Letter Warren Doane to Arthur Loew: "We now furnish for foreign use on each version of our pictures a dupe negative for the disc print and a dupe movietone negative STOP As to all pictures started from now on we will furnish a complete original negative for each foreign version which could be used not only for the disc prints but also for the movietone prints providing we could send the sound track separately instead of making a combination negative having the picture and sound track on one negative which has to be a dupe negative STOP For Canadian use we now send the picture on one film and the sound track on another and report for duty payment only the picture footage ignoring footage of the separate sound track STOP Believe if we could do this for all other foreign requirements customers could have much better quality of release print would be considerably cheaper for us to do this and would also enable us to save two or three days time in getting shipment ready Please advise."

April 2, 1930: WESTERN UNION Morty Springer/Arthur Loew's Office to Warren Doane: "PERFECTLY SATISFACTORY FOR YOU TO MAKE ONLY A PICTURE NEGATIVE AND SEPARATE SOUND TRACK NEGATIVE FOR ALL FOREIGN VERSIONS"

Here is the English translation of a Barcelona newspaper review in March 1930: "For the first time we saw yesterday in the cinema FEMINA something which we had been dreaming about for many years: that is a picture without titles, without more titles than 'METRO GOLDWYN MAYER presents Stan Laurel and Oliver Hardy in LADRONES, a picture with Spanish dialogue.' After this opening the picture starts, absurd, funny, like the comedies these artists usually present, but this time without being interrupted by annoying titles. We understood the whole picture due to the clear pronunciation of the artists, much more perfect than we would have supposed. The public was gratefully surprised. For the public which filled the house from end to end it was an agreeable surprise to see how easily these two comics had learned their Spanish lesson as announced by the advertisements. Perhaps their vocabulary does not surpass some hundred words, (the longest paragraphs are spoken by the chief of the police, an actor who by his accent and type seems to be Mexican) but the words are said correctly, so that they are perfectly understood and the plot is quite clear, and their mimicry is interpreted with the ease which characterizes them. We noted also that even in the tone of their voices they made their comicity [*sic*] apparent. Due to the perfect sound scenes every noise provokes a laugh. Especially the noises of the cats, the entrance in the house, and the sound scenes after the burglary are really great. These scenes are the biggest nonsense possible, but they are of great comicity. The public came out very pleased and praised the efforts realized by Metro Goldwyn, which this time have been crowned with success."

March 7, 1930 Postal telegraph Arthur Loew to Hal Roach: "Received cable from Lawrence quote Ladrones broke every known record Madrid grossing seventy thousand pesetas first week unquote received following cable from Argentina quote Ladrones and Speedway opened Porteno Buenos Aires yesterday to absolute capacity enthusiastically received STOP Believe Ladrones will gross more than previous years output Roach comedies unquote STOP This is great news however must advise you that there seems to be some disappointment about pictures with other stars...."

In April 1930 Charley Chase signed a new contract with Roach for $1,750 per week.

May 1, 1930 Postal Telegraph Arthur Loew to Hal Roach: "My impression in Europe makes me believe we should discontinue foreign versions all series except Laurel Hardy and possibly Chase whose pictures I have not yet seen STOP Incidentally Ladrones will gross thirty thousand dollars in Spain and Une Nuit Extravagante will also do very well STOP Please wire me complete report on Monsieur Le Fox."

May 7, 1930: WESTERN UNION Hal Roach to Arthur Loew: "CHASE COMEDY ENTITLED FAST WORK WHICH WAS WELL RECEIVED BY NEW YORK OFFICE RUNS THREE REELS IN SPANISH VERSION AND IS BETTER WITH SPANISH CAST THAN WITH ENGLISH STOP THIS COMEDY HAS CAFÉ SEQUENCE AND IN THIS SEQUENCE WE COULD ADD ANOTHER REEL OF SINGING AND DANCING WHICH WOULD MAKE THIS A SHORT FEATURE STOP ADDITIONAL COST WOULD PROBABLY BE TWO THOUSAND DOLLARS PLEASE WIRE YOUR DECISION AT ONCE."

May 9, 1930: WESTERN UNION Arthur Loew to Hal Roach: "BE-LIEVE ADVISABLE ADD SINGING AND DANCING SCENES TOO FAST WORK STOP...."

May 17, 1930 Sonin of Buenos Aires: WOULD HAVE DONE YOUR HEART GOOD TO HAVE HEARD MOST MARVELOUS RECEPTION ACCORDED VIA NOCTURNA PALACE THEATRE YESTERDAY STOP LAUGHS PACKED SO CLOSELY MANY MISSED STOP CRITI-CISMS BEST PAPERS MARVELOUS STOP POSITIVELY SET FOR LONG RUN"

June 9, 1930: Postal Telegraph Arthur Loew to Hal Roach: "Spain re-ports as follows quote Charlie [sic] Chase speaks perfect Spanish and was a revelation unquote am asking France for report on his French."

June 9, 1930 WESTERN UNION Night letter Hal Roach to Arthur Loew: "Thanks for your wire have finished five reel Chase comedy en-titled LOCURAS DAMOUR STOP Think this will be very well received in Spanish countries and the music and dancing we put in to extend this to feature length I believe does not hurt the picture in any way."

June 10, 1930 WESTERN UNION Hal Roach to Arthur Loew: "CAN YOU DETERMINE FOR US HOW MUCH ADDITIONAL MONEY WE WOULD BE JUSTIFIED IN SPENDING ON SPANISH AND FRENCH VERSIONS TO MAKE OUR SHORT COMEDIES WITH LAUREL AND HARDY AND CHASE INTO SHORT FEATURES THIS CAN BE DONE AT TIMES FOR LESS THAN TEN THOUSAND ON SOME PICTURES AND ON SOME MIGHT RUN TO TWENTY THOUSAND THIS PRICE WILL NOT INCLUDE MAKING OF ORIGINAL FOREIGN VERSION OF THE SHORT PICTURE BUT FOR THE ADDITIONAL FOOTAGE TO MAKE IT INTO A FEATURE PRICE INCLUDES BOTH SPANISH AND FRENCH VERSIONS STOP THE PARTICULAR QUESTION I AM ASKING IS CAN YOU GROSS CONSIDERABLY MORE ON FEA-TURE LENGTH COMEDIES THAN ON SHORT COMEDIES"

June 11, 1930 Arthur Loew to Hal Roach: "IMPOSSIBLE DETER-MINE HOW MUCH YOU SHOULD SPEND TO MAKE COMEDIES FEATURE LENGTH STOP TEN THOUSAND FOR TWO VERSIONS DOES NOT SEEM TOO MUCH HOWEVER ADVISE GOING EASY SINCE WE SHALL SOON MEET MORE COMPETITION WHEN AT-TRACTION BECAUSE OF NOVELTY WILL DIMINISH STOP WE CAN GROSS CONSIDERABLY MORE IN FEATURE LENGTH COM-EDIES THAN SHORT ONES IF THEY ARE GOOD STOP HOW MUCH MORE IS DIFFICULT TO DETERMINE"

May 20, 1930 letter from Arthur Fiedelbaum to Laudy L. Lawrence, Paris, regarding *Glueckliche Kindheit Der Koenig* and *Winterwetter*: "...I requested you to immediately cable New York to stop the production on further comedies inasmuch as these three comedies are practically useless for us... all the German dialogue is in very poor German spoken by the comedians. This in itself would not be such a great detriment to the quality but in addition, the comedy itself is exceedingly slow. This in addition to the fact that whatever German is spoken consists of absolutely matter of fact statements containing not one iota of humor and making these comedies very dull and dreary. If the characters had said something humorous in poor German, the results would undoubtedly be great but it is no great pleasure for a German audience to sit through two reels of noncommittal matter of fact conversation spoken in bad German.

"If any further comedies are to be made for Germany will you kindly communicate to the Studios that the use of a straight man speaking good German would be advisable and also that something witty and funny should be given to the comedians to say in their broken German.

"The French comedy which was shown with THE KISS at the Madeleine used the straight man in the form of Laurel's wife and in addition the French dialogue of Laurel & Hardy was at times either humorous or fitted well into a humorous situation." Handwritten top left corner of this typed letter: "Hal Roach—I do not agree entirely but there may be something to it."—A.W.L.

June 17, 1930 Letter from Allan Byre, MGM-France to Arthur Loew, Aboard SS. *Leviathan*: "Chase's French enunciation very pleasing but first impression golf comedy unfavorable. I must say that we were all very enthusiastic about Charlie [sic] Chase's French enunciation. Incidentally, I happened to be talking to Letsch who told me that his Spanish enunciation was so very good. It seems obvious then that Charlie Chase has a decided gift for languages. I sould [sic] say his French is really very good French; with a little more practice he should certainly arrive almost to a stage of perfection.

"I am afraid we were not so enthusiastic about his comed [sic]... The dialogue was not good French, this is the definitive statement made by Lauzin. Of course, golf is a game that is played in France only by a strictly limited few, with the result that a good many of the gags were lost on our little audience, but I feel very encouraged by the possibility of Charlie Chase in French comedies."

In July 1930 Hal Roach purchased a Travel Air Cabin monoplane with a Wasp motor to use in visiting various cities across the United States and for his frequent journeys to New York. The following month he hired 29-year-old pilot James B. Dickson from Evanston, Illinois at a salary of $125 per week plus expenses. In his contract it is indicated that "Plane will be used entirely for general transportation and nothing of stunt or trick nature." Roach would purchase several more private planes during the early 1930s. He preferred Lockheeds.

Hal Roach's will October 17, 1930: "It is my desire that Warren H. Doane be at all times retained as General Manager, he to have full charge and control, as such, of the corporations' affairs, under the direction of my trustee [Bank of America], and to be relieved only for good cause and cogent reasons."

Hal Roach's salary at the time was $1,500 per week. His new vice president Ginsberg earned $500 per week.

November 19, 1930: "Hal Roach anxious to go to Mexico in interest of his Spanish pictures."

November 19, 1930: Hal Roach to Arthur Loew: Invites him to Mexico. Mexico Manager offers Laurel & Hardy 25% of the gross for one week's appearance in Mexico City.

December 1, 1930: Hal Roach to Arthur Loew: "Just received message that you wanted to leave for Mexico right away. Was that in a rational moment or not?"

1931 RELEASES:
EIGHT OUR GANG TWO-REELERS (PLUS TWO SPANISH SUBTITLES)
SEVEN CHARLEY CHASE TWO-REELERS AND ONE THREE-REELER (PLUS THREE SPANISH VERSIONS, FOUR SPANISH SUBTITLES)
THREE LAUREL & HARDY TWO-REELERS, THREE THREE-REELERS AND A FOUR-REELER (PLUS THREE SPANISH SUBTITLES, TWO SPANISH VERSIONS, ONE FRENCH VERSION)
FIVE BOY FRIENDS TWO-REELERS AND ONE THREE-REELER (PLUS TWO SPANISH SUBTITLES, ONE SPANISH VERSION)
FOUR TODD & PITTS TWO-REELERS AND ONE THREE-REELER (PLUS TWO SPANISH SUBTITLES)
ONE FEATURE (PARDON US) (PLUS SPANISH, FRENCH, GERMAN AND ITALIAN VERSIONS)

January 7, 1931: WESTERN UNION Warren Doane to Arthur Loew: "SO FAR HAVE COMPLETED WITH LAUREL & HARDY FIVE FRENCH VERSIONS ONE OF TWO REELS TWO OF FOUR REELS ONE OF FIVE REELS AND ONE SEVEN REEL STOP NET GROSS REPORTED SO FAR SEEMS VERY SMALL STOP THE CURRENT PIC-

TURE IS DIFFICULT TO MAKE IN SPANISH AND FRENCH AND IF YOU ARE AGREEABLE WE WOULD RATHER MAKE ONLY SPANISH VERSION AS COST OF FRENCH VERSION WOULD BE APPROXIMATELY SAME AS SPANISH VERSION OR SOMEWHAT GREATER AND IT MAY BE FRENCH VERSION WOULD NOT JUSTIFY ITS COST STOP PLEASE ADVISE QUICKLY SO CAN PROCEED"

January 7, 1931: WESTERN UNION Arthur Loew to Warren Doane: "IN REPLY YOUR WIRE TODAY SATISFACTORY ELIMINATE FRENCH VERSION NEXT LAUREL HARDY."

February 10, 1931 Arthur Loew to Hal Roach: "You might be interested to know that the first release of the Laurel Hardy picture "THEIR FIRST MISTAKE" was made in Guatemala (Spanish), and that it was a sensational success."

Undated and unsigned letter to Arthur Loew: "Unidentified man told Stan Laurel that he believed Laurel & Hardy's *Ladrones* in Spanish "meant more to the audience" than the Norma Shearer picture playing with it which only had English dialogue and cut in Spanish silent titles. Also, this man believes "the chain exhibitors in Mexico were putting it over on the exchanges by booking pictures from them for certain definite theatres... for second runs."

March 31, 1931: Benito Erb, MGM Director of Publicity Hungary: "I am glad to inform you that the popularity of Laurel & Hardy is ever rising in Budapest." (Their names were used in a successful stage play: *I have tickets for a Laurel & Hardy show.*)

June 16, 1931 WESTERN UNION Hal Roach to Arthur Loew: "CONGRATULATIONS ON RECEIVING YOUR PILOTS LICENSE CAPTAIN DICKSON DOES NOT FEEL THAT HE HAS ENOUGH EXPERIENCE WITH TYPE OF PLANE YOU SUGGEST TO MAKE ANY RECOMMENDATION"

In January 1932 Hal Roach purchased "The Spirit of Fun," a Lockheed-Orion low-wing monoplane with a cruising speed of 175 miles per hour.

January 14, 1932 WESTERN UNION, Arthur Loew to Hal Roach: "BESIDES MEXICO CITY WOULD LIKE TO MAKE OVERNIGHT STOPS AT GUATEMALA PANAMA CITY LIMA AND LONGER STOPS IN SANTIAGO BUENOS AIRES AND RIO STOP I MAY LEAVE YOU IN RIO AND SAIL FOR EUROPE...."

January 1932: Arthur Loew loans Hal Roach $10,000 payable $1,000 a week.

January 19, 1932: FOR RELEASE: MGM Publicity states "With the intention of making an intensive survey of motion picture markets in central and South America, Hal Roach, producer, and Arthur Loew, vice-president of Loew's Inc., started this morning on an airplane cruise of approximately 20,000 miles. They will visit fourteen countries in Central and South America, returning to California in about four weeks...

"The prime purpose of his and Loew's journey is to ascertain if conditions in the countries they visit warrant resumption of foreign version production."

January 20, 1932 response: David Blum, Director, World-Wide New Service MGM New York City went ballistic. To Henry Ginsberg: "A story containing this item is apt to cause untold embarrassment to both Arthur and Hal during their trip since each country they pass through will not only feel that it should have Spanish productions, but that they should be produced locally. We, in M-G-M, are mighty happy that despite the necessity for synchronizing in German, French and Italian, we have never been forced to do this in Spanish. Certainly, the Hal Roach Studio is happy in the realization that for a few hundred dollars they can make a superimposed title version for Latin America which, if synchronized, would cost a few thousand and, if shot straight in Spanish, would cost a few tens of thousands. Any suggestion, no matter how vague, that there is the remotest possibility of resuming foreign version production might do incalculable damage."

Despite the publicity snafu, the air journey to Central and South America and back went perfectly. They visited fourteen countries and traveled nearly 20,000 miles in four weeks. Air travel and speed records were broken; theirs was the first private plane ever to reach Lima, Peru. The three men had the time of their lives. Only one tense occasion occurred when the governments of Chile, Colombia and Peru each wanted to fine Roach $10,000 because he had not obtained proper clearance papers when they left those countries. Roach purchased forty polo ponies in Chile and had them shipped to California by boat. Then he let Arthur Loew off in Rio De Janeiro so he could take a Pan American Airways commercial plane to Miami where he was due for a business meeting. Roach and Dickson then flew three days from Sao Paolo, Brazil to Lima, and from Lima to Panama in ten hours and twenty minutes, stopping to refuel only twice. The newspapers reported Roach wanted to break the Panama to Mexico City speed record by starting the trip at 6:30 a.m. and arriving by nightfall.

In Mexico City the fliers picked up Mrs. Roach and would attempt another record, the first one-day flight from Mexico City to Los Angeles, with only two stops to refuel.

When all returned safely on February 24th, Roach told waiting reporters that Hollywood film stars are more popular in South America than Spanish-speaking players. A second surprising discovery, said Roach, was that English versions are more popular with theatergoers than Spanish versions. He discovered that thirty percent of the theaters in South America are still unwired for sound, and in these, sound films are run silently with subtitles in Spanish.

In theaters where sound equipment had been installed, Hollywood-made pictures were screened just as produced with dialogue in English.

The reverse was occurring in Europe at this time. English-speaking movies were being BANNED. In addition, re-shooting their comedies in three or four foreign language versions was costly and time-consuming and the practice was abandoned in 1931, by which time post-production dubbing had been perfected.

"Last year foreign versions of all pictures were made which consisted of approximately 90 to 100 foreign versions... The studio has done away with the foreign interpreters, stenographers, cutters and of course the entire foreign staff necessary for the Spanich [sic], German, Italian and French pictures."

And movie showmen had been predicting that the talkies would establish English as the universal language

March 14, 1932: A.M. Morty Springer, Culver Export Corporation, MGM New York City: "Send dupe negative of 'Any Old Port' without dialogue to France. There is a police ordinance in France prohibiting the exhibition of motion pictures with English dialogue. There are one or two theatres now existing that have the permission of the Police Department to exhibit English dialogue productions but the expense involved in serving these two theatres does not warrant the cost of sending a print to Paris. As an experiment we are going to release 'ANY OLD PORT' with just a musical accompaniment and if it is successful, we will release all of the Laurel/Hardy comedies in this manner and possibly some of the other subjects. There is also a restriction in Italy against English dialogue pictures and we undoubtedly will try the same thing there."

June 28, 1932: Morton Springer, Culver City Export Corp. of MGM to Henry Ginsberg:

"Please prepare a musical score without dialogue (the same as 'Any Old Port') of the Laurel-Hardy subjects listed below: 'The Chimp,' 'County Hospital,' 'Music Box,' "Save The Ladies' (combination of 'Come Clean' and 'One Good Turn'), 'Beau Hunks' and 'Helpmates' (combined), 'Another Fine Mess,' 'Our Wife'....." Since it is impossible to release English dialogue versions with any success in Germany, France and Italy, I suggest you go through the last three years' product other than Laurel Hardy comedies and let me know what subjects you think it would be worth while to make a musical... score... We will then send a print of each subject to Europe to determine whether it will be profitable to release additional subjects of the same series."

July 8, 1932: Henry Ginsberg to Morton A. Springer: "We will endeavor to score these pictures and eliminate dialogue as quickly as possible... Would it not be practical to put superimposed titles in one or two pictures as a try, and would this method be as acceptable to you as the picture without dialogue but synchronized?... there is less dialogue used in Laurel and Hardy subjects than any of the past subjects we have made. This is due, as you appreciate, to the type of work Laurel and Hardy do and the fact that they depend to a large extent upon pantomime. The Pitts-Todd, Chase, Our Gang and Boy Friends have at least 25% more dialogue in them, and that is why I ask if they would be marketable with superimposed titles in the language of the countries you mention. Effective with this year's product we are keeping down to a minimum on dialogue, and preparing our stories so as to get laughs out of action rather than out of the spoken title. "

July 18, 1932 Morton A. Springer: "Made a second version of each... The reason we cannot use superimposed titled versions is because we want to release these subjects in countries where English dialogue versions cannot be released such as France and Italy and possibly Germany (if we are able to obtain the contingent)... However, we still require the superimposed titled versions for all other territories."

September 14, 1932 Morton A. Springer to Henry Ginsberg complaining "We received the instructions for superimposed titles for 'Show Business' and "What Price Taxi'... I am sorry to say and with due respect to you and your organization, these instructions are very lousy. They seem to have lost entirely the point of clearly establishing the characters and the necessity of titles only where the story must be explained to the audience or where there is a comedy bit in dialogue that is not conveyed by the action."

September 19, 1932: Henry Ginsberg to Morton A. Springer: "Work on 'Show Business' done by Mr. Walker who is no longer with this organization. Mr. Currier is now taking care of the matter of superimposed titles and he has been instructed as to your requirements and the manner in which to handle this work."

November 15, 1932 Henry Ginsberg to Major Edward Bowes, MGM: "...we were advised of the poor quality of sound [*Show Business*] and we immediately corrected our sound situation here... I believe that the pictures following the one in question are more in keeping with Erpi's and our idea of standard sound."

November 29, 1932: P.H. Cohen to R.C. Currier: "NOW WE'LL TELL ONE"—main title, cast and credit titles are displayed on the screen as electric signs and the noise of the electric current is the background of the sound track. We are puzzled exactly as to what can be done about this matter in superimposing titles in the foreign languages. We would either have to have a special sound track for reel 1 of this subject so that when we remove the English title the noise of the electricity would not be hard [*sic*] which of course would be unexplainable to an audience when seeing the flashes of the titles on the screen, or else, we would have to have negative main titles made up by yourselves in the various foreign languages... If we are to use the English main title as is and superimpose the foreign titles right over the English title, it would be impossible to read the title in either language."

February 17, 1933: Arthur Loew to Henry Ginsberg: "Not long ago we talked about dubbing PACK UP YOUR TROUBLES in French and Italian. I am convinced that this will be well worth your while... At the present time we have our own dubbing studio in Rome and are building one in Paris. I estimate that an Italian version will gross between thirty and forty thousand dollars and that a French version will gross between fifty and seventy-five thousand dollars. I am quite sure that we can dub the two versions for a total of ten thousand dollars. Since we shall dub on bootleg equipment there will be no royalty payable to ERPI or anyone else."

February 20, 1933 Henry Ginsberg to Arthur Loew: "Go ahead and dub 'PACK UP YOUR TROUBLES' if both can be made at a cost of $10,000. I assume, however, that our arrangement will be 60-40 and at such a time as you recoup out of the 60% cost of the dubbing, prints and any other deductible items that come into distribution, we will then split on a basis of 50-50."

In 1932 *Photoplay* published a letter from one Magdalena Hansen of New York City. She wrote that she took her Norwegian sister, who spoke no English, to movies three times a week. "It was surprising to see the work of talking pictures as an English teacher to a foreigner. At the same time they were entertaining. By seeing the actions of the players and hearing them speak at the same time, my sister picked up the language very quickly. Both she and I are grateful for the invention of talking pictures and I hope others will experiment in the same way."

Meanwhile, the English versions:

January 17, 1930: Premiere of *The Rogue Song* at Grauman's Chinese Theatre. This lavish two-strip Technicolor musical feature produced by MGM, directed by Lionel Barrymore and starring Metropolitan Opera star Lawrence Tibbett contained scenes of comedy relief with Laurel & Hardy that were directed by Hal Roach, who received no screen credit.

By the end of the 1929-30 season, according to Randy Skretvedt, the Laurel & Hardy talkie shorts earned $143,678.35 almost double the profits of the previous season. However, due to the looming Depression, it would be their last profitable season for two years. Stan's salary in 1930 was nearly $75,000; in 1931 it would be $104,000. Ollie earned $53,000 in 1930; he would be paid $77,333 in 1931. The Laurel & Hardy series would lose $25,000 in the 1930-31 season and $166,447.88 in 1931-32 even though their worldwide popularity continued to soar.

October 10, 1930 W.B. Zoellner, Resident Manager MGM Oklahoma City to Hal Roach: "'The Laurel and Hardy Murder Case' is billed over Clara Bow in 'Love Among Millionaires.' Newspaper ads have 80% taken up with Laurel & Hardy over Clara Bow who is supposed to be a big box office star, in a first run picture. This situation certainly proves very conclusively what the exhibitors in this neck of the woods think of Messrs. Laurel and Hardy."

October 27, 1930 D.E. Fitton of Harrison, Oklahoma referring to Our Gang's *Teacher's Pet*: "...it was the opinion of our patrons that we asked, that the music was detrimental to the picture. We have found this to be the case with features, but more so with this comedy as the child's voice is not as strong as the adult. This comedy would have been much improved had the music have been left out."

November 5, 1930 Hal Roach's reply: "The music on the print he received may have been a little too loud, but if you take the music out altogether the scratches and surface noises are very apparent and we expect to cover this up by having a slight musical background. However, we will watch very carefully to see that our music is kept at the right volume so that it does not affect the dialogue."

October 29, 1930: Robert Lynch to Hal Roach: "It is my opinion that [Charley Chase's *High C's*] is the best one that he has ever made... the way that music is worked in there is the last word."

November 19, 1930 Hal Roach to Robert Lynch: "Midst the surrounding gloom it is most pleasant to receive your cheery message. We are all working not to make the rest of the Chase Comedies as good as HIGH C'S but to top it."

December 3, 1930 MGM London to MGM New York City: "I think it would be best to advise the Hal Roach Studios that their new method of introducing comedies via spoken titles [recited in unison by cute blonde 13-year-old twin sisters Beverly and Betty Mae Crane] is beginning to meet with disfavor. At first it was considered somewhat of a novelty but now in rougher communities particularly, with the habit of speaking back to the screen, there is a tendency on the part of such audiences to speak the lines in conjunction with the two girls."

December 3, 1930 Felix F. Feist to Hal Roach: "Just finished looking at Boy Friends comedy 'Love Fever'... we might just as well make up our minds that this is another series that you will have to give up if you can't find better material or get more comedy into it... There must be some clever and fertile minds in that great center of motion picture production—Los Angeles, Culver City, Hollywood, etc.—that can conceive plots that suggest comedy situations, if not funny lines... [*Love Fever*] is the fifth one we have had of a series of eight, and there is only one, 'Ladies Last,' that had the semblance of Hal Roach comedy flavor. If it is your idea to continue this series next year, a very strenuous effort should be made on the remaining three to have them excruciatingly funny."

In late 1930 Hal Roach directed a feature for MGM entitled *Men of the North*. It starred Gilbert Roland, the Mexican-born Latin Lover, incongruously as a French-Canadian Mountie. (Contemporary viewers have commented that his accent is decidedly South of the Border.) Roland's co-star was Barbara Leonard, who was multilingual, and that proved useful as she also appeared in all four foreign language versions, Spanish, French, Italian and German.

Variety's review of December 17, 1930: "Mildly diverting romance of the French Canadian wilds holding some fine shots of dog teams mushing through snowstorms carrying the Northwest Mounted. Well balanced cast and good direction most of the way but the story lacks a sympathetic character during most of the footage. The final twist, which makes the villain the hero, apparently lacks the punch anticipated... Roland and

Miss Leonard both turn in good performances ably supported by Arnold Knoff, Robert Elliott and George Davis...."

December 22, 1930 Mr. C. Ayres, MGM London to Hal Roach: "I have often thought what a fine starred comedian they could make of James Finlayson, and recently, from several quarters it has been asked 'Why doesn't Hal Roach feature Finlayson?' (Perhaps in a series of Detective Comedies.) You have probably noticed that there is always a joyful titter among the audience when Finlayson makes his appearance in our comedies."

"Hal Roach believes four assets are needed for a girl to succeed in talking pictures: 1) versatility, 2) charm of personality, 3) good looks, not beauty, 4) a voice which records effectively.

The ability to project her personality into any type of portrayal. In order to do this she must be two persons, her real self and her screen self.

I place personality before beauty because it means more in the advancement of a film career

Pleasing combination of face and figure. Brunette or blonde, both have an equal chance

A good voice. Without this, the other attributes are of no avail. A girl may be versatile, charming and beautiful but if her voice records with harsh raspiness or unpleasing tonal quality, she will have no chance on the speaking screen."

July 11, 1932: WESTERN UNION Henry Ginsberg to Felix Feist: "NUMEROUS CHANGES MADE IN LAUREL HARDY FEATURE SLOW SPOTS TAKEN OUT ADDITIONAL FOOTAGE CONTAINING REAL LAUGHS INSERTED AND LAST REEL AND A HALF OF PICTURE MUCH STRONGER STOP PREVIEWED AGAIN LAST NIGHT... YOU WOULD HAVE BEEN VERY ELATED OVER RESULTS STOP PICTURE CLOCKED MORE THAN TWO HUNDRED AND SIXTY LAUGHS STOP...."

July 16—September 7, 1932: Numerous telegrams regarding the problems with synchronization for *Pack Up Your Trouble* New York City premiere. Although sound on disc recording was largely abandoned by 1931, "In 1932," wrote Ron Hutchinson of The Vitaphone Project, "there were still over 3,000 U.S. theatres that could only exhibit in the disc format, which is why discs continued to be pressed long after studios had stopped direct disc recording and editing." But one wonders why the studio would send a major theater in New York City a feature with sound discs at that late date.

July 16 Henry Ginsberg to W.D. Kelly, MGM New York City: "We are today sending to you a print of the feature PACK UP YOUR TROUBLES. This print is the only print in our possession, the negative has not as yet been conformed... This print has been played around with a great deal, cut many times, re-assembled and cut again. I trust you will give instructions that particular care be taken in its handling so that we run into no difficulties at the preview."

July 22 Henry Ginsberg to W.D. Kelly: "...naturally we are discouraged to learn that the showing of our picture PACK UP YOUR TROUBLES in your projection room was out of synchronization. We here cannot account for this condition because one of the sets of records sent you was run with the picture three times prior to its shipment... Under the circumstances we are now concerned as to whether or not the theatre chosen for preview will be so equipped as to properly project the picture with records... We are shipping you tomorrow two preview sets of records. If during rehearsal either of these sets go out of synchronization the preview is to be abandoned and the print shipped here so that we can arrange to take off a sound on film print. We have used records on this picture for four previews and for at least twenty runs of the entire picture in our projection room, and the situation that occurred in the East has never once occurred here."

July 23 Telegraph Kelly to Hal Roach: "...WE JUST TRIED THE NEW SET WHICH CAME AIR MAIL AND FIND THEY ALSO [are out of synch]... WE ARE USING VICTOR CHROME NEEDLE AND BEST WESTERN ELECTRIC EQUIPMENT BUT CANNOT PREVENT [going out of synch] STOP MY SUGGESTION IS THAT... RECORDS BE MADE ON SIXTEEN INCH SHELLAC WHICH WOULD ALLOW SUFFICIENT RANGE OF NEEDLE TO TAKE CARE OF SOUND IN THE PICTURE."

July 26 Kelly to Henry Ginsberg: "WE ARE SHIPPING BACK TO YOU TODAY PRINT PACK UP YOUR TROUBLES AND TWO SETS OF RECORDS STOP COULD NOT KEEP REEL ONE IN SYNCHRONIZATION THEREFORE CANNOT ARRANGE PREVIEW WRITING"

July 28: Letter from Kelly to Henry Ginsberg: "I fully realize that it must seem rather strange that you could run the records out there and we could not run them here. Our Engineering Department handled the entire matter and I stood by and watched and it was impossible to get reel #1 through on the last two sets. Therefore we could not go ahead with the preview because if we had trouble with reel #1 it would ruin the whole effect and my personal opinion is it would be entirely too risky from your own point of view.

"My suggestion is that in cases of this kind you ought to use 16" records for preview work particularly comedies where you have so much sound of the type that is difficult to record in the disc because of the wide range of the needle in recording low frequency sounds... I personally checked the records on my Victor testing machine which was made for me in the days when we used records generally and got them by fine, but not when put on the regular projection equipment, and you might also want to know that the original set of records sent on broke down in many places throughout the entire picture."

August 1 letter Henry Ginsberg to Kelly: "Rather than take any chance with records we are conforming the negative and will within the next week ship you a print sound on film, for a theatre preview in the East."

August 6 letter Henry Ginsberg to Kelly: "As advised by Currier, a movietone print of Pack Up Your Troubles was shipped to you yesterday... I trust you will get together with Dave Loew so a preview can be arranged immediately."

Also on August 6 Henry Ginsberg wrote to Felix Feist: "Yesterday we forwarded a new print of Pack Up Your Troubles sound on film. You will have no difficulty with this print."

August 12 Western Union "PACK UP YOUR TROUBLES WILL BE PREVIEWED IN NEW ROCHELLE MONDAY AUGUST TWENTY SECOND STOP DELAY IS CAUSED BY NEW YORK STATE CENSOR BOARD ASKING THAT WE MAKE ELIMINATIONS...."

August 23 Henry Ginsberg letter to Kelly: "We appreciate that some of our recent productions have not been up to par as far as sound is concerned... A few of our pictures which had deficiencies in certain spots was caused more by the fact that these pictures were produced in a silent form with the dialogue dubbed in, which of course has been found to be unpractical, in addition to causing inferior sound. We have gone further, however, and have for the past week brought our sound equipment up to what we believe a standard that will overcome any deficiencies in the future."

August 25 Postal Telegraph Felix F. Feist to Henry Ginsberg: "PRACTICALLY EVERY PREVIEW CARD EXPRESSED REPULSION AT PIE THROWING EPISODE WHICH HAL AGREED SHOULD COME OUT STOP ALSO DISCUSSED WITH HAL INSERTING SOMETHING TO ELIMINATE ABRUPTNESS OF CHANGE FROM GARBAGE SCENE

TO SCENE WITH EDDIE BABY AND SCOTCH WOMAN WHICH HE ALSO AGREED TO FIX UP STOP WITH THESE TWO ELEMENTS STRAIGHTENED OUT OKAY GO FORWARD WITH PRINTING AS PICTURE SET FOR SEPTEMBER FOURTH RELEASE...."

August 30 Western Union Henry Ginsberg to Kelly: "PLEASE PHONE STAN LAUREL WARWICK HOTEL AND ARRANGE SCREEN FOR HIM IMMEDIATELY PRINT PACK UP YOUR TROUBLES STOP FOLLOWING WHICH YOU CAN RETURN PRINT TO US...."

September 7 Kelly to Henry Ginsberg: "...WE CAN EASILY MEET RELEASE DATE OF SEPTEMBER SEVENTEENTH STOP HAVE YOU ONE MOVIETONE PRINT OF OLD VERSION WHICH YOU CAN RUSH OHIO FOR CENSORSHIP...."

At last, the issue of talkie presentation was finally resolved. Movietone or sound on film would be the standard from then on; this was virtually the last gasp of the sound disc presentation of talking motion pictures, though Ron Hutchinson wrote, "My friend bandleader Vince Giordano read some very late circa 1934 correspondence to Roach from a theatre owner complaining about still sending discs for a Chase short."

Meanwhile, the continued international popularity of Roach's stars in any language or recording format was uncontestable. *Movie Classic* magazine October 1932:

"Laurel & Hardy top all Hollywood in international popularity. There is a theatre on the main street of Vienna that runs nothing but Laurel & Hardy comedies, giving four shows a day! There hasn't been a change in the program for months and the S.R.O. sign is always out... The kings and emperors of at least three countries command private showings of all new Laurel & Hardy releases. They are as big a hit somewhere East of Suez as they are at your neighborhood theatre. South America literally cries for their films (which have Spanish versions). They are one Hollywood team whose profits are with honor in any country. Czechoslovakia brought out a national coin with Laurel on one side and Hardy on the other (worth a few cents)."

6

Dirty Work
Laughing Through the Depression
1931-1935

HAL ROACH STUDIOS 1931 PUBLICITY:
"Making two-reel comedies is a serious business at the Hal Roach Studios. The studio is a well-organized factory of fun, not a merry madhouse. The laughter machinery runs with perfectly-oiled smoothness, and the precision of carefully-timed production. The comedians, at whose antics the whole world laughs, move about their business with the dignity and decorum of men in any profession. Their buffoonery, their slapstick clowning, is confined solely to the hours they spend before the cameras and microphones. Away from the stages, they drop their masks, and become themselves, keen-minded business men, whose job it is to make the world laugh. That job itself, is enough to make any one think seriously. Being funny is the hardest work in the world… Businessmen forget their early morning [conventional] grouches, if any, in trafficking in the tangible.

"But the makers of comedy, no matter how gray the day or how dreary the outlooks, must seek the elusive laugh, capture the unseen smile… The natural comic, the life of the party, who convulses his gang with his tricks and antics, would probably be a woeful flop on the screen. The successful comedians of the films are usually the most quiet and retiring of gentlemen. The stars of the Roach two-reelers would pass unnoticed in any crowd of amateur funmakers. They would be the audience, not the clowns… Even the great Henry Ford, disciple of efficiency, might learn a lesson or two from the precision and machine-like operation of Hal Roach's Culver City mirth factory.

"Every week, encased in its neat tin container, a two-reel film emerges from the assembling room, ready for a long and merry life in countless

149

projection rooms. Each tin box holds twenty minutes of trouble—chasing mirth for the doctors, lawyers, beggermen and chiefs of the world. Then the comedy manufacturers settle down to the production of a newer and funnier, faster and furiouser film."

"It is impossible to tell in advance what the public is going to like in comedy pictures," said Mr. Roach in 1931. "It is always a question of making our picture, using your gags and then trying them out. No one can tell in advance whether the audience are going to laugh their heads off at a certain gag or whether they will pass it by as tame and boresome."

"As told by Oliver Hardy: 'We had spent a strenuous day on a dimly lighted set at the studio working on 'The Laurel & Hardy Murder Case' and in order to film some night scenes we worked until midnight. We were pretty weary from being chased by spooks, ghosts and weird looking characters. Stan and I were getting ready to leave the studio and as I was ready first I went to his dressing room and called him. His room was cloudy with cigarette smoke and as I opened the door and didn't find him I thought he must have left, but I walked in to see. The light was bad and the most alarming sounds were coming from the closet. The property man had left a couple of trained bats in the closet and when I opened the door they flew past my head with white sheets trailing over them. My jaded nerves nearly collapsed but I managed to get outside where Stan was getting the laugh of his life."

More 1931 Publicity:

"Stan Laurel and Oliver Hardy, when they are not trying to outdo each other in talking about their fishing and golfing, discuss the possibility of anyone being able to perfect a rocket capable of carrying scientists to Mars. The recent balloon trip into the stratisphere [*sic*] was watched with keen interest by the famous comedians. [This must be the May 27, 1931 feat undertaken by August Piccard and Paul Kipfer who, from Germany, reached the record breaking altitude of 51,775 feet in a spherical, pressurized aluminum gondola.]

"...Thelma Todd reads practically everything pertaining to the sciences of other planets. Her literary trend runs to biographical sketches of such men as Professor Albert Einstein and other noted foreign scientists. The study of relativity and fourth dimension also has its place in the thoughts and conversation of this talented screen star." She was also reported to have the "widest bed in Hollywood" (at nine feet across).

"Ollie is one of filmdom's finest golfers, yet Stan's first game was 187 strokes for 18 holes and his golf partner accused him of cheating! Ollie golfs in the low 70s and has won 22 cups in tournaments. Stan goes deep sea fishing off his 34 foot cruiser. His latest catch was a 190 pound Marlin swordfish. Hal Roach is the only left handed polo player on the West Coast. Charley Chase enjoys ping pong.

"The chauffeur for Charley Chase says he was leaving the hospital after an operation, dropped a coin in a street scale to get his weight. The machine ejected a small card bearing a picture of Charley Chase with the inscription, 'Your Favorite Movie Star,' and printed on the reverse side, 'You are a perfect specimen of physical fitness and never bothered by illness.'"

"Laurel and Hardy agree, as a team, that there is nothing like giving something to someone who is needy to snap out of the blues. Just think of someone who is in need and go out and do something for them and it is sure to bring a sense of relief from depression. Get your mind off yourself, is their slogan."

"During a conference in Roach's office, when he left the room to get a document Stan and Ollie slipped off their shoes to sneak out but just down the steps Roach caught them. 'We were caught like mice in a trap.'" A photo of this incident can be seen on page 192 of this book.

"I was the luckiest fellow in the world," Roach said in 1931. "I found an Englishman, Laurel, and a boy from Georgia, Hardy, neither of whom was anything at all alone. I put 'em together and the combination spelled comedy applesauce with lots of money for all of us."

"Mr. Roach told of a new comedy series now being made at the Hollywood studio," declared *The Atlanta Constitution* on April 7, 1931. "This brings ZaSu Pitts and Thelma Todd together as a feminine team. In the series [Roach] said, they are small town girls who go to a big city, where Thelma Todd believes all the time they are going to meet prominent society and business people and become rich overnight, while ZaSu Pitts just knows it can't be done. The first of these pictures has just been made and will be released in the near future."

"During the filming of *The Pajama Party*," stated Roach publicity that year, "ZaSu Pitts accidentally pushed Hal Roach, who was directing, into the swimming pool."

In August 1931 Roach signed a new agreement with MGM for an indeterminate period of years for the production and distribution of forty comedies of approximately two reels in length and one feature length production, *Pardon Us*, starring Laurel & Hardy.

September 1931: Budget for 1930-31 season which included thirty-two two-reelers and one feature *Pardon Us* was approximately $1,700,000. In 1931-32 the budget was $1,500,000 forty two-reelers.

October 1931: Promotions among the Roach personnel: Warren Doane, Vice President and General Manager since 1920 made Director of the Chase series to alternate with James Horne. Benjamin Shipman, legal advisor and business manager promoted to Doane's former post as General Manager. L.A. French, with Roach since 1919 as head of the Purchasing Department retains that post as well as becoming Assistant General Manager. R.C. Currier, Morey Lightfoot and Anthony Mack become Directors.

October 22, 1931 Telegraph Hal Roach to David Loew: "I WANT HENRY GINSBERG TO ACT AS ASSISTANT TO ME HANDLING WHATEVER IS NECESSARY TO BE HANDLED IN THE EAST AS WELL AS ASSISTING IN PRODUCTION HERE."

On October 30, 1931 Hal Roach and his friend Will Rogers arrived in Mexico City in Roach's private plane piloted by Captain James Dickson. A large crowd greeted them and they were met by Captain R.E. Cummings, military attaché of the United States Embassy.

"Mr. Roach said one of the principal objects of the visit was to close a deal for the Mexican polo team to visit Los Angeles and play there on December 5" stated The *New York Times*. The teams did play on the stated date in Los Angeles. The Americans defeated "the clever and hard-hitting Mexican players eleven to ten."

Roach began practicing polo under the tutelage of Will Rogers when the latter arrived in California to star in his series of shorts for Roach in 1923. But left-handers like Roach were barred from playing polo. His skill, however, so impressed the chairman of the local polo club that the rules were changed. Roach eventually had his own string of polo ponies along with Rogers. In 1934 Roach won the West Coast open championship and played regularly with other Hollywood polo enthusiasts including Jack Holt, Spencer Tracy, Robert Montgomery and James Gleason.

November 16, 1931: Henry Ginsberg comes to Hal Roach Studios. Ginsberg has been painted as something of a villain by other writers, or at least criticized for his parsimonious methods: "Ginsberg was a Producer and Exhibitor with no feel for comedy production whatsoever and his continual cost-cutting measures slowly chipped away at the creativity and morale of the Roach staff. The Lot of Fun would never be so fun again" wrote Richard M. Roberts in *Smileage Guaranteed*.

Randy Skretvedt in *Laurel & Hardy The Magic Behind The Movies* wrote, "…Ginsberg sought to cut costs wherever and however he could, and he didn't make many friends in the process." Anita Garvin says Stan called him 'The Expeditor.' He was always trying to get everyone to work as quickly as possible." Richard Currier was quoted as saying "Everybody hated Ginsberg." Even Charley Chase's daughter June had a negative comment: "All of Daddy's problems there really started with Ginsberg. My mother always said not to trust him...." But these criticisms may be unduly harsh, as the circumstances of the Depression and other threats to the Hal Roach Studios seem to have warranted Ginsberg's disciplined approach.

Brian Anthony and Andy Edmonds, in their 1998 biography of Charley Chase, *Smile While the Raindrops Fall*, report that Ginsberg was hired by Roach as a condition of a large loan granted to Roach by the Bank of America. "Ginsberg was to supervise production costs, keeping them down wherever possible... Ginsberg insisted Charley Chase cut down from three-reelers to two which Chase resented; in January 1932 Chase quit the studio." He returned in June with a new contract for the 1932-33 season that included a raise to $3,000 per week and with the proviso that his brother Jimmy (at $750 per week) be hired as his unit director. But Chase was only allowed to make two-reelers from then on.

Whatever has been written about Ginsberg, his own correspondence reveals him to have been a man who had formed his own film distribution company in 1925, enjoyed film comedy and shared with Roach the enormous joy his daughter had for the Our Gang kids; Ginsberg wanted to see the film comedies maintain a high quality; he was an astute businessman who was dedicated to preserving and improving the profitability of the Studio by avoiding time wasting and inefficiency among the often, let's admit it, capricious employees. And two facts stand out dramatically in Mr. Ginsberg's favor. Whatever Richard Currier has been quoted as having said about him, Currier actually sent Ginsberg an apology letter admitting to his own bad behavior and hot temper AFTER he had been terminated. And there is correspondence showing that Ginsberg fought to prevent the MGM higher ups from terminating the Our Gang series in 1933.

David Loew in New York City had written to Hal Roach on November 18, 1931: "Henry [Ginsberg] left for the Coast yesterday and I sure can say that I never saw anybody in my life more enthusiastic over a job than he. I think he accomplished more in knowledge and results in one week than ordinarily is accomplished in a month... We were riding home the night before he left and he made a crack to the effect that he is so wrapped up in the work and it has held his interest so much that he would work for nothing in order to see the outcome, and my only hope is that he proves satisfactory to you as I feel in my heart he will."

Meanwhile, although Chase would be cutting down the length of his shorts, Laurel and Hardy had began experimenting with making even longer movies. One of the first was *Beau Hunks*, a four-reeler.

"I think that is my favorite Laurel and Hardy picture," Roach told me in 1973. "Where they join the Foreign Legion. I had the cheapest leading lady in that one, by the way. [His eyes twinkled as he said this.] Jean Harlow was a friend of mine, and we used only her photograph as the girl that jilts Babe."

Jean Harlow was indeed grateful to Hal Roach, who after all had given her her start in the movies back in 1929. But it wasn't an easy start. Jean Darling, a child actor and Our Gang kid from 1927 to 1929 recalled her experiences with Jean Harlow to the author eighty-four years later:

"One day when I was sitting by the lake listening to Jean Harlow's tale of woe about everything about her was wrong according to the powers that be, her eyebrows, her voice, her walk and she was starving to death because she had been put on another diet. Just then Roach came up. 'You two come with me,' he said, bundling us into his car. On reaching Max Factor's Jean and I were placed in adjoining chairs and her dark hair was bleached to match mine. And photos of Hal Roach and the two blonde Jeans appeared in the rotogravures nationwide."

In her autobiographical article 'The Authentic Story of My Life' as told to Eleanor Packer in the *New Movie* magazine of October 1934, Jean Harlow wrote: "...overnight I jumped from the extra rank into the femme leading role with Stan Laurel and Oliver Hardy. I wouldn't trade anything I own for my experience in those comedies. There was a friendliness and camaraderie about that small studio entirely different from the impersonality of the larger places. No one was too busy to help and advise. Stan and 'Babe' realized my ignorance and did everything in their power to make me feel at home and at ease. I felt that I was receiving invaluable training in the school from which some of the best known screen players had been graduated.

"After I had played in two comedies, Hal Roach offered me a five-year contract. When I signed that contract, I thought that I was definitely deciding the course of my life...

"As luck would have it, Grandfather and Grandmother, who rarely went to motion picture theaters, chose for one of their rare visits the theater in Kansas City where the Laurel and Hardy comedy was playing. Today we all can laugh over their horrified surprise when they saw me, dressed only in black lace teddies, appear before them on the screen. But no one was laughing then. It was a heartbroken and more than angry grandfather who telephoned me that night and both begged and demanded that I stop motion picture work at once...

"The next day I explained the situation to Hal Roach. I shall always be grateful for his complete understanding. He released me from my contract and Jean Harlow became Harlean Carpentier McGrew once more." It wasn't long, of course, before Jean Harlow returned to the screen and ultimate super stardom when she met a chap by the name of Howard Hughes.

November 13, 1931 Laurel & Hardy attended the World Premiere of *The Champ* with a list of luminaries that included U.S. Vice President Charles Curtis, James Rolph, Jr. (the then Governor of California), Hal Roach, Joe Rivkin, Thelma Todd, Louis B. Mayer, Clark Gable, Joan Crawford, Norma Shearer, Jackie Cooper, Ramon Navarro, Buster Keaton, Anita Page, King Vidor, Lionel Barrymore, Pola Negri, Dolores Del Rio, Bebe Daniels, Constance Bennett, Ann Harding, Robert Armstrong, Irene Dunne, Joseph von Sternberg, Warner Baxter, Janet Gaynor, W.S. Van Dyke, Lewis Stone, Marlene Dietrich, Heda Hopper, Mack Sennett and so many other great celebrities of the day.

December 2, 1931: Henry Ginsberg letter to Warner Bros. associate Jacob Wilk in New York City: "Things are breaking very marvelously for me. I am terrifically happy, and have found in Mr. Roach an associate that is so entirely different from anything in the business that it really astounds me. I am to make my headquarters here [Culver City] and will bring my family out in the next few weeks."

December 1931 News from Hal Roach Studios: "Henry Ginsberg, eastern film executive who arrived here last week from New York, was made vice president and general manager of the Hal Roach Studios, Inc... Mr. Ginsberg, who assumes his new position at once, will relieve Mr. Roach of many routine business affairs of the organization. Mr. Roach plans to concentrate on production activities. L.A. French will act as Mr. Ginsberg's assistant while Benjamin Shipman, who succeeded Warren Doane as general manager six weeks ago, will become business manager and legal advisor of the firm."

December 8, 1931 J.D. Williams & Associates "Specialists in Special Pictures" 11 W. 42nd Street, New York City to Henry Ginsberg: "Hammons... is going into three and four reel comedies to counteract the double bill program. This I believe is a mistake as he has nothing of sufficient value to take the place of the double bill that contains names, and if he is not able to give the theatre the extra draw in the four reel comedy, it is of no more value to the exhibitor than two separate subjects each of two reels... In the first place, only about 20% of the country is showing double bills, and those that are doing so is not for the reason that they are doing so in order to just give quantity of footage. Their aim is to have two pictures of drawing power. I note here some of the houses are showing *An American Tragedy* and *Get Rich Quick Walingford* on the same bill, and it is not likely that this class of theatre will buy a four reel Andy Clyde to take the place of either. If Clyde has drawing power sufficient to counteract either of the above pictures, then he is strong enough to be put into a full length feature, and derive the benefits of the single feature theatre. The theatre that runs single features will not pay much more for a four reel comedy than for a two reel, for he can buy a two reeler and a couple of single reels at a much less price and have a varied program."

Henry Ginsberg: "The short comedy is an integral [impregnable was crossed out!] part of a theatre program; along with the News Reel and cartoon it is the feature attraction where children are concerned. It is this trade that the sophisticated drama and the too-talkie motion picture has chased away from the theatre... The double feature in reality is an example of impulsive showmanship, giving no thought to its future as an institution of entertainment. Double featuring has further hurt the child trade—it gave them more feature-length films, but excluded its only hold on child trade, the comedy.

"The showing of double features is on the wane! It bettered the theatre receipts for a short period, then over-fed the public, taking from them a most important theatre policy, namely, diversified entertainment. This is now recognized and from present observation the double feature will practically become extinct within the next year."

Two years later, the double bill issue was still of concern:

February 20, 1933: Fred Quimby Personal Postal Telegraph to Henry Ginsberg: "WITH CHAOTIC CONDITION OF MAJOR CIRCUITS FROM WHICH WE RECEIVE OUR IMPORTANT SHORT SUBJECT REVENUE PLUS DOUBLE FEATURE EVIL THERE WILL BE VERY PERCEPTIBLE SHRINKAGE IN NINETEEN THIRTY TWO THIRTY THREE COMEDY REVENUE THEREFORE CANNOT IMPRESS UPON YOU TOO FORCEFULLY IMPORTANCE OF REDUCING NEGATIVE COST ON BALANCE OF PICTURES TO BE DELIVERED TO ABSOLUTE MINIMUM."

February 27, 1933: 275 cards re double feature presentations "representing about two million women" all are against double-bills. About six exceptions, stating they are in favor of the present situation from an economic standpoint."

1932 RELEASES:
NINE OUR GANG TWO-REELERS
EIGHT TODD & PITTS TWO-REELERS
SEVEN CHARLEY CHASE TWO-REELERS
SIX LAUREL & HARDY TWO-REELERS AND TWO THREE-REELERS
SIX BOY FRIENDS TWO-REELERS
FOUR TAXI BOYS TWO-REELERS
ONE FEATURE, LAUREL & HARDY'S PACK UP YOUR TROUBLES

January 6, 1932: The *Wall Street Journal*: "HAL ROACH NET $91,752 IN 57 WEEK PERIOD (to August 29, 1931)."

In January 1932 Ginsberg wrote to Louise Brecker of Roseland, New York City, with the idea of making "a few comedy shorts" with Duke Ellington and his band. A couple of days later he corrected himself, stating he meant Cab Calloway.

By February 1st Ginsberg had moved to 525 Canon Drive, Beverly Hills.

On February 17, 1932 Ginsberg wrote to Leonard Ginsberg, 40 West 77th Street, New York City: "Dear Len—Very thoughtful of you to send me the letter about RCA's progress with television—this sounds rather interesting—information of this kind is always valuable if for no other reason than to see the trend that amusement business is taking." Ironically, just the month prior Arthur Jefferson, Stan Laurel's father, was interviewed in *Picturegoer Weekly*. "The talkies came and killed the silent," he reflected. "The old order changeth. What will they give us next—talkies televised direct to our fire-sides? I wonder. I wonder."

February 22, 1932: Memorandum Henry Ginsberg to Hal Roach: ZaSu Pitts offered thirty-five weeks contract first year $1,250 per week, second year $1,500; third year $1,750; fourth year $2,000; fifth year $2,500.

March 14, 1932: Henry Ginsberg letter to Louis Swartz, New York City: "Learned last week about Harry Goetz' departure from Paramount. This is rather a shock as I assumed he was pretty well set there. I don't know just what the business is coming to when people of Harry's character cannot be appreciated and afforded the proper opportunities in a company as large as Paramount... Fortunately enough, in our studio there is no element of political intrigue and under the circumstances a man can do a day's work and rest easy when he gets home."

March 18, 1932 Henry Ginsberg letter to David Loew, MGM: "In connection with 'The Nickel Nurser', Fred Quimby advised me here that it was one of the best pictures that Chase made...."

April 8, 1932 letter from Fred [Quimby?] to Henry Ginsberg: "I notice in the poll taken by the Hays Organization, from several hundred thousand questionnaires sent to people throughout the United States as to which type of motion picture they preferred, the majority of answers indicated they liked slapstick comedy best. I understand these questionnaires were sent to a large list of college presidents, teachers, professional people... and the answers from these people, very much to my surprise, indicated that they liked slapstick comedy better than any other type of comedy."

April 9, 1932: Henry Ginsberg: "...it is my personal opinion that this will be one of the worst theatre summers in the history of the motion picture business, and if my belief is correct you can possibly imagine what will happen to such companies as Fox, RKO and Warners with the huge losses they are taking in their theatres."

April 29, 1932 Henry Ginsberg to David Loew: "Tomorrow is my birthday and we are going to have dinner at Hal's and then attend the opening of 'Grand Hotel.'"

April 29, 1932: Henry Ginsberg to Thomas W. Gerety, MGM New York City: "If you boys in New York would relax and laugh heartily when you are screening a Roach comedy, you too would look as young as I do without a make up man."

In April 1932 Fred Beck of Hollywood, writing a magazine article, asks Ken Porter:

" What gag produced the biggest laugh in any Laurel & Hardy picture?

In Mr. Laurel's opinion?

In Mr. Hardy's opinion?

Mr. Laurel thinks the bunk sequence in 'Pardon Us'... drew the longest and loudest laughs from the audience. This scene was not in the script at all but enacted merely through spontaneity on the part of Laurel & Hardy after the camera started its grinding. It is a long sequence, but not monotonous because of its extreme pantomime. Laurel is clad in long underwear and heavy socks while Hardy wears a long flannel nightgown. Both of them attempt to get into a jail bunk, third tier up, which ordinarily would accommodate but one person. Eventually up on the bunk both try to settle comfortably for the night, but after much twisting, squirming the bunk breaks down."

Funniest gag in the opinion of Oliver Hardy: "The tack gag in 'Beau Hunks.' Sprinkling tacks on rock floor to capture army of barefooted riffs. "Mr. Hardy adds that the success of this gag was due to its unexpectedness on the audience, and its being so different and an entirely new gag."

After the historic and epic plane trip Roach, Loew and pilot Dickson took to South America in January and February, June through September brought more news items about their flights. "HAL ROACH PLANE BREAKS HAWKS' EAST-WEST RECORD" screamed one headline on June 17, 1932.

"Smashing two transcontinental flying records, Captain James B. Dickson, piloting a plane owned by Hal Roach, set the ship down at Clover Field at 6:41 p.m. yesterday. Dickson's flying time from Newark, N.J. was 14 hours and 49 minutes.

"This broke the westbound record set by Captain Frank Hawks, who in August, 1930, flew from New York to Los Angeles in 14 hours and 50 minutes.

"It also broke the passenger-carrying record as there were three passengers in Dickson's plane...

"In the plane with Dickson were Arthur Loew, vice president of Lowes, Inc.; Harry [sic] Ginsberg, general manager of Hal Roach Studios, and William Meinicker, South American representative of Metro-Goldwyn-Mayer...."

June 18, 1932: Henry Ginsberg letter: "We left New York at sunup Thursday in Hal Roach's plane and arrived in Los Angeles at sundown the Same day, breaking past records in coast to coast aviation circles. You can see by this that in addition to becoming a producer I am now a transcontinental flier—most anything can happen to you when you move to Hollywood!... My only disappointment is in the fact that the City of Los Angeles did not hold a parade in our honor!"

Just days later newspapers reported that Roach's plane, traveling from Los Angeles to New York, after bettering Lindbergh's transcontinental flight record up to that point, was forced to land at Ames Airport in Pennsylvania due to a heavy fog bank. "His time for the distance was about an hour less than Colonel Lindbergh's." The passengers continued to New York by train.

In July, returning west, they landed at Colorado Springs in eleven hours and fifty minutes. From Colorado to Los Angeles took five hours and nineteen minutes.

July 6, 1932 letter from T.Y. Henry, NY: "Due to ERPI about reaching the saturation point in theatre sales and the fact that their non-theatrical sales are nil, due to lack of pictures, etc. many of us were 'washed up'... among them being myself."

Henry Ginsberg's response: "Conditions are as bad if not worse out here than they are in New York. The entire industry is more or less in an upheaval and there are a great many executives out of work; in fact, every type of help is over-abundant here."

August 17, 1932: Henry Ginsberg to David Loew: "Everything is coming along nicely and we are pretty well ahead on our product for this year. We are quite happy, particularly in the fact that our negative costs for the season so far show a difference in costs of between 35 and 40%, and from our observations here the quality is being maintained. I note from the papers that theatre conditions in the east are improving; at least I hope so. It's about time this depression was over."

By December Henry Ginsberg would write, "The so-called depression hit this place [Hollywood] after it did New York, and there are so many out of work, including capable executives, that it really is pathetic."

The flip side of nepotism:

August 4, 1932 Henry Ginsberg to Felix Feist: "Hal's brother Jack has been working at the studio for the past five years [since 1927]. He is about 35 years old [actually he was forty-two]. On account of being Hal's brother the boy has been terribly handicapped and naturally does not make the strides that he ordinarily would were he in an organization of strangers. Hal has felt that he would like to have him join Metro's Foreign Department. Would you consider placing him in your Los Angeles Branch at no compensation until such time as he receives sufficient experience?... Hal feels quite confident that among strangers he will absolutely make good." [Would he have to change his last name?]

October 4, 1932 Henry Ginsberg to David Loew: "If we thought a plan of this kind practical we would be unable to do anything until after the current season, as Miss Todd has a definite contract for five more pictures which are still to be made in the Pitts-Todd group."

November 29, 1932 Henry Ginsberg letter: "...it looks as though I am going to be a permanent resident of Los Angeles inasmuch as I signed a new contract covering a few years."

December 16, 1932: Letter from "Dick" [Currier] to Henry Ginsberg: "shocked" that he was let go, however, "...I realize you were right in telling me that I hadn't been showing the proper respect, in checking up on myself I can see where I have been overbearing and cocky, I'm very sorry for this and would have welcomed some one calling it to my attention, I realize that

I have a personality that is very unlikeable and unless I guard against it at all times it crops out and I don't realize it until I get a jolt, sit down and analyze myself, and I'm sorry to say that in this case it was to[o] late."

Harvard School Report Card for Hal Roach Jr., month ending January 29, 1932. English C, Arithmetic C-, History C, Science D (Lack of diligence and effort), Manual Training B, Drawing C, Gymnastics C, Military Record C.

Hal Roach's tax liability for 1922-26, 1928 and 1930: $37,510.84 owed March 8, 1932 per the Treasury Department.

May 1932: "A bill has recently been introduced in Congress to prohibit the importation of foreign motion picture stars. All future foreign stars, according to the proposed bill, must have merit and distinction to get in. Yet Garbo hadn't a nickel's worth of merit to her name for all the American films knew. And now look. And Dietrich's greatest successes were made in this Same land of the free. Marie Dressler was no great shakes as an actress in Canada. But she won the Academy prize just the Same."

May 10, 1932: The *Los Angeles Times*: "Even before Harold Lloyd finishes his current comedy, *Movie Crazy*, he is already thinking about his next production... he is strongly considering an original story by Hal Roach. In this story he would play the role of a young veterinary surgeon with all sorts of theories concerning his profession...."

May 27, 1932 Hal Roach to C.B. Wrightman, Standard Oil, Wichita, Kansas: "Received nine polo ponies from Chile... A great many of the Argentine ponies come from Chile and the prices there are about one-fourth the Argentine price... Margaret and I are leaving Sunday morning for a week with Wallace Beery and his wife at his cabin in the High Sierras."

July 29, 1932: Lew Maren to Thomas W. Gerety, MGM New York City: "Studio is still looking for beautiful, talented girls. Paulette Goddard was released due to her unwillingness to cooperate... Mr. Ginsberg informed me to eliminate all the old Chase photographs as his present series will reveal the comedian in an entirely new characterization."

This new characterization Charley was trying out was a milquetoast or "Nance" character who had decidedly "gay" or effeminate traits. There was more farce injected into these comedies, as well as gay humor, which was tolerated during the Pre-Code era of Hollywood. His 1930 short *Fast Work* had explored these facets; they were very pronounced in *Now We'll Tell One* and *Mr. Bride* ("one of his funniest comedies," according to Anthony and Edmonds). There were even elements of science fiction inserted into the new Charley Chase plots.

August 17, 1932 Henry Ginsburg to H.E. Roach, c/o Arthur Loew, Glen Cove, Long Island, New York: "[Elmer] Raguse is not in New York. He is with Fox Studios out here. I am communicating with him in an endeavor to get him back and start with us when we open."

August 30, 1932 Hal Roach to IRS: WESTERN UNION: IMPOSSIBLE FOR ME TO BORROW ANY MONEY FROM BANKS IN NEW YORK OR HERE CAN BORROW AN ADDITIONAL TEN THOUSAND DOLLARS FROM THE COMPANY ON MY SALARY STOP WOULD LIKE TO SUBMIT AS COMPROMISE THE FIVE THOUSAND YOU NOW HAVE AND ADDITIONAL TEN THOUSAND AS SETTLEMENT ASSURE YOU THAT I MADE A SINCERE EFFORT TO RAISE ADDITIONAL MONEY AND THAT LAWYER ASSURES ME THAT I WOULD BE CRIMINALLY LIABLE FOR ANY GREATER AMOUNT OF LOAN FROM CORPORATION...."

September 2, 1932: IRS WESTERN UNION: "RELATIVE YOUR TELEGRAM PROPOSED OFFER INADEQUATE CONFER WITH COLLECTOR."

1932: Lew Maren, Publicity Director. The previous August Miss Harriet Parsons, daughter of Louella O. Parsons the Hearst movie writer, started as a member of the publicity staff to write gags, humor and amusing feature material.

Also had issue with the Ohio Film Censor for Our Gang's *Hook and Ladder*. On September 12, 1932: Hal Roach wrote to Dr. B.O. Skinner, Director of Education, Division of Film Censorship, Columbus, Ohio: "Dear Sir: This is to certify that under no circumstances do the Hal Roach Studios, Inc., ever subject dumb animals to any cruelty during the filming of motion pictures, and particularly not in OUR GANG comedies. The animals have as much fun out of their work as do the children. This is a matter to which I personally give a great deal of attention, as my love for animals is such that I would not tolerate anything but the utmost care and considerate treatment when animals are used in our pictures."

For years Laurel and Hardy had been insulated from the world as they worked steadily at the Hal Roach Studios, unaware of the true extent of their popularity. In 1932, this all changed. That summer they went on a tour of Europe and huge crowds flocked to them wherever they went.

July 5, 1932: Dave Blum, MGM New York City to Stan Laurel and Oliver Hardy: "THE CUNARD LINE TO WHOM WE SELL PICTURES WOULD LIKE TO SHOW A LAUREL & HARDY COMEDY DURING YOUR TRIP ON AQUITANIA BUT WILL ONLY DO SO UPON WORD FROM YOU

THAT SUCH SHOWING WOULD NOT BE EMBARRASSING TO YOU STOP PLEASE WIRE ME YOUR WISHES IN THE MATTER"

Henry Ginsberg's reply, Same date: "IT IS OKEY FOR CUNARD LINE TO SHOW LAUREL AND HARDY COMEDY DURING THEIR TRIP STOP IF IT CAN BE ARRANGED THE BOYS WOULD LIKE EITHER THE COUNTY HOSPITAL OR THE MUSIC BOX THEIR MOST RECENT PICTURES SHOWN"

July 16, 1932 Ken Porter to T.W. Gerety: "Two weeks ago we placed life sized dummies of Laurel & Hardy in a haberdashery store window in Hollywood. So much attention did these figures draw that it became necessary for special police to disperse the crowds, as the store in question was next door to Warner Bros. Theatre and the usual crowd attending the Theatre was diverted to the comics."

Thomas W. Gerety, an MGM executive in New York City, wrote to Henry Ginsberg on July 18: "Well, we finally packed Laurel and Hardy off to Europe and things are comparatively normal once more. Following the small luncheon at which all the sales executives of our company were present, we held a couple of press interviews and spent the balance of the afternoon shooting newsreel footage of them seeing New York from Broadway in an open hack. It did not take New York more than thirty seconds to realize that Laurel and Hardy were in town. Times Square put on a mob act and made it almost impossible to do a thing... The way the mob turned out to see them the other afternoon, was the most amazing demonstration of their popularity that anyone could possibly ask for. Every member of the organization that had the pleasure of meeting them feels that they are a couple of regular fellows, and that they can have most anything they want...."

Lew Maren, Roach Publicity head, released the following on August 22, 1932:

"Laurel & Hardy... will arrive in Hollywood September 12th. A surprise welcome-home celebration is being planned by film stars and friends on the event of their sixth anniversary under the banner of the Hal Roach Studios. It was on September 20, 1926 that Laurel & Hardy were officially teamed together by Mr. Roach. Since then they have made more than forty short comedies and two feature length productions.

"Plans for the homecoming are being handled by Thelma Todd and ZaSu Pitts. The delegation will include the entire roster of Our Gang kids, Charley Chase, Dorothy Layton, Muriel Evans, Billy Gilbert, Ben Blue and other screenplayers."

On September 1st Gerety wrote to Ginsberg: "Laurel and Hardy arrived okay on the Paris yesterday... They told me that their trip has been a very hectic one in that they have been pursued continuously by representatives of the press, civic and theatrical officials and the entire population of several European countries. In spite of the fact that their trip afforded little recreation they feel that they have accomplished a great deal of good and I am sure that they have a much deeper and broader understanding of the appreciation that the public has for them. It should be an inspiration to them in the continuance of their work. I am sure that after they have had a few days of real rest after they return to California they will be in great shape and spirits to continue with their production plans...."

They returned all right, but not exactly in "great shape." A publicity release revealed "Stan Laurel put on fifteen pounds and Oliver Hardy added seventeen pounds to his weight while in Europe. Laurel is now on a buttermilk reducing diet." While their weights were up, their spirits dropped when they learned that the Hal Roach board of directors voted in a meeting on November 25, 1932 to suspend their contracts and salaries from July 10 to September 12, the period of their trip. Stan was docked $19,200 and Ollie $15,200. According to Richard Lewis Ward, "Relations between Roach and Laurel became so strained at this point that... Roach felt compelled to inform MGM of the very real possibility of a breakup of the team of Laurel and Hardy...."

But Felix Feist of MGM wired Roach "...WE CANNOT SUBSCRIBE TO ANY PLAN THAT WOULD BREAK UP THE TEAM AS IT WOULD INVALIDATE ALL PRESENT CONTRACTS AND IT WOULD IN OUR OPINION ALSO MEAN FOREGOING A VERY VITAL PART OF YOUR SETUP SO RECOMMEND YOUR DOING EVERYTHING NECESSARY TO MAINTAIN PRESENT STATUS OF TEAM AND WIRE US THAT SETUP IS TO CONTINUE."

The studio sang a different tune a year later:

May 1, 1933: Henry Ginsberg telegram to Mat O'Brien: "PLEASE ENDEAVOR COMMUNICATE LAUREL & HARDY TELL THEM METRO WOULD LIKE THEM MAKE APPEARANCES IN EAST FOR FOUR WEEK PERIOD FOR WHICH THEY WILL PAY FIVE THOUSAND PER WEEK RAILROAD AND HOTEL EXPENSES STOP THEY COULD USE THEIR RAG ACT AND METRO WOULD ALSO PAY FOR THIS ACT AEVISE [sic] AS SOON AS POSSIBLE WHETHER THEY WOULD CONSIDER ABOVE OFFER AND CONVEY TO

THEM THAT I WOULD LIKE VERY MUCH TO HAVE THEM DO THIS IF AT ALL PRACTICAL. REGARDS"

The reply came three weeks later: May 22, 1933: Mat O'Brien to Henry Ginsberg: "HARDY DESIROUS TRIP PANAMA RETURNING HERE JUNE ELEVENTH... LAUREL AND HARDY NOT IN FAVOR OF PERSONAL APPEARANCES VERY MUCH THANKS FOR OFFER"

"Women chased them all over the place," says Roach, "so when they came home, Laurel fancied himself a real ladies' man. He had a beautiful home in Beverly Hills, and a lovely wife, but she divorced him and he started running around with punks."

According to Randy Skretvedt in his book *Laurel & Hardy The Magic Behind the Movies*, Roach considered Stan's divorce from his first wife Lois "the tragedy of Laurel's life....She handled him beautifully; she was also his agent. When I made a financial deal with Laurel, I made the deal with her, not with Stan. If there was anything at the studio that was wrong, she was the one who came to me. I tried to talk her out of the divorce, but she said, 'Hal, it's not worth it.' So that was that."

"As I said before," Roach explained to me, "Laurel was the greatest gag man, but he was the worst when it came to story construction. His concept of story construction was just damned childish. And when he came back from this tour, he became more and more difficult to work with. On the set of *Fra Diavolo* he resented the fact that Dennis King, the operatic star, had the lead, and was constantly insulting him."

But at least Laurel's failings were overlooked by the rest of the film community, for in November 1932 The Academy of Motion Pictures Arts and Sciences awarded a certificate to Laurel & Hardy's three-reel classic, *The Music Box* as Best Short Subject (Comedy) for 1931-32.

The Music Box "takes a simple laboring job (two men carry a piano up a long flight of stairs), and makes it a perfect little epic of monotonous futility, ornamented with odd little lyrical moments...." observed Raymond Durgnat in his study of film comedy, *The Crazy Mirror*. "It's the myth of Sisyphus in comic terms, a little hymn to the uselessness of work, a study in absurdity."

What is not generally known is that the Academy did not simply view *The Music Box* and declare it a great short. There wasn't even a category for Best Short Subject until the latter part of 1932. On July 5th Henry Ginsberg had written to Mike Levee at the Academy of Motion Pictures Arts and Sciences, "Would it not be in keeping with the Academy's purpose to include in your yearly awards some token of recognition for the accomplishments of the comedy and short subject producer, player, writer and director?"

Apparently the Academy thought that to be an excellent idea and they subsequently sent a letter to the various studios months before the Awards ceremony stating: "All producers of short subjects to submit product for consideration for recognition in the annual Awards of Merit program of the Academy. List should be sent by October 18, 1932 for subjects of 3,000 feet or less first publicly exhibited in the Los Angeles District during the year ending July 31, 1932."

"Recognition of the importance of the short comedy in motion picture entertainment by the Academy of Motion Pictures Arts and Sciences," wrote Ginsberg, "will in the final analysis, immeasurably benefit the theatre and its patrons. The annual awards will act as an incentive for producers, directors and players to strive for greater perfection in their respective fields… When it is considered that the short comedy constitutes at least forty percent of a motion picture theatre's performance, the significance and importance of this type of entertainment can not be questioned. The Academy's recognition is progressive, vital, stimulating. It will serve as an impetus toward the creation and the production of more novel and entertaining short attractions. And the sum and substance of it all will inevitably benefit the theatre and its patrons."

July 21, 1932: Academy of Motion Pictures Arts and Sciences letter to Henry Ginsberg: Invitation to become an Associate member of the Producers branch of the Academy. Dues $1.00 per month. $15.00 initiation fee.

August 15, 1932 Fred Quimby telegram to Ginsberg: "HAVE DIFFICULTY GETTING CAPITOL THEATRE NEW YORK USE LAUREL HARDY MUSIC BOX ACCOUNT LENGTH PICTURE RUNS THIRTY MINUTES HOWEVER THEY WILL USE IT PROVIDING YOU WILL GIVE US AUTHORITY CUT PICTURE TO TWENTY MINUTES WHICH I THINK CAN BE DONE WITHOUT HARM TO PICTURE YOUR CUTTER COULD GIVE US INSTRUCTIONS HOW TO CUT PICTURE REGARDS"

Henry Ginsberg responded the same day: "APPROVE CUTTING MUSIC BOX FOR CAPITOL RUN. CUTTER SUGGESTS REEL ONE—ELIMINATE FROM SCENE 32 TO END… REEL TWO OPEN AS IS… RUN TO TITLE THAT AFTERNOON SCENE 27 AND CUT AT TITLE… PICK UP AT SCENE 43 AND CONTINUE THEN CUT AFTER HARDY EXITS AND ELIMINATE TO SCENE 22 INCLUSIVE STOP PICK UP AT SCENE 23 AND CONTINUE AS IS TOTAL ELIMINATION 734 FEET"

October 13, 1932 telegram Fred C. Quimby to Henry Ginsberg: "OUR OPINION NICKEL NURSER, PAJAMA PARTY CHOO CHOO OR SPANKY STOP REGARDING LAUREL HARDY HARD TO DECIDE BETWEEN COME CLEAN ANY OLD PORT MUSIC BOX"

October 17, 1932: Hal Roach Studios submits *Music Box*, L&H; *Nickel Nurser*, CC; *Pajama Party* Pitts-Todd; *Spanky*, Our Gang.

Meanwhile, the Our Gang series had reached its tenth anniversary by 1932. Director since its inception, Robert McGowan, reckoned more than 100,000 kids had been interviewed during that time and about thirty-seven youngsters had enjoyed the distinction so far. "One in approximately 3,000 kiddies has a chance of becoming a film rascal" stated a release. On February 11, 1932 the *Our Gang* short *Free Eats* premiered, notable for the first screen appearance of three-year-old George McFarland, better known as "Spanky." The little boy's Aunt Dottie in Texas had noticed a trade magazine advertisement from Hal Roach Studios in Culver City, California, requesting photographs of "cute kids," so she sent pictures of her nephew. The response was an invitation to make a screen test, which was so favorable that portions of it were included in Spanky's screen 1932 *Our Gang* entry, aptly entitled *Spanky* released on March 26th. Spanky became an instant star.

June 20, 1932: "With a sudden display of temperament upon his introduction to Mary Pickford, little 'Spanky'... was told by the famous star that he would never be a Jackie Cooper. 'I don't wanta be Jackie Cooper, I wanta be 'Spanky' was the wee gangster's reply."

August 1, 1932 Bob McGowan claims he filmed forty-seven scenes in *Free Wheeling*—a record for one Our Gang short. The previous record was thirty scenes.

August 29, 1932: "DID YOU KNOW THAT... Mary Pickford's favorite actor is four-year-old Spanky, member of Our Gang kids?"

September 5, 1932: Dickie Moore and Spanky had a spat and refused to work together. For the first time in twelve years of handling the Gang kids, McGowan was forced to use a "double" for Spanky. The kid quarrel was patched up by *Birthday Bliss* when McGowan brought around a big birthday cake for Jacquie Lyn. Jacquie was the little girl being cared for by Laurel & Hardy in *Pack Up Your Troubles*. *Birthday Bliss* was her only appearance with the Gang. In fact, it was her last movie and she completely disappeared from the public eye for the next sixty years. Jacquie was rediscovered by the Sons of the Desert because of a home movie taken by Stan Laurel which Jacquie playing with Stan's daughter Lois. The brief film was featured on a video that Jacquie's son had purchased for her in the early 1990s. In the introduction to this video, Lois asked the whereabouts of Jacquie, and the long-retired child actress contacted the address given in the video and was ultimately reunited with Lois. She subsequently became an honored guest at the 1992 Sons of the Desert convention in Las Vegas, where she finally got to re-meet her former boss. Jacquie passed away in 2002 at the age of seventy-three.

September 23, 1932 Hal Roach Studios letter to Captain James B. Dickson:

"Dear Sir, Your employment with this corporation is terminated this day, at your request, to permit you to accept an engagement with Mr. Arthur Loew and to act as his pilot with him on his foreign trip."

The same day Dickson signed an agreement "in consideration of your lending me your aeroplane for use on my foreign trip, I agree to indemnify you against and hold harmless from any and all liability claims, demands, judgment suits... I agree to return the plane to you on in as good order and condition as it is delivered to me, ordinary wear and tear excepted, at or about the middle of December, 1932."

"The Spirit of Fun" was transported from Los Angeles to Sydney, Australia aboard the S.S. *Monterey*, disembarking on October 13th. From there, Dickson, Loew and Loew's friend attorney Joseph Rosthal began an incredible journey from Australia to Singapore, Bangkok, Hanoi, Shanghai, Mandalay...

October 23, 1932 Arthur Loew telegram to Hal Roach: "FLIGHT INDESCRIBABLE MAKING HISTORY IMAGINE AUSTRALIA TO SHANGHAI FIVE DAYS ACTUALLY THIRTY TWO HOURS IN AIR STOPPING FIVE IMPORTANT CITIES EN ROUTE PACKED FULL EDUCATION BEAUTY LAUGHS THRILLS GLORIOUS RECEPTIONS NAKED CHILDREN HALF NAKED WOMEN KIND BUT FILTHY NATIVES EXTRAORDINARY SINGING DANCES IF THIS IS BUSINESS BRING ON MORE WORK LOVE AND ALL ARTHUR"

By November 3rd they were flying over Bombay, India and crossed the breadth of India to Calcutta in one nonstop flight which was a first time record. From Karachi, then to Basra, then Bagdad. On November 9th they were over Assuan, Egypt and mid-November landed in Capetown, South Africa. By the time they had reached Johannesburg they had traveled 18,000 miles in seven weeks, often traveling at 200 miles per hour.

"Business was the real object of the youthful director of the Metro-Goldwyn-Mayer Corporation in making this world tour," reported a newspaper article, "and he arrived in Johannesburg in time to be present at the opening of the company's new theatre there. 'We are not out to break records,' he told an interviewer, 'but we can't hold the machine back.'"

"These American travelers in the course of their world tour had in seven days seen seven of the world's most famous rivers—Ganges, Indus, Tigris, Euphrates, Jordan, Nile, Zambes; and it was their desire to add the Victoria Falls to their list of world spectacles… If the present trip had been completed 'The Spirit of Fun' would have toured every continent in the world within one calendar year."

But the present trip was not completed. On the afternoon of November 17, 1932 shortly after taking off from Victoria Falls, the motor failed (later determined to be due to the high altitude and unexpectedly thin oxygen in that region). The plane clipped the top of some trees, turned three somersaults and crashed to the ground. Killed by a broken neck was pilot Dickson. Only slightly injured but suffering from shock were the passengers Arthur Loew and Joseph Rosthal.

"Loew's Life Saved By Heroic Pilot," reported the *International News Service*. "Although he lost his own life in the accident, Dickson probably saved Arthur Loew, American film magnate, and Joseph Rosthal of New York from death or serious injury when their plane crashed at Victoria Falls, it was learned today. Captain Dickson, who was piloting the plane in which Loew was making a world tour, cut the switch when he saw that a crash was inevitable. The pilot was catapulted from his seat into the whirling propeller and was almost decapitated, but Loew and Rosthal escaped with slight bruises."

Dickson was six days shy of his 32nd birthday. He left behind a young and pregnant wife. He was buried in South Africa with a Rhodesian military funeral.

Fred Quimby wrote to Hal Roach: "Yesterday when we learned about Jimmy Dickson's death it was a terrible shock to everyone, and there was a genuine feeling of sadness throughout the Home Office. Jimmy's lovable character won him many admirers and friends here, and from the many splendid comments that I heard it seems as though everyone in the organization knew him. Felix Feist was very much upset when he heard about the accident, and the same thing was true with me. I can understand how badly you must feel, and I wanted you to know we regret the loss of such a fine fellow."

Hal Roach wrote to Dickson's parents in Evanston, Illinois: "I join with you in sorrow for one of the grandest men I have ever known, your son."

Dickson's father replied, "Dear Mr. Roach, we greatly appreciate your kind sympathy and your expression of your high estimate of our son who has been a loved and valued member of our family circle. His association with you was a joy to him and added much to the pleasure of his work."

On November 28, 1932 Hal Roach received a letter from Dickson's widow Margaret. "I shall always be glad that James had two years of wonderful experiences with you. He was so happy with you and enjoyed your companionship and admired you so greatly. I wouldn't have had his life otherwise... I hope this experience of James' does not in any way spoil your pleasure in flying. I am so sure we go when our time comes anyway."

December 6, 1932 Postal Telegraph Hal Roach to Arthur Loew SS *Warwick Castle* en route to Southampton, England: "LOVELY BABY GIRL ARRIVED MRS. DICKSON AT GOOD SAMARITAN HOSPITAL."

Hal Roach and Arthur Loew made arrangements so that she received financial assistance for several years to come. And Roach continued to fly.

Meanwhile, life went on at the Hal Roach Studios:

October 5, 1932: Lew Maren to T.W. Gerety: "Director James Parrott has been eliminated from the list [of studio employees]. Some friction between the director and the studio, and his chances being given an assignment is problematical."

November 26, 1932: A brush fire swept through the Hal Roach Ranch and destroyed several sets and "prop" automobiles.

"John Hill, a watchman at the ranch, was painfully burned about the head and arms in aiding firemen to halt the flames," a newspaper reported. "He was taken to the University Hospital in Culver City. The fire reached the Roach property shortly after noon and burned for about three hours before it was extinguished... the loss probably would reach several thousand dollars."

Harvard School, Hal Roach Jr.: December 16, 1932: English C, Spanish D (Lack of diligence and effort), Ancient History C, Algebra B, Military Record, B.

December 1932: Problems with the tax man. IRS claims he owes $50,000 back income tax. Roach responded: "First: The salary of $1,500.00 which is now my sole income, belongs half to Mrs. Roach, on which she has in the past paid the income tax and which is turned over to her every week. Therefore, my weekly salary is actually $750.00 instead of $1,500.00.

"Second: I am under no contract to the Hal Roach Studios, a corporation which has made no money for the past three years and the salary is subject to change at any time and can only be paid while the studio is in operation which, in this particular year will probably be 40 weeks." He requests a payment plan.

December 1932: Walnuts sent to all executives of MGM New York City. What—no hard boiled eggs?

December 17, 1932 Robert Lynch, MGM Pennsylvania to Hal Roach: "I just received the box of nuts, for which kindly accept my sincere thanks. In view of the fact that the film business is driving the average exchange man nutty nowadays, I am wondering if you sent those nuts to help the good work along...."

December 21, 1932 Morton Spring, MGM New York City to Hal Roach: "Was mortified when an expressman walked into my office and said, 'Nuts to you, sir.' However, after closer examination I saw that he meant nothing personal but was delivering a package from you. Up to the time of the receipt of your package, 'nuts' only played a certain part in my life but now the cook is trying to use them up in a hurry and I get them in everything except the soup."

1933 RELEASES:
SEVEN CHARLEY CHASE TWO-REELERS
SIX OUR GANG TWO REELER
SIX TAXI BOYS TWO-REELERS
FIVE LAUREL & HARDY TWO-REELERS
FOUR TODD & PITTS TWO-REELERS
THREE TODD & PATSY KELLY TWO-REELERS
TWO LAUREL & HARDY FEATURES

FRA DIAVOLO, Laurel & Hardy's first Comic Operetta:
January 1933 contracts:
Thelma Todd $1,000 per week
Henry Armetta, Innkeeper, $700 per week
James Finlayson $600 per week
Lucille Brown, Zerlena, $150 per week
January 30, 1933: Thelma Todd is recovering from an auto accident. Slight fracture of her shoulder and rib and abrasions of the left hand.

February 13, 1933: Thelma Todd "has recovered sufficiently... to report to Hal Roach Studios to portray the role of Lady Pamela in the comic opera Fra Diavolo."

Nineteen thirty-three was a tough year for Hollywood. It was the depths of the Depression.

February 4, 1933: Henry Ginsberg letter to Dave Loew, New York City: "Things are surely happening in the business. From the outlook it appears that many changes will take place out here. The receiverships and reorganizations taking place will no doubt make for a better business. I hope so, anyway."

On March 8, 1933 the Academy of Motion Pictures Arts and Sciences issued an Emergency Resolution: "...in view of the National banking emergency, unless immediate and radical steps are taken on the part of all employees, all the studio... and other activities of the companies will have to be suspended at once and for an indefinite period. The facts presented were so serious as to justify the assertion of the producers that without the acceptance by all employees of substantial cuts in salaries, effective March 6, 1933, and continuing for a period of eight weeks, the payrolls can no longer be met. The producers propose that all salaries above $50 per week be reduced 50 percent with a minimum pay of $37.50 per week; all salaries of $50 and under be reduced 25 percent with a minimum pay of $15 per week. In view of the fact that the only alternative to the cut appears clearly to be the cessation of all motion picture activities of all kinds... by all studios, the Board of Directors of the Academy recommends to all its members and other employees that they accept the proposal and give it their wholehearted support."

Understandably, a large number of workers resented the imposition of pay cuts, no matter what the reason, and there was labor unrest in Hollywood.

The Pinkerton's National Detective Agency, Inc. sent a report "dealing with Communist conditions as they pertain to the motion picture industry" directed to Henry Ginsberg on March 15, 1933: "Joseph M. Casey, a local representative of AFL theatrical superintendent sent a letter to John Spaulding of the Theatrical Workers Union of the AFL "who is a Communist sympathizer" stating that "the motion picture owners of the nation took advantage of the banking holiday to put the workers of the industry in an unfavorable light and the workers' side of the controversy has not been correctly presented... Casey claims that after a survey of the entire situation, he has found that half billion or more dollars were taken in at the box office of the theatres during 1931, while the pictures shown at the theatres represent a cost of only one hundred fifty million dollars. Casey asks...what has happened to the money, since the studios get only

13 cents on the dollar that goes into the box office, which would amount to $195,000,000. He also says… if the studios spent only $150,000,000 during this period, there should be a profit of $45,000,000 somewhere, but instead there are only large deficits.

Casey concluded that it is up to organized labor to find out where the money went to and if necessary a federal investigation will be requested…."

March 20, 1933 Henry Ginsberg letter: "Since the reopening of the banks and the activities of Roosevelt it appears that there is a little more confidence around. Things have been rather hectic on the coast for the past few weeks, although they are beginning to have a brighter outlook."

Back in February 1933 Henry Ginsberg wrote to Arthur Loew: "During our summer close it was [Hal Roach's] thought to go to Europe with a view to finding a good French or English comic. Instead of making tests he figured on taking along a writer and assistant director, getting together both French and English comics who he might otherwise test and instead make two comedies abroad. From these we could then determine their talents and at the Same time produce two subjects that might have commercial value in the foreign market."

March 29, 1933: Lew Maren to Gerety: "The last L&H comedy 'The Best Man' has been changed to ME AND MY PAL. The boys posed for 12 negatives on this comedy, and agreed to do some special stuff in the gallery in order to meet the stipulated number of stills with each production. I expect to get this material tomorrow, if kidding and ribbing comics can be depended upon to keep their word…."

April 4, 1933: Lew Maren to T. Gerety: "Babe Hardy has taken a powder. His promise to pose for additional stills for 'Me and My Pal' is like a thousand others. He scrams, forgets appointments, and then alibis. I could tell you plenty, but the point is that there isn't a chance of getting the stills. Stan is marvelous, and regrets he can't do anything about it…."

April 21, 1933: Gerety to Maren: "While the stills on the Laurel & Hardy subject are for the most part quite similar and devoid of action I think we can get by with them in view of your difficulties in getting additional stills."

In April 1933 it seems everyone was going on vacation: Bob McGowan left for Europe for six weeks. In London Roach signed English comedians Douglas Wakefield and Billy Nelson to long term contracts. He wrote that audiences abroad still like slapstick comedy. He also hired Jack Barty, who became most memorable as Mae Busch's insane butler in the 1934 short *Oliver the Eighth*. Thelma Todd also went to London for two months for

British International Pictures after completing eight comedies with ZaSu Pitts. Oliver Hardy planned a trip to Havana. Stan went fishing off Catalina, then decided to head up the Pacific Coast to Victoria, British Columbia. Charley Chase stated he would go to the desert, changed his mind and went to London, Paris and Berlin instead. Spanky McFarland and Tommy Bond returned to their respective homes in Dallas, Texas. It was noted that Dickie Moore, Stymie, Echo and Pete the Dog would be stay-at-homes.

April 22, 1933 Henry Ginsberg letter regarding a boy not given work at Hal Roach Studios: "My work here is a great deal more important than preventing personalities from playing in our pictures. All people who in any small way meet with our requirements are given an opportunity, as we are more anxious to find personalities than we are to discourage them."

April 1933: Telegram: "MISS PITTS IS NOT INTERESTED IN THE DEAL AS OUTLINED IN YOUR LETTER OF APRIL 22ND HOWEVER SHE ASKS ME TO THANK YOU FOR OFFER"

In April 1933 Billy Gilbert was hired for the role of Spike in Production #475 for $300 per week less twenty percent on loan from Sennett Pictures Corp. for one week.

Quite puzzling is the June 29, 1933 letter from Harry De Shon of the Edward Small Agency sent to Henry Ginsberg: "This will announce the availability of H.M. (Beanie) Walker, who has just returned to Hollywood after completing a world tour. Before going abroad he completed the adaptation and dialogue of 'Salt Water' and the dialogue on 'They Just Had To Get Married' for Universal. Will you kindly communicate with us if you are interested in his services?"

What? This is the one and only "Beanie" Walker who was associated with Roach from the early silent days and was one of the main members of his staff for many years. Why couldn't Beanie himself just have picked up the phone, called his former boss directly and said, "Hal, I'm back in town. I'm ready to return to the studio?"

And on November 2, 1933 Jack E. Gardner, Agent, sent this letter to Henry Ginsberg: "Ed Kennedy is starring on his second six-picture two reel contract at RKO, and having lots of time between pictures is available for directing."

And on December 13, 1933 agent Dave Kay wrote to Ginsberg: "May I respectfully submit the name of Anita Garvin who I believe you know very well. I would greatly appreciate you considering the above person in your coming pictures." Agents for Shemp Howard and Jimmy Durante also offered their clients' services, to little avail.

Perhaps the strangest solicitation of an actor to the Hal Roach Studios at this time was from Jim Crosby of Frazee Motion Picture Technical Research Laboratories in Hollywood. On July 25, 1933 he sent the following letter to the Hal Roach Studios: "If you want a good bet in a comedian, Stan Laurel's brother Ted is your man. He is a very versatile comedian and I think that he is one of the best light comedians in the game; why not try him out...."

There is no letter indicating what the response was, but a few days later, on August 2, 1933 came another letter addressed to Henry Ginsberg this time from Edwin Frazee, apparently the owner of the Frazee Motion Picture Technical Research Laboratories: "Am sorry that Stan Laurel has taken the stand he has, as I am most interested as I produced his first motion picture, and it is not fair to Hall [sic] who has been the means of his steady climb... Ted Jefferson, the undisputed brother of Stan, who in my estimation is a better comedian and more versatile... He does not wish to succeed through the use of the name that Stan is useing [sic] so has decided to use his own name, 'Ted Jefferson' and not Laurel."

In any event, there is also a letter Frazee sent to William Koenig, General Manager of Warner Bros.: "I take great pleasure in introducing Ted Laurel, brother of Stan, of the team of Laurel and Hardy. Although Ted wishes to use his own name, Jefferson, to make his progress, and is not asking nor wishing to climb on Stan's name...."

Koenig sent this letter to Hal Roach with the note: "Enclosed is a letter which you might find very interesting. Maybe you can use him for a double." But not for long. In December 1933 the unfortunate Edward "Teddy" Everett Jefferson died from a heart attack at the dentist's office following an intake of laughing gas for a tooth extraction. He was thirty two.

May 15, 1933: Bob McGowan: "People never grow up. They just get a little smarter, and don't get any sense until they're over thirty-five."

May 22, 1933: Henry Ginsberg: "Unfortunately, this studio being so small, I find myself with at least ten people who ordinarily should be eliminated but who must be kept on the payroll. I have tried every possible way to eliminate this condition but it is somewhat beyond my control and I hesitate to further encourage it."

The following telegram illustrates that Henry Ginsberg was not such a villain. In fact, it appears he saved the Our Gang series from cancellation in 1933:

May 24, 1933 Western Union Henry Ginsberg to Bob McGowan, Astor Hotel, New York City: "WHILE I WAS IN NEW YORK SELLING DE-

PARTMENT WAS MOST INSISTENT THAT GANG BE ELIMINATED THIS WAS MOST DISCOURAGING TO ME AND I FINALLY GOT THEM TO ACCEPT AT LEAST SIX SUBJECTS NEXT YEAR STOP I BELIEVE IT MOST IMPORTANT THAT YOU SPEND SOME TIME WITH QUIMBY AND GET ALL POSSIBLE SUGGESTIONS AND IDEAS SO THAT WE CAN FEEL ASSURED THAT THE FIRST GANG MADE NEXT YEAR IS A TYPE SATISFACTORY AND WITH THE POSSIBILITY OF REVIVING THE SERIES I SUGGEST THIS TO YOU FOR OUR MUTUAL BENEFIT."

In early July 1933 Henry Ginsberg announced that more than $1,600,000 would be spent by the Hal Roach Studios during the current year in producing forty-four shorts and two feature-length features.

Scores of actors and actresses will be used," it was reported in the *Los Angeles Examiner* of July 2nd, "and the production program will necessitate the hiring of 1000 skilled craftsmen. Six different units now are preparing material for production.

"Laurel and Hardy will make six short films; Charley Chase is scheduled to direct and star in eight comedies; Thelma Todd and Patsy Kelly will also appear in eight comedies; Our gang, directed by Robert McGowan, will be in six comedies.

"Six musical comedy subjects, with Billy Bletcher and Billy Gilbert, will be produced. Douglas Wakefield and Billy Nelson, London music hall favorites, will appear in ten comedies, in which they will be featured with Don Barclay, former Ziegfeld Follies comedian.

"Writers now on the Hal Roach staff are Royal King Cole, Frank Terry and Stanley Rauh."

Meanwhile, the labor problems of earlier in the year did not go away. On July 22, 1933 Pinkerton reports: "Columbia Pictures Sound Department strikers are being infiltrated by...Communist organizers... The Theatrical Workers Union of the Trade Union Unity League through the John Reed Club Organizers... are now being prepared to spread the strike in other studios unless the agreement is signed...."

A July 25, 1933 letter from the Nick Harris Detectives to Personnel Manager, Hal Roach Studios: "Appreciating the fact that you may need the assistance of my organization during the acute labor emergency... I feel privileged at this time to make you a very generous offer in supplying guards, under-cover operators, peace officers, non-technical men of any and all descriptions as well as a high type of personal body guards to accompany Studio Executives or shadow them with or without cars."

On July 26, 1933 *The Wall Street Journal* headline ran "STUDIOS FIGHT STRIKE... The walkout of 665 sound technicians at midnight Saturday is seriously affecting operations of the various motion picture studios involved. Some 30,000 employes [sic] will be out of work unless the strike can be overcome.

"Studios are advertising for additional sound technicians to take the place of the striking union men.

"The studios affected include Warner Bros., Metro-Goldwyn-Mayer, Universal, Educational, R.-K.-O., Paramount, Fox, Hal Roach, United Artists, Harold Lloyd Corp. and Columbia Pictures."

That same day another letter from Nick Harris Detectives: "Informant reports: 'The strike picketing authorized by the Executive Committee of the Communist Party today was in full operation, concentrating their efforts to create a general tie-up of the entire motion picture industry...the aim of the Communist Party is to fight the Recovery Act to a finish because the act is in favor of the Capitalist class and not in favor of the Workers... Every union of the AFL having to do with studio employees, and the International Brotherhood of Electrical employees, are composed of at least 20% of Communist members and many of whom are so-called under cover Communist agitators. In every craft union of the AF of L the membership of these unions has at least 10% of the union membership composed of Trade Union Unity League members. The Trade Union Unity League is a subsidiary of the Communist Party and the Communist Party membership in Los Angeles and suburbs reaches the 60,000 mark."

August 2, 1933: Henry Ginsberg to David Loew: "We have had a few hectic weeks here due to the strike. We have been working, however, for the past week, using a non-Union crew and doing the best we can under the circumstances. I personally feel that the strike situation will be cleaned up within the next two weeks...."

Fortunately the situation calmed down by the late summer of 1933 and all those under-cover agents and bodyguards became unnecessary. It was business as unusual once again.

August 31, 1933 Postal Telegraph Bob McGowan to Norman McLeod, Paramount Studios: "UNDERSTAND JEAN DARLING IS BEING CONSIDERED FOR ALICE IN WONDERLAND JEAN IS A CLEVER LITTLE GIRL AND HAS HAD EXTENSIVE VAUDEVILLE EXPERIENCE WAS OKAY WITH ME UNTIL SHE GREW UP IF POSSIBLE GIVE KID BREAK. REGARDS"

Nearly 7,000 girls auditioned for the coveted role of Alice. Eighty years later, Jean Darling, who had appeared in the Our Gang comedies from 1927 to 1929, was still disgruntled about it. "I had the part of Alice, dressed like Alice, publicity as Alice," the ninety-one year old Miss Darling wrote to the author in November 2013, "and still didn't get the contract!"

Paramount decided to bypass Bob McGowan's suggestion of Jean Darling and to star an unknown girl named Charlotte Henry. Well, that was Paramount Pictures, and Mr. McGowan obviously had little influence there. It is interesting to note that when the Hal Roach Studios made *Babes In Toyland* the following year, it was NOT Jean Darling who played Bo-Peep but—Charlotte Henry. At least Miss Darling did appear in that movie, as the character Curly Locks, though she was uncredited.

September 28, 1933 *Los Angeles Examiner*: "Hal Roach, cinema tycoon, yesterday had a meeting of Los Angeles business and social leaders at the Biltmore, at which time he outlined plans for the formation of the Southern California Jockey Club, a program calling for 400 memberships at $5000 each on a profit-sharing basis... Roach has the inside track if he can put over his altruistic project. He seems optimistic about his outlook, despite conditions and times, and says that the response has been favorable."

Among the celebrities who contributed $5000 to the formation of the new racetrack were Joseph Schenck, Oliver Hardy, Darryl Zanuck, Harold Lloyd, his old partner from the Rolin days Dwight Whiting, A.P. Giannini of Bank of America, director Frank Borzage, who had known Roach since the days they were both extras back in 1914, actor Robert Montgomery, Chico Marx and Arthur Loew.

It took over a year of wheeling and dealing, but when Roach and San Francisco dentist Dr. Charles H. Strub united to form the Los Angeles Turf Club they were able to bankroll the construction at a cost of a million and a quarter dollars and preside over the opening of the beautiful Santa Anita Racetrack in Arcadia, California in December 1934. Santa Anita Park, which occupies 320 acres and has a grandstand that seats 26,000 is still going strong eight decades later.

In 1933 Mack Sennett, Roach's long time rival was finally forced out of the business and numerous letters, some rather pathetic, flooded the Hal Roach Studios from actors and other motion picture veterans seeking work.

Including a few former Roach employees. In May 1933 the Affiliated Credit Exchange Collection presented a claim against Mickey Daniels for $25.00.

"He has ignored our correspondence, and has failed to indicate any intention of paying this balance." The studios wrote back, "His contract expired April 23, 1932 and since that time he has worked for the Hal Roach Studios only as an extra actor or on a time basis as an actor... October 15 to 22, 1932."

Another boy met with an unfortunate fate that October of 1933. In an incident eerily reminiscent of Harold Lloyd's tragic accident of fourteen years earlier, but even worse. Fourteen-year-old George Alexander was wandering "a film battle field" apparently owned by the Hal Roach Studios [at his Ranch?], found a prop bomb on the ground and picked it up. It exploded, and he completely lost his right hand. A lawsuit in the amount of $100,000 was filed against the Studio; however, Superior Judge Elliott Craig "ordered the jury to return a directed verdict in favor of the Hal Roach Studios, Inc."

August 26, 1933 Henry Ginsberg to David Loew: "We have engaged William Seiter, who has done some good work, to direct [the next feature, Sons of the Desert]. We are quite enthusiastic about the story and also about Seiter, and I think we will really turn out a good feature."

Mae Busch contract September 27, 1933 for the role of Oliver Hardy's wife, Prod. F-4 [Sons of the Desert] $350 per week to being October 2, 1933 for not less than one week

Dorothy Christy signed October 3, 1933 as Stan Laurel's wife for $500 per week

David Bennett, Dance Director, $350 per week

October 19, 1933 Henry Ginsberg to Arthur Loew: "This week we have shipped to New York the first picture of the All Star Series. This is one of the three pictures made thus far and featuring the English comedians, Douglas Wakefield, Billy Nelson and Jack Barty. I personally believe their popularity in England should greatly benefit the playing time and rentals of those subjects in which they appear. If you are of the Same impression would you be good enough to call this matter to the attention of the British offices so that we may receive full benefit from their box office value abroad."

October 20, 1933 Arthur Loew to Hal Roach: "From all indications, FRA DIAVOLO will gross somewhere between $750,000 and $1,000,000. I thought that it would be wise for you to know this in the event that it would be possible to include some music in their new feature. Of course the music must fit in properly with the story and must not be just thrown in."

October 26, 1933: Henry Ginsberg: "Next month I celebrate my second year as a Californian. We love the living here and I am very happy in my work."

1934 RELEASES:
NINE CHARLEY CHASE TWO-REELERS
NINE TODD & KELLY TWO-REELERS
EIGHT OUR GANG TWO-REELERS
SEVEN MUSICAL TWO-REELERS
FOUR LAUREL & HARDY TWO-REELERS
THREE IRVIN S. COBB TWO-REELERS (PLUS ONE UNRELEASED)
ONE LAUREL & HARDY FEATURE

As January 1934 would mark the twentieth anniversary of Hal Roach's career as a motion picture producer, he decided to throw a lavish party at his studio on December 7, 1933. The guest list included 400 of Hollywood's leading luminaries. "It started as a dinner, turned into a dance, and concluded with a vaudeville revue," stated the *Los Angeles Examiner*.

There was a national radio hook up to capture the speeches headed by Will Rogers. It was noted that a young up and coming cartoon producer, Walt Disney, was there, attending his first Hollywood party.

"Louis B. Mayer, head of Metro-Goldwyn-Mayer, particularly lauded Roach's achievements and value in the film industry. In response to all this tribute from high places, Mr. Roach in turn gave credit to such screen luminaries as Laurel and Hardy, Thelma Todd, Charlie [sic] Chase and Patsy Kelly for much of his success."

December 11, 1933: Letter from Henry Ginsberg: "We had a lovely party here last week in celebration of Roach's 20th anniversary as a comedy producer. A good time was had by all and we now contemplate cutting the salaries of some of the help in order to offset the expense of the party."

Hundreds of distinguished guests celebrated Roach's twenty years as a movie producer; several bands performed, ten MGM police officers, twelve "special policemen" and three uniformed firemen protected the partygoers, and six bartenders kept them all happy. The event was broadcast on radio and Charley Chase made an amusing speech:

"When I first joined Mr. Roach it was supposed to have been for one picture. I have just finished my fourteenth year. As the comics say, 'I knew it wouldn't be permanent.' However, Mr. Roach is the best boss I ever had; in fact, the longest and dumbest, as the others always got wise to me in about two weeks."

"At about this time I went to New York to buy *Babes in Toyland*," Roach explained to me in 1973. "On the train coming back, I rewrote the story to center it around Laurel and Hardy. The antagonist is this giant spider who has a Rube Goldberg-type apparatus, with tubes and things that extracts liquids of Love and Hate. Stan was to be 'Simple Simon' and Ollie, of course, 'the Pieman.'

From May to June 1934 Hal Roach traveled to Alaska aboard the luxury yacht owned by New York financier E.F. Hutton for a bear hunting expedition. The papers reported that he returned from Alaska "brown, fit and smiling" via United Airlines, having bagged "two grizzlies and four black bears." A couple of months later he was all set to fly off to New York in his new airplane when he was forced to enter the hospital for an appendectomy. Two days later his wife and daughter were injured in automobile smash up. Fortunately their injuries were minor.

Irvin S. Cobb (1876-1944) was a prolific American author and columnist from Kentucky. He wrote popular stories about the rural folk who lived in the countryside of the Good Ole U.S.A. in the late 19th century. He was also a newspaper reporter and covered some major world events such as the Russian-Japanese Peace Conference for the *New York Evening Sun*. His reporting about World War I for the *New York World* made him the highest-paid staff writer in the United States. He authored more than 300 short stories, several of which were made into silent films. In his fiction Cobb was a homely homespun literary populist in the tradition of Mark Twain. There was a bit of the ham in him, so he was not averse to acting, coming across as a sort of country cousin to the likes of W.C. Fields. He was also a friend of Will Rogers, and so Cobb's talents made him a perfect fit for the Hal Roach Studios. Or so it was presumed.

Roach tried. Cobb was paid $5,000 a week – more than any other actor on the lot, according to Randy Skretvedt. Stan Laurel was making $3,500 per week and both Oliver Hardy and Hal Roach earned $2,000 per week at that time. Four Irvin S. Cobb shorts were produced for the 1934-35 season. The first one was *The Ballad of Paducah Jail*, based on one of Cobb's own stories, and was released on October 20, 1934. "The

Cobb series [slated to be comprised of six shorts] was so unpopular with exhibitors," wrote Richard Lewis Ward, "that it was canceled after only four films, one of which was not even released to theaters." Soon after that, the All-Star series was retired.

Cobb quickly went on to have real Hollywood success when he collaborated with the great director John Ford on two Will Rogers classics. *Judge Priest* released in September 1934 was based on Cobb's own stories and was adapted for the screen by two of the best scriptwriters in Hollywood at the time, Dudley Nichols and Lamar Trotti. The following year Cobb performed as an actor only, playing Captain Eli in another nostalgic look back to a bucolic America, *Steamboat Round the Bend*. Both are excellent films, two of Ford's and Rogers' finest.

Grace Rosenfield, who had been Henry Ginsberg's stenographer since the twenties and had been working in the New York Office since 1932 was assuming more and more responsibility. With Hal Roach about to travel to New York, his Culver City secretary Ruth Burch sent a friendly letter to Mrs. Rosenfield.

"I am sure you will enjoy your work with Mr. Roach. He is a perfectly grand person and keeping up with his activities is an inspiration in itself… Mr. Roach's ideas of what he wants are very definite and you will always find out that they work out pretty well. I've found him to be a man who gives instructions and expects you to use your own initiative in executing them in whatever way produces the most satisfactory results—without asking any more questions than are absolutely necessary.

"Above all else, don't ever be nervous or worry, for you are so conscientious, that if you do your best in a calm, easy manner, you will be sure to please. And when you understand Mr. Roach better, you will appreciate and admire him more than you do now."

Grauman Chinese Theatre Premieres: December 6, 1934 Laurel & Hardy's two-reeler *The Live Ghost* was shown along with the William Powell-Myrna Loy feature *Evelyn Prentice*. Just a week later, the Patsy Kelly-Thelma Todd short *Bum Voyage* played along with the George Arliss feature *The Last Gentleman* co-starring Edna May Oliver. (It's a pity that great eccentric character actress never performed with Stan and Ollie.)

Late in 1934 Charley Chase collapsed at the studio after having completed *The Four Star Boarder*. The doctors told him he had to stop drinking—or die. Chase recovered enough to complete three more shorts into the spring of 1935. Then he took about five months off to recuperate. When he returned to the Hal Roach Studios in September 1935 he was quite thin and looked older than his forty-two years. And he just didn't seem to be able to stop drinking for long.

1935 Releases:
Eight Todd & Kelly two-reelers
Seven Charley Chase two-reelers
Seven Our Gang two-reelers
Two Laurel & Hardy two-reelers
Two Features (Laurel & Hardy's *Bonnie Scotland* and *Vagabond Lady* with Robert Young)

For the January 10, 1935 premiere of Garbo's *The Painted Veil* at the Grauman's Chinese Theatre they screened Charley Chase's *Fate's Fathead*.

January 26, 1935: Sam W.B. Cohn to Joe Rivkin, New York City: "...I am now making a film subject showing intimate 'behind the scenes' views of our various stars with an introduction by Hal Roach. This is for the use of M.G.M.'s Traveling Studio... It will be a couple of weeks before I complete this as it is being held up by Charlie [*sic*] Chase, who is out of the city at this time."

January 31, 1935: Cohn to Rivkin: "Swell article on Hal E. Roach NOT Hal *C* Roach in *Film Daily*. I have just about completed the filming of the studio tour subject... with the exception of the Charlie Chase sequence... Charlie has been quite ill and if I do not hear from him in the next few days I shall ship the film without his sequence."

February 1935: Eli Danziger succeeds Al Feinman as head of Short Subject Publicity.

February 8, 1935: Ships trailer just completed to MGM Exchange, Dallas

March 1, 1935: *Tit For Tat* was screened at the Chinese Theatre with *One More Spring* starring Janet Gaynor and Warner Baxter. The classic Laurel & Hardy short featuring Mae Busch and Charlie Hall, reprising their roles from 1934's *Them Thar Hills*, would be nominated by the Academy Awards for Best Short Subject, Comedy, but would lose to Robert Benchley's *How To Sleep*.

March 4, 1935: Joe Rivkin to Sam W.B. Cohn: "...saw the studio reel you made and liked it very much, as did everyone else."

March 11, 1935: Sam W.B. Cohn to Joe Rivkin: "Charley Chase will complete his current production, 'Okay, Toots,' Wednesday. His daughter,

Polly Parrott, is making her screen debut in this comedy. She is eighteen years of age and is a very attractive and talented young lady."

March 18, 1935: Sam W.B. Cohn to Joe Rivkin: "Our present intention is to go ahead with the picture co-featuring Oliver Hardy, Patsy Kelly and Spanky McFarland."

March 28, 1935: Laurel & Hardy's two-reeler *The Fixer Uppers* was shown at Grauman's Chinese Theatre along with *Folies Bergère* starring Maurice Chevalier and Merle Oberon.

March 28, 1935: *The Film Daily* gave the Our Gang short *Beginner's Luck* a laudatory review: "It is a knockout. One of the finest offerings from this kid ensemble that the Roach Studios have ever turned out…. Spanky: "This kid is immense….It's feature caliber in short subject meter." Which was Roach's goal all along.

March 28, 1935: Sam W.B. Cohn to Joe Rivkin: "The picture [*Vagabond Lady*] was very well received with scores of laughs and got a big hand at its conclusion."

Vagabond Lady was the first non-Laurel & Hardy feature length film Roach had produced in eight years, not since *No Man's Law* in 1927. (The feature he directed in 1930, *Men of the North,* was produced by MGM.) *Variety's* review: "This just misses being a charm picture…Chief trouble seems to be that someone got too ambitious and loaded the tale with satire which is not always funny…Evelyn Venable…plays Josephine with a dash and genuine comedy spirit…." Contemporary viewers have found mild-mannered Robert Young and generally somber Evelyn Venable (who was so terrific in *Death Takes a Holiday* the year before) difficult to warm up to in a "madcap comedy." *Vagabond Lady* lost money for the Studios, while the Laurel & Hardy features had always shown a profit.

April 9, 1935: Sam W.B. Cohn to Joe Rivkin: "…we have signed up Jimmy Finlayson who used to be on this lot and also was with Mack Sennett for several years, to play a prominent role in support of Laurel & Hardy in their forthcoming feature…Fin is scheduled to sail from England tomorrow…I received a call from Louella Parsons, who had got wind of the Finlayson story, which she is breaking tomorrow, Wednesday. Although she insisted in having the yarn exclusively, I asked her to agree to letting me give it to the trade journals as well."

May 1935 The *Hollywood Reporter*: "Hal Roach is expected to be placed in charge of all short subject productions for MGM." The article went on to state Roach would replace an ailing Harry Rapf, but two days later MGM had decided to keep Rapf in charge of the short subjects. "Some powerful executives at MGM considered Roach too independent," opined Anthony and Edmonds.

May 20, 1935: Sam W.B. Cohn to Joe Rivkin: "You will undoubtedly be pleased to learn that the Gang's fan mail is increasing every week. Undoubtedly this situation is brought about as a result of the excellent comedies that are being turned out and the splendid exploitation and publicity that is being given them."

June 27, 1935: Sam W.B. Cohn to Joe Rivkin: "Mr. Roach is again at the Studio following his polo accident last Sunday. His jaw was fractured and his upper lip severely lacerated to say nothing of the loss of a couple of teeth. His father C.H. 'Dad' Roach, returns from the Good Samaritan Hospital Saturday after a two weeks rest following a minor heart attack."

Hal Roach was back playing polo July 21st at the Riviera Polo Grounds. In early August he was aboard ship bound for a Honolulu polo tournament when he cracked a rib while engaged in a boxing match with his son.

August 1, 1935: Signed Jimmie Savo, comic. When he arrived a few months later he did not cooperate with publicity and his wife snuck away. Her name is NOT "Nita Farina." Jimmy Savo to begin his picture middle of November with Isabel Jewell (though she's not signed yet) and "Spanky."

According to her Mini Biography on the IMDb, "Little Darla [Hood] made an unscheduled, impromptu singing debut at the Edison Hotel in Times Square [New York City] when the bandleader invited her onto the stage, and the crowd roared in appreciation. By sheer chance, a Hal Roach agent (Joe Rivkin) spotted the four-year-old scene-stealer, tested her, and signed her to a long-term (seven year) contract at $75 a week."

On August 15, 1935 word came to the Hal Roach Studios that his great friend, Will Rogers, had perished in a plane crash in Alaska along with his pilot, Wiley Post. Rogers was fifty-five years of age. Roach had already ended his flying career months earlier. In March 1935 his secretary Ruth Burch had written to a pilot who was inquiring about possible employment: "Mr. Roach has sold his airplane and is, therefore, not seeking the services of a pilot." A couple of months after Rogers' death, Roach himself wrote to another pilot: "At the present time I have no ideas of owning a plane."

September 9, 1935: Sam W.B. Cohn to Joe Rivkin: "The Hood youngster arrives tomorrow—but on what train and at what time nobody around here seems to know. However, we have decided not to make a big fuss over her arrival as in previous instances such publicity has rebounded when the kids failed to make good."

September 11, 1935: Joe Rivkin to Sam W.B. Cohn: "Hope the Hood child arrived okay...I hope you like her as much as I do. I think she has great possibilities and Metro has already inquired as to a loan-out for her. Also Warners."

September 12, 1935: Sam W.B. Cohn to Joe Rivkin: "Little Darla Hood is certainly a darling and looks as though she should go a long way."

September 14, 1935: Sam W.B. Cohn to Joe Rivkin: "I think your pet, 'Our Gang Follies of 1936' is going to be a honey. The rushes look great and everyone around the lot is highly enthusiastic over it. Although Darla Hood's part is very small owing to the fact that she arrived here after the picture went into production, she will show to good advantage and will have at least one solo number. 'Spanky' gives a great performance and your pal, 'Alfalfa,' is unusually cute in his rendition of the song, 'The Object of My Affection.' More than one hundred kids are seen in the picture including a number of specialty singers and dancers assembled from the various professional schools in and around Los Angeles. I am indeed sorry that this picture is not going out in four reels instead of two as it looks like a real hit."

September 19, 1935: Sam W.B. Cohn to Joe Rivkin: "I am to take [the 'Our Gang' kids] down to the San Diego Fair Saturday where they are to be the honor guests. We are getting a wonderful lot of publicity out of this and it will be a great treat for the kids."

September 26, 1935: Sam W.B. Cohn to Joe Rivkin: "The 'Our Gang' appearance at the San Diego fair last Saturday was a tremendous success from every standpoint. Besides getting front page art breaks in the San Diego papers three days running, we were successful in getting the *Hearst Metrotone News Weekly* to cover the event and any number of outside still photographers were also on hand to photograph the kids. Thousands of kids turned out to greet the little 'rascals' and the parade through the grounds was a triumphal procession."

October 2, 1935: Stan Laurel to Philip L. Gildred, Managing Director, California Pacific International Exposition, Balboa Park, San Diego, California: "Upon Mr. Hardy's return to Los Angeles this morning I learned that he expects to leave the city again tonight on a business trip and will not return until the day we begin production on 'The Bohemian Girl.' This being the case, it will be necessary for us to decline your kind invitation to be honor guests at the San Diego Exposition on Saturday, October 12, and inasmuch as we will be actively engaged in production for the ensuing several weeks, we cannot plan to be with you on any future date until after the 'Bohemian Girl' is finished which will be sometimes in November. Both Mr. Hardy and I extremely regret our inability to accept your kind invitation. Cordially yours."

September 30, 1935: Sam W.B. Cohn to Joe Rivkin: "I am afraid it will be impossible to get any holiday art with Laurel & Hardy as they do not go in for that sort of thing anymore. It's difficult enough to get straight pictures of them as you may imagine…."

On October 5, 1935: Charley Chase's first two-reeler since his collapse the previous year was released. *Nurse To You!* happened to be the first of some of his best comedies in years.

October 11, 1935: Luncheon for press and preview of *Our Gang Follies of 1936* was "grand and glorious."

October 21, 1935: Joe Rivkin to Sam W.B. Cohn: "We have arranged a real Hollywood World premiere at the Capitol Theatre for *Our Gang Follies.* We have invited every prominent picture child in the East as well as children of public celebrities such as Grover Whalen, Mayor La Guardia, Jack Dempsey, Fanny Brice, etc….Other child artists who will be present are Baby Rose Marie, Mary Small, Mitzi Green and numerous others."

October 23, 1935: Sam W.B. Cohn to Joe Rivkin: "This [Hal Roach Studios publicity] stunt has gone over tremendously and there is hardly a block in Los Angeles that is not plastered with 'Spanky's' likeness. Yesterday, I had the occasion to take Darla Hood to the Hall of Records to have her contract approved and on each floor of the building was a large mounted Community Chest poster with 'Spanky.' The twenty four sheet billboards are all over town as are pole cards and other outdoor advertising." Rosina Lawrence signed this week to seven year contract by Hal Roach. She is the first of a contingent of new players to be added to the roster of players by the Roach Studio during the ensuing ninety days… According to Roach, he will shortly announce the signing of several other new players who will form the nucleus of a stock company. This is in accordance with his recent announcement that he will produce more features in 1936."

October 25, 1935: Western Union telegram, Sam W.B. Cohn to Joe Rivkin: "OWING TO ILLNESS MAE BUSCH WILL PROBABLY BE REPLACED IN CAST STOP"

October 26, 1935: "WE ARE GOING AHEAD WITH THE PRODUCTION WITH THE ASSUMPTION THAT MISS BUSCH WILL BE SUFFICIENTLY RECOVERED TO RESUME WORK BEFORE THE PICTURE IS COMPLETED."

October 30, 1935: Sam W.B. Cohn to Joe Rivkin: [Trying to get photos of Laurel & Hardy for Adams Hat Store]: "…it would be impossible for me to secure any further cooperation from the boys on anything that smacked of a commercial tie-up. This applies to publicity art as well as to display advertising. Since Stan acquired a manager several months ago and under the terms of his new contract, he is now out for cold cash on all such propositions. Under these circumstances, it will be futile for me to approach him on the subject as the first thing he says to me now when I do so is, 'How much?' I had occasion to find this out just the other day when I endeavored to get him and Babe to pose for a tie-up with the Standard Oil Company which would have meant forty thousand dollars worth of display advertising in more than one hundred metropolitan newspapers for 'The Bohemian Girl.' Instead I used Thelma Todd and Antonio Moreno."

November 1, 1935: Joe Rivkin to Sam W.B. Cohn: "...Have ANTONIO MORENO or Charlie [*sic*] Chase. Do not necessarily have to have LAUREL AND HARDY for these photographs. Get anybody that is available on the lot. [Their letters must have crossed in the mails.]

November 2, 1935: [Referring to getting photographs at the train station of David Loew coming to work at Hal Roach Studios.] Sam W.B. Cohn to Joe Rivkin: "...the arrival and departure of motion picture executives in Los Angeles has ceased to be 'hot news.'"

"This kid [Darla Hood] has received more publicity than any youngster that has ever joined the 'Gang' I believe, and I sincerely trust that she lives up to it. I think she has great possibilities and should go a long way if properly handled. Don't you?"

November 1935 *Liberty* magazine reviews *"Our Gang Follies of 1936."*

November 19, 1935: *Variety*: "Production on Jimmy Savo's starrer *Alone Alas!* [with a cast including Isabel Jewell, Leon Errol, 'Spanky,' 'Alfalfa,' 'Buckwheat,' 'Porky,' Paul Dominick, Edward Gargan and Robert Homans] was stopped by Hal Roach for a sweeping rewrite job after six days in work. Unless doctored satisfactorily, studio may scrap the picture and take $50,000 loss expended to date. Director Gus Meins, Harry McCoy and studio writing staff will give the script a two weeks' going over. Cast is being kept intact."

Jimmy Savo (1892-1960), who had been praised as a great pantomimist by no less than Charlie Chaplin, had appeared in a few silent films in the 1920s and would appear in a few talkies in the 1930s. He achieved acclaim for his performance in the original 1938 Broadway production of *The Boys From Syracuse*, but he never did make a film for Roach.

December 11, 1935: Sam W.B. Cohn to Joe Rivkin: "'Our Gang' goes into production tomorrow on *King Gang* a comedy in which the little 'rascals' put on an amateur contest. Fred Newmeyer, who was one of the first directors ever hired by Mr. Roach, has returned to the studio to direct this."

December 13, 1935: Joe Rivkin to Sam W.B. Cohn: "Will you please advise Mr. Roach that in the new smash hit on Broadway, called 'BOY MEETS GIRL,' there is a scene where one of the actors is asked whether he has had any previous motion picture experience and he replies have just finished a picture for Hal Roach. This is a great plug for us and would appreciate your calling Same to Mr. Roach's attention."

December 17, 1935: "'BONNIE SCOTLAND' selected as the first picture to be played at the newly erected Metro Theatre in Calcutta, India.

December 6, 1935 Western Union telegram, Sam W.B. Cohn to Joe Rivkin: "THELMA TODD CONTRACT READS QUOTE IT IS SPECIF-ICALLY UNDERSTOOD AND AGREED THAT THE ARTIST IS TO RECEIVE FIRST FEATURED BILLING AFTER THAT OF LAUREL & HARDY END QUOTE."

On the morning of December 16, 1935 the beautiful, vivacious Thelma Todd, who had recently completed filming her scenes for the upcoming Laurel & Hardy musical *The Bohemian Girl*, was found dead in her car in the garage of her seaside café. There has been much speculation as to how the 29-year-old beauty met her end. Books have been written about it and they are continuing to be written about the tragedy. In 1991 a television movie, *White Hot: The Mysterious Murder of Thelma Todd*, based on the book *Hot Toddy* was produced which provided one of many versions of the events. I had the opportunity to discuss this movie with Mr. Roach at that time and to ask him about his theories. This can be found in Chapter nine.

December 17, 1935: Sam W.B. Cohn letter to Joe Rivkin: "I know you must have been shocked to hear the tragic news about Thelma Todd. It came as a terrific blow to everyone here and we are as much in the dark about the whole matter as are the authorities."

Brian Anthony and Andy Edmonds relate in their book *Smile While the Raindrops Fall* that several Roach staffers received Christmas cards from Thelma, who had mailed them the day before she died.

"Charley Chase received her card and broke into tears... Though their affair ended years before, the two had remained close friends." Charley and Thelma Todd had appeared together in twelve talkie shorts from 1929 to 1932. Charley wanted to create a permanent comedy team with Thelma, but this idea was nixed by Roach who teamed Thelma with ZaSu Pitts and then with Patsy Kelly.

Hal Roach released a public statement: "She was a favorite with everyone on the lot, from the lowliest employee to the highest. She apparently was joyous and happy and seemed to enjoy her work."

William Donati, in his book *The Life and Death of Thelma Todd* (2011) wrote, "At Roach Studio there was a meeting: Thelma's scenes in *The Bohemian Girl* should be cut; audiences would be distracted to see Thelma singing of love and life when she is dead." Even today, however, there is a version which can be seen that contains nearly two minutes of Thelma singing a gypsy love song near the beginning of the movie. Her hair is dark as befits a gypsy—perhaps the only time this blonde was a brunette in the movies. She has that same radiant smile and looks as though she could live forever.

The 1932 Lincoln Phaeton that Thelma had died in was sold for $550. Alice Todd, her devoted mother, took her urn of ashes home to Lawrence, Massachusetts and kept it with her for the next thirty-four years. When Mrs. Todd died in December 1969 at the age of ninety-two, Thelma's ashes were buried with her.

Thelma Todd was the embodiment of the carefree, fun and light-hearted glamour of Hollywood in the 1920s and early 1930s, and her death at the end of 1935 was almost a harbinger of great changes that were to come. The year 1936 would prove to be one that would see the Hal Roach Studios evolve from that era and change forever.

Hal Roach Studios greet the arrival of sound. Warren Doane, Stan Laurel and Oliver Hardy and the crew from The Victor Recording Company of Camden, New Jersey at their sound truck in November 1928. Photo courtesy Craig Raguse, grandson of Elmer Raguse.

Hal Roach watches as Elmer Raguse of the Victor Recording Company tests the sound disc for the newly installed Western Electric equipment for the production of talking movies in November 1928. A technician examines other equipment in the background. Photo courtesy Craig Raguse, grandson of Elmer Raguse.

The platinum blonde at the start of her film career early 1929. Jean Harlow appeared in several Hal Roach shorts before becoming a star. Photo courtesy Delmar Watson.

In the spring of 1929 the trades announce that Hal Roach talkies had arrived and were ready to be screened at those movie theaters that had been wired for sound.

Laurel & Hardy first worked together at the Hal Roach Studios in 1926. They became an official team the next year and had achieved worldwide fame by the time they were featured in *Picture Play* magazine in November 1930.

The Boss catches his two leading employees sneaking out of a meeting c. 1931.

Laurel & Hardy peruse an issue of *New Movie* magazine on the set of their classic 1930 short *Brats* in which they played themselves as well as their own children.

One of the ads which Laurel & Hardy Hardy posed for in 1930 was for the Schalk Chemical Company, makers of Savabrush paint brushes.

By 1933 there was a new cast of Our Gang kids, including Stymie Beard and George "Spanky" McFarland. The series was almost axed by MGM execs that year, and the Series was very probably saved due to the defensive action of the often-reviled Henry Ginsberg.

The newspapers loved to cover Hal Roach's adventures. The intrepid world traveler owned his own plane and with his pilot James Dickson broke world records during their business trip to South America with MGM exec Arthur Loew in early 1932.

The public eagerly awaited Laurel & Hardy's second feature length film released in 1932 to coincide with their crowd-drawing visits to New York City and Great Britain. Courtesy USC.

Hal Roach very occasionally would do a "Hitchcock"—make a cameo appearance in one of his own movies. Here he plays a prisoner in Laurel & Hardy's first feature film *Pardon Us* (1931). Photo courtesy Dave 'Lord' Heath, *Another Nice Mess* website.

Harold Lloyd, Bebe Daniels, Hal Roach, Mrs. Marguerite Roach and Mildred Davis (Mrs. Harold Lloyd) at the twentieth anniversary party Hal Roach threw to Commemorate twenty years as a motion picture producer in December 1933. Photo courtesy USC.

Louis B. Mayer, head of MGM and Will Rogers with Hal Roach, December 1933. Photo courtesy USC.

Jean Harlow, by 1933 a superstar, always remembered her days at the Hal Roach Studios fondly, and brought her beloved mother Jean Bello to the twentieth Anniversary party. Photo courtesy USC.

Hal Roach, Theda Bara, Will Rogers and Charley Chase celebrate at Hal Roach's party in December 1933. Photo courtesy USC.

Patsy Kelly and Thelma Todd with their director Gus Meins at the 1933 party. Photo courtesy USC.

Silent serial star Ruth Roland, Harold Lloyd, Mrs. Mabel Roach (Hal's mother) and Mildred Davis (Mrs. Harold Lloyd) at the 1933 party. Photo courtesy USC

George "Spanky" McFarland and Pete the Pup endorse the Spanky Bar, one of Our Gang's many tie-ins. Courtesy USC.

The press made a big fuss when David Loew left MGM's New York City parent company Loew's Inc. to come work for Hal Roach as VP in 1935. But his tenure lasted only a few months. Left to right: David Loew; Hal Roach; Mrs. Loew; Mrs. Henry Ginsberg; Mrs. Morton Spring (wife of NY Roach exec); and Henry Ginsberg.

Celebrating their twenty-first wedding anniversary in 1937 is Marguerite and Hal Roach. The party also celebrated the twenty-first birthday of Vittorio Mussolini, son of the Italian dictator, much to the dismay of many in Hollywood.

Hal Roach with movie pioneer D.W. Griffith, who came to Culver
City for six months in 1939 to assist with several productions,
including *One Million B.C.*

Having avoided military service in World War I, fifty-year-old
Hal Roach was finally sent "over there" in 1942. Celebrating his
departure, left to right: S.S. Van Keuren, Roach's cousin, Vice
President and Production Manager of the Studio; Margaret Roach,
Hal's daughter, sitting on her grandmother Mabel's lap; standing is
Jack Roach, Hal's older brother; seated is Mabel's sister, Maude Van
Keuren, who lived at the Studio with her; and Major Hal Roach.
Photo courtesy Craig Raguse, grandson of Elmer Raguse.

7

Of Mice and Men
The Changing Ways of Hollywood
1936-1940

IN MAY 1935 Grauman's Chinese Theatre began showing double features. Roach's first feature since he began making them with Laurel and Hardy was *Vagabond Lady,* and it was screened at the Chinese Theatre in June along with *Public Hero Number One* starring Lionel Barrymore and Jean Arthur. Finally Laurel & Hardy's own feature *Our Relations* had its World Premiere at Grauman's on November 18, 1936. It was shown along with the feature *Reunion* starring the Dionne Quintuplets.

Laurel and Hardy's "graduation" from the all-talking two-reel length to features was gradual: they were prominent guest stars in MGM's extravagant, all-star talkie feature, *The Hollywood Revue of 1929*, and had major roles in *The Rogue Song* in 1930. Their first full-length starring feature, *Pardon Us*, was released in 1931 and they alternated making features and two- and three-reelers until 1935, after which time they made only features. There has been some debate as to whether or not Laurel and Hardy should have gone into feature production at all. Many critics have said that they were at their best in the shorter films.

"I couldn't agree more, "said Roach. "Comedy should not exceed forty-five minutes. You've got to save the best for the last: build the gags as you go along. You need a hell of a story to carry even thirty-five percent of a picture. But there was no market for two-reelers in this country anymore. The double feature killed two-reel comedy."

In addition to the triumph of the double feature presentation, there was another innovation that had reached a level of supreme proficiency.

"Animated cartoons took over the business!" Roach explained to author Mike Steen in 1969. "It was impossible to compete with them, because they had an unlimited ability to fantasize. You can make drawing-

199

board characters like Mickey Mouse, Betty Boop, Popeye, and Pluto do almost anything… Animated cartoons were so good and unique and so popular that I had to go into the making of full-length comedies."

Though Roach ceased production of comedy shorts in the late 1930s, other comics persisted in the genre. Edgar Kennedy had a successful series that lasted up to his death in 1948, Leon Errol's popular series lasted until his death in 1951, Andy Clyde's series lasted until 1956, and the Three Stooges were producing shorts in 1958. Nevertheless, Laurel and Hardy made their last short in 1935 and went on to concentrate on feature-length productions, the first in 1935 being *Bonnie Scotland.*

1936 RELEASES:
FIVE CHARLEY CHASE TWO-REELERS
FIVE OUR GANG TWO-REELERS
FOUR OUR GANG ONE-REELERS
THREE NON-LAUREL & HARDY FEATURES
TWO LAUREL & HARDY FEATURES
TWO PATSY KELLY & LYDA ROBERTI TWO-REELERS
ONE PATSY KELLY & PERT KELTON TWO-REELER

In January, Henry Ginsberg, for the past five years the vice president and general manager of the Hal Roach Studios offered his resignation. "The retiring Roach executive assigned no motive for his action and declined to indicate reasons behind his desire for contract termination," reported The *Los Angeles Times.*

"Ginsberg's departure may have allowed everyone a sigh of relief," wrote Anthony and Edmonds, "though at least he was a known evil. No one knew what to expect when David Loew was appointed the new general manager of the studio."

But no one had time to discover what changes David Loew might make, for he suddenly resigned in March to form his own production company and produced a series of Joe E. Brown comedies which the star himself considered "a mistake." The reason for the unexpected departure of Roach's long time friend and advisor only three months after he had arrived, and who had been given a fantastic going away party in New York shortly before moving to Hollywood has never been given.

In March 1936 Fred Quimby wrote to Hal Roach: "I think the Our Gang Comedy—SECOND CHILDHOOD—is one of the cleverest Gang

Comedies you have ever made. The old lady—Zeffie Tilbury—turned in a fine performance and the kids worked very well with her. She will make a great hit with the public. Possibly it would be a good idea to use her in some of the one reel Our Gang productions."

Ms. Tilbury who was blind but you'd never know it watching her on the screen, had played the Gypsy Queen in *The Bohemian Girl* released a couple of months prior to *Second Childhood*. She actually replaced Thelma Todd, who had died on December 15, 1935, just days after the first preview of *The Bohemian Girl*. Zeffie Tilbury (1863-1950) would go on to play memorable grandmothers in two John Ford classics, *The Grapes of Wrath* (1940) and *Tobacco Road* (1941).

The first convention of European Laurel & Hardy Clubs was held in Paris in August in connection with the showing of *The Bohemian Girl* and set the greatest attendance and box office receipts of any picture ever shown there.

The Bohemian Girl was not so well received in other countries. It was banned outright in Germany due to the Gypsy element; in Hungary censors demanded that the scenes involving Hardy comically holding up and robbing a gentleman be deleted, and in Japan the shots of Hardy's wife, played by Mae Busch, kissing her lover Devilshoof (Antonio Moreno), as well as "any mention of her affection for Devilshoof" were instructed to be cut.

The Bohemian Girl was the final Roach film to feature "the ever popular Mae Busch" (as Jackie Gleason would often declaim during his 1950s TV show). So memorable as Oliver Hardy's shrewish wife or as a floozy or shady lady, Mae Busch had been working quite steadily at the Hal Roach Studios since 1927 after achieving fame early in the decade in features directed by Erich von Stroheim as well as starring with Lon Chaney in his silent classic *The Unholy Three*. Yet after leaving the Hal Roach Studios Mae Busch's appearances in the movies were to be in tiny and often uncredited roles right up until her early death in 1946 at the age of fifty-four.

A pair of red boots (take note, future colorists) might be considered the reason for her disfavor and decline. "On October 19, 1935," stated a report in the Hal Roach Collection, "Miss Busch reported that the boots she was wearing in a gypsy scene of BOHEMIAN GIRL had caused her feet and legs to become infected. She reported to the Community Hospital, Culver City, the medical institution which takes care of all [Hal Roach Studios] insurance compensation cases. Dr. C. Lewis Gaulden reported... that Miss Busch had a chronic condition which could not possibly have been caused by the boots in question."

However, Miss Busch filed a lawsuit against the Hal Roach Studios on November 30th. But the attorney for the American Motorist Insurance Company, in a letter to Hal Roach's personal secretary Ruth Burch, was firm. "We still believe that the condition that Mae Busch has suffered from is in no way associated with her employment and that is the position that we are taking... her troubles are of long standing and not the result of her employment with your studio."

May 28, 1936: "C.H. 'DAD' ROACH SUCCUMBS AT 76" declared the headlines. "From the ranks of filmdom's beloved pioneers, death yesterday claimed Charles H. 'Dad' Roach, father of Hal Roach and secretary-treasurer of the studio his son heads. Mr. Roach died at the University Hospital in Culver City of a heart ailment. He was taken to the hospital last Saturday night. In an adjoining room was his wife, Mrs. Mabel B. Roach, ill of a severe cold...

"Mr. Roach, who was 76, had been secretary-treasurer of the Hal E. Roach Studios since 1918 when he came to Los Angeles from Elmira, N.Y., where he had lived for 35 years. He was born in Alexandria, Va.

"With his wife, he made his home in an apartment at the studio. He was beloved by all members of the Roach film companies, some of whom recalled yesterday that it had been his chief pleasure to supervise distribution of pay checks, handing the checks to star, extra and laborer alike, with a smile and a cheery greeting.

Another newspaper noted, "He took pride in every film released, every sound stage built—in fact they'll tell you he watched the construction of every building on the lot to see what went into it and how the work progressed."

Columnist Marion Nevin wrote, "We have heard many times about the friendly atmosphere that was part of the Studio. You felt it every time you visited their sets, and we attribute a large part of the 'homey' welcome to Mr. Roach's friendly hello."

Columnist R.A. Cronin wrote, "Horse racing in California lost a staunch friend in the passing of Charles H. Roach, who helped organize and finance the Santa Anita Jockey Club....Never missed a racing day during the two seasons at the Arcadia plant in spite of the fact that he was 76 years of age. All his life he was an enthusiast over the thoroughbred and oftentimes visited the Santa Anita barns before the races to size up this horse or that. He rarely made a wager over a horse race."

Dwight Whiting, Dad's predecessor as Secretary-Treasurer in 1918, sent Hal a letter of condolence: "...no doubt you enjoyed, outside of an ordinary father and son relationship, his good comradship [sic]. The hell of it is, they don't make really nice people such as Dad was very often, and when they are gone, it is a loss of course impossible to even think about replacing."

Telegrams and letters of sympathy poured into the Studio, from the likes of Jack Warner, Darryl Zanuck, Cecil B. DeMille, Dr. Giannini of Bank of America and Frank L. Shaw, the Mayor of Los Angeles, and from actors Patsy Kelly, Marie Mosquini, Daphne Pollard, Charlie Murray, Johnny Downs and Jean Darling's mother Dorothy Darling. Dad's entire $10,000 estate went to his widow, Mabel.

The following week Hal and his family moved from their two-story, five bedroom, four bath Italian Renaissance home in the historic Berkeley Square section of Los Angeles where they had lived since 1920 into a huge Colonial-style mansion in Beverly Hills. The new mansion boasted five kitchens and six bedrooms and included a swimming pool and tennis court. The household staff was comprised of butler, maid, cook, house boy, the Japanese gardener and his assistant, a laundress, a night watchman, the relief night watchman, a personal assistant for Mrs. Roach and a projectionist on 24-hour call for screenings in the basement. Mr. Roach also employed a chauffeur armed with a revolver and who carried a police badge issued by the Culver City Police Department.

Roach lived in this home until 1961 when he moved to a more modest single story house in Bel Air where he spent the rest of his life. He outlived that palatial Beverly Hills mansion, which was torn down in 1989.

Less than a month later, the newspapers announced another demise: "CHARLIE [sic] CHASE, HAL ROACH BREAK UP ASSOCIATION," ran the *Chicago Daily Tribune* headline of June 14, 1936.

"The impresario of laughs, Hal Roach, has discontinued making short comedies with, of course, the exception of the perennial dozen starring the juveniles, 'Our Gang.' He will concentrate his producing talents on long comedies from now on. Even Laurel and Hardy are out of the two reel class. Charlie Chase, before beginning his free lance career, will take a long vacation." Chase had been at the Hal Roach Studios for seventeen years and had appeared in, according to the *Chicago Daily Tribune*, 240 comedies.

Charley Chase's 1936 project *Bank Night* started out to be a feature. When it was previewed *Variety* noted "Best thing to be done... is to cut it to a short...." Which is exactly what they did, and called it *Neighborhood House*. Released in May of 1936, it was Charley Chase's final short for the Hal Roach Studios.

Chase did appear in one Hal Roach production after that, Patsy Kelly's first starring feature-length film, *Kelly the Second*, a slapsticky romp dealing with boxing and gangsters, with Charley in a secondary role. Fred Quimby, Manager of the Short Feature Department in New York, wrote to Roach in May of that year after seeing a rough cut. "...everyone in the Theatre Department thought that the picture was very poor, however, yesterday morning Messrs. Rodgers, Lichtman and Connors saw the picture with the Foreign Department and they said that they considered it a satisfactory Class B production."

A week later Quimby sent the following Postal Telegram to Roach: "PREVIEWED KELLY SECOND LOEWS GRAND THEATRE TO CAPACITY HOUSE APPROXIMATELY TWENTY FIVE HUNDRED PEOPLE STOP AUDIENCE REACTION VERY GOOD CONTINUOUS LAUGHTER FROM BEGINNING TO END PERSONALLY RATE PICTURE VERY GOOD STOP...."

Variety's review on October 17, 1936: "*Kelly the Second* probably will be welcomed in the duals, because it is filled with humorous moments. But it is too lightweight in plot and accomplished results to stand up alone in most spots. In Patsy Kelly and Charley Chase, Metro has teamed two of its ace comics from short features." *Variety* noted that the seventy minute length had been further cut down by fifteen minutes, "and that helps a lot."

Charley Chase had at last allowed his prematurely gray hair to show in this film.

"Charley was summarily fired from the Hal Roach Studios in May 1936" wrote Anthony and Edmonds. "...No one has ever received a completely satisfying explanation for Chase's dismissal. Roach, many years after the fact, gave conflicting reports. He blamed Ginsberg, though it was unlikely that the powerful v.p. could make such a decision on his own. Further, Ginsberg had left the studio months earlier. Roach later claimed that Chase was too ill to continue working, which was clearly not the case. His health was fragile. Perhaps there were other, more personal reasons."

"Charley Chase was a closed chapter in Roach's life," concluded Anthony and Edmonds. "...after Charley left the studio the two never spoke again."

The following year Charley Chase appeared in one Technicolor short distributed by MGM, and then moved to Columbia Pictures, where he starred in twenty-one comedy shorts before his untimely death from alcoholism at the age of forty-six in 1940.

Hal Roach licensed the rights to Charley Chase's sound comedies to Film Classics, Inc. in 1949 and then relicensed them in the early 1950s to Regal Television. While the main titles were poorly remade, the quality of the prints were excellent. The films existed "in a kind of limbo for the next twenty years," according to Anthony and Edmonds. Their rights were eventually acquired by the Australian company Quintex and later in the 1990s by RHI, Inc. While every Columbia short is now available on two volumes of 'made to order' DVD's from Sony, only two Charley Chase Hal Roach talkies have ever been available on DVD, *Whispering Whoopee* (1930) and *On The Wrong Trek* (1936) because the copyrights weren't appropriately renewed and they've fallen into the public domain.

In the spring of 1936 the Our Gang kids embarked on a personal appearance tour to several cities in the Midwest. During the last leg of the tour, in Detroit, Spanky came down with measles. Little Darla suffered the same malady a couple of weeks later.

Once back in Culver City that July five grown-up members of the original "Our Gang" film comedy troupe came to the Hal Roach Studios and met in person the six juvenile funsters who were carrying on the comedies. The occasion was the fifteenth anniversary of the starting of the first "Our Gang" comedy, and Fred Newmeyer, who directed the first film back in 1922, was present to greet Mary Kornman, Joe Cobb, Johnny Downs, Jack Condon and "Farina" Hoskins.

The 1936 "Our Gang" kids were there too: "Spanky" McFarland, Darla Hood, Carl "Alfalfa" Sweetzer, "Porky" Lee, Baby Patsy and Billie "Buckwheat" Thomas. And Gordon Douglas, the current "Our Gang" director. Mrs. Fern Carter (1893-1961), who had been the teacher for the "Our Gang" players for fifteen years, was there also. Messages from Jackie Cooper, Mickey Daniels and Dickie Moore were read.

"The children to a great extent run the lot," read a 1936 *New York Times* article. "They have access to all of the offices, and all shooting is scheduled in accord with their lives, their schooling and the play periods. Strict rules govern their conduct and that of the parent assigned to watch over them. Their salaries are determined by their public appeal. They start in at $40 a week, but Spanky, who is almost a star in his own right, receives $1,250 a week. Most of the parents put the money away against the children's later life and their schooling. The father of one boy, however, thought that his son's $500 a week entitled him to the life of a movie star, and Roach had to go to court to protect the lad's earnings from the parent.

"When a child joins 'Our Gang' the rules which govern him are explicitly given, and parents are called into the Roach offices for infractions. No child is frightened or coerced into doing anything he doesn't wish to do. Parents must keep hands off during working hours. School and recreation periods must be adhered to. Every comfort must be provided child and parent on the set. No child can be scolded or spanked on the set. All disciplining must take place at home, away from the eyes of the others. All children must be treated alike; there can be no favorites as far as the crew is concerned.

"Instead of ponderous conferences by executives from which, rather laboriously, the names of stars emerge on other lots, the picture crew determines the nicknames of the Roach youngsters. When they join the gang the carpenters, electricians, camera men and others are in contact with them constantly, and they give them their names. Roach believes that better results are obtained this way, for generally the titles have reason. Of the present gang the boys on the stage named 'Spanky,' 'Buckwheat' Thomas, the successor to 'Farina'; 'Alfalfa' Switzer, who is very much the farm boy, and 'Porky' Lee, who is as chubby as his name indicates.

"In handling them Roach operates on the theory that the loss of an ice cream cone is as much a tragedy to a child as a million dollars to an adult. Therefore they are never allowed to become accustomed to false values, and the nickel cone is their standard of life and affluence. Their toys come, for the most part, from the prop shop and are implements that have been used in pictures. They have others that smack of the dime store, and they are constantly trading and making deals.

"There is a complete turnover in the 'Gang' personnel every three or four years. The members are replaced one at a time and each grows into his part naturally. The 'movie mother menace' being so acute, Roach refuses to interview any who come to the studio. He may miss some prospects but he saves himself a great deal of grief. Parents must submit photographs."

From 1934 to 1936 the Our Gang shorts were directed by Gus Meins who had been working for Roach since 1932. He was born in Frankfurt, Germany in 1900 and came to the United States as a boy. At the age of sixteen he was working as a cartoonist at the *Los Angeles Evening Herald*. A few years later he was a gag writer for Fox Film Corporation and in 1922 was directing comedies for Mack Sennett. At Roach's he directed four of the Thelma Todd-ZaSu Pitts shorts and then eleven with Thelma and Patsy Kelly to 1936. He also directed some sixteen Our Gang shorts, one Charley Chase short in 1933 and three for the *Taxi Boys* series. His final assignment for Hal Roach was directing the Patsy Kelly-Lyda Roberti feature *Nobody's Baby*.

Apparently Meins left the Hal Roach Studios due to "artistic differences" in 1937. He went on to direct B movies at Republic. In 1940 he was arrested on a morals charge. The *Reading* (Pennsylvania) *Eagle* stated he was accused of "sex offenses against six youths." The website *Death in Toyland* by a Thomas Mine states that there were three boys in his basement. When he came home after being released on bail he allegedly told his son Douglas, "You probably won't see me again," and drove off in his car. His car was found days later in the brush with his dead body inside. Apparently he died from self-inflicted carbon monoxide poisoning. According to Thomas Mine, "Since the case against Gus Meins never came to trial and the charges were filed by minors and thus sealed, the question wether [*sic*] he is innocent or not remains open." The *Reading Eagle* article of August 5, 1940 concludes: "His widow was under a physician's care today." Hopefully the Our Gang kids remained blissfully unaware of this incident. Did any of them question whatever happened to their Uncle Gus?

On July 23, 1936 Roach sent a letter to the one man he was beholden to during his years associated with M-G-M, Nicholas Schenck, President of that great studio's parent company Loew's Inc., wherein he confirmed the new direction he would now be taking his Studio:

"My dear Nick:

"I think my change-over to feature length pictures is going to work out very successfully, both for Metro and myself.

"Our organization, and the quality of our pictures, is improving daily. I feel that, by the time we reach the end of the season, you will be more than pleased with the results obtained from our studio, and I feel that one Studio, devoting its entire time and attention to the developing of comedy features is a decided asset to this industry.

"My best to both you and Pansy. I hope you are both coming out soon. Sincerely."

Also on the same day Hal sent the above letter to Schenck, he sent a general letter addressed to various MGM Division Managers in major cities throughout the United States. As he had done since the early silent days, Roach was eager for professional feedback.

"We are doing everything possible to build a competent organization for the development of feature comedy pictures. Your criticism and suggestions on these pictures will be greatly appreciated. As you know, I have no representation in the field except Metro, so any information you can give me as to how the pictures go, or what subjects or effects appeal to you, will be very helpful. Also, let me know how you like the people we are featuring."

It's interesting that he wrote "the people we are featuring" rather than "the actors we are employing."

Metro's New York office took exception to the fact that Roach had written directly to the District Managers, rather than addressing his issues to the head office. Roach sent what amounted to an apology letter, acknowledging that he "had forgotten about the rule that such communications must first be sent to the New York office." He went on to explain, "Until we have several features on the market to make a comparison, we will be shooting in the dark as to cost and quality, so if we can secure the information as to just what our pictures are doing in the different theatres and how they are received by the trade, it will assist us greatly in planning our future product."

"In about 1936 my studio began feeling its way into features to see what we could make that would be profitable. The only thing we had suitable was Laurel and Hardy. We started making full-length features with them, but that wasn't enough to keep the studio busy. We began to search for story material."

"By the beginning of 1936," Anthony and Edmonds had written, "Hal Roach was resigned to the failure of his attempts to bolster interest in his short subjects... But the market for quality shorts was dwindling. Roach had to adapt if he was to survive... Hal Roach was never one to look back. Even in his nineties he was far more interested in initiating new projects than reminiscing about former glories. So when it became apparent that feature production was his only recourse, he unsentimentally forged ahead."

Maybe too Hal Roach was growing up. He was forty-four years old, after all, no longer the young go-getter of the teens and twenties, and as Hollywood was maturing, so was he. On August 14, 1936 The *Los Angeles Times* announced "HAL ROACH TO RETIRE FROM POLO. Hal Roach, motion-picture producer and southpaw polo star, yesterday announced his retirement from the mallet field in favor of his position as president of the Los Angeles Turf Club. From now on Roach, a three-goal polo player, will devote all his spare time from his own business to the advancement of horse racing at Santa Anita. He has already given away his top pony Gentilla, to the famous Tommy Hitchcock. Roach has been playing polo since 1924 and has often been a hard-riding member of Midwick's celebrated fours."

"HAL ROACH CARRIES ON 'Our Gang' and Laurel and Hardy Survive Despite the Double-Bill Menace" declared The *New York Times* on August 30, 1936.

"The double-feature mania which has gripped the nation has killed one of the cinema's most flourishing institutions," the article went on, "the slap-stick comedy factory. Most of them have given up the ghost. Hal

Roach, however, has adapted himself to the times by renouncing the two-reelers for the more respected multiple-reel films. The man who once said that there is nothing as funny as a custard pie in the face still clings to his theory—with certain amendments. The pie must be composed of sterner stuff than was used ten years ago and it must be tossed a little more artfully.

"The baggy trousers and the chalked face have been abandoned for the time being by the Roach players. He believes that some day public taste will demand them back. Until that time he will concern himself with eight full-length comedies a year and twelve one-reelers with 'Our Gang.' Charlie [sic] Chase has departed from the lot since his attempt at feature work met with public apathy; the art of Laurel and Hardy will be limited to features; Patsy Kelly has been teamed with Lyda Roberti, who has replaced the late Thelma Todd, and there will be an all-star musical each year with all the Roach comedians, including the 'Gang.'"

In August Roach reduced the Our Gang comedies to one reel in length beginning with *Bored of Education* which would be the second (and last) Hal Roach short to win an Academy Award for Best Short Subject, Comedy.

Mr. Cinderella, starring Jack Haley (who had replaced Jimmy Savo), was released soon thereafter, a zany comedy with Haley as a barber pretending to be a millionaire. The New York censor, however, had insisted that they "Eliminate views of Jack Haley swimming in the nude, where his naked body is visible through the water." Presumably once the nudity was deleted, *Variety* reviewed the movie, declaring Mr. Cinderella a "swiftly moving, light comedy... made half-way palatable by the tidy performance of chief featured players."

On September 30, 1936 Fred A. Purner, Director of Publicity and Advertising wrote to Miss Grace Rosenfield, MGM New York City: "'Bonnie Scotland' has beaten all box office records for their [Laurel & Hardy] productions, and the 'BOHEMIAN GIRL' is keeping pace with it or running a bit ahead...."

That fall King Edward VIII of England requested Laurel & Hardy's latest feature, *Our Relations* be screened at Balmoral Castle in Scotland for a private royal viewing.

General Spanky, released in December 1936, and co-directed by Our Gang's Gordon Douglas and old timer Fred Newmeyer, who had directed some of Harold Lloyd's best features in the 1920s, was the one and only excursion the Our Gang kids made into the feature film realm, an experiment very reluctantly agreed to by MGM. The unusual aspect of it was that the film was set during the Civil War, and the fact that Buckwheat plays a runaway slave makes contemporary viewers uncomfortable.

Charles Tatum, of *efilmcritic.com* wrote, from the perspective of the 2010s: "The film is not as blatantly racist as *The Birth of a Nation,* or even the stunning minstrel number from *Babes in Arms,* but I see a lot of explaining to children who might catch this and begin asking questions. The screenwriters (it took four to write this?) treat slavery and the Civil War as inconveniences. I realize this is a film made for the family, and there are a number of funny episodes strung together, but watching little Billie Thomas asking strange men if they would be his new master, or having Spanky claim Buckwheat as his slave to avoid a fight with other kids, is still something I had never seen onscreen before, and trust me, I thought I had seen it all."

By contrast, blogger Jeffrey Hill suggests "…Time has twisted this picture from the wholesome boundaries of its intended domain to something that today's social climate cannot tolerate. It runs counter to some very basic ideas we have about children, sex and race (and yet, it is not racy). No producer would touch *General Spanky* today because its very fiber is now offensive, and yet, ironically, its heart is so purely innocent and benign that it requires a sense of guilt in order to abhor it…

"*General Spanky* is funny because, whether it was intended to or not, it upholds these comedy truths: it challenges accepted social behavior; it confronts the rational world with irrationality; and it is surprising in its ignorant audacity. This movie will cause you to squirm more than you will laugh, but it is that very characteristic that makes it resonate long after the viewing. Moments that seemed trifling grow in the digestion. Buckwheat as a willing slave is an uncomfortable image. This movie is an archival crystal ball that gives a sense of how segregation affected racial comedy. It is to Buckwheat's merit that he still can come across funny instead of tragically sad."

In any event, there were no further Our Gang features.

1937 Releases:
Eleven Our Gang one-reelers
Four Features (one starring Laurel & Hardy, one as guests)
One Our Gang two-reeler

And there were almost no further Laurel & Hardy features either, as Stan Laurel, according to The *Hollywood Reporter* in early March 1937 "is staging a one-man sit-down strike on Hal Roach." It was announced that he had filed incorporation articles for his own company, Stan Laurel Productions with a capitalization of $100,000."

"Oliver Hardy, Laurel's partner," continued the *Hollywood Reporter*, "is under contract to Roach for two years more, and unless Laurel can be persuaded from his sit-down position, the famous team of comics will be separated. Hal Roach, who admits the holdout, says the new incorporation is all Greek to him."

Photoplay May 1937:

"At last, from all indications, you have seen the final Laurel & Hardy picture—which will be sad news to a million or so movie fans. Stan Laurel refused to sign a new contract with Hal Roach and has incorporated himself as a motion picture concern. Reports have it he is financed from New York banking circles and will start production soon. Hardy stays at the Roach studios. But can you imagine seeing one without the other? Like reading about Damon when there is no Pythias."

In January 1937 the *Chicago Daily Tribune* announced "HAL ROACH 45; MOVIE SUCCESS for 23 YEARS."

"Those who began reading about Hal Roach and his comedies about the same time they started hearing about Mack Sennett and the Christie Brothers, might imagine Roach as a dyspeptic graybeard, but such is not the case.

"A jolly, round faced, suntanned hearty looking fellow with just a trace of gray in thick and curly dark hair, Roach still applies youthful pep to his personal activities and to his film enterprises.

"And his bank roll also retains the vigor and heartiness of those early days. It was not so with Sennett and the Christies, whose studios have been closed for some years. Roach announces he is planning the biggest production schedule of his career for 1937 and that it will include six musical comedies of full length...

"Roach also is organizer and president of the Los Angeles Turf Club which operates the horse racing at Santa Anita Park, ranks as a four goal polo player, is a top amateur tennis player, boxer, and wrestler.

"His new home in Beverly Hills is one of the most impressive in the movie colony. His wife, a social hostess, their son, Hal Jr., and their daughter, Margaret, comprise his family."

The *Los Angeles Times* also ran a piece about Roach in January 1937 recalling him during the early years as a "Typical Movie Sportsman."

"...the old Locker Room Gang at the Los Angeles Athletic Club...'knew him when.' It was the locker room, the showers and the handball courts of the L.A.A.C. that Hal Roach embarked [on his movie] career that finally put his name on that Turf Club stationery. The old locker room gang was a motley assortment of young men, most of whom, like Roach, had been places and seen things and all of whom liked nothing better than the tortured muscles, blinding sweat, fierce competition, and hot arguments that are part of the life of young athletes.

"Among them, with Roach, were a rising young actor named Charles Ruggles and his brother Wesley, a bulgy-muscled giant named Noah Young, a pair of knockabout comedians named Harold Lloyd and Snub Pollard and a whole raft of other young huskies who mauled one another about and, while they may have dreamed of the accomplishments that have since been theirs, probably never expected to realize them…

"All the time the old locker room gang stuck pretty well together and Roach had a handball and squash court at the studio where the old-time perspiration, cheating and arguments were carried over from the L.A.A.C. days. Johnny Weissmuller and his pal Stubby Krueger, with Tom Gallery, an ex-squash champion, occasionally came down to play…

"It was as a polo player at Midwick Country Club that Roach and Carleton Burke, then Midwick captain and hard-riding back, became close friends and when the passage of the California horse-racing bill opened the field for a track which should rank with the best in the country it was only natural that Hal Roach should head the group of enthusiasts, who talked so much of the dubious financial possibilities of this 'sporting venture' that they had an awful time getting enough money together to start it. And if you see a group of grinning guys including Roach, the Ruggles boys and Harold Lloyd milling around on the bridge between the grandstand and the Turf Club—it's just the old locker-room gang cutting up old touches…."

In the meantime, back at the studio, following the sudden death of Thelma Todd, Roach had chosen Polish-born sexy blonde entertainer Lyda Roberti to co-star opposite Patsy Kelly, yet they made only two shorts. So in 1937 the two gal comics were teamed in the feature *Nobody's Baby* which was released in April. *Variety* called it "an agreeable comedy with songs." B.R. Crisler in the *New York Times* assessed the movie from the vantage point of Hal Roach's—even at that date—historical legacy.

"The name of Hal Roach has stood impregnably for so many generations, like a stone wall of conservatism in comedy," Crisler wrote, "that hardly any one will be surprised if the most revolutionary thing about his latest brainchild, *Nobody's Baby*, at the Rialto, is the fact that it runs to more than two reels. [Was he ignorant of all the other features Roach had produced up to that time?] Yet the dated farce and slapstick are so well buttressed by the vitality and strictly contemporary gagging of Patsy Kelly—the belle of the brawl—… that at times they almost can't be recognized…

"In a word or two at the most, the picture is pure Hal Roach, who has no more been changed by the procrustean expedient of stretching himself to feature length than the Supreme Court was changed by being housed in an air-conditioned building." [How's that for being considered up-to-date?]

Poor Lyda Roberti's career didn't go too far after that. She died of a heart attack just a year later, at the age of thirty-one.

In June 1937 Hal Roach Jr. graduated with honors from his military school and, according to the *Los Angeles Examiner*, "Hal Sr. was so pleased he's starting the boy today in his first job as second assistant director on the Roach lot."

"One of my contract writers came across the Thorne Smith book *Topper* and brought it to me," Roach told me in 1973. "I liked the idea of the invisible ghosts do-good couple and the comic situations that were potential to get them involved with."

Topper is the story of a happy-go-lucky couple who die in an automobile accident and come back as ghosts to harass the living, in the form of a stuffy middle aged couple Cosmo and Mrs. Topper. Roach originally wanted W.C. Fields to play Topper. He settled for the delightful character actor Roland Young. Billie Burke played his daffy wife. As for the fun loving younger couple, Roach was determined to cast up and coming Cary Grant.

As they were next door neighbors and often shared the swimming pool together, "Weekend after weekend Roach badgered Grant," wrote Geoffrey Wansell in his biography *Cary Grant, Dark Angel*. "…Grant liked Roach and admired his films a great deal," added Grant biographer Marc Eliot, "particularly his silent comedies, so as a favor to him, he decided that if Roach agreed to make a percentage deal and the film could be done quickly enough, then he would say yes."

Wansell wrote that Cary Grant had suggested Jean Harlow for the role of his wife, but Roach preferred Constance Bennett, "who was much less to Grant's taste. Nevertheless, she brought a chemistry to her role… But [Grant] did not care for the film or his performance. It came as no surprise to him when the *New York Times* called it 'rather a heavy consignment of whimsy.'" The public did not agree with *The New York Times'* and Cary Grant's dim assessment of *Topper*. After it was released on July 16, 1937 it "was a huge success" wrote Marc Eliot. "It went on to be the second highest grossing film of the year, a giant career leap for Grant as well as a solid financial investment that paid off in huge dollar dividends. It was by far the most popular and best Cary Grant film to date...."

The story of two frolicking ghosts was a most unusual subject for audiences in 1937. The reviewer for *Variety* seemed impressed by the special effects yet was uncomfortable with the frivolous tone by which the dead were depicted.

"...Hal Roach, heretofore identified with obvious action comedy and, with the assistance of Norman McLeod, as director, has produced as weird and baffling a tale of spiritualism as the screen ever has seen... It is carefully made, excellently photographed, and adroitly employs mechanical illusions of cinematic composition and trick sound effects...

"Effort to excuse the story's absurdities on the theory that the intent is farce comedy does not entirely excuse the production from severe rebuke. Fact also that the living dead always are facetious may be shocking to sensibilities. Some of the situations and dialog offend conventional good taste... *Topper* will be talked about both in and outside the industry.

"The skill with which camera and sound effects have been accomplished sets a standard for mechanical excellence. Settings are elaborate. But whether word of mouth advertising will be sufficient to overcome the obstacles which this type of story always combats is questionable. Probably not."

The *New York Times* review of *Topper* focused on another aspect, how well the tone and feel of Thorne Smith's story translated to the screen: "We honestly regret our inability to shout hurrah for *Topper* because everybody seems to have tried hard to make it click... But whimsy is a delicate and perishable commodity and nobody need be blamed for the slight soilage... Mr. [Roland] Young and his fellow players are responsible for whatever success an otherwise completely irresponsible film enjoys...."

The year 1937 was quite a turbulent one for Hal Roach. In May a Wild West party was thrown at his Ranch by MGM executives and their sales force as part of the MGM sales convention, and a young starlet accused one of the salesmen of a sexual assault. She filed a half-million dollar lawsuit against not only the salesman in question, but against Hal Roach, because the alleged crime occurred on his property, and two MGM officials. In November Superior Court Judge W. Turney Fox ordered the young woman, Patricia Douglas, to amend her charges or drop the action.

Miss Douglas said the studio officials were guilty of conspiracy by virtue of staging the party. Judge Fox ruled the act of conducting the affair was not sufficient evidence to involve them in the damage suit. Seventy years later, a film, *Girl 27*, was made of the incident by first time director David Stenn, who had penned biographies of Clara Bow and Jean Harlow.

Variety reviewed *Girl 27* on January 21, 2007: "...muckraking *Girl 27* milks a sad real-life story with shameless abandon... Appointing himself [Stenn] her confessor and new best friend, he presses for details of the 65-year-old [*sic*] incident she's struggled to forget. He convinces her—congratulating himself at length for doing this service—that she will only experience peace and 'vindication' if she tells the world her story once again. But onscreen evidence suggests the process provided more pain than healing in her final months. (She died last year.)

"Stenn leaves no opportunity unseized to interview himself and express his anger at the injustices endured by his subject—oblivious to the fact that he's using her in a violative fashion as well."

In September 1937 a real scandal of international proportions directly touched Hal Roach and threatened all the decades of goodwill he had created.

Roach courted controversy and almost censure when he traveled to Rome and entered into negotiations with dictator Benito Mussolini to produce four Italian operatic films. "Mussolini was getting nothing out of it except his desire to make good pictures in Italy," said Roach.

"[Mussolini] looked at all the good American movies, and he looked at all the bad Italian movies, and he went nuts. He said, 'Why, with the great literature of Italy, the great paintings, the great music, are we so behind in motion pictures?' And it made him eager for Italy to do something important in the motion-picture industry because he thought it too, was an art... I don't know why I was the person they got hold of and invited to Italy to discuss the deal. Anyway, I went to Rome, but I didn't want to make a deal, so I kept making it tougher. The tougher I made it, the more determined Mussolini became. I was to make four pictures for world distribution, ten pictures for European distribution, and forty pictures for Italian distribution. The Cinecittà Studio, a ten-million-dollar studio, was turned over to me, as well as eight million dollars in credit from the largest bank in Italy... Young Vittorio Mussolini, the dictator's son, was to be my partner."

Sailing with Roach to the U.S. on his return trip to Culver City was Mussolini's 21-year-old son Vittorio, who was eager to learn the movie business. His arrival was resented by many in Hollywood. The Italian military takeover of Ethiopia, with tons of mustard gas dumped from airplanes like "deadly rain" upon the Ethiopian people and lands the previous year was still fresh in the world's memory; at the time both the Soviet Union and the United States refused to recognize Italy's control over the small African nation. Even longtime Roach employee, little actor Sammy Brooks, was quoted as saying, "How can you condone a man who just dropped bombs on all those black people in Ethiopia?" However, according to the *Encyclopedia Brittanica*, "Although Mussolini's aggression was viewed with disfavour by the British, who had a stake in East Africa, the other major powers had no real interest in opposing him."

Roach conceded to author Mike Steen in 1969 that this association became a hot-button issue because of misunderstanding.

"…there was a problem from the beginning," explained Roach, "since the motion picture industry is a Jewish business, and Italy was a Fascist country. But Mussolini was not anti-Semitic. That's the first thing I asked him. I said, 'Any sanctions against Jews? If so, no deal.' And he assured me not and gave me all the dope… There was no Jewish problem in Italy until it was created by Hitler." It was not until a year later, in September 1938, that Mussolini enacted the Manifesto of Race which declared Italians to be the descendants of the Aryan race and anti-Semitic laws against the Jews of Italy were imposed. Although this was not the case at the time of young Mussolini's visit to Hollywood (in fact, the Dictator Mussolini had mocked Hitler's racial theories in his speeches of earlier years), the party Roach threw for the young Mussolini was reportedly shunned by many in Hollywood. But by how many? The contemporary *Los Angeles Times* article describing the Roach-Mussolini event lists an enormous number of Hollywood's elite, who were certainly naïve regarding the beginnings of a nightmare that would soon engulf the world.

"Since he was from a Fascist country and there were so many refugees here, some with Communist leanings, who had fled Germany, there was a movement to ignore him. I gave a large party for him. Some Jewish people who were in the motion picture business called other people and asked them not to come. But because they asked them not to come, they came as protest. I mean, people like David O. Selznick and Louis B. Mayer, these people came."

The *Los Angeles Times* called the September 28th party "one of the most brilliant social events of the season." It was not only a celebration of the 21st birthday of Il Duce's son, it was marked the 21st anniversary of Mr. and Mrs. Hal Roach's wedding.

"Over the tennis courts of the Roach estate in Beverly Hills," described the *Times*, "a gigantic canvas was stretched in the manner of a circus tent. A portable dance floor was arranged in the center and two orchestras, one Hawaiian and the other, a popular dance orchestra, alternately provided music. Buffet service established in the four corners of the pavilion, were typical of a different nationality.

"At one, Chinese food was served, with Chester Gan, Chinese character actor, [he appeared in *Vagabond Lady*] presiding as host. The amiable Hattie McDonald [McDaniel most likely] of radio fame received guests where succulent Southern dishes were arrayed.

"In another corner, where the colorful Spanish singer Stelita, served as hostess, Spanish food was in order. Paul Porcasi, Italian character actor, presided at the Italian buffet. In each instance those attending the buffet, booths were dressed in native costumes.

"A birthday cake for the honor guest was a huge chocolate one weighing more than thirty pounds. It was decorated with Italian and American flags and centered by a big candle with the national colors of Italy. A wedding cake to commemorate the anniversary of Mr. and Mrs. Roach's marriage was equally large and elaborately surmounted with decorations in white frosting.

"More than 300 members of the upper strata of society and filmdom were present to pay respects to the distinguished visitor. Young Mussolini, after dancing first with his hostess and with Miss Margaret Roach, chose many a famous star for his partner during the rest of the party hours which carried over until close to dawning.

"First on the long list were Dolores Del Rio, Constance Bennett, Billie Burke... Guests included... A.H. Giannini... Messrs. And Mmes. Fred Astaire... Warner Baxter... Wallace Beery, Ralph Bellamy, Jack Benny... Milton Bren, Clarence Brown, Joe E. Brown, John Mack Brown, Fredric March... Leo McCarey... Adolphe Menjou, Lewis Milestone, Robert Montgomery, Frank Morgan, Harmon O. Nelson, Eugene O'Neill... Dick Powell... Harry Rapf... Alden Roach... John Monk Saunders... David O. Selznick... Donald Ogden Stewart, Hunt Stromberg... Franchot Tone... Spencer Tracy, W.S. Van Dyke, S.S. Van Keuren, George Wallis, Raoul Walsh... William Wellman, Dwight Whiting... Sam Wood, Ed Sullivan, Robert Young, Darryl Zanuck, Joseph Schenck... Messrs. And Mmes. Charles Boyer, Tod Browning, George Burns, Leo Carrillo, Irvin Cobb... Gary Cooper... Bing Crosby, Cecil B. DeMille, Walt Disney... Douglas Fairbanks... Errol Flynn... George Jessel, Al Jolson, Allan

Jones, Harry Lachman... Harold Lloyd, David Loew, Edmund Lowe, Ernst Lubitsch, Anatole Litvak... Edward J. Mannix... Countess Dorothy Di Frasso... Mrs. Will Rogers... Mrs. C.H. Roach... Frances Marion... Ginger Rogers... Gloria Swanson... Virginia Bruce... Patsy Kelly... Lola Lane... Carole Lombard, Anita Louise, Geraldine Fitzgerald... Janet Gaynor, Paulette Goddard... Sonja Henie, Lili Damita, Loretta Young, and Messrs. Joe Mankiewicz... Herbert Marshall... Norman McLeod, Antonio Moreno... George Raft, Charles Ruggles, Wesley Ruggles, Randolph Scott, George Brent... Brian Aherne... Lionel Barrymore, Gilbert Roland... Charles Chaplin... Ronald Colman... Nelson Eddy... Carl Laemmle Jr... Cary Grant... Tyrone Power, Will Hays and Oliver Hardy."

Social triumph it may have been, the party was a political fiasco. Young Mussolini cut his Hollywood visit short and Roach quickly abandoned his Italian cinematic adventure. No Roach-produced Italian comic operas were ever filmed and five years later Roach showed the world what he thought of Mussolini in the early 1940s: he made two comedies lampooning the Italian dictator and his Axis cohorts Hitler and Hirohito.

At least the 1937 impasse with Stan Laurel was resolved. In October Roach signed a two-year, four picture deal with Stan Laurel Productions. Laurel was to be paid $2,500 per week and $25,000 per feature, the first to be the musical *Swiss Miss*.

Scarcely had the Mussolini-induced storm passed when Roach was involved in another screaming headline. "$200,000 GEM RAID STAGED IN HOLLYWOOD" ran the headlines on October 19, 1937. "Hal Roach Store Robbed in Real Movie Style; Girl and Man Bound by Pair." Hal Roach and a partner had opened a swank jewelry store on Sunset Strip that catered to many screen stars. On the morning of October 19 the store manager and his clerk was surprised by two revolver brandishing bandits who bound and gagged them, emptied the vault and were in the process of clearing the window display when the postman arrived. They bound and gagged him as well, and made their getaway. The lady who owned the dress shop next door happened to be outside and watched them flee; she managed to jot down their license plate number.

The bandits' abandoned car was found on Melrose Avenue. Among the loot was a $10,000 bracelet belonging to actress Simone Simon left for repairs, and jewelry belonging to Billie Burke. One diamond valued at $25,000 was also taken.

1938 RELEASES:
SEVEN OUR GANG ONE-REELERS
FOUR FEATURES (TWO WITH LAUREL & HARDY)

Roach was focused on his movie endeavors, however, his new project being a feature length comedy *Merrily We Live* starring Constance Bennett, Brian Aherne, Patsy Kelly and Billie Burke (did she have her stolen jewelry returned to her? Or let's hope she was insured). Perhaps the term "screwball comedy" hadn't been invented then, for in November 1937 Frank N. Seltzer, at that time Director of Hal Roach's Publicity and Advertising Department, wrote to Dr. Frank C. Baxter, a Professor of English at the University of Southern California (and later the host of Hal Roach Jr.'s TV show *Telephone Time*) "...to coin a new word that will describe the exact type of comedy we are trying to create in our current picture *Merrily We Live*. For obvious reasons we feel that the recognized terminology of farce, slapstick, satire or zany comedy is inadequate for our needs if we are to achieve distinction. What we want is some mouth-filling word that has a lilt and a ring to it."

The special care given *Merrily We Live* was proven by research. The number of laughs per picture at various screenings from 1938 to 1941 for six Hal Roach features from *Block-Heads* to *Topper Returns* were carefully counted during previews and adjustments were made accordingly. *Merrily We Live* came in at number one with an average of 231 laughs; *There Goes My Heart* received 221 laughs; whereas *Block-Heads* received a mere 161 laughs and *Zenobia* (admittedly not an out-and-out comedy) was last at 144 laughs. *Merrily We Live* has an airy, refreshing pace and the ensemble cast work together seamlessly. The comedy is now available on DVD at Movies Unlimited.

Clarence Kolb as the father of this zany clan has amazing zest and even does some impressive pratfalls, remarkable for a man of sixty-four. Yet *Variety* in its March 1938 review felt that "Most of the fun comes from a fine performance by Billie Burke. On the production side, Roach and Milton H. Bren, executive producer, give the film extravagant settings, equal to the best. Picture is in the high cost bracket."

Yet Frank Nugent of the *New York Times* chided the story of *Merrily We Live* as being a rip off of the much better *My Man Godfrey*, the classic 1936 comedy which starred William Powell and Carole Lombard.

But when Roach's next "zany comedy," *There Goes My Heart*, was released six months later, Nugent was livid. "*Merrily We Live* had all the earmarks of *My Man Godfrey*," he wrote in October 1938. "And *There*

Goes My Heart is *It Happened One Night* sans the transcontinental bus… Frankly though, we prefer our revivals straight and with the original casts; imitations so seldom do justice to the source work… The small talk grows pretty microscopic at times, and most of the fun is lost when you know from the first reel how everything is going to turn out. This admittedly is a prejudiced report: we can't help being prejudiced against copy-cats."

Regarding Roach's mid to late '30s excursions into "highbrow" comedy reminiscent of the movies being made by the major studios of the day, in 2014 an uncharitably harsh yet perceptive Facebook critic echoed Frank Nugent's contemporary attitude back in 1938:

"And this is the kind of stuff that Roach aspired to make! Even a $2000 profit on [Laurel & Hardy's *Our Relations*] meant that everyone's salaries were paid, the studio overhead was covered and MGM got their cut. Not a bad day's work. But to hemorrhage money [by] making third-rate versions of Capra or McCarey… madness. [Data supplied by Richard Lewis Ward reveal that *Vagabond Lady* lost over $156,000 and *Nobody's Baby* over $140,000.] Instead of feuding with Stan and firing Chase, Roach should have given them the keys to the studio and gone off to play polo for a decade or two."

Variety's critic in 1938, on the other hand, didn't seem to care a whit whether *There Goes My Heart* had copied any other movie. The reviewer was rapturous: "Picture is top-notch comedy drama with plenty of zip and zing and geared to garner important coin up and down the line, and generate holdover business in a number of spots. Picture contains many elements necessary to provide enjoyable entertainment. Script, with its comedy passages, is brilliantly magnified in transference to the screen through capable and inspired direction by Norman Z. McLeod. There's a closely-knit story which is generally lacking in a picture containing as many wholesome laughs and comedy sequences as this one. Getting under way at the start, yarn moves with increasing pace, with no letdowns, and McLeod has skillfully guided it through dramatic episodes with a lightness and deftness that retains the sparkle and charm necessary in a comedy-drama—but too seldom secured.

"Patsy Kelly, slimmer by forty pounds, is outstanding… Picture is given every advantage of smart and substantial production and rates A caliber throughout."

On June 18, 1938 the 169th and final Our Gang short was released by the Hal Roach Studios, entitled *Hide and Shriek*. That year he sold the

18-year-old series to MGM, which continued to produce them as one-reel shorts until 1944.

Earlier in 1938 it was announced that Hal Roach's daughter, 18-year-old Margaret, would begin a film career when she was assigned a speaking role in a Pete Smith short. "She took the name of 'Diane Rochelle,' she said," stated the *Hartford Courant*, "so she wouldn't trade on her father's reputation." Margaret would also appear uncredited in the Laurel & Hardy feature *Swiss Miss* the following year. She had credited roles in a three of her father's features and streamliners from 1939 to 1941 and uncredited walk ons in a few streamliners thereafter. In a display of Hollywood history irony, Ms. Roach also had uncredited bits in Cecil B. DeMille's *Union Pacific* (1939) and can be seen as a Showgirl walking up the stairs in Laurel & Hardy's post-Roach feature *A Haunting We Will Go* (1942).

She ended her Hollywood acting career with two "exploitation" low budgeters, *Test Tube Babies* (1948) and *The Devil's Sleep* (1949). Of the former, one viewer commented that "*TEST TUBE BABIES* is a sleazy and horrid little film that is actually much worse than Ed Wood's 'masterpiece', *PLAN 9!* In every conceivable way." Another commentator: "It's pretty clear that the filmmakers are skeezing lowlife themselves. The perfect meld of form and content!" Regarding *The Devil's Sleep*: "This film is a lot of fun," wrote one viewer. "It's stupid, campy, and downright weird and pointless. A good one." Another: "Definitely one of the better examples of the genre! While this isn't as funny as either *Reefer Madness* or *Test Tube Babies*, it's still something of an entertaining time-capsule movie. It's entirely ludicrous of course. And its exploitation efforts are commendable—women seem to strip down as much as possible at every given opportunity—while its heroically bad acting is a delight to see, with some characters clearly reading their lines off bits of paper. All-in-all, a good laugh." Interestingly, Hollywood nepotism is rampant throughout *The Devil's Sleep*. Charlie Chaplin's first wife, Lita Grey Chaplin, plays the tough lady Judge Rosalind Ballantine, and Mildred Davis, Harold Lloyd's wife and second leading lady, appears as the character Tesse T. Tesse in what was perhaps her only talkie. And speaking of Hollywood nepotism, Mildred and Harold's son, Harold Lloyd Jr., starred a few years later in another one of these strange exploitation quickies entitled *The Flaming Urge*. But that, of course, is for another story.

Meanwhile, getting back to the more civilized period of the late 1930s, Hal Roach's relationship with Stan Laurel was deteriorating.

"We were always fighting," he told me. "Another disagreement we had was with the picture *Swiss Miss* [1938]. For some damn reason Laurel wanted a gorilla to appear in the Alps, which was ridiculous. But he also contributed a lot of great gags to his pictures; for example, the great tickling scene in *Way Out West* [1937]. As for Hardy, he was no problem. He'd do anything you wanted him to. He was a good actor and devised all his mannerisms, but he wasn't interested in the writing or gag end. He'd just like to play golf or cards or drink."

In June 1938 the newspapers announced that Hal Roach Jr. "just 20" had been promoted to associate producer on the next Laurel and Hardy comedy *Block-Heads*, their 90th film for Roach. In August, two days before the release of the film, Roach fired Stan for alleged breach of contract. The *New York Times* noted: "There are vague and distressing rumors that Laurel and Hardy are about to dissolve their screen partnership. T'would be a pity, as almost any one will admit...."

Despite The *New York Times*' disappointment, *Variety*'s skepticism and Cary Grant's tepid view of the film, the ghost-comedy *Topper,* was such a big box office hit that Roach made two sequels. The first, screened at the end of 1938, was *Topper Takes a Trip,* with the same cast, minus Cary Grant, who only appears in flashback. (Following the cast credits at the beginning of the movie there is the title "Grateful acknowledgement is expressed to Mr. Cary Grant for his consent to the use of scenes from the original film "TOPPER.") *Variety*'s reviewer found it to be "a delightful, very entertaining comedy." The *New York Times* reviewer, however, was not so generous.

"*Topper Takes A Trip* is a case where the spirits are willing but the freshness is weak... the law of diminishing returns is one not even a dematerialized terrier can romp through... There is, after all, such a thing as an excess of spirits...."

The spirits were raging between Hal Roach and Stan Laurel. Roach accused Laurel of drinking on the set and getting into all sorts of marital mishaps with his numerous ex-wives and fiancées that involved the police. On August 12, 1938 the Hal Roach Studios terminated Laurel's contract.

1939 Releases:
Five features (Two directed by Hal Roach)

As Oliver Hardy still had several months left on his contract, Roach teamed him with a former silent comedy star who had been working as a gag writer, Harry Langdon. The new feature was called *Zenobia*, a light period comedy set in the antebellum South (ideal for the Georgia-born Hardy). The delightful Billie Burke played Oliver's ditzy wife, but Harry Langdon, who had not had a success in many, many years and had long lost the baby-faced innocence for which he was identified, was rather bland and unmemorable. *Zenobia* did not do well at the box office, and there seemed to be no possibility of a series of Langdon-Hardy teamings, if indeed one had ever even been contemplated.

"...Slender story provided does not warrant the amount of footage," declared *Variety* in March 1939. "...on the whole, comedy is strained. Things just seem to drift away without achieving much audience interest... Hardy demonstrates he can easily handle straight comedy without resort to familiar slapstick, but is handicapped by material provided. Langdon has but a few moments to work with Hardy, so an estimate on their work as a team must wait for future pictures."

The *New York Times* likewise expressed some disappointment. "By all the productional rules of thumb, in the mastery of which Mr. Roach bows to no man, *Zenobia* should, in fact, be a very funny picture. And it is... the humor might even, with inspired treatment, take off into stratospheric fantasy. Mr. Roach has failed to achieve this final, aerial felicity, but in the lean days which slapstick has currently fallen upon, only the professional killjoy is going to look a horse laugh in the mouth.

"...Harry Langdon's pale and beautifully blank countenance... has probably already excited the artistic jealousy of Mr. Laurel. As for Stepin Fetchit, he is getting as stylized as James Joyce; it is now almost impossible to form any idea of what he is trying to say."

Mr. Laurel, artistically jealous or not, at least was not one to sit idle: it was announced that he would join Mack Sennett's corporation and star in a series of comedies produced by Roach's old rival. This plan did not materialize. In April of 1939, Stan Laurel and the Hal Roach Studios reached an out-of-court settlement and both Laurel and Hardy signed separate, but concurrent, one-year contracts with Roach.

It's interesting to examine Stan Laurel's contract, which was for one year's service from April 15, 1939 as an ACTOR and/or PERFORMER, and as a WRITER and/or DIRECTOR. These duties are clearly if generally described: "...said Artist, in addition to rendering services to STUDIOS as an ACTOR, shall, as designated by STUDIOS, also render services in assisting in the writing and direction... it is contemplated that during the period of said employment, the ARTIST will assist in writing, composing and preparing necessary stories and story material for such photoplays, and render services in connection with the direction, or assisting in direction of such photoplays. The ARTIST, however, is primarily an actor. STUDIOS will employ other writers to originate and prepare story material, and ARTIST's only obligation is to assist in such preparation by oral suggestion, and not by physical writing… ARTIST has waived story approval, which ARTIST had under previous contracts, but such stories must be primarily about LAUREL and HARDY as the principal characters; be in keeping with the characters they have created; be consistent with making the photoplays hereunder at low cost; and lend themselves to easy and ready comedy treatment." His compensation was $2,500 per week, for not less than forty weeks during the year for up to four four-reel comedies.

In light of his recent bad publicity, there was a clause entitled CONDUCT OF ARTIST. "Artist agrees to conduct himself with due regard to public conventions and morals and agrees that he will not do or commit any act or thin that will tend to degrade or disgrace him in society, or bring him into public hatred, contempt, scorn or ridicule, and/or that will tend to shock, insult or offend the community, or ridicule public morals or decency, or prejudice the STUDIOS, or the motion picture industry in general. STUDIOS, however, realizes that ARTIST is now engaged in matrimonial difficulties with his present wife, and that on previous occasions former wives of ARTIST have started litigation and/or caused publicity. Publicity and conduct reasonably incidental to such matters shall not be a breach of ARTIST."

The comedy team of Laurel & Hardy had been saved once again! That year Roach loaned Laurel and Hardy for the first time in their career to another studio. Independent producer Boris Morros starred the boys in *The Flying Deuces*, their second excursion to the Foreign Legion, following *Beau Hunks* eight years earlier. Harry Langdon was hired as a staff writer and Roach player James Finlayson came along. Charles Middleton, the original commandant in their 1931 four-reeler repeated his role in this popular feature, which was released by RKO-Radio Pictures.

And popular it was. In a letter dated December 2, 1939 the branch manager of RKO Radio Pictures, Inc. in Philadelphia, Mr. F.L. McNamee, wrote to Roach, "FLYING DEUCES is doing a most unusual business… played State Theater in Allentown for a full week to $1350.00 gross in a house that normally does about $900." Other theaters in Pennsylvania also had "unusually big grosses. The Park Theater, Reading opened this picture Sunday December 3rd to $1707.00 (the third biggest Sunday in the history of the theater) being topped only by GUNGA DIN and SNOW WHITE."

A triumphant Stan and Ollie returned to the Hal Roach Studios and made what turned out to be their final two features for Roach, *A Chump at Oxford* and *Saps at Sea*. Both of these vintage comedies included a supporting cast made up of the comics who had been with the boys since the silent days. But when Laurel and Hardy's contracts with Hal Roach expired on April 5, 1940, a whole era drew to a close. It was decided that Laurel and Hardy would not renew their contracts with Roach and the comic triumvirate of Hal Roach and Laurel and Hardy would never work together again. Stan Laurel planned to become an independent producer and produce the "Laurel & Hardy comedies" himself, but this was not to be.

In 1938, Roach became a producer for United Artists, where he made a distinguished production of John Steinbeck's *Of Mice and Men* starring Burgess Meredith and Lon Chaney Jr., and the prehistoric fantasy *One Million B.C.*

July 16, 1937 *Evening Independent*, St. Petersburg, Florida: Lewis Milestone signed to direct *Road Show* by Eric Hatch; Marc Connelly, author of *Green Pastures*, to write screenplay. This is Hal Roach's next production following *Topper*."

However, nearly a year later, the *Los Angeles Examiner* carried this item: June 3, 1938: "Roach Sues Milestone for $339,000 in Row over Film

"When a screen director begins work on a picture, should he follow studio instructions and make it a comedy, or his own ideas and turn out a serious drama?

"This question is concerned in a suit, amounting to $420,661 filed yesterday by Hal Roach Studios, Inc. in reply to an attachment suit brought by Lewis Milestone, film director."

Milestone asserted that he had worked for ten weeks and was properly paid the agreed $5,000 per week, but that the production was suspended and he was discharged because Roach did not like the fact that Milestone was turning his comedy into a drama. Milestone subsequently sued to recover $60,000 in salary for the suspended weeks and $21,661 as a penalty.

"In its response the film studio...demanded that Milestone make good the loss suffered in the production delay, which claims amount to $339,000, including $89,000 paid him and Marc Connelly, screen writer, for script work."

February 20, 1939 *Palm Beach Daily News*: "Details are now being worked out whereby Lewis Milestone directs *Of Thee I Sing* to star Jack

Benny "as his second Hal Roach Production." Victor Moore to recreate his stage role. This 1931 political satire musical, book by George F. Kaufman and Morrie Ryskind, music by George Gershwin, lyrics by Ira Gershwin— what a great movie that would have been! Alas, it was never made into a Hollywood movie in the 1930s. In fact, it was not until 1972 that a television version appeared, greatly altered, starring Carroll O'Connor, Cloris Leachman and Jim Backus.

In May 1939 came *Captain Fury*, directed by Roach himself, and starring Brian Aherne as an Irish rebel fighting his way out of an Australian penal colony with a band of hearties. "Here is a lusty outdoor melodrama on the familiar Robin Hood format," declared *Variety*. "There's action, gunplay, fast riding, surprise attacks, some broad comedy and a few dashes of romance... Picture is the first chore for Hal Roach as a director in several years. Job is moderately successful, with tempo kept at a good pace to overcome minor shortcomings in the script...."

A special screening of *Captain Fury* was presented at the Australian Pavilion of the British Empire Building at the New York World's Fair on May 23rd. L.R. MacGregor, Australian High Commissioner at the Fair, and W.G. Van Schmus, Managing Director of Radio City Music Hall hosted "a specially invited audience."

The *New York Times* stated "The picture [has a] remarkable resemblance to any and all other picaresque screen melodramas since the dawn of the cinema. No resemblance whatever to life, of course."

In the spring of 1939 pre-production commenced on Laurel & Hardy's comeback feature, *A Chump at Oxford*. Someone must have been worried about using the actual institution of Oxford University in the movie, and sought the professional advice of a well known legal authority in Washington, D.C., an attorney who specialized in copyright, trademark, and entertainment law. On May 27, 1939 Fulton Brylawski wrote to the Hal Roach Studios, "So long as your picture does not libel Oxford University, the fact that the locale of the picture is laid there... would not subject you to any possible liability."

Hal Roach Jr., barely twenty-one, served as associate producer. Longtime veteran Alf Goulding directed; and the usual cast and crew who had been supporting Laurel & Hardy for the past twelve years contributed, along with a few newcomers. It's interesting to see what salaries were paid to the cast: James Finlayson, $450 per week; Wilfred Lucas $375; Forrester Harvey $750; Charlie Hall $400; Peter Cushing $350. Oliver Hardy's stand-in was paid $118.50 per week, whereas Stan Laurel's stand-in received $99.00. (Was this based on poundage?) Charlie Rogers, co-writer received $412 per week. Originally slated as a 42-minute "streamliner" to be released in February 1940, the footage was extended to sixty-three minutes and finally released in the U.S. and Europe early in 1941.

Lots of old timers from the silent days were still churning them out at the Hal Roach Studios. But one veteran would never return. On May 10, 1939 James Parrott died at the age of forty-one. The papers said it was a heart attack. Others believe his demise was self-inflicted due to his numerous ailments, addictions and alcoholism. He had stopped directing in the mid 1930s but did receive credit as a writer for the Laurel & Hardy features *The Bohemian Girl, Way Out West, Swiss Miss* and *Block-Heads.*

"There has been a tendency in recent years to minimize the contribution of Jimmy Parrott to both the Laurel and Hardy and Charley Chase comedies," wrote Anthony and Edmonds in 1998. "This was primarily due to the fact that Stan Laurel never accepted directorial credits on his own films. Contemporary historians, correctly believing that Laurel never received the recognition he deserved, now overcompensate and seem to suggest he was the only creative person behind the camera. In many ways Jimmy Parrott was the quintessential director of Hal Roach comedies. Never hurried, he tended to stress character and human eccentricities. His films were filled with subtle, quirky throwaway gags that often become evident only after repeated viewings, but add considerable charm and depth to the productions."

"The films were a creative collaboration, both behind as well as in front of the cameras. Magnificently talented as they were, both Stan Laurel and Charley Chase benefited greatly from gifted directors. And a large measure of a director's effectiveness, especially on the Roach lot, was being able to work amiably with the stars, offer creative suggestions, and gain the confidence and respect of the actors."

Within days of James Parrott's death, Roach sought out a Hollywood director who had indeed gained the confidence and respect of film actors years previously, but whose talents and abilities were being neglected.

"My old friend D.W. Griffith would come every day to the set of *One Million B.C.*, recalled Roach in 1973. "I felt sorry for him and put him on the payroll." In this Mr. Roach had forgotten a few facts during the intervening years. He had actually written to Griffith, who was at home in Kentucky, offering him to come to California and assist him at his studio.

As far back as 1926 Roach had the idea of hiring Griffith to make a series of dramatic shorts. In a telegram to Mr. Griffith on December 26, 1926 he had written, "I FIRMLY BELIEVE THE RESULT WOULD BE SOMETHING WHICH MIGHT REVOLUTIONIZE THE INDUSTRY."

But even then D.W. Griffith was considered a Hollywood has-been. *Photoplay* in March of 1927 had observed: "D.W. Griffith is back in Hollywood groping about for a theme worthy of his megaphone. We hope he finds one that will bring him back to the position that he earned and held for years as our finest director. His golden throne has been melted by inferior productions and the metal fashioned into medals for a dozen directors who were unheard of when D.W. was making motion picture history."

"Hollywood today is a sterile film Detroit with emotions as standardized as automobile parts," reflected D.W. to writer Jim Hart in an article published in *Liberty* magazine in June of 1939 from his home in Kentucky.

"We have moving pictures that do not move," reflected Griffith as he chain-smoked. "Activity is mistaken for action; sex for love; and sound effects for suspense. If history remembers at all the people responsible for such an assembly line, it should only be for the vandalism they have wrought in a medium that could have ranked with art and literature."

Griffith had been inactive from the "sterile film Detroit" he himself had helped to build for nearly a decade.

In his 1984 biography *D.W. Griffith, An American Life*, author Richard Schickel wrote that Hart felt that Hal Roach must have read this article and this prompted him to offer Griffith employment. "But both Mrs. Griffith and Roach himself remember the circumstances differently," wrote Schickel. "She recalls Griffith simply deciding to return to the Coast to look for work, and Roach remembered being moved at the sight of Griffith at loose ends in Los Angeles 'not doing a damned thing... one of the great geniuses of the business.'" [Hal Roach to Richard Schickel].

The evidence leads to other conclusions. In the Hal Roach Collection there is a mimeographed letter from the Hal Roach Studios dated May 13, 1939 addressed to

"Mr. D.W. Griffith, La Grange, Oldham County, Kentucky.

"Dear David:

"Our program for next year includes: HOUSEKEEPER'S DAUGHTER, which is a comedy murder mystery. The screenplay "OF MICE AND MEN" which will be directed by Lewis Milestone. "1,000,000 B.C., a prehistoric picture, something like THE LOST WORLD, only with an authentic period. CAPTAIN CAUTION by Kenneth Roberts, a very fine sea story, and probably TURNABOUT by Thornton Smith, a novel comedy in which a man and wife change places.

"With the exception of Frank Ross (Jean Arthur's husband) who is a very good business man and who has not had too much experience in pictures, I have no other producer on my lot.

"I personally am directing two or three of these pictures. Therefore I need help from the production side to select the proper writers, cast, etc., and to help me generally in the supervision of the pictures.

"My thought was that you could come to our studio without any pretentiousness at the start and see how you would work into any capacity into which you would fit, for which I would pay a modest salary until such time as we could determine both whether you liked the association and whether you would add sufficient value to our pictures to justify additional compensation.

"During this period I thought of your salary somewhere between $500.00 and $1,000.00 a week.

"Upon receipt of this, please let me know your intentions and if there is any further information you desire, please contact me. Kindest regards, Sincerely, Hal E. Roach."

On May 22 Griffith sent Roach the following postal telegraph: "LETTER RECEIVED TODAY ACCEPT YOUR OFFER WILL DISCUSS SALARY WHEN WE MEET SURE WE CAN AGREE ON TERMS AS OUTLINED IN YOUR LETTER LET ME KNOW WHEN YOU WANT ME AND I WILL LEAVE ON RECEIPT OF FARE TO AND FROM CALIFORNIA FOR WIFE AND SELF REGARDS D.W."

Griffith and his wife arrived in California in June and remained on the Roach payroll for six months, during which time he assisted with the pre-production of *One Million B.C.* at the salary of $600.00 per week.

"The one thing D.W. Griffith did on *One Million B.C.* was discover the lead for that picture, Carole Landis," said Roach. Griffith pointed out the blonde starlet to Roach as "the girl who can run like a deer." Roach was so impressed with her that he signed her to a two picture a year contract. Not only did Carole Landis appear as the female lead in *One Million BC.*, but she was also starred in *Turnabout, Road Show*, and *Topper Returns*.

In June 1939, a year after Hal Roach had filed the lawsuit against director Milestone for his mis-direction of the aborted 1937 project *Road Show*, they had at last come to an agreement. Milestone would direct a feature length drama *Of Mice and Men*, based upon the acclaimed novel by John Steinbeck that was enjoying an equally successful run as a Broadway play. Writer Eugene Solow would adapt the screenplay and he and Milestone joined Steinbeck for several weeks at his home in Los Gatos, California to work on the script. "...we are working on a final script of Mice," Steinbeck wrote his agent on June 22nd, "and it sounds very good to me."

July 24, 1939 *New York Times*: "Negotiations were opened today by Hal Roach with Warners for the loan of Humphrey Bogart for the role of George in *Of Mice and Men*. Previously Roach had sought James Cagney for the part. Lewis Milestone, who will produce and direct, expects to begin work early next month."

"While his own studio [Warner Bros.] paid seemingly little attention to furthering Bogart's career," wrote A.M. Sperber and Eric Lax in their 1997 biography *Bogart*, "other producers, thanks to *Dark Victory*, were looking seriously at him... The most frustrating offer that couldn't be taken came from Lewis Milestone, the director of *All Quiet on the Western Front*, who wanted Bogart for John Steinbeck's *Of Mice and Men*. It was a quality part that hadn't come Bogart's way since *Dead End* and [Bogart's agent Sam] Jaffe pleaded with Warners to loan him out. No, the studio answered, they needed Bogart for *The Roaring Twenties*, and since they didn't know what his assignment after that would be, they were making no picture commitments. *Of Mice and Men* went on to a Best Picture nomination."

August 28, 1939: "With The Hollywood Reporter" by Frederick C. Othman, U.P. Hollywood Correspondent. "If two top movie makers hadn't gotten into a fight and started slapping lawsuits at each other *Of Mice and Men*... might never have been turned into a movie.

"But fight there was, between Hal Roach, who made millions as a custard pie comedy producer, and Lewis Milestone, director of such pictures as *All Quiet on the Western Front* and *Front Page*. When John Steinbeck wrote *Mice* and it became an outstanding stage hit, Milestone obtained the rights to make it into a movie.

"All the producers laughed at him. They said they didn't intend to sink their money into any picture wherein the two leading characters were psychopathic cases: one addicted to petting animals so roughly he killed them and the other loving his partner so much he shot him through the head to save him from a lynching party.

"Milestone countered with the assertion that *Mice* was one of the most powerful stories of this age; that it had a poetic quality; that it would make a magnificent movie. 'Haw,' the producers said, and sucked on their cigars.

So Milestone signed to do another picture with Roach. They had an argument; Milestone sued Roach, Roach countersued.

"When the anger cooled, they agreed that after all they were grown up intelligent men. They settled their differences out of court—and part of the settlement was that Roach would finance Milestone's production of *Mice*.

"So now the studio which has turned out more comedy hits perhaps than any other is engaged in making a movie destined to hit the customers between the eyes with an emotional sledge hammer. There never has been a better piece of irony than that..."

Several actors were considered for the role of Lennie, the big, dumb migrant worker with a penchant for anything soft and furry. Broderick Crawford and baseball player turned actor Guinn "Big Boy" Williams were considered, but when Lon Chaney Jr. played Lennie in the Hollywood stage production of *Mice* and received fourteen curtain calls, the choice was obvious.

Finding a run-down California ranch to film *Of Mice and Men* turned out to be a problem, as so many of them had been modernized. At last it was decided to build a ranch on land in Agoura, California.

"Fifty carpenters spent $40,000 and eight days erecting nine ranch buildings and a windmill," reported Othman.

"We asked Milestone whether he believed enough cash customers would see the picture to pay expenses. He said frankly that he didn't know.

"I remember when we previewed *All Quiet*, he said. "The experts all said that I had made an artistic success and a financial fizzle. Then the picture went out and made millions.

"When the producers talk about making commercial movies, they're talking about neither fish nor fowl but tripe. All I know is that *Of Mice and Men* distinctly will not be tripe. It is a great story. I know that. And I'm not going to worry about its success at the box office."

Meanwhile, Roach produced AND directed another feature for 1939 release.

September 26, 1939: Unsigned letter to William Wilkerson, the founder and publisher of *The Hollywood Reporter*, most certainly written by Roach: "Dear Billie: Deferring to the suggestions made in your review of *Housekeeper's Daughter*, I shot several additional scenes and we are previewing the picture again this Thursday evening September 28 at the Alexandria Theatre in Glendale at 8:30 p.m. I would deem it a personal favor if you would be good enough to cover it again at that time."

"Best laugh riot in years," was the consensus of a Denver sneak preview.

"Happiest audience we've seen in a long time," stated The *Loew-Down* report.

"Constant flow of laughs," declared The *Exhibitor News.*

"Excellent! It is one of the most intelligently produced, most highly entertaining comedies that has been made in years," boasted *Harrison's Reports.*

"Here is a broad farce which many times bubbles over into burlesque of the early Mack Sennett and Harold Lloyd era," said *Variety* of *The Housekeeper's Daughter* in September 1939. "It's a smacko laugh generator... Critics may tab it as hokey and corny, but it's top laugh entertainment. Hal Roach, who personally directed, dug back into the handbook of silent comedy technique and brought out some nifties to piece together here... *Housekeeper's Daughter* is a wacky farce...."

The *New York Times*: "For a really strenuous exercise in slapstick, it is still necessary to go to that past master of unsubtlety, Hal Roach, of whose collected cinematic editions *The Housekeeper's Daughter*... is the funniest specimen in years and years... its broad and boisterous and irresponsible humors, acted with gusto by a cast of cinema veterans, are all that a lover of direct comic action and a hater of mere innuendo could possibly desire... The cast is superb...."

December 21, 1939: Personal letter to Roach from A.C. Blumenthal, wealthy real estate developer and theatre chain promoter: "I could not let the occasion pass without expressing to you how much I like your picture 'The Housekeeper's Daughter.' Apart from the fact that everybody around me in the theatre fell on their sides laughing, I personally thought the... picture was most entertaining...."

Yet not everyone was laughing, least of all, if one were to believe the December 1939 article in *Photoplay*, stars Joan Bennett and Adolph Menjou.

"...one horrible picture like *The Housekeeper's Daughter* could have killed a star bigger than Joan Bennett... fortunately Joan can weather it because she is beautiful and promising enough and not so abnormally high salaried that producers can't still take a chance with her... Adolphe [Menjou] had signed for it, as Joan had, after reading the book, which they both liked, but without seeing the script, which was impossible... when they got to work they couldn't escape because of their contracts... every time Joan left the set for any reason whatsoever [Menjou] would hurry to her side. 'Don't leave me here alone in the middle of this picture,' he'd cry, 'Joan, you promise to come back'... It was only by such kidding that they managed to live through the picture at all... they knew how awful it was from the very first take... for actors do know a lot more about stories than they are given credit for knowing... Miss Bennett says she will never again go into a picture on which she has not seen the full script."

Parenthetically, Mr. Menjou was paid $50,000 for six weeks of work on that film; Miss Bennett received $30,000 for the same time period, probably the highest salary The Hal Roach Studios had paid to any performers up to that time.

As if the *Photoplay* put-down weren't bad enough, *Hollywood* magazine noted that Joan Bennett was less than happy with Roach for something even worse than what she considered a bad script. She filed a lawsuit to have posters of *The Housekeeper's Daughter* torn down because "he had put out bill posters indicating the character she played... was nicer to the boys than any nice girl should be."

To emphasize her displeasure, Miss Bennett (or her lawyers) sent a letter of protest to dozens of ladies' societies and film organizations around the country. That missive states, in part, "I find that some of the advertising and publicity material designed to exploit a picture in which I appear—*The Housekeeper's Daughter*—is of a distasteful and undignified nature... To remain silent would be an intimation that I approve of or acquiesce in such methods of motion picture exploitation. This construction would be exactly opposite to the fact. In justice to the motion picture industry I may state that such violation of good taste are rare. But that is no reason I should submit to interpretations that might be damaging to my standing as an actress and, worse, to my standing as an individual."

The offensive ad campaign ran as follows: "Five Men Ran After The Housekeeper's Daughter... Who Treated Them Like She Hadn't Outer!" "Five Men Tried to Keep House with The Housekeeper's Daughter... But Keeping House Was Not in Her Line!" "She Couldn't Cook, She Couldn't Sew, but Oh how she could so and so!"

According to James McKay in his book *The Films of Victor Mature*, Joan Bennett "hailing from a respectable acting dynasty... didn't see the funny side [of this publicity] and promptly harnessed the support of 2,600 women's clubs countrywide in her objection to the tongue-in-cheek slogans. The press had a field day with the protests, which simply fueled publicity for the film."

"The resultant publicity," concurred *Hollywood* magazine, "made that somewhat less than sublime film a four-star box office hit."

In her autobiography written some thirty years later, Joan Bennett stated, "The ads implied a vulgarity that simply wasn't there and had nothing to do with the film, which was a bland comedy, and not a very good one at that."

A much more compliant participant in *The Housekeeper's Daughter*, and who helped to make it a hit, was the appearance of a new star—Victor Mature. Born in Louisville, Kentucky to Austrian immigrants, Mature was spotted by Hal Roach Studios Vice President Frank Ross while performing at the Pasadena Playhouse. Roach signed him and cast him as Lefty, the lovesick gangster. Immediately some 20,000 fan letters (some reports say 30,000) were sent to the new bobbysoxers' heartthrob, convincing Roach to put the young man under contract, cast him as the lead in *One Million B.C.* and *Captain Caution*, and then loaned him out to other studios.

Years later, in the May 1972 issue of *Interview* magazine, Mature talked about filming *The Housekeeper's Daughter*. He was directed to slap Bennett in one scene. "He overdid it and accidentally knocked her wig off which made Bennett extremely angry. When Roach approached Mature with a serious expression, the actor feared the worst, but the mogul simply whispered to him, 'Next time hit her a little harder.'"

"I didn't win the battle with Hal Roach," concluded Ms. Bennett in her autobiography, "but I have an idea he knew he had a worthy adversary by the time I was through."

The Housekeeper's Daughter was banned outright in Jamaica by the Chief Censor under the Cinematographic Law of the British West Indies. No reason was given to the Hal Roach Studios, despite Hal Roach himself writing two letters to the Chief Censor requesting an explanation.

Despite his difficulties with Miss Bennett, Roach wanted to cast her in the third trilogy to his "Topper" series which was tentatively entitled "Topper Behaves" (released in 1941 as *Topper Returns*). Miss Bennett quit because she felt her part wasn't good or prominent enough.

"Why do you say that Joan Blondell has a better part than you?" Roach is reported to have asked Miss Bennett. "Blondell plays a disappearing ghost." "'The trouble is that she doesn't disappear enough,' snapped Miss Bennett as she swept out of his office." Carole Landis played the role.

Happier news resulted from Mr. Roach's next 1939 release. *Box Office* review of *Of Mice and Men* on December 30, 1939: "Hal Roach's screen version…is a triumphant production in every department…flawless casting and masterful direction of a delicately wrought screenplay."

Variety, January 3, 1940: "...a most sincere job of expert screen crafts-manship... the players have been excellently selected for their respective assignments."

William K. Everson gave a glowing assessment: "A superb example of remaining entirely faithful to the content and structure of a literary work, yet transposing a story originally told exclusively through dialogue into visual terms, *Of Mice and Men* was powerful, gripping, almost unbearably poignant—and beautifully acted.... Despite unqualified raves from the critics, the film was not a huge success. After the froth and never-never-land of the mid and late thirties, audiences just weren't ready for such a grim and uncompromising film...."

Hal Roach himself had a practical down-to-earth assessment:

"I don't think [*Of Mice and Men*] failed to be a big box-office smash be-cause it was such a heavy and psychological picture. It was that word 'mice' in the title. Right away we lost all the women."

"Everyone thought he was crazy," wrote Florence Fisher Parry of Lewis Milestone in her February 18, 1940 newspaper column "I Dare Say" regarding his wanting to make *Of Mice and Men* into a movie. "The book might be a literary gem of the first water... but it had a morbid theme; it had an 'unhappy' ending; it hadn't a glimmer of glamour of romance in the whole story, it was about bindle-stiffs who slept in their underwear and washed (when they washed) out of a tin basin. What would the fans make of a picture like that?

"Finally Hal Roach said he'd sponsor it. He put about $200,000 in it, about the smallest sum ever invested in a Class A picture. Milestone got a ranch, a good photographer, a good cast, and in about six weeks the picture was finished. It was one of the finest motion pictures ever made. It is as good a picture as the novel was a novel...

"Now this film was a purely experimental film. So was *The Grapes of Wrath*, its only rival today in stark unsparing film drama. So was *Pasteur* and *David Copperfield* and *Snow White* and almost every truly great advance in motion picture making. I doubt if any exhibitor, free to select any one of these films before their completion, would have risked leas-ing them. Buying them in block, among a lot of sure-fire box-office films, they knew that by the terms of their 10 per cent elimination clause they wouldn't 'have' to show them if they didn't click.

"The Neely Bill is before the House of Representatives. If it should pass, there would be no more experimental films, or prestige films; and the industry, from a creative standpoint, would stop stock still and stay there for lack of the kind of initiative and risk and daring that is required in any creative field."

Senator Matthew M. Neely of West Virginia proposed this Anti-Block Booking Bill in May 1935 for hearing in 1936; it was finally brought before the House of Representatives in 1940. Earlier, in the House, Indiana representative Samuel B. Pettengill originated a sister proposal.

"At initial glance, the Neely-Pettengill bill seemed an ideal rallying point for all independents. However a provision designed to undermine blind bidding alienated many of the producers. Since many distributors sold their movies before they were produced, theaters complained that the sparse information upon which the theaters based their purchases was altered during the production process. In a well-intentioned effort to improve the bargaining position of the theaters, the Neely-Pettengill bill required all films to be presented to exhibitors with a 'complete and true synopsis' of the movie, including plot details, scene analysis, and character information. Any person who sold a film without a synopsis, or knowingly provided false data, would be subject to fine or imprisonment.

"Requiring all Hollywood producers to adhere to a detailed synopsis throughout production was a laughable concept in the major studios which relied on test screenings and reediting to hone their movies before each release. The independent producers also found the provision objectionable. While some independents were known for a methodical approach to film production, many of the creative producers resorted to on-the-fly filmmaking, molding the productions with quick decisions and last minute changes. The unpopular provision left most independent producers apprehensive of the bill, and made Neely an easy target for the Hollywood resistance."—*Hollywood Renegades Archive* website by J. A. Aberdeen

"To compel any Producer to be bound in advance of Production to standardized, machine-like production of motion pictures is too abhorrent to ever contemplate."—David O. Selznick.

"The Neely Bill is but another example of Government needle-nosing," continued Mrs. Parry in her February 1940 article. "Its passage would disrupt, cripple, and all but ruin the fourth major industry in our country... It would encourage monopoly by encouraging the industry in the hands of a comparatively few companies of unlimited financial resources, and do to the death all independent producers, men who, like Samuel Goldwyn, Walter Wanger, Walt Disney, Charlie Chaplin, and now Hal Roach, have consistently striven for originality and freshness in their productions.

"The tragic thing about such legislation as the Neely Bill is that it is supported by minority laymen agitators who know nothing whatever about the functionings of the motion picture business, but whose active little pressure groups wield vast influence upon the representatives who regard their shrill and always articulate plaints a cross-section of public opinion for the simple and sad reason that those worthies in the House and Senate do not hear concerted protest launched by the very ones whom such absurd legislation would affect most directly: the MOTION PICTURE FANS THEMSELVES."

In June 1940 the bill was deemed "unworkable."

Meanwhile, D.W. Griffith continued his work at the Hal Roach Studios through the second half of 1939. In addition to discovering Carole Landis, he made title suggestions (he wanted to call One Million B.C. Before Adam), he gave his input regarding the opening dialogue sequence and he was one of the first to view the rough cut of Of Mice and Men.

Griffith's non-directing assignment came to an end in December 1939. He did NOT quit nor was he fired by Roach as certain persistent rumors suggest, fueled no doubt by the erroneous statement published by the otherwise impeccable William K. Everson that "D.W. Griffith, who had signed to direct amid much publicity (his first film in almost a decade), was removed from the picture." The evidence uncovered to date reveals that Griffith's tenure was strictly a six month general assignment and that he requested his credit not appear on the screen.

Richard Schickel wrote "Richard Reynolds [D.W.'s] chauffeur, would recall Griffith saying as they headed home from the studio, 'These young whipper snappers don't know what they're talking about, they don't even know the technique... they try to ignore me... but I really know. I was born with it, I started it, I invented it...'"

1940 RELEASES:
FIVE FEATURES (TWO DIRECTED BY HAL ROACH)

Perhaps Griffith requested no screen credit for One Million B.C. because he sensed it would not be a resounding critical success. Indeed, its reception following the premiere at the California Theatre in San Diego on March 27, 1940 was decidedly mixed.

"Hal Roach's pretentious production... is a good try, but doesn't jell," said Variety in its first review. "The whole thing still smacks of Saturday matinee serial offerings." On May 1ˢᵗ appeared another critique: "*One Million B.C.* looks something like 1910 A.D... it's that corny. Except for the strange-sounding grunts and monosyllabic dialog, it is also another silent. Hal Roach, who has spent a lifetime making comedies, goes to the other extreme as producer of the prehistoric spectacle. He may be discouraged from doing something along these lines again, since all indications point to disappointing grosses."

The *New York Times*: "Not in the last million years, conservatively speaking, has the screen witnessed anything to equal *One Million B.C.* in which Hal Roach, the comedy king, takes a bargain-counter excursion into paleontology...."

While *Film Daily* burbled "Thrill-Packed Screen Novelty... Direction Excellent, Photography Corking," *Picture Reports* of April 20ᵗʰ was rather scathing: "As a mixture of Tarzan and Lost World... this one should gross about enough to return its negative cost if that figure isn't very high. If it does, Hal Roach's son will have gotten some directorial experience at the customer's expense and no one but the exhibitor is likely to get hurt. While a lot of genuine effort and extremely clever special effects and photography undoubtedly went into this picture, the result is still amateurish by today's standard...."

In any event, *One Million B.C.* received Oscar nominations for the special effects and for the music score (by Werner Heymann).

Next to be released was *Turnabout*, a fantasy-comedy based on the 1931 novel by *Topper* creator Thorne Smith (1892-1934) and directed by Hal Roach. It is a risqué tale about a husband and wife who, through some magic hoo-doo, get their personalities and gender roles switched. Had Roach made *Turnabout* the way he wanted to during the Pre-Code era of relaxed censorship in Hollywood, it would have been a wild, anarchic gender-bending romp. But after mid-1934 the Production Code had taken a stern Puritanical grip on exactly how freewheeling and "loose" morality could be presented on the screen. Joseph Breen, the notorious head of the Production Code Administration, the censorship organization which passed or rejected scripts and movies, was at the height of his powers in 1940. (He would remain head of the PCA until 1954.) When he read the *Turnabout* screenplay he wrote to Roach, among other objections: "This characterization of Mr. Pingboom as a 'pansy' is absolutely unacceptable, and must be omitted from the finished picture. If there is any such flavor, either in casting, direction, or dialogue, we will not be able to approve the picture."

Roach, as producers did in the early 1930s ignored this warning and cast Franklin Pangborn, the ultimate "pansy" character actor of the 1930s, in the role of Mr. Pingboom. (Who else?) When he submitted the movie for the Code seal, it was, of course, rejected.

"After the deletion of a number of Pingboom's lines," wrote Richard Barrios in his book *Screened Out* in 2003, "the PCA granted the certificate, after which the Code-sanitized *Turnabout* proceeded to run afoul of the Legion of Decency… So more material with Pingboom was eliminated… Thus denatured, *Turnabout* went on to mild critical response and indifferent box office returns."

"A hilarious sally into the field of droll fantasy," stated the review in *Box Office* in May 1940, possibly imagining those deleted scenes and lines were still there. "…this stands as one of the season's funniest and most unusual comedies. It's definitely not for the kiddies."

"Presumably the scenarists thought they had a screamingly funny idea," opined The *New York Times* reviewer. "…and undoubtedly there will be a good many folk who agree. Although this department maintained a stony silence there were guffaws and giggles in many parts of the house. Call it a question of taste… 'Corny' was the word muttered by a starboard partisan yesterday." "Corny"—even in the *New York Times*.

Variety, in describing *Turnabout*, dropped that word "corny" again. "Direction, in attempting to hew to satirical lines, drops into corny slapstick that grooves in to the silly and ridiculous category too often… Deep cutting could have eliminated at least a reel… In the metropolitan areas, the swish characteristics assumed by [John] Hubbard might pass, but there is a chance that audiences in the hinterlands and family houses might take offense…."

"Nevertheless," concluded author Barrios, "the mere existence of *Turnabout* makes it a key marker in the evolution of gays in the movies. Roach's audacity in making and releasing it is, under the circumstances, extraordinary. And for all its compromised unevenness you can still feel, as Roach puts Landis and Hubbard and the cast through their fey-frenetic paces, the cheerful whiff of sedition in the air."

No mean feat, considering the moral temper of the times. In fact, it was decades later when a letter Breen had written to a Catholic priest surfaced, illuminating just where this Hollywood censor was coming from: [Hollywood consists of] "a rotten bunch of vile people with no respect for anything beyond the making of money. Here we have Paganism rampant and in its most virulent form. Drunkenness and debauchery are commonplace. Sexual perversion is rampant...any number of our directors and stars are perverts. Ninety-five percent of these folks are Jews of an Eastern European lineage. They are, probably, the scum of the earth." (Quoted in *Lion of Hollywood: The Life and Legend of Louis B. Mayer* by Scott Eyman.)

While we're on the subject, the Hal Roach Studios produced comedies replete with "gay" characters and "gay" gags from its earliest days. Drag, same-sex flirting, cross dressing, implied and explicit improprieties of all types were staples of slapstick comedy and Hal Roach delighted in exploring it all. They don't call him a "pioneer" for nothing. In fact, he'd take the cross dressing one step further the year after *Turnabout* was released with his streamliner *All-American Co-Ed* (not even mentioned in Barrios' book on "gay" Hollywood), where practically the entire male cast sings and dances in full drag. And the year after that came *Dudes Are Pretty People* with Grady Sutton as a fey cowboy "not giving John Wayne much to worry about," as Barrios noted, with his "elaborately billowing kerchief."

Shortly after *Turnabout* was released Hal Roach invited Hollywood reporters to a lavish afternoon reception at fashionable Ciro's, where he was to introduce Carole Landis as the "Ping Girl," "the silliest and most unsavory title of several," claimed Eric Gans in his biography *Carole Landis, A Most Beautiful Girl*, "during that era forged on the model of Clara Bow's 'It Girl' or Ann Sheridan's 'Oomph Girl.' Maybe he should have invited Mr. Pangborn as the "Ping Boy," but that might have been going a bit TOO far, even for Hal Roach.

"The day before her scheduled reception," wrote Gans, "quarter-page announcements signed by Carole appeared in *The Hollywood Reporter* and *Variety* proclaiming that she did not intend to be present at the press conference 'to ping, purr or even coo.'... The publicity, deliberate or otherwise, obtained by this incident swiftly provoked a spread in *Life* on June 17th—the best coverage the iconic photo magazine would ever give her." The name of the *Life* magazine article: "Carole Landis Does Not Want to Be Ping Girl." Shades of Joan Bennett's distaste for *her* publicity involving *The Housekeeper's Daughter* some six months earlier.

But more serious matters than the dissatisfactions of leading ladies would challenge Hal Roach in the coming year. The end of a great movie triumvirate would occur, along with financial hardships and the sudden death of a loved one. As if those difficulties weren't bad enough, problems that would fell a lesser man than Hal Roach, the War in Europe would soon engulf the world and disrupt and alter the lives of everyone.

8

Saps At Sea
After Stan & Ollie
1940-1948

IN MAY 1940 Roach released *Saps at Sea*, Laurel & Hardy's farewell film for the Lot of Fun. With a running time of slightly less than an hour, it is a nostalgic look back at a comedy style that was soon to become obsolete. Old veterans appeared for the last time with the boys, most of them uncredited. Along with James Finlayson, Harry Bernard, Richard Cramer, Charlie Hall and James C. Morton were Sam Lufkin, Patsy O'Byrne, Jack Hill and Mary Gordon. Mack Sennett star Ben Turpin, who had last appeared in the Laurel & Hardy 1931 two-reeler *Our Wife* as the cross-eyed Justice of the Peace who marries Laurel to Hardy (!), had a cameo appearance in this comedy as a cross-eyed plumber who can't get his pipes straight. The story and/or script was devised by such old stalwarts as Charley Rogers, Felix Adler, Gilbert Pratt and Harry Langdon.

But as ever, Hal Roach was focused on the future. A six million dollar production schedule for 1940-41 was announced in May 1940, "the costliest in the company's 25-year-history." Six features were announced: *Broadway Limited* with Victors McLaglen and Mature, *The Unholy Horde* with Lon Chaney Jr., *Fiesta*, a musical, *Topper Returns* (which Roach will direct), *Road Show*, to be directed by Gordon Douglas, and *Niagara Falls*, a romantic comedy. As it turned out, *Broadway Limited* starred only one Victor, McLaglen (Dennis O'Keefe played the other male lead), *The Unholy Horde* was never made, *Topper Returns* was directed by Warner Bros. veteran Roy Del Ruth, and *Road Show* was directed by Roach himself. *Fiesta*, while filled with the images of colorful native costuming, with lovely music and dancing, fell apart in the story department; the rhythm and flow at the beginning came to a screeching halt due to long stretches of static camera work (as though filming a stage play, so reminiscent of the primitive talkie musicals of 1929), along with pretty lame slapstick performed by some not very talented unknown comical types.

Ever relishing variety, Roach's next movie was a seafaring action-adventure set during the War of 1812.

Motion Picture magazine, August 1940: "Impromptu on-the-set party took place the other lunchtime on the set of *Captain Caution*, the Hal Roach picture which contains so many of the old-time vaudeville headliners... Appearing in the picture are Leo Carrillo, Fred Sweeney, Roscoe Ates, El Brendel and the Metzetti troupe—all of whom appeared on the same bill at the old Orpheum Theatre in Los Angeles 'way back in 1911... To commemorate their reunion, the actors put on a lunchtime vaudeville show for the members of the picture's cast and crew... Quipped Leo Carrillo when they had finished:—'No wonder vaudeville's dead. We killed it.'"

A rip-roaring seafaring tale set during the War of 1812, *Captain Caution* starred Victor Mature, Louise Platt (fresh from John Ford's magnificent *Stagecoach* wherein she played the demure heroine), Leo Carrillo and Bruce Cabot.

It's interesting to see what the salaries were in those days. Victor Mature, who was under contract to Roach, received $300 per week. Louise Platt received $1,000 a week for five weeks; Leo Carrillo $3,000 per week for four weeks; Bruce Cabot $1,500 for five weeks; Roscoe Ates $400 for four weeks; and the sailor extras were paid the going rate of $66.00 for one week's work.

The director was Richard Wallace, who had helmed several of Roach's 1926 All-Star comedies, including *Raggedy Rose* with Mabel Normand and *Madame Mystery* with Theda Bara, which he co-directed with Stan Laurel. Later in the '40s Wallace distinguished himself with such features as *A Night to Remember* (1942), *The Fallen Sparrow* (1943), *Sinbad, the Sailor, Framed* and *Tycoon* (all 1947).

When *Captain Caution* was first submitted to the British Board of Film Censors it received a TOTAL rejection on the grounds that the picture represented Great Britain in an unfavorable light. When 237 feet were deleted, the filmed was passed.

Box Office review of *Captain Caution*, August 3, 1940: "Few preceding motion picture sea stories have more completely ensnared blood-tingling action and adventure... a robust melodrama to completely sate the appetites of all who relish red meat on their celluloid menus."

"Although the picture holds plenty of robust action, excitement and knockabout battles," went the *Variety* review, "it never quite makes up its mind whether to be a straight adventure drama or a Gilbert and Sullivan operetta presentation of the subject. As a result, *Captain Caution* is a strange hodgepodge of effects... Attempts to develop drama and romance misfire continually, and the battles aboard ship—although geared to the spectacular—obviously show their staging when sailors start tumbling before they are hit. Battlers drop to the deck and overboard like tenpins, apparently happy in withdrawing from the scuffle."

"The small boys were having a fine time on Saturday at the Globe," wrote Theodore Strauss of the *New York Times*. "The carnage was terrific, with extras falling like flies; flaming sails plummeting amidships; masts crashing all around; amid the din of battle the men, hearty fellows that they are, dispatching each other with a wonderful sense of timing, and pretty ladies looking wide-eyed at all the blood-letting. So do the small boys. Half the time one doesn't know which side is which, but no matter, this is for children under twelve, not over... *Captain Caution* is a slapstick version of the long voyage home—without a compass."

Ultimately, *Captain Caution* did not exactly set fire to the box office; and the *New York World-Telegram* called Mature's performance "bluntly, amateurish."

Some thirty-two years later Victor Mature was asked by *Interview* magazine writer J. Marks for some comment about his former boss and director Hal Roach. "Mature described him as a very nice man who appeared to have lots of confidence in his team."

After *Captain Caution*, Roach loaned Mature to RKO and made $3,000 a week for his services in *The Shanghai Gesture*. Mature was paid $450 a week. Then 20th Century Fox took over Victor Mature's contract in November 1941 for a reputed $80,000 and increased the actor's salary to $1,200 per week.

But despite all this productivity, "The year 1940 saw the Hal Roach Studios at the brink of financial ruin," as Richard Lewis Ward so starkly stated. The studio was in debt to the tune of $2.6 million. At that time, Hal Roach was earning $1,450 per week; his son $125 per week.

"In 1940 I was called back into the Army," Roach told authors Bernard Rosenberg and Harry Silverstein in *The Real Tinsel* (1970). "I immediately wrote and said, 'I don't want to be a colonel; I just want to get out of the Army.' They let me out."

Times were getting tough for Mr. Roach and his studio. Perhaps that is why he decided to sell his stock in the Los Angeles Turf Club and step down as president of the organization that ran the Santa Anita Racetrack he had been so instrumental in forming some six and a half years previously.

The following month, in October 1940, the *New York Times* ran the following article: "WIFE SUES HAL ROACH...Mrs. Margaret Roach, wife of Hal Roach, film producer, filed suit today for separate maintenance and requested a temporary order 'freezing' all of his assets except those needed in the actual conduct of business. Her suit charged her husband with 'cruel and inhuman treatment.'

"She asked an equitable division of the community property and $2,125 a month as temporary support for herself and their 19-year-old daughter, Margaret, whose custody she seeks." [Apparently Marguerite was calling herself Margaret these days, which was the way her daughter spelled her first name.]

1941-43 RELEASES:
THREE FEATURES (ONE DIRECTED BY HAL ROACH)
TWENTY STREAMLINERS

Nineteen forty-one did not begin auspiciously for Hal Roach. In January it was announced that he had filed a lawsuit for over $1 million against his former associates, Loew's, Inc. and Metro-Goldwyn-Mayer Distribution Corp. based on breach of contract, alleging that the defendants charged excessive advertising and distributing costs against some 350 motion pictures produced by Roach under contract to MGM since 1926 and transferred to Loew's in 1936.

Two months later, the defendants filed a counterclaim for $500,000 asserting "that the methods of computing profits and expenses," stated the *New York Times*, "...had been known and approved by the plaintiff. On the other hand, it was asserted, improper claims by the Hal Roach organization had cut the share of profits to which the Loew organization was entitled."

On February 21 newspapers reported that Roach and "his estranged wife" had settled their property differences. Mrs. Roach dismissed her pending maintenance suit for $2,125 a month and agreed to receive $1250 a month, one-half of her husband's interest in the Hal Roach Studios and their mansion in Beverly Hills. "Mrs. Roach stated that she will not obtain a divorce because of her religion."

Meanwhile, glad to be free from military duties for the time being, and undoubtedly needing a distraction from his marital woes, Roach finally made *Road Show* the way he had wanted to when he had first brought Lewis Milestone onto the project back in 1937—as a comedy. And this time he directed it himself. But it wasn't entirely successful.

"This one starts out with promise of some good solid laughs," stated *Variety* in February 1941, "but quickly hits a detour into ancient film technique... Hal Roach retains all of the old-fashioned ideas of comedy technique in his direction and as a result, picture is a disjointed hodge-podge of situations aiming at comedy peaks but seldom achieving that aim... Story is a synthetic and extended tale... and there's a series of minor attempts at comedy to string things along for sufficient footage and running time."

Bosley Crowther of the *New York Times* put it this way: "...Mr. Roach's latest comic effort, compounded out of madness and confusion, strives much harder to be funny than it actually is, and often its figurative flailings strike the funny-bone with little effect. In other words, the slapstick, in this instance, has the shape of a boomerang. And that is passing odd, for Mr. Roach, as every one knows, is an old hand at farcical contrivances, and the story by Eric Hatch, from which the present film is incubated, provides ample scope for madcap fun... But somehow the humors have a way of flattening out before they explode, and most of them have no more point than that on the end of a club...."

Roach's wife Marguerite Nichols passed away suddenly at the age of forty-five. A newspaper article by an unknown writer dated March 18, 1941 described the tragedy:

"Estrangement Forgotten as Mrs. Hal Roach Dies. In death all troubles end... As the shadow of death crept into a room at the Good Samaritan Hospital yesterday the marital differences of Mrs. Marguerite Roach and her husband, Hal Roach, motion picture producer, were solved poignantly, tenderly. When the drama of life reached its end for Mrs. Roach, there no longer was any estrangement.

"Her husband knelt at her bedside. His hand held hers. His prayers mingled with her own and those of their children, Margaret, 19, and Hal Roach Jr., 21.

"In those last moments before death gently lowered the curtain, the troubles of Mr. and Mrs. Roach, which were climaxed when they made a property settlement agreement three weeks ago, were forgotten.

"Instead, the thoughts of the man who wept and the woman who lay dying were upon the happiness they had known throughout much of their quarter century of married life.

"On the threshold of the most permanent of all separations, there were reconciliation, reunion, mutual affection, a renascence of their love.

"After an illness of only a week, Mrs. Roach died of pneumonia. She was stricken ill last week in her home at 610 North Beverly Drive, Beverly Hills, only a short time after her return from a trip to Honolulu... It was her strik-ing beauty that first brought her to Roach's attention when she was given a role in one of the first pictures he directed and produced, in 1918 [*sic*]...."

Another article of the same date stated: "The passing of Mrs. Hal Roach has left many of us sad, for she was one of the loveliest women this writer has ever known, so sweet and kind. In all the years I have known Margaret [*sic*], I have never known her to utter an unpleasant word about anyone. Ironically enough, a letter just came from her, written from Honolulu, in which she told me what a grand time she was having and how many wonderful people she had met... Our sympathy goes to Hal Sr., who never left her bedside after she was stricken, and to young Margaret and Hal Jr., who can be comforted by the beautiful memories she leaves to them and to her friends."

Ironically, just three days after Marguerite Roach's passing, the third and last of the ghost-themed *Topper* films—*Topper Returns* was released, on March 21, 1941. Although quite enjoyable by today's standards, with a deft mixture of old dark house melodrama emoted in grave terms by the likes of such classic pros as H.B. Warner, George Zucco and Rafaela Ottiano, contrasted with the excellent timing and comic delivery of eternal favorites Joan Blondell, Roland Young, Billie Burke, Patsy Kelly and Eddie Anderson, Theodore Strauss of the *New York Times* was not impressed. "The bug-eyed fright of Edward Rochester Anderson notwithstanding, we still hold that even a ghost may become a common bore if it (?) stays around too long... a rather sluggish ghost-hunt... The actors chime in with a will on all the non-sense... But for all their efforts they can't conceal that *Topper Returns* is old stuff. All of which indicates that one may raise a ghost, but hardly the ghost of a ghost." Perhaps critic Strauss had not considered that it had been four years since the first *Topper* movie, and that a whole new flock of children would be seeing this comedy-ghost story for the first time and hence would hardly find the movie a "bore."

Hal Roach's last full length feature before the U.S. entered World War II was *Broadway Limited*. Old timer Harry Langdon was one of the writers on that rather derivative and lightweight script, earning $350 per week. The 75-minute comedy starred Victor McLaglen and Marjorie Woodworth, with support from two of Roach's comedy stars from the 1930s Patsy Kelly and ZaSu Pitts, an interesting teaming in that they had both worked separately with Thelma Todd. Second unit location footage of a train coursing through the countryside was supervised by Hal Roach, Jr., who worked in cooperation with the officials of the Pennsylvania Railroad for these scenes.

"Mildly funny Class B farce," said *Variety* on June 18, 1941. "Direction is speedy and the production passable."

The *New York Times* reported "The best and worst that one can say concerning *Broadway Limited* is... the only difference between this and *Twentieth Century* [the 1934 screwball classic starring John Barrymore and Carole Lombard] is that that film started down the tracks with a full head of steam and *Broadway Limited* starts off without a thimbleful... [The actors] recite their lines with great force, as if to compensate for the script's total lack of wit or comic invention...."

Believing that four-and-a-half-reel "featurettes" would replace the "B" pictures that had replaced the two-reel shorts, Roach then produced about twenty "streamliners," as they were dubbed, released by United Artists between 1941 and 1943. They were for the most part lightweight comedies featuring such players as ZaSu Pitts, Slim Summerville, William Tracy, James Gleason, Marjorie Woodworth, Joe Sawyer and William Bendix, and are all but forgotten today, though they have recently been shown on Turner Classic Movies to enthusiastic contemporary response, judging by the viewer comments on the IMDb. Many may also be viewed for free on the Internet via The Internet Archive and Hulu.

"I had to fight U.A. like hell to convince 'em [to distribute his streamliners]. But they made me $1,800,000 and I still think my streamliners would've caught on if I hadn't been called to active duty in Europe."

Certainly contemporary reviews of these streamliners expressed little appreciation for Roach's latest product. Bosley Crowther of the *New York Times* reviewed *Tanks a Million* in October 1941. This was the first of five streamliners of 1941-43 to star William Tracy (1917-1967) as Sergeant "Dodo" Doubleday and Joe Sawyer (1906-1982) as Sergeant William Ames, his cohort-at-odds. Laurel & Hardy were actually considered for these roles, but they declined. Tracy had the sort of innocent baby face charm of Harry Langdon; Sawyer was his gruff counterpart.

Crowther noted that "If the first of Hal Roach's 'streamlined features'—his new comedy, *Tanks A Million*—is a fair sample of those to come, then we must confess a certain disappointment. For 'streamlined feature,' it would appear, is just a fancy Fifth Avenue name for a five-reel instead of a two-reel slapstick comedy—or a five-reel instead of an eight reel, if you prefer." If that weren't bad enough, Crowther decides "... star William Tracy... plays the kid without any real comic distinction."

In 1973 Hal Roach seemed quite reluctant to talk with me about his professional career during and after World War II, and I didn't persist. It was a long time later that I learned some of the details.

Three months before the attack on Pearl Harbor, in September 1941, Hal Roach became a grandfather; a seven and a half pound girl was born to Hal Roach Jr. and his wife, the former Dolly Hunt.

On July 24, 1942 "I got a notice to report to Fort MacArthur," recalled Roach. "They told me, 'Your commission said that in the event of a national emergency, you could be called six months after your retirement date.' I was forty-eight [actually he was fifty]. I was overweight. Everything. But I couldn't even get three days' deferment, and there I stayed for four years. I fought just the Americans." Roach was commissioned a major in the Photographic Division of the U.S. Army's Signal Corps. From Fort MacArthur in San Pedro, California, south of Los Angeles, Roach was sent to Wright Field, near Dayton, Ohio; he also was stationed at Eglin Field near Orlando, Florida, as well as in Washington D.C

On August 31, 1942, 50-year-old Hal Roach married his second wife, 29-year-old Lucille Prin (1913-1981), a secretary with the American Society of Composers and Publishers. This marriage lasted nearly forty years, until Lucille's death in April 1981. They had four daughters, Elizabeth Carson Roach born December 26, 1945, who lived for less than nine months, passing away "at home following an operation" according to a newspaper account, on September 6, 1946; Maria May Roach (born April 14, 1947); Jeanne Alice Roach (born October 7, 1949); and Kathleen Bridget Roach (born January 29, 1951). His oldest daughter, Margaret whom he had had with Marguerite Nichols, was nearly thirty years older than his youngest daughter Kathleen.

In October 1942 the Army Air Signal Corps took over the Hal Roach Studios. In 1943 Roach was sent to England to serve with the Eighth Air Force Film Unit to record the activities of bombers and fighters there. He also made trips to New York.

"...the studio was taken over by the Army and the Air Force," said Roach. "It was closed for four and a half years. During this time, I had pictures out and was able to accumulate a considerable amount of money."

Several streamliners produced at the Hal Roach Studios before the military occupied "Fort Roach" were released during the War. They included two bizarre slapstick comedies parodying and caricaturing Hitler, Mussolini and Hirohito, in a style that seemed to combine Charlie Chaplin's *The Great Dictator* (1940) with The Three Stooges shorts *You Nazty Spy* (1940) and *I'll Never Heil Again* (1941).

"As psychopathology became the dominant narrative mode for explaining the Führer phenomenon," wrote Sabine Hake in her 2012 study

Screen Nazis: Cinema, History and Democracy, "mockery and ridicule emerged as the preferred form of political denunciation."

The Devil with Hitler was released first. Dead ringer Bobby Watson played Hitler, Joe Devlin, a jut-jawed "Bonito" Mussolini, and George E. Stone was "Suki Yaki"—er, Hirohito. Alan Mowbray seemed to be miscast as "The Devil Himself" for he comes across as a slightly more animated version of the proper English butler he played in *Topper.* It's too bad they didn't get the lean and mean Charles Middleton for the role of the Devil, as he could sneer with more menace than any villain in Hollywood; he had a face and a voice that could strike terror.

The premise of this frantic film is that the Board of Directors of Hell has put the Devil on notice that they intend to replace him with Adolf Hitler unless he can get Hitler to commit a good deed. This doesn't make much sense, because even Adolf Hitler didn't have to answer to a Board of Directors, therefore, why should the Devil? Or did he? Hmm. So often Hitler has been portrayed, even today, as a demi-god whose iron will brought about the Third Reich. Maybe this Mr. Roach was trying to slip in some sort of a message here. Perhaps this great friend of children was showing them with these slapstick comedies that the three bogeymen terrorizing the civilized world were human, after all, and susceptible to the same laws of chaos and physics as the rest of us. And maybe that their kind could not have achieved nor maintained their power without some sort of "Board of Directors" backing them up.

The second Axis farce, *That Nazty Nuisance,* was released nearly a year later. The plot has our three wacky dictators traveling to a desert island to sign a treaty with an Arabian-type leader and getting mixed up with a pillow-throwing Orangutan and a shipwrecked crew of American seamen. The *New York Times* never bothered to review these films, but *Variety* did.

"Wacky in its entirety," was the way *Variety* put it reviewing *The Devil with Hitler* in October 1942, "much slapstick is included in the action... Roles of the Axis leaders are exceptionally well cast... Picture has been ably directed by Gordon Douglas and has a good pace."

Variety in 1943 found *That Nazty Nuisance* "...a funnier and better-made Roach streamliner than recently to come from this mill... even the slapstick is well done... Glenn Tryon, who also is listed as associate producer, directs with imagination for such a small-budgeter...."

After the War, when American movies were at last exhibited in Europe again, The French Ministry of Information banned *The Devil with Hitler* (and presumably its sequel). According to the *Hartford Courant* of May 17, 1947, "The censors ruled that showing characters so closely resembling Hitler and other high Nazis might provoke disorder, despite the film's burlesque character." Apparently the French censors failed to read the disclaimer at the end of those films: "The events and characters depicted in this photoplay are fictitious, and similarities to actual persons, living or dead, is purely coincidental." Perhaps that was funniest gag of them all.

The *New York Times* did review the final two streamliners released by Hal Roach during the War. In his July 1943 review of *Prairie Chicken* Bosley Crowther opined, "Just forty-seven minutes of old-fashioned slapstick... We thought they had stopped making such pictures about twenty years ago."

Later that month, fellow *New York Times* reviewer Theodore Straus called *Calaboose* "feeble foolishness... The gags belong to the declining period of the two-reel comedy, which hasn't yet recovered."

"In 1943," writes Richard W. Bann in his essay "Film Preservation, Another Fine Mess" on his website laurel-and-hardy.com, "producer George Hirliman's Film Classics contracted with Roach to re-release much of the studio's post-1928 product. The company was obliged by its agreement to remove the roaring lion-head logo and all of the M-G-M trademarks from the Roach comedies, however, and in so doing replaced or defaced most of the creative and artistic original main and interior production credits title cards."

There is documentation indicating that Roach bought the rights to all his MGM and United Artists releases in 1944, but according to Bann, "Film Classics' license expired in 1951. Robert Savini's Astor Pictures was one of several distributors who picked up theatrical reissue rights in succession. Concerned only with short term box-office returns, like so many others, the laboratory abuse of negatives continued."

The carefree world of the teens and 1920s and even the Depression 1930s had indeed vanished. The change affected everyone, including the great comedy team of that remarkable time. In 1940, after leaving Roach and with the war raging in Europe soon to engulf the world, Laurel and Hardy embarked upon a Red Cross tour followed by a 12-city U.S. stage show tour which lasted to the end of the year.

In 1941 they returned to the cinema screens via slick but empty productions for Twentieth Century-Fox and MGM, huge film factories where the boys were allowed none of the creative freedom they had enjoyed at the intimate Hal Roach Studios. They were forced to follow scripts written by those who seemed completely unfamiliar with Stan and Ollie's characters and comedy style.

"Stan and Roach, whatever their differences, were one in their love for comedy" wrote John McCabe in *The Comedy World of Stan Laurel.* "Hal Roach needs no finer monument than the vast footage of first rate comedy bearing his name... But at Fox, Stan was told at once that he had no autonomy. He was to do pictures the studio way or not at all...."

Laurel and Hardy were getting on in years, too: they had changed physically. All those years of pratfalls seemed to be taking their toll on these once-agile comedians who were, after all, now in their mid-fifties. Ollie was no longer pleasantly plump—he was obese. Stan no longer had a youthful bean pole figure—he was potbellied and the shock of red hair that used to stand straight up now was thinning and lay limp on his head; he looked tired and decidedly middle-aged. The Boys did retain their special charm, but that wasn't enough to counteract the mediocre scripts they were forced to work with, except on rare occasions. But their fans loved them no matter what they were in; their forties films were screened at the prestigious Grauman's Chinese Theatre as they had been in the thirties, and Laurel & Hardy remained pretty popular during the war years, even though these later films were often mediocre, and even following the phenomenal success of that younger comedy team, Abbott & Costello, whose brash style and rapid patter had swept the country in 1941. The war-torn world apparently needed laughter and comedy however tired, and were happy just to see those two old slapstick clowns on the screen.

After a half dozen dismal efforts, culminating with *The Bullfighters*, Laurel and Hardy contented themselves with a 1947 European stage tour (including a Royal Command Performance in London) and stage tours from 1952 to 1954 in England, where they never lost their popularity. They made one final film, *Atoll K*, in France in 1950-51. It was scantily released in the U.S. three years later. Their last notable appearance together occurred unexpectedly—as surprised guests on the television show *This Is Your Life*, which aired on December 1, 1954. Ironically, in the early 1950s that rival team of Abbott & Costello were filming their weekly television series at—yes, The Hal Roach Studios.

The post war period was a time of challenge for Hal Roach as well. "After the war I returned to Hollywood and started making the 'streamlined comedies' again, with United Artists putting them with a longer feature to make up a double bill," explained Roach in a 1969 oral history to author Mike Steen. "However, United Artists came out with about ten bad pictures which nobody wanted. They couldn't sell them to the exhibitors; therefore, they couldn't sell my comedies... United Artists went through a very bad period," said Roach, "and when they flopped, Metro-Goldwyn-Mayer gave me a contract to make these streamliners."

"When World War II broke out I joined the Air Force," is the way Mr. Roach put it to me in 1973, "and when I came back, I didn't want to make comedies anymore." Well, perhaps he would have liked to have forgotten, but Roach did make a few comedies when he resumed command of The Hal Roach Studios in 1946. But to post World War II America, they were not too much to laugh at.

Once Hal Roach was discharged from the Army Air Forces as a lieutenant colonel he received a letter of commendation from Lieutenant General Ira C. Eaker, deputy commander of the Army Air Forces, for turning over his entire Culver City motion picture plant to the Army in October 1942. Eaker's position as commander of the Eighth Air Force led to his becoming the model for the fictional Major General Pat Pritchard in the acclaimed 1949 war movie *Twelve O'Clock High*.

By mid-November 1945 Roach was happily back at his Studio (or at least he had begun to receive his mail there; news reports announced that the War Department would be transferring the Army Air Force Unit from the Hal Roach Studios to Lowry Field, Denver, Colorado 'about' January 1st, 1946). Wherever he was, Roach decided to resume producing streamliners. Since 1944 Hal Junior had been working for Rainbow Productions, a corporation controlled by Leo McCarey, David Butler, Bob Hope, Bing Crosby and others. The first picture Rainbow produced was *The Bells of St. Mary's*. Roach Jr. left Rainbow for only seven or eight months when he joined the military in February 1945, during which time it was reported he worked on training films. Once discharged following the War, Junior helped his dad reestablish production at the Studio while also continuing to work for Rainbow. In mid-1947 he began to devote full-time to his father's studio.

Though work was definitely going on at Hal Roach Studios at the time, on December 21, 1945 Hal Roach Jr. wrote to someone seeking a writing position, "The United States Army has not vacated the Studio premises as yet and it is very indefinite before we will contract for more writers...." However, there is a memo dated three weeks prior to that stating that "The following production numbers have been assigned to cover the first three pictures: F-54 Robert McGowan Unit [*Curley*], F-55 Fred Guiol Unit [*Here Comes Trouble*], F-56 Bebe Daniels Unit [*The Fabulous Joe*]." Could it be that the Roaches had started working at the Studio alongside the remaining military personnel? Or perhaps they worked elsewhere until the official announcement of resumption of the Hal Roach Studios in March

1946? Or was Roach Jr. just telling a white lie to soften the rejection of a job-seeking writer?

Junior was certainly working for his dad during those last months of 1945 as he was attempting to secure the rights to *Babes In Toyland* once again to remake it as a streamliner, but the negotiations fell through. He also had the idea of producing one streamliner a year based upon the Topper character and wanted to bring back Roland Young for the title role, as well as star him in two or three additional pictures a year. Those plans did not work out either.

Former silent comedienne Bebe Daniels returned to the Hal Roach Studios for the first time in twenty-seven years, since 1919 when she was leading lady to Harold Lloyd. This time she was to take on a new role: producer. Her first assignment was the streamliner *The Fabulous Joe* a fantasy about a talking dog concocted by Hal Roach Jr. with such dubious stars as Marie Wilson and Donald Meek.

The announcement was published on January 21, 1946 by the *Los Angeles Times*: "HAL ROACH SETS RE-ENTRY DATE. Hal Roach has officially set March 4 as his date for re-entering the producing field. 'The Fabulous Joe,' which is to be supervised by Bebe Daniels, his star of other years, will be first before cameras. Army engineers are now taking terminal inventory at the Roach establishment, which was used for a big war project. All Roach pictures, 12 being listed for this year, will be in Cinecolor." Shooting for *The Fabulous Joe* was set to commence the end of April 1946.

1947-48 Releases – All filmed in Cinecolor:
Hal Roach Comedy Carnival
Part 1 – *Curley*
Part 2 – *The Fabulous Joe*
Lafftime
Part 1 – *Here Comes Trouble*
Part 2 – *Who Killed Doc Robbin*

By late June 1946 principal photography on the first streamliner *Curley* had been completed. Roach originally wanted to produce all his new films in Technicolor, however, Herbert T. Kalmus had advised him back in December 1945 "…we are sold out to capacity for the entire year 1946, with a long list of producers and pictures waiting to get in…." In those days, a producer could not simply purchase Technicolor film stock and begin shooting; the three-strip process required a special bulky and very heavy Technicolor camera that could only be rented along with camera technicians and a "color supervisor" to maintain standards. So Roach decided to film in Cinecolor, a system which could produce acceptable color pictures at a fraction of what Technicolor cost and it could be used in modified black and white cameras. Cinecolor had been used to film the Max Fleischer cartoons, while top cartoon producer Walt Disney had an exclusive contract with Technicolor.

Curley was a kids' picture in which old Our Gang director Robert McGowan was credited as producer and story writer. MGM had granted Roach permission to produce a children's movie as long as he did not use the name Our Gang. *Curley* was released, on a dual bill with *The Fabulous Joe*, under the umbrella title *Hal Roach Comedy Carnival* over a year later, in August of 1947.

Hal Roach Studios veteran Fred Guiol who had been there since the early 1920s, was in the midst of directing *Here Comes Trouble*, another Cinecolor streamliner, which reunited William Tracy and Joe Sawyer as Doubleday and Ames for one last time, former sergeants, now civilians after the War. Originally Shelley Winters was announced to play the secretary "Dexter," but that role went to Australian-born Patti Morgan, who was little heard from since.

Here Comes Trouble was cleverly written, with lots of plot twists and a well directed chaotic chase scene at the end wherein all is resolved for a satisfying happy ending. Despite the comedy, this film showed that there could be just as much chicanery, double crossing, murder and mayhem in civilian life as there had been during the war. *Who Killed Doc Robbin* was another kid picture, and Roach's last. *TV Guide's* assessment: "You've seen it all before."

Meanwhile, a lawsuit in New York's U.S. District Court was in full swing between the Studio and Film Classics, the distributor of many of his films. On April 20, Attorney Charles Schwartz reported to Roach, "Money judgment paid yesterday [$35,000] in suit against Film Classics. They will appeal which gives you back TOPPER. In connection with the institution and prosecution of the suit, Miss Rosenfield was most helpful and cooperative and contributed substantially to its successful outcome."

Grace Rosenfield was Hal Roach's New York City sales rep and had worked for him since 1932 and would stay in his employ for some eighteen years.

July 1946: Ground was broken at the Hal Roach Studios for the building of a new $200,000 sound stage as part of a $750,000 expansion program. The *Los Angeles Times* stated "Roach has slated 12 feature comedies in color for 1946-47 release. Two have been completed and a third is now in production."

In September it was announced that Roach signed an agreement with producer Walter Wanger to form a new "major motion picture producing organization." Wanger (1894-1968) began as an assistant to Jesse L. Lasky at Paramount in 1921 and worked his way up in the organization before leaving in 1931. By 1936 he owned his own production company with an impressive roster of stars and was enormously successful by the time of the announced partnership with Roach.

Supposedly the combine was going to establish offices in New York, London and Paris "for the acquisition and development of new stars, story properties and technical talent." In reality, Wanger leased some office space at the Roach lot as well as used the Roach sound stages to film some scenes for the huge box office bomb *Joan of Arc* (1948) starring Ingrid Bergman.

As Roach explained the situation in a letter to a potential investor in 1951, "In 1946, we entered into a contract with the Walter Wanger Corp., whereby they were to rent one-third of the Studio for $300,000 per year for five years. Their first picture 'Joan of Arc' was a failure and they went broke. However, on the strength of this contract, we borrowed $1,500,000 from R.F.C. [Reconstruction Finance Corporation] to enlarge our plant with the thought that the revenue from the Wanger contract would pay off the R.F.C. loan. Then you know what happened to the motion picture business."

Wanger wasn't the only producer Roach had problems with at that time. Edward Small (1891-1977) like Roach was an independent movie producer from the silent era, and he would still be working through the 1960s. But Small was very unlike Roach in that he did not publicize himself; he was completely unknown to the world outside of Hollywood. Small had started out as a talent agent in New York, moved the agency to Hollywood in 1917 and began producing films in 1924. His output was modest but prolific and did some of his work uncredited, as on Alfred Hitchcock's *Witness for the Prosecution* (1957). His last movie was *The Christine Jorgensen Story* (1970).

On September 18, 1946 Edward Small sent a very angry letter to Roach: "...Several months ago, we worked out the major terms of a two-year agreement for the purpose of making a number of pictures... [but we received a letter from you] to our surprise terminated all negotiations, abruptly closing the door to any further opportunity to discuss the matter. This, in my opinion, is a very crude way to do business—without even the decency of considering our position and the damage that might have been occasioned by your action...."

"Three days after the receipt of your letter, it was announced that you had made a deal with Wanger for the studio. We certainly have a basis for questioning whether you were dealing with us in good faith. I think there is such a thing as goodwill even in Hollywood...

"Our agreeing to assume the obligation of $300,000 minimum stage space rent over a period of two years apparently was considered a good business transaction for you until something better, in your opinion, came along, and thereby we have been a very useful convenience. And so out of a sense of principle, I have a right to express my opinion of the whole negotiation when I say this is a mighty shabby way to do business."

Of all the business correspondence between Mr. Roach and his Hollywood colleagues that have been deposited in the USC Collection, letters covering over forty years of Hollywood history that I have discovered heretofore, this was the ONLY one that expressed anger or criticism of Mr. Roach's morals or business methods. Of course, some old sour puss cynic such as Clarence (Mr. Crutch) Wilson might just say that all the correspondence showing our hero in an unfavorable light had been dumped off the Brooklyn Bridge. Well, it takes all types to make the world, as Mr. Roach demonstrated time and time again.

It's interesting that the sum of $300,000 is exactly what Roach said was the amount Wanger would pay. One may wonder if it gave Mr. Roach small comfort to have known that back in 1939 his erstwhile adversary, Joan Bennett, who had been such a thorn in Mr. Roach's side due to *The Housekeeper's Daughter* ad controversy, also caused trouble for Edward Small. In her autobiography, Ms. Bennett admits to having thrown at Mr. Small, during the filming of *The Man in the Iron Mask*, "a small, lethal jar of cold cream."

Around this time Roach began renting out studio space to other independent producers to generate income, a practice he continued throughout the remaining years of his studio's existence.

By November 1946 Roach's secretary, Edith Udell, was able to write to the Hal Roach Studios New York Sales rep Grace Rosenfield, "The Studio is bustling with some activity again although we do not start retakes on TROUBLE until next Monday. It is nice to see a lot of the faces back again for lay-offs at this time especially, can be rather unpleasant."

Mrs. Rosenfield meanwhile, aside from her sales rep duties, was always on the lookout for new talent for the Hal Roach Studios. In one letter alone she recommended three performers who all became successful in Hollywood: Jesse White, Danny Thomas and Jules Munshin. Munshin she called "a combo of Bert Lahr, Groucho Marx and even a bit of Durante... Honestly, Hal, he is a real find...." Munshin would become famous in the major movie musicals *Easter Parade* (1948), *On the Town* (1949) and *Silk Stockings* (1957), among others. Jesse White and Danny Thomas, of course, both had long and successful careers in television. Mrs. Rosenfield also discovered a gawky young performer named Alice Pearce, she with the post-nasal drip, while she was performing on the nightclub circuit in New York. Mrs. Rosenfield sent Roach three 8x10 headshots of Alice Pearce with the note, "this girl definitely belongs on our lot." Within two years Ms. Pearce had scored in *On the Town* (along with Mrs. Rosenfield's other recommendation) and had a long career in television, most notably as Samantha's nosey neighbor, the first Gladys Kravitz, on the TV series *Bewitched* from 1964-66.

During 1946 Hollywood Union workers were protesting and threatening to strike to the point where it was being called a "crisis." The shadow of the "Communist menace" made its first appearance too by 1947 and numerous letters were received at the Studio offering services of counterintelligence. But Roach was only interested in solving the problems of profitable movie making, not engaging in ideological battles.

But there was one battle he was willing to fight, and that was race discrimination.

Curley, the movie about all-American kids, was banned by the Memphis, Tennessee Censor Board. Lloyd T. Binford wrote to the Hal Roach Studios, "The Memphis Censor Board... is unable to approve your picture with the little Negroes, as the South does not permit Negroes in white schools nor recognize social equality between the races, even in children."

It was Grace Rosenfield, in the New York office, who urged Mr. Roach to legally challenge and oppose this racial censorship. And Roach agreed. He, together with Eric Johnston, president of the Motion Picture Association, and Gradwell L. Sears, president of United Artists, challenged the Memphis Censor Board's decision in the Tennessee Supreme Court in September of 1947 and vowed to take the matter all the way to the federal courts if necessary.

They pointed out that within the past few years Binford had banned all footage of Lena Horne, Eddie "Rochester" Anderson, Pearl Bailey, Duke Ellington and Cab Calloway from films. Johnstone called *Curley* "a wholesome comedy of delightful American children" and that the ban was "nauseating."

"The Memphis Board's action is outrageous," said Johnstone in an official statement. "It is un-American. Surely the board does not speak the mind of the millions of fair-minded citizens of the South who believe in freedom of speech. We count on their support."

Producer Roach stated, as reported by the *Chicago Defender*, "Young children of various races play together without friction until their elders inoculate them with the venom of race prejudice. The aged Binford is still fighting the Civil War, apparently forgetting that white and Negro service men fought and died together."

"Sears of the United Artists Corporation, said, 'If Binford can ban a motion picture showing white and colored kids playing together, then tomorrow some other Binford may ban the use of newspapers in printing pictures showing the Brooklyn Dodgers or a group of permanently disabled soldiers or sailors of different races in a veterans hospital. Negroes and fair-minded white citizens the nation over will eagerly watch the progress of this important case.'"

"In a curious twist," reported the *Memphis Flyer*, "the court actually upheld Binford's ban on *Curley* but ruled that he could not ban future performances just because they included Blacks. Binford grumbled, 'Well, we'll just have to pass those pictures now.'"

"Four years in uniform gave Hal Roach time to think," wrote Otis L. Guernsey Jr. in his column in the *New York Herald Tribune* in mid 1947, "and the first result of his ruminations will have an August release under the title *Comedy Carnival*. This portly, longtime impresario of celluloid laughter, who looks like a member of the Cleveland Chamber of Commerce and has been making pictures in his own studio since 1914, admits that he might have gone along grinding them out in the same old way, 'possibly making them a little worse each time.' But the interval spent in uniform gave him time to reflect on his chosen profession, examine it in new perspective and, he believes, discover its big error. Something, Roach believes, is wrong with film comedy; and that something is the long running-time.

"'I'm out with a message,' Roach stated emphatically to this department last week. 'It takes a mighty good comedy idea to sustain a show for an hour and a half. We've got to stop padding them, make them shorter and funnier.'

"Roach knows that he cannot change the conventions of feature length over night. His compromise is *Comedy Carnival*, which combines two featurettes under one title. The first, running for about forty-five minutes, is what the producer calls a 'kid comedy' along the 'Our Gang' lines. The second, going fifty-five minutes, has Walter Abel, Marie Wilson and a talking dog. The idea is that the two together can be shown as one big feature—or, in a few instances, can be separated and run individually with one of those two-hour dramas."

However, instead of the twelve films planned, only four productions were completed by the end of the 1946-47 season. When *Here Comes Trouble* and *Who Killed Doc Robin?* were finally released in 1948 under the umbrella title *Lafftime*, all *Variety* would report was that they were "okay for lower half of dualers." Pre-production paperwork had been prepared for five more projects: F-58 *Cradle And All* to be directed by Fred Guiol, F-59 *Mr. Wilmer* to involve Harve Foster, Bebe Daniels and Jack Jevne (from a novel brought to Roach by Antonio Moreno), F-60 *The Glicket Cat* which was to have been a combination live action and animation, F-61 *Speck*, another kid picture to be directed by Robert McGowan, and F-62 *Circus Story*, co-written by Dick Wesson who would later become a noted television series writer. None of these productions were made, nor the three additional color pictures planned, due to the deteriorating economic condition in Hollywood at that time. "Roach blamed United Artists and their sluggish sales force for the poor nationwide performance," wrote Richard Lewis Ward. The contract between Roach and United Artists was cancelled in early 1948.

In the spring of 1947 as all these lightweight comedies were awaiting release, the Hal Roach Studios began negotiations with writer Philip Yordan, whose controversial play *Anna Lucasta* had been a recent hit on Broadway. "The most important American comedy drama in twenty years," acclaimed the *New York World-Telegram*. Certainly the Roach Studio could have benefitted from having another prestige picture, for not since *Of Mice and Men*, seven years earlier, had a truly great movie of a pedigreed literary origin been produced by Roach.

The play's producer, John Wildberg, wrote to Roach, "Whether we get together on this property or not, I certainly want to express my keen delight at having met you and the great desire that I have to work with you and your organization." But the play *Anna Lucasta* was not an easy sell as a Hollywood movie. Primarily because Anna Lucasta was a prostitute.

Joseph Breen of the Motion Picture Association of America, the successor to Will Hays, wrote to Roach, "…I regret to feel compelled to advise you that this material is thoroughly and completely unacceptable under the provisions of the Production Code… This unacceptability is suggested, first of all, by the general, overall low tone and immoral flavor of the story. The characterization of Anna as a prostitute is treated, in our judgment, in a thoroughly unacceptable fashion… In addition, the details of the loose conduct of a number of the characters... together with the frequent vulgarities, blasphemies, etc. all add up, in our judgment, to the general unacceptability of this story."

The property somehow managed to pass the censor's ire two years later when *Anna Lucasta* was produced by Columbia Pictures with Paulette Goddard in the starring role; ironically, she had been briefly under contract to Roach in the early 1930s. A Black version of *Anna Lucasta* was released by United Artists in 1958 starring Eartha Kitt and Sammy Davis Jr.

In April 1947 Hal Roach became a father again. Lucille gave birth to a daughter, Maria Eugenia. In December of that year, Roach attended the wedding of his eldest daughter, 26-year-old Margaret, by his late first wife Marguerite. The groom was 43-year-old Robert Livingston, a cowboy actor working at Republic Pictures. The couple would have one son and divorce less than four years later.

In October 1947 J.J. Felder, Vice President of Favorite Films Corporation wrote to Grace Rosenfield: "We are interested in acquiring world distribution rights for television, 16mm and 35mm, on all the short product produced by your Company and released by Metro over a period of years, and such features that Metro distributed for you. Also to be included are the features and streamliners originally distributed by United Artists which we are at present handling for the domestic distribution also in certain foreign countries... For the acquisition of the exclusive rights of the subjects as outlined for a period of 10 years from the date of delivery, we offer you a cash consideration of $25,000.00 upon the signing of the contract which is to be considered as an advance against a 50/50 distribution deal. The advance and print costs are to be recouped by us on the basis of a 50/50 deal... Our experience in the television field during the past year convinces us that now is the opportune time to hit on all cylinders before the market is flooded with product and made available for its use. Therefore, if we can take advantage of the present situation by placing the Hal Roach product before the television public today, together we can mutually gain the desired maximum financial results...."

Handwritten at the bottom of this letter by Hugh Huber, "We told Grace to close the deal."

Early in 1948, soon after having canceled his contract with United Artists, Roach signed a six picture deal with MGM and the *New York Times* announced that there was renewed activity at the Hal Roach Studios.

Although Roach had sworn off owning airplanes in 1935, by the late forties the Studios possessed a Lockheed Lodestar. Charles Easton was the pilot, Mark Miller, co-pilot. They were both on the Studio payroll for combined salaries of $255 per week. Apparently Roach sometimes would fly without his pilots. On November 11, 1947 *The Film Daily* reported that the previous Sunday he and his wife were winging their way from Hollywood to New York. "The producer, flying his own plane, was delayed temporarily due to a heavy blizzard which forced a landing in Minneapolis."

Blizzard or not, Roach was ready to go places. "Then the reality of the postwar Hollywood retrenchment hit," wrote Ward. "Having persuaded MGM to take him back as a producer, Roach was unable to obtain financing for the new series of pictures." MGM refused to advance Roach any money, and the contract was canceled. It wasn't just Roach. All of Hollywood was facing an industry-wide recession, and it was deepening.

"...we regret to advise," wrote Hal Roach Jr. to a job applicant in January 1948, "that we are not in active production at this time. As a matter of fact, many of our employees are on lay-off."

In May 1948 Roach became so desperate that he offered to sell his studio to the Air Force for $4.5 million. The offer was declined. A few months later the Air Force brightened Mr. Roach's gloom, if only for a brief period of time, by inviting him to preside as the Chairman of their Entertainment Committee for "Operation Wing-Ding," the grand Air Force Reunion and Jamboree to be held for three days in September at Madison Square Garden in New York City. It was a major event. Joshua Logan, the Broadway and Hollywood director and writer, who was a captain in the Air Force units in Europe during World War II, was the event's Producer; World War II hero General James H. Doolittle was Chairman of the Board that included Clark Gable, gunner and observer with the Eighth Air Force advancing to the grade of Major; Merian C. Cooper, director-producer who had been with the 20th Bomb Group in France during World War I; Jack L. Warner of the American Expeditionary Force in World War I and instrumental in organizing the Air Force's first motion picture unit in World War II; J.H. "Jock" Whitney (he invested in Technicolor in the early days and put up half the money for *Gone With the Wind*; later he became U.S. Ambassador to the United Kingdom) who was a colonel in Europe during World War II; and James Stewart, Air Force private who became colonel and chief of staff of a bomber wing with the Eight Air Force in Europe.

A special high speed airliner was secured to transport a variety of celebrities to the event from Los Angeles to New York City and back, including Bob Hope, James Stewart, Paul Lukas, Bebe Daniels and her husband Ben Lyons, Jack Warner, Mr. and Mrs. Hal Roach and Dinah Shore. Joe E. Brown and Bill Holden would meet them in New York. On September 24th the entire 48th Street Theatre on Broadway was reserved for all the guests of "Operation Wing-Ding" to enjoy Joe E. Brown's performance in the stage comedy *Harvey*.

After that extravagant gala event, when Roach was back at his office in Culver City, he had to write to an actor requesting work: "Unfortunately, there is a great deal of unemployment in practically all the studios at the present time and I cannot give you any encouragement whatsoever for an acting part in the immediate future."

That immediate future looked grim for the entire movie industry as attendance fell and box office receipts dwindled. And then one morning in November of that year of 1948 Hal Roach received a four-page letter from E.F. McDonald Jr., President of the Zenith Radio Corporation of Chicago.

"…Years ago I learned that in a period of transition it may be fatal to not move swiftly," wrote McDonald. "The motion picture industry, as seen from where I sit, is at that critical stage today, and the problem is much more acute than it was when sound film replaced the silent flicker. Railroads smothered the stage coach, automobiles replaced the horse, movies took over the theater, and radio swallowed the phonograph industry. Now television is moving swiftly to take over the entertainment business.

"You are beginning to feel the impact… There are only 800,000 television sets in the United States. Yet your theaters have already felt the bites of sharply reduced audiences when events of great public interest are televised. More dangerous is the fact… that the purchase of a television set is followed by a sharp fall off in movie attendance, which continues even after the novelty of television set ownership has worn off. What will this trend do to your box office when 2,000,000 television sets (10,000,000 viewers) are added next year, and still more in the following years?…

"…television knocks at the producer's door… a revolution in show business is in full swing—unrealized by many, as most new movements are at the beginning. Television is destined to be the new entertainment medium, the greatest entertainment medium the world has ever seen, and it is already much later than many people think…."

Hal Roach read that letter long and hard. And so did his son. And they both chuckled. Zenith Radio President McDonald wasn't telling them something they didn't already know. Two months prior to receiving that letter, in September of 1948, Roach was in New York City attending a business luncheon at the St. Regis Hotel. Among the businessmen there was Robert Swezey, Vice President of the Mutual Broadcasting Company.

In a letter to Roach on September 28, once he had returned to Culver City, Roach's New York rep Grace Rosenfield wrote, "Mr. Swezey conveyed over the telephone... [that] your presentation was most impressive to the Board and that the consensus of opinion was that you know more about television than several other motion picture producers who recently contacted Mutual along similar lines."

On October 15, 1948 Hal Roach wrote to Mrs. Rosenfield: "We are going to make pictures for television that will cost on the average of $24,000 per hour...."

A new era was about to begin and the Hal Roach Studios would become the first Hollywood motion picture production company to convert exclusively to producing films for "the greatest entertainment medium the world has ever seen."

Trade papers announce the return of Lieutenant Colonel Hal Roach to the motion picture industry at the end of World War II.

Ground is broken for the expansion of the Hal Roach Studios in 1946. Watching the Boss make the first strike is left to right, Hal Roach, Jr.; S.S. Van Keuren and Bebe Daniels, former comedienne and actress, now a Roach producer.

By 1949 the Hal Roach Studios had completely converted to television production. In addition to producing their own shows, they rented space and facilities to other television companies.

Longtime Roach executive Warren Doane greets Stan Laurel during the December 1954 *This Is Your Life* television show which honored Stan Laurel & Oliver Hardy.

Hal Roach's second wife Lucille with ZaSu Pitts, who starred with Thelma Todd in a series of shorts in the 1930s and returned to the Roach lot over twenty years later to film television's *The Gale Storm Show: Oh! Susanna*, 1956-60.

Father and son producers at the height of their television success. Three years later the studio would file for bankruptcy.

Catalogue cover for the four day auction in 1963 during which all the equipment and paraphernalia at the Hal Roach Studios were sold.

The author loved watching the comedies of Laurel & Hardy as a boy and was inspired to become an actor specializing in comedy. In 1970 at the age of seventeen he made this drawing, little knowing what the future would bring.

In 1980 a plaque was placed nearby and dedicated to commemorate the Hal Roach Studios in Culver City, California. Mr. Roach was there for the event.

The author visits Hal Roach at his home in March 1982 when the producer was a hale and hearty 90 years young. Photo by Rick Greene.

The author played James Finlayson in a comedy short produced by General Motors in 1990. Laurel & Hardy Universal City California impersonators Jeffrey Weissman and Bevis Faversham played the Boys, and "Buster Keaton" even appeared in the cast. I showed this short to Hal Roach in 1992 and he cried "I thought that really was them!" with the first glance he had of the talented duo.

At the home of Hal Roach in May 1992. I had first met him nineteen years earlier. On this last visit I showed him some films I had been involved with and got to meet Richard W. Bann who took this photo. Mr. Roach at 100 still had all his marbles.

Hal Roach in his bedroom, May 1992 with his hunting dog Tripper. Photo by author.

Hal Roach signs a 1920 photograph of himself for the author in May 1992. Photo by author.

Hal Roach's last hurrah, his last public appearance at the Sons of the Desert Convention in Las Vegas in July 1992 with his friend and associate Richard W. Bann. Laughing 'til the very end. Photo courtesy Richard W. Bann.

Film Pioneer Hal Roach, Comedy King, Dies at 100

■ **Hollywood:** Producer paired Laurel and Hardy, created 'Our Gang' series and was a key figure in TV.

By DENNIS McLELLAN
TIMES STAFF WRITER

Movie producer Hal Roach, who teamed Laurel with Hardy and turned a talented yet unaffected group of child actors into "Our Gang" during a career that spanned silent one-reelers and television situation comedies, died Monday at his Bel-Air home.

His 100th birthday in January, celebrated at the Motion Picture and Television Home in Woodland Hills, produced what proved a final outpouring of sentiment and public attention to the film industry's oldest pioneer.

He had been in relatively good health despite his age, said Richard

Please see ROACH, A20

Hal Roach in January

Front page news: The *Los Angeles Times* announces the passing of Hal Roach on November 3, 1992.

9

Racket Squad
Television Pioneers
1948-1963

THE OFFICIAL OPERATION of a New York metropolitan television station began on April 30, 1939 via the RCA-NBC transmitter atop the Empire State tower in New York City. The first broadcast covered the inauguration of the New York World's Fair and the opening speech by President Franklin D. Roosevelt. From 1939 to 1941 CBS presented a number of programs, mostly in the evening, for the several thousand who had receivers. One of the first notable shows following the World's Fair Opening was *The Wednesday Night Program* which featured Hal Roach alumnus from the 1920s, Martha Sleeper.

In 1940 NBC began to relay some telecasts to the General Electric station in Schenectady, New Jersey, thus forming history's first network of sorts. But by January 1940 barely 1,200 television sets had been sold due to the poor quality of the programs as well as the high price of the television sets.

"Commercial television first saw the light of day," wrote Tim Brooks and Earle Marsh in their *The Complete Directory to Prime Time Network and Cable TV Shows 1946-Present* "July 1st 1941 when both CBS and NBC were granted commercial licenses (so that neither one could claim to be the first)."

"World War II put a stop to everything," wrote Brooks and Marsh. "Little was telecast during the war years except for some training programs." In 1944 DuMont Laboratories was granted a license to operate as a network.

It wasn't until after World War II officially ended in September 1945 that the development of television as a commercial enterprise began in earnest. In fact, the BBC, which began the world's first television network transmission in 1936 and stopped on September 1, 1939, did not resume television broadcasting until June 7, 1946. That was the year several network series began in the United States. Most television programs in the early years were produced by the advertisers themselves.

Interestingly, the very first public mention wherein the name Hal Roach and television were linked was as early as May 11, 1945 when the *Los Angeles Times* published a brief notice under the headline "ROACH GOING INTO TELEVISION SPHERE." "Hal Roach, who plans to resume his film work as soon as his studio is released by the government, will also enter the radio and television field. About $300,000 will be used in financing enterprises through 11 counties in the south of California and in Arizona and Nevada, it is indicated. Leland H. Driver will serve as general manager." Always planning for the future. However, when Roach resumed production in 1946 it was with filmed streamlined motion pictures, and he was to focus his efforts on motion pictures well into 1948.

Hal Roach was interviewed by Mike Steen in *Hollywood Speaks* in 1969 regarding his entry into television.

"After the war I returned to Hollywood and started making the 'streamlined comedies' again, with United Artists putting them with a longer feature to make up a double bill. However, United Artists came out with about ten bad pictures which nobody wanted. They couldn't sell them to the exhibitors; therefore, they couldn't sell my comedies. United Artists went through a very bad period, and when they flopped, Metro-Goldwyn-Mayer gave me a contract to make these streamliners.

"I had made the deal with Metro that I would finance the pictures myself. When we were ready to go into production, we found out we didn't have the money to finance them. A large amount of money had disappeared. I don't want to say how, but not very legally. So that's when we went into television production."

Despite what the *Los Angeles Times* had reported in May of 1945, it seems that it was early in 1946 when Roach earnestly began exploring the possibilities of television. He was in discussions with E.A. Tracey, President of Majestic Radio and Television Corporation of Chicago, who wrote to Roach on March 22, 1946 to advise him that "The plant in Burbank is moving along but not as fast as I had hoped...." In July Tracey wrote to say that his company was making thirteen-tube television sets.

On July 8, 1947 the Academy of Motion Pictures Arts and Sciences released a Confidential Research Council Report on Television to its members. It described the first demonstration of a large screen color theater television made by RCA that had taken place on April 30th. While the color was better than ever seen before, it still did not match the quality of the color of projected motion picture film. "Color television cameras and transmission facilities, however, have not yet been developed," said the report, "and many problems remain to be solved before this type of equipment could be demonstrated commercially as a normal size theatre picture."

As far as color television for the home was concerned, "color telecasting by CBS has been discontinued after the recent FCC ruling and no other home color process is expected to be developed commercially for several years. Home black-and-white television is continuing to make rapid strides, particularly in the East, both from a technical and entertainment standpoint."

The broadcast of the 1947 World Series baseball games, from September 30 to October 6, brought television its first mass audience. The games were telecast in New York, Philadelphia, Schenectady and Washington, D.C. President Harry S. Truman is reported to have watched the games on the first television set in the White House. The World Series was seen by 3.9 million people, 3.5 million of them in bars. "After that," wrote Brooks and Marsh, "TV ownership was contagious." The Motorola VT-71 of 1947 priced at $189.95 was the first television set to be sold for under $200, thus making television affordable for millions of Americans. By the end of 1947 The United States had 44,000 licensed television receivers, with some 30,000 of those in the New York City area alone.

CBS delayed its entry into network service because it was trying to get the FCC to approve its color system. It did not, and RCA's all-electronic color system was eventually chosen several years later. Reluctant to wait any longer, CBS began feeding programs over its own small network early in 1948.

Comedian Milton Berle became television's first superstar, and his show was rated number one for three seasons, from 1948-1951. Home television ownership in 1948 was less than two percent of the U.S. population when Berle began; it soared to fifty percent by 1953 and then to over seventy percent when he left the air in 1956. By the early 1960s, ninety percent of American homes had at least one television set.

It wasn't until January 11, 1949 that television networks were able to extend their signal from New York to the Mississippi River, and coast-to-coast television was at last achieved in September 1951. During these early years, virtually all programming originated from New York City and were transmitted "live."

In January 1948, far-sighted Grace Rosenfield wrote to Roach, "The thought occurred to me that due to their popularity [*Amos 'n Andy* on radio] a series of short subjects featuring these characters may have tremendous value in the television field at a future date...." *Amos 'n Andy* would indeed become a CBS television series three years later—and be filmed on the Hal Roach Studios Culver City lot.

On February 17, 1948 Robert T. Thompson, Majestic's Chief Engineer, wrote to Roach, "Majestic shipping today laboratory sample of our Model 30TV792 which has been set up for the television channels in the Los Angeles area... We are enclosing instructions for installation and operation of this receiver...."

Roach wrote to Tracey at Majestic soon thereafter, "We will either set up our own sales organization [for television distribution] or have them handled through one of the sales agencies now handling transcription for radio. This idea looks hotter every day."

Yet belts were being pulled pretty tight at the Hal Roach Studios at this time. In responding to an appeal for a donation to the Society of Motion Picture Engineers, Hal Roach Jr. was forced to reply, "...Unfortunately, however, circumstances at the Studio within the last year during which time we have been idle, make it impossible for us to extend any financial assistance at this time."

Virtually forced to by circumstance and historical timing, father and son would become the first major Hollywood producers to convert a movie studio to television production. Articles of Incorporation for the Hal Roach Television Corporation were initiated in April of 1948 even as negotiations with MGM to produce theatrical films were in progress.

The *Los Angeles Times* reported on April 28, 1948 that "Lois Moran, well remembered from film appearances in the past, is busy again, this time in a television picture, 'Your Witness,' being made by Telepix, Robert Longenecker organization, at Hal Roach Studios."

Writing to actress Margot Grahame in London the following month, Roach revealed the dire financial straits his studio was in. "...Due to general conditions in the motion picture business, we have been out of production for almost a year. I had hopes that we would resume activities long before this time... we have severed our association with United Artists and now have a contract with Metro Goldwyn Mayer for the distribution of a number of our pictures. Naturally, we are very pleased feeling that this is a very fine release.

"Due to the general business conditions in the picture industry, it has taken us some time to conclude the MGM deal and we are still working out the financial matters. However, the picture we have in mind to star you in is still on the schedule...."

But the MGM deal fell through and it was during Roach's September 1948 business trip to New York to meet with television executives that he became convinced television was indeed the wave of the future, and that he should devote himself exclusively to that medium. He put his thirty-year-old son, Hal Roach Jr., in charge of production. The first meeting of the Hal Roach Television Corporation took place on December 6, 1948. Roach let a newspaper reporter know that he was planning to create a new kids' television show. Immediately the Studio switchboard was flooded with telephone calls "to say nothing of telegrams, letters and personal visits from mothers with children who want to get into our *Puddle Patch Club* television series." Nothing seems to have come from that early television concept.

Of historical interest is the fact that Hal Roach began his television pioneering with his old rival Mack Sennett, who had ceased production when his studio went into bankruptcy back in 1933. On December 1, 1948 Roach wrote to Grace Rosenfield: "Mack Sennett has a fifteen minute comedy with Donald Novis singing a very beautiful song. The negative is in good shape and he has an old print. Would you please check around and see what can be done about selling this picture for television... I would like to assist him as a personal favor to him."

A few days later Mrs. Rosenfield replied, "...as you know, through numerous contacts, I may be in a position to [approach distributors or direct book to stations]... and thereby enable Sennett to retain 100% of the revenue, rather than release a substantial portion for distribution fees...."

Roach wrote to Sennett at the Garden Court Apartments in Hollywood, "Do you have a print that can be shipped to New York?"

Down Memory Lane, a seventy minute television special comprised of four Mack Sennett shorts and narrated by Steve Allen, was broadcast on television on August 2, 1949. Sennett himself appeared in a brief cameo at the end. According to reviewer Les Adams on the IMDb, "The shorts used were: *Sing, Bing, Sing* and *In the Blue of the Night*, both starring Bing Crosby; *The Dentist* with W.C. Fields; and *The Singing Boxer* with Donald Novis. There were also ten songs, many that became hits (in their time) and one that later became Crosby's theme song."

"Hal Roach Studio's Films Wholly for Television" read the headline of the *Daily Boston Globe* on December 22, 1948. "Hollywood, Dec. 21 (AP) Producer Hal Roach today said his studio will make films wholly for television. His studio thus becomes the first major Hollywood firm to enter the television field exclusively. He said shooting will start tomorrow on the first of six 30-minute video shows. He expects to have all completed by

Jan. 5. Average shooting schedule will be two days." The *Los Angeles Times* on Christmas Day added, "Hal Roach, who will concentrate on television films, plans no fewer than 18 series, samples of which will probably all be made within the next month or two."

In January, 1949, Roach stated in a newspaper interview: "The conversion of a large studio like ours to television points the way to leadership in this new industry for Los Angeles." How true those words remain.

A February 1949 newspaper article headlined "Hal Roach Jr. Pioneers Way in Pictures for Television." "Already in production, the company is producing films at the rate of 52 a year, or one a week. Each film will suffice for a half-hour program… Speed of these productions has amazed Hollywood. It completely upsets the leisurely time-consuming methods of making pictures… Films produced by Hal Eugene Roach Productions are priced at between $8500 and $10,000, which places them within reach of sponsors… Television and associated industries, he feels, within the next 10 years will be one of the first five industries in the United States."

Were the above facts related in the February 1949 article fanciful? For the truth was that Roach had outstanding loans of over $3 million and creditors were sitting on his board. He even offered to sell his studio to the U.S. Air Force yet again, and would try one last time in 1953, even when his television productions were doing quite well.

His son, too, was sold on television. "HOLLYWOOD TO BE TV CENTER PARLEY TOLD BY HAL ROACH JR. Hollywood, not New York City or Chicago," the *Chicago Daily Tribune* reported on March 10, 1949, "will become the television capital of the nation, Hal Roach Jr., executive vice president of Hal Roach studios, yesterday told the national television conference in the Palmer House… Altho many movie moguls are keeping a discreet silence, Hollywood producers, actors, writers, makeup and camera men, and even hair dressers, are enthusiastic about television and hope to get into it, Roach said."

But in June 1949 his father couldn't even pay an attorney the $750 that was owed him. "I am very well aware of the fact that the Hal Roach Studios owes your firm $750.00" Roach Sr. wrote on June 10th. "Unfortunately, we owe a great many hundreds of thousands of dollars besides this amount. We are doing our darndest to refinance and think we will. At the present time a creditors committee is watching every expenditure and our income is only sufficient to make it possible to bring in the small income to pay taxes and insurance and a skeleton crew to keep the studio in operation. Of course, nothing came out of the Metro deal…."

In August and September 1949 Hal Roach sent letters to the heads of fifty-two of the leading corporations in the United States announcing that he would beginning television programming in January 1950 and the subject would be "Industrial U.S.A." He offered to showcase their company in his television film. Some of the responses were decidedly negative, such as that of Franklin Bell, Director of Advertising for H.J. Heinz Company in Pittsburgh.

"...I cannot enthuse over the proposal to sell the American people via television," he wrote. "...So far as a mass market is concerned, television is still limited. And so far it does not by any means reach the kind of audience interested in industrial U.S.A." Allied Mills, Inc., Bon Ami, Procter & Gamble Co., The Pullman Co., Sears, Roebuck & Co., Standard Brands and the United Fruit Company were also uninterested in having any exposure on television.

But there were some takers. Positive responses came from E.F. Hutton, Union Oil and the New York Stock Exchange. As it turned out, Union Oil, which had already hired Roach to create an industrial film for them a year earlier, now gave him the green light to produce a forty minute film in Ansco Color to be screened for their Sixtieth Anniversary Celebration. It was a hit at both the New York City screening as well as the one in Los Angeles, where cocktails and a buffet were served at Perino's Restaurant, followed by the screening at the Wilshire-Ebell Theatre, one of the few elegant Broadway-styled theatres in Los Angeles. Roach could not attend due to having the flu.

On March 8, 1950 Reese H. Taylor of Union Oil wrote to Roach, "The splendid reception of the picture produced by your Studio, by our directors, shareholders, dealers and employees is proof that your Studio is ideally equipped to produce commercial films. We congratulate and thank you for a job well done." Richard Lewis Ward states that Roach even produced a commercial spot for Union Oil featuring an unknown starlet named Marilyn Monroe. Yet Roach wanted to do more than to make commercials and industrial films. What he really wanted to do was to produce films for television.

"'...as many people will be employed in television in a year as there are now in motion pictures,' predicted Hal Roach" to the *Hollywood Reporter* that fall. "...Hal Roach, longtime motion picture producer whose experimentation with video films for the past two or three years... entitle him to tread into the jungle of television clairvoyance with more authority than the average looker-into-the-future...."

"Even though New York advertising agencies are antagonistic to Hollywood now for fear of losing some of their intermediary identities when complete programs roll out of here abundantly in film cans, Roach foresees only local domination of production with full agency representation locally... Hollywood is now producing about 27 hours of motion picture programming weekly, relatively minor to the much greater capacity of television when stations go on the air seven to nine hours a day. All this is a cheering prospect to the talent and technicians here, one that Roach is certain of materialization in the near future when the elaborate plans come to happy fruition."

"'We will not get rich overnight,' said Roach, "though Roach predicted profit will be shown for 1951."

On October 27, 1949 he sent a letter relieving long time loyal New York sales rep Grace Rosenfield of her job, even though she seemed to be handling the new medium of television quite well. She had been with him since 1932 and had assisted the Studio in so many matters, most recently the lawsuit against the distributor Film Classics, which they won, and the battle with the Memphis Censor Board, as well as providing astute suggestions for programs and personalities for the new medium of television. Perhaps Roach felt she belonged to an earlier era. Certainly there were economic reasons.

"Dear Grace:

"It is with a great deal of regret that I find it necessary to write this letter.

"As you know, we have left the motion picture field entirely and are concentrating all our efforts on television. To that end, we have hired Mr. Schindler to represent us in the selling field, supplementing his service with that of Hal Jr. who will spend a great deal of his time in the New York office during the formative months necessary to successfully launch our television activities.

"Naturally, all of your activities have been concerned with motion picture representation and motion picture personalities; and I believe there is still a very good future for you in that line of endeavor.

"Our financial situation is such as you probably know, that it is imperative that we economize everywhere possible in order to carry ourselves while we are launching this new venture. In justice to our creditors who are being very lenient, and to RFC who holds a mortgage on the Studio, we also find it necessary to economize in every way possible.

"Since the position you now hold will be practically non-existent shortly, I can only inform you with regret that I am giving you a three months termination notice. During this three month period you can either continue on the job or take the three months for a vacation. I believe you will find no difficulty in securing another position to represent some other or several producers.

"Please believe me, Grace, this has been a most difficult decision for me to make. I deeply appreciate the loyalty and hard work you put in for us during the long years of our association. Please feel free to call upon us at any time for any references you may need.

"I shall look forward to seeing you on my next trip to New York. Sincerely, Hal E. Roach."

Herb Gelbspan continued to work in the New York office. Mrs. Rosenfield reportedly had planned to open her own sales and publicity office for motion picture independents; she was one of the producers of the 1952 Broadway revival of Noble Sissle and Eubie Blake's 1921 African-American musical revue *Shuffle Along*, but it only ran four performances. The following year she became a distribution agent for the Niagara Pulsator Corporation, manufacturers of personal massage devices.

On November 11, 1949 Roach wrote to Clara Beranger de Mille (1886-1956), the wife of Cecil's director brother William and a screenwriter from the early days of Hollywood. Mrs. de Mille was one of the original faculty members of the University of Southern California's School of Cinematic Arts, founded in 1929 which was a joint venture with the Academy of Motion Pictures Arts & Sciences.

"Dear Clara: There is an expanding market for new shows and ideas for television but the proper procedure is to submit the ideas to the sponsors back there [in New York City]. We have our eastern representatives for the purpose of submitting those ideas."

Apparently Roach liked one of Mrs. de Mille's television proposals and a couple of weeks later he wrote to her, "After several months of inactivity sponsors are again calling for new television show ideas. I would like to keep the material 'For Better or Worse' here as we are beginning to get new calls for show ideas."

Another USC faculty member, Wilbur T. Blume, had invited Roach to talk to the students at one of his classes. Much impressed, on September 23, 1949 Roach sent a letter to Mr. Slavko Vorkapich (1894-1976), famous as a creator of superb montage sequences in Hollywood movies of the 1930s and 1940s, then a professor at the USC Cinema Department.

"We are embarking on a rather extensive television program," Roach wrote, "For this program we are going to need a great many additional producers, directors, writers, actors and technicians. Most every type of program is contemplated—comedy, drama, musicals, scientific and educational.

"It was my thought that possibly your faculty could allow me to contact the students who are finishing the various courses so that we may have these groups augment our staff...."

In November Blume wrote to Roach, "...Prof. Vorkapich and I... are now considering establishing an experimental course for the Spring Semester in which a select group of graduate students might attempt to solve some of the production problems as suggested by you. I would like to thank you for taking the time to come down and look over our department. At present we do not have too many students to send you. However, in February at the end of this semester, and again next June, we will have several more whom we would like to recommend for your consideration."

November 11, 1949: Hal Roach to Wilbur T. Blume: "...I will be glad to meet with you at any time either here or at the University and will be awaiting word from you."

Several promising USC film students were indeed interviewed by Mr. Roach. It is not known how many, if any, became studio employees.

In late 1949 a lot of people still did not realize that Hal Roach had made the switch to television. On November 14, 1949, Roach Sr's secretary, Edith Udell, had to explain to an inquiring motion picture screenwriter: "The studio has recently entered into the television field and Mr. Roach is concentrating all his time and efforts in the production of films for television only." That month Apex Film Corporation signed a one year rental agreement with the Hal Roach Studios at $350 per day, $150 per day for exteriors, to begin filming their new series, *The Lone Ranger*. The era of television had truly begun.

But renting studio space was not enough. The enormous debt that had accrued since 1946 had to be dealt with and reduced. In 1950 there was a major financial reorganization of the Hal Roach Studios whereby general creditors accepted the proposal to transform in excess of one million dollars of liabilities into the net worth section of the company, thus placing the studio on sound financial ground. Vice President and Treasurer H.R.P. Lytle began pruning expenses, instigating a revision of the accounting procedures and effected substantial reduction in operating expenses.

"Since 1914 Mr. Roach has been a prominent figure in the film industry," wrote Lytle. "he has contributed much to the wealth of enjoyment that motion pictures have given this nation and the rest of the world. For over a third of a century Hal Roach has been a name associated with some of the screen's greatest achievements. The belief in his ability and his creative genius was pronouncedly evident at our meetings with creditors. Their general comment was to the effect that having known him for many, many years, they believed in his ability and were willing to go along with any sound and equitable plan that would enable the studio to properly plan for this anticipated increased volume of business. This feeling is, I am sure, prevalent among movie-goers all over the world and has convinced me that Hal Roach will become one of the greatest names in television which today is America's fastest growing industry."

"This proposed reorganization of ours," said Roach, "was deemed advisable in view of the terrific growth trends in the television film production field... Our group has felt that we should immediately prepare ourselves for what appears to be a big expansion in this branch of the motion picture industry."

As an economic measure, the Directors agreed to a salary cut on January 16, 1950. President Hal Roach's pay was to go from $750 a week to $500; Vice President and Treasurer Hugh Huber from $350 to $200 a week, Vice President S.S. Van Keuren would receive $275 instead of his usual $400; and Secretary Fred Wilkins' weekly pay would be reduced from $200 per week to $150.

At that time, early 1950, a dispute between Hal Roach and one of his trusted Vice Presidents, Hugh Huber (1897-1969), threatened to consume all the energy that was required to resolve the studio's financial problems and to gear up for television production. Hugh Huber had worked for Roach as the chief auditor since the mid 1930s. In January 1940 he had succeeded Frank Ross as a Studio Vice President and Director.

On March 13, 1950 Roach sent Huber a letter: "Dear Sir: During the period from January 25, 1945 to September 4, 1945 you transferred without any right, authority or permission from me the sum of $35,000.00 of my monies to Topical Products Corporation... when you were directly and financially interested in the TPC as an officer, director, stockholder and creditor thereof." This action had been concealed from Roach until February 9, 1950.

A further amount was discovered to have been taken, so Roach demanded Huber as well as Topical Products repay him $77,800.00. Huber denied guilt and resigned his post. Eventually a settlement was reached.

On March 17, 1950 a Memo To All Employees was distributed, signed by Hal E. Roach, President; H.R.P. Lytle, Executive Vice President-Treasurer; S. Van Keuren, Vice President-Studio Manager; and Hal Roach Jr., Vice President:

"We are glad to inform you that we are in the final stages of a financial reorganization of the company... We are now in a greatly improved financial position. This does not mean that we have any money to spare—or more to lose. It means simply that from now on we cut the buck—make a profit or else. That is a *must*. The outlook is good. We have in this lot a choice production property and facilities. And don't belittle TV—every day as the number of receiving sets increases, our outlook brightens... We have a fine organization of intelligent and highly qualified men and women—the vast majority of whom we believe love the company and are deeply loyal to it. We need your every help to do the job ahead—to cut costs, save money and increase productivity... Let's put the Roach banner ahead where it's been most of the many years since the birth of motion pictures."

In March 1950 General Motors Corporation hired Roach to film a motion picture titled *Headline* by a company new to Hollywood, Wolverine Productions, represented by the General Motors public relations department in Detroit. It was a 35mm seven-reel feature with a cast including Donald Crisp, Jeffrey Lynn, Marjorie Reynolds and Alan Hale Jr. It was produced for $250,000 with a 16-day shooting schedule.

Meeting Minutes, August 29, 1950: "Mr. Roach stated at some length his plans for getting the studio into further television production on a basis which would not alone give the studio production charges but would give it an interest in the pictures produced so that it would have a future income from these pictures."

Meeting Minutes, September 12, 1950: "Mr. Roach outlined to the Committee his plans to interview sponsors and their agents to try and line up television shows which would be produced by the Company with funds advanced by the sponsors. As most of these contracts have to be made in the east it requires that some officer of the Company spend several weeks running down prospects for this business and Mr. Roach proposed that he do this himself as soon as it is possible for him to get away for the required time. This type of business is so vital to the Company that it was felt the expenditure of money and time was fully justified."

Meeting Minutes, September 26, 1950: "It was clear that the studio could not break even on a rental business alone at the prevailing rates, except in the extreme case where all of the facilities were in constant use, which is never the case."

Meeting Minutes, October 6, 1950: "Mr. Roach reported on the matter of production of television pictures for Magnavox and stated that the maximum budget the sponsor would allow for a 55 minute picture was

$23,500.00... If the picture runs over the budget the Company pays the excess... While the start in this type of business with such a sponsor is most desirable, the Committee felt that it should have further information before making a decision."

Meeting Minutes, November 24, 1950: "The New York television stations are utilizing 27 live action shows, which Mr. Roach considered could be better performed through the use of motion picture film and the costs of such live shows had now reached the point where the costs of motion picture facilities could more equitably compete with live shows on television. Mr. Roach stressed the need of the corporation to have a proper sales organization to contact and sell the facilities and the studio organization's ability to the various advertising organizations and to the sponsors of television shows. The consensus of opinion of the majority of the other Directors was that in view of the lack of funds to launch such a sales campaign with the delay in recouping such costs that the corporation could not incur such expenses at this time.

"Approved payment for Roach's trip Back East $619.07."

Meeting Minutes, April 27, 1951: "Hal Roach Jr. is negotiating with Robert Lippert to produce 13 motion picture productions of one hour each during the first year and 26 like productions during the second year. $30,000 per picture. Also negotiating a series of television shows *Don't Be a Sucker*, one half hour at $11,500 each. [This became *The Stu Erwin Show* aka *The Trouble with Father*.]

Memo to Hal Roach from S. S. Van Keuren, June 11, 1951: "Companies located on the lot: APEX FILMS: two pilots completed, *Cavalcade of America* and *Texas Ranger*.

ROLAND REED PRODUCTIONS: *Trouble with Father* [Stu Erwin]

SHOWCASE PRODUCTIONS: *Racket Squad*

WALTER WANGER: Two features

C.B.S.: *Amos 'n Andy* series

ABBOTT & COSTELLO: TV series and one feature...

TV Spots for: Hunt's Foods, Pabst Blue Ribbon, Boluva Watch, Admiral... etc."

According to author Ward, what really saved the Roach Studios from economic ruin was the 1951 sale of the Our Gang shorts to television for $200,000 which permitted a settlement of the debt and the return of control of the studio to Hal Roach.

"Roach has finally succeeded in getting his financial position in shape whereby he can see a little daylight," he was able to announce to an MGM executive on July 6th. Soon, instead of just renting space for such

TV shows as *Abbott & Costello* and *The Lone Ranger*, the Hal Roach Studios began producing their own television shows.

Meeting Minutes, August 2, 1951: "Total Amount Due Creditors: $284,325.12. Amount at 60% Settlement: $170,595.07."

"Hal Roach Makes Money in TV" declared a *St. Petersburg Times* headline on October 19, 1951. "HOLLYWOOD—(AP)—The movie colony shuddered with disbelief two years ago when Hal Roach became the first major studio to go all out for television movies.

"But Prexy Roach now discloses that the company is operating in the black—a feat that some of his scoffers can't equal.

"'Business is good and getting better all the time,' he comments. *Amos & Andy, Beulah,* and *Racket Squad* are some of the Roach-made TV shows."

TV Guide explained it this way in their major story on Hal Roach Jr. *The Man Who Bet on Television* in their June 11, 1955 issue. "Hal Jr. came back to his father's studio to announce that television was the coming thing. His father, forward-thinking to the point of being ahead of his time, agreed."

However, "…the motion picture industry reacted to television exactly like the theatrical industry did when motion pictures came in," explained Roach in *The Real Tinsel* by Bernard Rosenberg and Harry Silverstein (1970). "Theater people would not hire an actor who worked in a movie. They would not let an actor, producer, or a director, or anybody else who had anything to do with legitimate theater in pictures. The theater should have owned the business instead of fighting it."

But the Roaches were ready to challenge those antiquated attitudes. Except they differed on what to produce. Junior wanted to turn out profitable half-hour films in a hurry. The "old man" (only 58) saw TV broadcasting hour shows—and longer. So they made two hour-long films *The Three Musketeers* and *Hurricane at Pilgrim Hill*, which *TV Guide* said were still sitting on the shelf several years later, but Richard Lewis Ward states "received a strongly favorable reception upon their late 1950 airings on CBS as part of the normally live, New York-based *Magnavox Theater.*" Additionally, Roach Sr. wanted to have multiple sponsors per show, rather than one advertiser identified with one show as was the radio model, though it would be five years before NBC announced its "revolutionary magazine concept, its 90-minute 'spectaculars'—big shows with two and three sponsors."

"Junior, meanwhile, borrowed money and plunged into his first TV film venture, *The Stu Erwin Show.*

"'They all thought I was an idiot,' [Roach Jr.] says, 'and it actually helped. Left me with nothing very serious to live up to.'"

The Hal Roach Studios as a television entity was up and running. The comic Stu Erwin had originally appeared in a Hal Roach silent two-reeler *A Pair of Tights* in 1928. His half-hour domestic sitcom lasted five seasons and 130 episodes. Then came the TV series *Racket Squad* starring Reed Hadley for 98 episodes. Interestingly, many of those episodes were directed by Erle C. Kenton (1896-1980), who had originally worked for Mack Sennett. Kenton later directed, ironically, several Abbott & Costello features in the 1940s. Appearing in two episodes of *Racket Squad* was Johnny Downs (1913-1994) an Our Gang kid from 1925-27 and a juvenile lead in Roach's *All-American Co-Ed* in 1941.

In 1952 the highly popular *My Little Margie* debuted, starring Gale Storm, Charles Farrell and Clarence Kolb (memorable from the 1938 Roach feature *Merrily We Live*). The domestic comedy lasted 126 episodes to 1955. Hal Yates (1899-1969) who had directed several memorable silent Roach shorts in the 1920s returned to directed ninety episodes. *My Little Margie* was so successful that it led to a spin-off, *The Gale Storm Show (Oh! Susanna)*, for an additional 125 episodes from 1956 to 1960. ZaSu Pitts made a welcomed return to the Roach lot after many years to co-star.

"Yes, I heard they were running some of our old pictures on TV. They use them here every week, have been for the last three years. The sad part is we don't get any revenue from them at all. Anyway, it keeps our name in front of the public which keeps us from dying out altogether." – Stan Laurel in a private letter, February 4, 1953.

Even though television was proving to be so successful, Mr. Roach still apparently hankered to produce motion pictures as well. On July 7, 1953 he wrote to Nicholas Schenck:

"I believe there will be a scarcity of good features this fall. Your sales organization could sell six additional pictures without increasing your sales cost. We have learned in the last three years how to make pictures at a low cost… because we had to meet television prices. We can now make a feature in color for $150,000 that will look like $300,000 or more. We would like to make six of these features a year for you. We would make one as a sample and if you did not like it, you could cancel the rest. We will make these pictures on any basis you suggest. You can buy them outright, release on percentage or give us a profit after the picture has grossed a given sum. We can finance the picture if you agree to reimburse us ($150,000) when negative is delivered. I think you will be more than pleased with the quality we can obtain for this amount of money.…"

Nicholas Schenck, July 20, 1953: "In the general scheme of things as they are to-day, we do not feel that it would be advisable for us to release this type of picture...."

Hal Roach to Nicholas Schenck, August 3, 1953: "...sorry we cannot make pictures for you again... Please do not completely dismiss this idea for I think we can give you some very profitable pictures."

In November 1953 Roach was able to write to an investor, "From a dollars and cents standpoint, we are doing quite well at this time; at least the studio is in the black and it looks like it will be until after the first of the year... [Cinerama and Todd-AO large screen process] want to make one big picture that would utilize practically all the facilities of the Studio at the time and then do nothing until they get an idea of the audience acceptance to this type of production. Therefore, we would run into the same situation as we did on *Joan of Arc* whereby it would be necessary to clear out our present tenants to service this type of picture. It is not practical for us as they would not go into continuous production, particularly at this time."

In December 1953, still thinking "prestige," there was some talk about producing *The Life of Goya* to be co-financed with Rota Film of Spain and to star Hedy Lamarr as the Duchess of Alba "and either Marlon Brando, Van Heflin or Charles Laughton as Goya." In a letter to Ignacio Ortiz de Mendivil in Madrid Roach wrote, "The *Goya* script is being worked on at the present time...." However, nothing came of this project.

By 1955 Roach had no less than ten television series on the air. They included *My Little Margie* with Gale Storm, *Passport to Danger* with Cesar Romero, *Public Defender, Screen Directors Playhouse*. Also being filmed at the Hal Roach Studios, but produced by others, were *The Life of Riley, Amos 'n Andy, So This Is Hollywood, It's a Great Life* and *You Are There*. On March 1, 1955 newspapers announced that Sr. had sold The Hal Roach Studios to his son for $10 million. "The purchase included the 18-acre plant in Culver City, all rights to the features, TV productions and story material and star and creative personnel contracts... The father will become a member of the board of the new corporation, Roach Jr. will be president, and Sidney S. Van Keuren, Charles Meacham and William Hinckle, directors." [*Los Angeles Examiner*, March 1, 1955.]

Roach Jr. was eager to continue his father's comedy legacy on television, and had already been planning a new series of one-hour color specials to star Laurel and Hardy. It was to be called *The Fables of Laurel & Hardy*.

In January 1955 Stan Laurel had written, in a private letter, "We are at present negotiating with Hal Roach Jr. to make six one hour shows a year for TV, & have another meeting next week. They are to be costume pictures in Color, fairy tales—done in the manner of an English Panto-mime, like 'Babes In The Wood,' 'Jack the Giant Killer,' etc. similar to the picture we made *Babes In Toyland* which besides TV, can be played in the Theatres Abroad where we still have a big following. Have had one or two offers to make a series of 39 shorts, but it's too much hard work, plus the difficulty of material... Think it will work out this time as we don't have Roach Sr. to contend with & his 'you know what I mean' stories—however will let you know if & when the deal is closed."

Unfortunately, Oliver Hardy suffered a stroke just ten days before filming was to begin, and the project was abandoned. Unable to move or speak, after eleven bedridden months, poor Oliver Hardy at last passed away on August 7, 1957.

From 1956-58 Hal Roach Jr. had in production *The Charlie Farrell Show* (another spin-off from *My Little Margie*), *Telephone Time*, *Blondie*, *Love That Jill*, *The Veil* hosted by Boris Karloff, *Code 3* and *The Count of Monte Cristo*, all highly popular. While television production boomed, these were truly the waning days of the studio system for the movies. In 1957 Louis B. Mayer (who had been ousted from M-G-M in 1951) died; that same year his be-loved studio lost money for the first time in its thirty-three year history.

On November 7, 1956 Hal Roach Studios and Onyx Corporation filed a civil action in the United States District Court against Charles H. Tarbox dba Film Classic Exchange, George Bagnall & Associates and NBC "for in-junction, damages and other relief, for copyright infringement and unfair competition." The Complaint states that between 1915 and 1929 Hal Roach produced approximately 600 silent films "which have gained world wide acclaim as 'Hal Roach Comedies.' In November 1934 Pathé Exchange, Inc. "did assign in writing to Roach, Inc. all the right, title and interest... to all of the copyrights of said motion pictures [the ones produced through August 1927]...." Roach, Inc. duly renewed copyright for the titles after the initial 28 years elapsed (the most recent films of 1927 lapsing in 1955) and therefore was the lawful proprietor to these films. Roach then signed an agreement in 1953 with Comedy Corporation of America granting them exclusive license for five years "for the purpose of distributing, and licens-ing others to distribute certain motion pictures which are the subject of this action for exhibition on television throughout the world." Comedy Corporation of America appointed Onyx Pictures Corporation as its sole and exclusive agent in 1954 "to market through the medium of television in the United States, Alaska and Hawaii" those films.

However, state the Plaintiffs, "commencing on or about January 1, 1952, and continuously since then, defendant Tarbox, in concert with defendant George Bagnall... have largely copied the prints or negatives, or both, of certain of plaintiff Roach's copyrighted motion pictures... and have licensed or otherwise authorized numerous persons throughout the world, namely defendant NBC... to publicly perform these motion pictures... and have thereby engaged in unfair competition and unfair trade practices against plaintiffs, to plaintiffs' irreparable damage." The lawsuit lists 138 comedies in question, but states "the number of motion pictures copied and publicly distributed... by Tarbox, Bagnall... is considerably in excess of the above amount. However, said defendants' operations have been so far flung, and their acts of infringement so numerous that a precise count of their infringing motion pictures is not now possible."

In a deposition on January 14, 1958, Charles H. Tarbox stated that he had presented Hal Roach's silent comedies to be aired on NBC television because, "In the last conversation that I had with Hal Roach Sr. [in 1950], he said that they had no interest in these comedies, that they had been disposed of, and that he had no concern at all with what we did with the comedies."

But merely unlawfully showing Roach's old silents on television wasn't the only infringement Tarbox, et al were being accused of: "In addition, said defendants have altered or wholly deleted the titles, title cards and billing credits of many of the original motion pictures...." They also alternated "the sequence of scenes and deleted entire scenes by reducing their length... In addition to the acts of unauthorized alteration... defendants... have seen fit to add a musical soundtrack of their own choosing to each copied motion picture, the original of which were silent comedies. They have done this without the permission of plaintiff Roach, and despite its objections. Said musical soundtracks are tasteless and cheap and detract further from whatever artistic merit has survived said defendants' acts of mutilation.

"Further, without the permission of plaintiff Roach, and despite its objections, defendants... have affixed plaintiff Roach's trade name to defendants' inferior copies... and have represented their copies as 'Hal Roach Productions'... and have consciously created the impression, false though it is, that plaintiff Roach was actually associated with defendants... Defendants... have represented, and at all times herein set forth, and do still represent, that the motion pictures they are distributing are genuine Hal Roach Comedies, when, in truth, they are nothing but shoddy shadows of plaintiff Roach's original artistic endeavors, and said defendants have so spoiled the market with their inferior product and have caused such public confusion by their false representations of the origin of said inferior product, and of the ownership of distribution rights in Hal Roach Comedies as a class, as to have dissuaded many persons from evincing any further interest in publicly performing any Hal Roach Comedies on television, or by other media, and have thereby materially impaired plaintiffs' ability to license the public performance of their genuine motion pictures...

"Defendants... continued foisting on the public of their spurious and inferior motion pictures under the guise of being genuine Hal Roach Comedies can only have an injurious impact upon the success of plaintiffs' contemplated comedy productions. A large portion of today's theatre going audiences and television audiences has never seen a genuine, full length Hal Roach comedy motion picture, or an authorized, carefully edited television version as distributed by plaintiff Onyx, and such audiences are thus unprepared to judge between good and bad comedy. Comedy as represented by said defendants' mutilated copies of plaintiff Roach's original motion pictures, as herein described, is bad comedy, which despite said plaintiff's objections, is made to bear its name. This forced mis-association is unfair and harmful to plaintiff Roach—for public distaste which is acquired today is not easily divested tomorrow.

"Further, many of the so-called Hal Roach comedies which defendants... are distributing and vending are so bad in print quality and editing that audiences laugh at the comedies themselves as ludicrous examples of poor picture making rather than at the antics of the performers. This misdirection of audience attention is also unfair and harmful to said plaintiffs.

"Much of the success of the comedy motion pictures produced by plaintiff Roach's predecessors is traceable to the careful selection and delineation of the characters featured in each of said motion pictures... the quality of the characters created and developed by plaintiff Roach's predecessors has been cheapened and the characters degraded and the value of their future use to plaintiff Roach in contemplated motion pictures has been materially diminished, to the detriment of said plaintiff." Damages in the amount of $250,000 were requested.

The case dragged on for two and a half years, and finally on July 21, 1959 the Judge issued an Order of Dismissal For Lack of Prosecution. Apparently one or both parties simply failed to file the proper motions in a timely manner; in Roach's case perhaps it was a sense of giving up, for by then his studio was in bankruptcy and the gates to the Lot of Fun were shuttered.

Meanwhile, there was a renewed interest in Laurel and Hardy's classic comedies. The exposure of Roach's shorts on television inspired Robert Youngson to create a "compilation film"—a feature comprised of various clips from many comedy shorts. Working with Herbert Gelbspan as associate producer, *The Golden Age of Comedy*, released in 1957, was a great success. This was followed by *When Comedy Was King* (1960), *Days of Thrills and Laughter* (1961), and *30 Years of Fun* (1963). Several more retrospective compilation comedy films were released after this, and will be mentioned in the next chapter.

Oliver Hardy had died before the first of these films were released, but Stan Laurel basked in a warm glow of the affection from a new generation. Although he had opportunities to continue acting, Stan refused: his career had been made with Oliver Hardy, and since his partner was gone, he was determined to remain in retirement. In 1961 he received an Honorary Academy Award "for his pioneering in the field of cinema comedy."

On May 28, 1958 the *Los Angeles Examiner* had the following headline: "Pennsylvania Firm Buys Roach Studios." The Scranton Corporation of Scranton, Pennsylvania acquired all outstanding stock of Hal Roach Studios. "Included in the deal were the $12,500,000 18-acre [*sic*] studio, all existing television and motion picture properties, and the entire film library of the Roach organization. No figure was given. Hal Roach Jr. will continue as president and executive producer of the studios, to be operated as subsidiary of Scranton and will become a director of the corporation." The purchaser was Alexander L. Guterma, described as "a New Yorker, president of F.L. Jacobs Company, which owns controlling interest in the Scranton Corporation."

In August 1958 it was announced that "a major expansion program into many phases of the entertainment business" would be launched by the Hal Roach Studios. The seven sound stages had already been remodeled "at a cost of more than $500,000." A multi-million dollar program for the 1958-59 season was announced, to include 20 feature-length films, six new television series, formation of a releasing organization for theatrical and TV films, and "talent and program divisions to institute a concentrated search for new faces and literary material."

The following month the world's largest radio network, the Mutual Broadcasting Corporation, was sold to Hal Roach Studios at a price in excess of $2 million. Guterma, the new president of the network, said Mutual planned to branch into television. Roach Jr. would be board chairman of Mutual. Roach Jr. said buying the network is an "important step in my studio's plan to move into many phases of the entertainment industry." He also announced a $1 million project to make the Hal Roach Studios the first major Hollywood film production center to be fully equipped for videotape operation.

Some five months later, on February 16, 1959 the *Los Angeles Examiner* revealed that "Guterma, 44, surrendered to Federal authorities yesterday and is out on $5000 bail on charges of failure to report sales of stock in violation of regulations of the Securities Exchange Commission. Authorities have said they are investigating charges of fraud against Guterma which involve millions of dollars." Because of this development, and according the *New York Herald Tribune* of February 16, 1959, Roach Jr. bought the international financier's stock and became chairman and chief executive officer of the auto parts manufacturing firm which apparently controlled the Roach Studios "to protect the company's 6,000 employees."

A week later, Jerry Stagg, originator of the television series *Telephone Time*, sued Hal Roach Jr. and others in the amount of $635,000 for conspiring to defraud him of his fair share of profits in the seventy-one half hour shows.

In early March 1959 Roach Jr. sued Guterma for return of some stocks. "This suit," stated the *Los Angeles Examiner*, "was filed just before Roach was scheduled to appear before the Federal District Court in another matter—the Government's efforts to have the Jacobs firm declared unsound and have a receiver appointed. The Securities and Exchange Commission claims Roach 'has not demonstrated the business acumen or judgment' to deal with the complex financial affairs of the far-flung holding company."

On March 22, 1959, the Scranton Corporation, which controlled the Hal Roach Studios, ousted Hal Roach Jr. and shut the studio down on April 3rd. Stan Laurel sent his former boss a letter that very day:

"My Dear Hal:

"I was deeply shocked to hear about the Studio situation & felt I would like to express my sincere regrets. It's difficult to realize that such a thing could happen to you—I am terribly sorry Hal, but I know you have great fortitude & courage, & will come through 'Flying Colors!'

"Even tho' we've had our little differences in the past Hal, I want you to know I have always held great admiration for you & have many fond memories of our association.

"You have many friends Hal, so I am not alone in wishing you well & lots of good luck in your hour of misfortune, if anything I can do, please don't hesitate.

"My kindest regards and every good wish.

"Sincerely always: Stan Laurel."

In July, writing to another friend, Stan put a sort of film noir twist to the sorry situation: "...the trouble that Roach Jr. was in—it was the Scranton Corpn. a manufacturing outfit—probably making 'Black-Jacks,' they evidently tested one on young Hal & it worked perfectly—during his coma they purloined the Studio."

The studio might have been closed down, but there were still two more Hal Roach movies to reach the screens. On May 5, 1959 *Little Rascals Varieties* appeared, a feature-length compilation of five late '30s Our Gang shorts. The following month the musical *Go, Johnny, Go* rocked and rolled its way to the theaters with a rollicking cast that starred legendary radio DJ Alan Freed, rock musicians and singers Chuck Berry, Jackie Wilson, Ritchie Valens (in possibly his only on-screen performance), The Cadillacs, The Flamingos and Eddie Cochran. Rumor was that Buddy Holly and the Crickets were offered guest spots in this film, but their producer/manager turned the offer down, over the objections of the group—because they would not be paid! *Go Johnny Go* was reportedly filmed in five days earlier in 1958.

After the music died things were went from bad to worse for the folks associated with the Hal Roach Studios. On September 2, 1959 a Federal Grand Jury accused Mutual Broadcasting Network's former officials Alexander Guterma, Hal Roach Jr. and Garland L. Culpepper Jr., "of conspiring to use the radio network to spread propaganda favorable to the Trujillo government of the Dominican Republic... The grand jury charged that Guterma, Roach and Culpepper obtained $750,000 from Trujillo's government on or about last February 6 on the understanding that Mutual would disseminate political propaganda favorable to the Dominican Republic in the guise of genuine news items." (*Los Angeles Examiner*, September 2, 1959)

"I deny the indictment," declared Roach Jr. "I am not now, have not been in the past and would never be an agent for a foreign principal. I am absolutely confident that I will be cleared of the charges when the facts are presented in court." [Was it a coincidence that the housekeeper for Hal Roach Sr. in the 1980s was from the Dominican Republic?]

Guterma pleaded no defense to the charge that he failed to register as a foreign agent for the Dominican Republic. The same plea was entered by co-defendant Hal Roach Jr. on the charge he failed to file a registration on behalf of the Mutual Broadcasting System.

On June 25, 1960 the *Los Angeles Examiner* declared "Hal Roach 'Fall Guy,' Court Rules." He was fined $500 but escaped a jail term. District Judge Joseph R. Jackson said it would be "unconscionable" to jail

Roach, whom he described as "more sinned against than sinning." Jackson told Roach, "the record shows you received not one single penny of the $750,000."

According to the *Los Angeles Examiner*, "The propaganda never was broadcast and the Dominican Republic lost its money. Mutual is now under new ownership. Jackson said Roach was not the same type as Guterma, with whom he said Roach had an 'unfortunate association.' Guterma will be sentenced after an Appellate Court rules on his conviction in a stock fraud case in New York."

Although virtually exonerated, Hal Roach Jr. seems not to have recovered from these blows. In April 1960 he and his wife separated after twenty years of marriage. In June 1961 his estranged wife filed a restraining order against him after filing for divorce, charging that her husband, while intoxicated, had threatened her life. In September their "beautiful home" went on the market, and later that month Junior was charged with drunken driving; he faced a jury trial on November 29. In January 1962 Mrs. Alva Brewer Roach was granted an uncontested divorce. According to the *Los Angeles Times*, she testified her husband drank excessively and did not explain many absences from home. She waived alimony rights. The couple had a 20-year-old daughter, Penny.

In March 1962 Hal Roach Jr. filed bankruptcy papers. "About the only assets listed" stated the *Los Angeles Times*, "...were household furnishings and clothes valued at $623.50." The *New York Times* offered a different amount regarding his assets: $39,633 which included "oil property leases in Texas valued at $35,000."

"As to cash on hand, bonds and securities, stocks, automobiles, horses, sheep and cows, Roach answered: 'None.'" reported the *Los Angeles Times*.

Both newspapers agreed that among his other debts, totaling $1,050,082, Roach Jr. listed performance fees for actor Charles Farrell totaling $142,491.85 and $128,538.85 to actress Gale Storm. According to the *Los Angeles Times*, he declared his total earnings for 1960 to be $2,500 and for 1961 they were $500. The *New York Times* stated $2,500 were earned in 1961 and $500 were earned "so far this year [1962]."

Meanwhile, *Variety* on December 6, 1959 had reported that Hal Roach Sr. had flown to Puerto Rico hoping to convert a hangar at the San Juan Airport into a picture studio.

In March 1960 *Variety* reported that Roach Sr. would be "reactivating his studio, leasing it back from a group which will try to buy it from the court trustees, and set up an annual production and syndicated distribution program of eighty hour-long tv comedies and four theatrical features. Slate calls for a $8,420,000 outlay. Roach Jr. will not be associated with his father in the venture until he has cleared himself of two legal actions now pending, according to Roach Sr."

The Newark Evening News of May 3, 1960, interviewed Roach Sr., who said "I thought I was all fixed for an income of $60,000 a year for the rest of my life. One day I woke up and discovered I wouldn't be assured of that income. It was coming from Hal Roach Productions which was broke. So I had to go back in business."

The *News* said Roach "plans to recoup the $6½ million lost by Hal Roach Jr. in four months by creating a one-hour TV comedy show to include all kinds of comedy. He has approached Buster Keaton, Imogene Coca, ZaSu Pitts, Reginald Gardiner, and Eddie Bracken. 'I want to limit each performer to ten-minute routines.' He also plans 45-minute 'Streamliners' to complete a double bill with one of 1960's extra-length movies."

After the creditors turned off the lights in mid-production in 1959, the studios were used as overflow stage space for some television shows and such MGM productions as *Mutiny on the Bounty*, *The Four Horsemen of the Apocalypse*, and *How the West Was Won*. (These films were released in 1961 and 1962.)

McGarry and Me, a 30-minute pilot, was the very last television show produced at the Hal Roach Studios. It aired on CBS on July 5, 1960.

Author Larry Goldstein wrote very movingly: "The Hal Roach Studio is silent now. Occasional noises from rented sound stages are due to low-budget TV filming, but otherwise the Southern Plantation style building lies bleak and quiet and deathlike-with black asphalt fields stretching toward a barbed-wire boundary. The studio is all laughed out. The magic that once filled the Washington Boulevard landmark is gone. But the comic classics that were produced within its walls still serve, like chuckling ghosts, to recall that golden era when Stan Laurel and Oliver Hardy were the Hollywood ambassadors of fun, frivolity and foolishness."

In May 1961 those "bleak and quiet and deathlike" abandoned buildings were utilized as the location for the first episode of Season Three of *The Twilight Zone*. A young and lithe Elizabeth Montgomery and a youthful Charles Bronson portrayed survivors of an apocalyptic futuristic war wandering the empty buildings and forlorn streets; virtually the entire episode was silent—the characters rarely spoke. Ironic indeed.

In June, 1961, the *New York Times* reported that Hal Roach Sr. was planning to produce and direct feature length comedies in England at

MGM's Elstree Studio. Nine properties were said to have been "lined up," but none were produced. [I discovered why in 1988.]

Unfortunately, as described by *Variety* on June 27, 1962, "Hal Roach Jr. made a deal with big time operator Alexander Guterma, whose financial empire collapsed and with it went the Hal Roach Studios." *Variety* noted that Roach Sr. was due to receive from his son at the time of his retirement in 1955 "$2,319,161 payable monthly over a thirty year period... Father charges that funds to meet the payments were soon drained off in the form of allegedly illegal loans to Guterma... Roach Sr. filed a conspiracy suit in the New York Federal Court alleging fraud in connection with the eclipse and eventual bankruptcy of the Hal Roach Studios... Hal Roach Jr., was induced by the 'conspirators' to absorb them in the management of the company, in violation of a 1955 agreement between Senior and Junior."

The old days of Hollywood seemed to be over for sure: in an issue of *Variety* in 1962, former screen star Bette Davis put out a classified ad seeking work, and on September 17, a full-page ad appeared, declaring "For Sale At Public Auction on Oct. 19, 1962: The Hal Roach Motion Picture Studio!"

Even the decades-long friendship between Hal Roach and Harold Lloyd seemed to have been torn asunder. The *New York Times* on November 2, 1962 reported "Hal Roach Sues Harold Lloyd For a Breach on Old Films." A million dollar lawsuit between Roach and Lloyd? "The complaint charged that Mr. Lloyd and others have exhibited old Lloyd films crediting the comedian as producer, while Mr. Roach is entitled to credit as producer under an agreement signed with Pathé Exchange more than 40 years ago... Mr. Roach charged that the films were mutilated, abridged and distorted when recently exhibited, thus damaging his reputation and prestige as a film producer."

Was Roach referring to *World of Comedy*, the feature Lloyd released in May of 1962 which was comprised of a compilation of scenes from his earlier films? Did this lawsuit go to trial? Was it settled out of court? Whatever the outcome might have been, it's sad to contemplate that two such long-time colleagues would have ended up this way. Were they on bad terms at the end? Not at all, as I soon discovered. Business is business, but true friendship endures.

On December 20, 1962, Barton Fenmore of Ponty-Fenmore Realty Fund bought the fifty-three buildings including the Administration Building, seven sound stages, Optical and Special Effects Building, Dubbing Stage, Film Editorial Building, Make-up Department, etc., that comprised the Hal Roach Studios for a reported $1,326,000.

Nine days later, Mrs. Mabel B. Roach, the mother of Hal Sr., died at the age of ninety-six. It was reported she had long been in ill health. She was survived by her two sons Hal Sr. and Jack, sister Mrs. Maude Van Keuren who had lived with her at the studio, seven grandchildren including Hal E. Roach Jr., and nine great-grandchildren.

There was a brief ray of light during all this bad news: The *New York Times* on January 24, 1963, stated that the studios "would be renovated and kept in service as a film studio." Alas, on May 22, 1963, the *Times* had to announce: "Decision to raze the studio had been reached after four months of unsuccessful efforts to operate it as a studio."

The cameras did turn one more time at the Hal Roach Studios before it was closed forever. An MGM-release, the offbeat *Dime with a Halo* starred five boys playing Mexican street urchins and BarBara Luna, the young Broadway star, as an underage stripper. This black and white low-budgeter directed by Boris Sagal reached the screens in May 1963. Set in a tawdry border town, it was the final production filmed at the doomed Culver City studio.

Fifty years later, BarBara Luna recalled to the author that all the interiors of that little movie, neglected by MGM as they were focusing all their attention on Marlon Brando and the filming of *Mutiny on the Bounty* at that time, were constructed and filmed on the virtually abandoned Roach lot, including the replication of a sleazy Tijuana strip club. "I knew the studio had a lot of history," recalls BarBara (who prefers to be called Luna) "but it was shabby and quiet. We were the only unit filming there, and not much was going on."

"WALLS TUMBLING DOWN: Studio That Fun Built Soon to Be a Memory," is the way Lee Bastajian put it in the July 28, 1963 *Los Angeles Times* article. Bastajian noted that Hal Roach wasn't crying about it.

"'No,' declared producer Hal E. Roach, "I have no feeling of regret. Passing of the studio has no effect upon me. It's just brick and mortar.'

"However, more than just brick and mortar bubbles to the surface when Roach thinks of what the studio once was.

"'I do regret,' he added, 'the passing of the studio as a place for the filming of comedies.'

"The development of a shopping center and a residential complex is planned on the site where Roach established his fun factory in 1919 and made laugh-getters like Harold Lloyd known around the world.

"'The developers are making a mistake,' he exclaimed. 'They could invest a half million in making comedies and make a million a year. They won't make that kind of money in markets and apartments.'"

"As he talked," Bastajian wrote, "Roach left little doubt that he is itching to get back into the thick of the business… he is full of $200 million ideas to save television which he thinks is 'throttled by Madison Avenue and the sponsors. It needs freedom.' 'It hasn't improved in ten years,' said Roach. '… There are 47 million homes with television sets. Each is a potential theater. Collect $5 annually from each and you'd have more than $300 million with which to operate. You could use name stars to produce films—without relying on a sponsor for financing.'

"Sidney Van Keuren, for many years manager of the studio, summed up his former boss's accomplishments: 'He was one of the most rugged individuals in the business. The things he did on the screen were his own creation. He was willing to gamble, to stand or fall on his own ideas.'"

Or to jump, as fellow New Yorker Steve Brodie did back in 1886 from the Brooklyn Bridge—and survive.

During the first four days of August 1963 the studio paraphernalia was auctioned off by the Milton J. Wershow Company, known as "the Sotheby's of the industrial world" as noted by *Business Week* magazine.

Auctioneer Wershow told *The Wall Street Journal* the week prior to the auction, "It is impossible to estimate what we will get out of the contents." He expects buyers from other studios to spend from $100,000 to $200,000 on technical equipment. But other items are hard to appraise.

"There are, for example, thousands of still photographs of such former stars as Harold Lloyd, Mary Pickford [*sic*] and Will Rogers; 5,000 to 10,000 pairs of drapes, six buses complete with 1956 license plates, an assortment of colored bathtubs and hot water heaters; one Model A Ford; one 1941 Chevrolet panel truck; several complete tool shops, one old-time steam engine and one antique thunder and lightning machine."

"Sets for sale include caves, mountains, jails, ocean ships and a permanent city street where 1,500 TV shows were made."

"Everything's for sale at Hal Roach Studios," declared the *Los Angeles Times* on August 2, 1963, "including the catwalks on the sound stages and the cheese slicer in the commissary…

"Marvin Hatley, 59, music director at the plant for 15 years, came around to reminisce and perhaps to buy," stated the *Times*.

"'I worked here for years and knew everyone on the lot,' he said. 'We're sad that this thing should go to the wall. Roach gave so much happiness to the world.

"'I want to buy some of my musical scores back. I wrote all the music for Laurel & Hardy, Charlie [*sic*] Chase, Our Gang, Capt. Fury. Hal Roach told me the other day that he's going to make a lot of movies again and when he gets started he's going to hire me as his music director.'

"Bud Graves, 80, who preceded his brother, Stax, as head of the still department, was on hand with more than 2,000 other people. He wanted to buy some of his old photo equipment.

"'I feel very bad about the sale,' he said. 'I went over and looked at my name in a concrete slab. I put it in with a penny 30 years ago. The penny's gone, but my name's still there.'

"Byron (Bones) Vreeland, 61, errand boy, laborer, grip, plant superintendent, assistant manager and manager in his more than 30 years [*sic*] with Roach, wasn't interested in buying.

"'It's bound to hurt,' he said. 'I've spent all my adult life here. I see things auctioned off that I probably had to fight both Roaches to buy in the first place.'"

According to his biography on IMDb, Vreeland had worked for Roach since 1919 when he was hired as a carpenter. He was head of the Grip Department from the late 1930s to the late 1940s and became Studio Superintendent in 1949. From 1955 to the very end he was the Studio Chief (CEO).

"Mr. Roach treated his workers like family," observed former Our Gang member Tommy "Butch" Bond. "He kept employees for twenty or thirty years. You saw the same electricians, prop men, special effects men, and cameramen. They were pros who knew what they were doing. They had been doing it for years and years. Roach trusted them and kept them through good times and bad. Only if he couldn't trust their work would he let them go."

After the four-day auction, from August first through the fourth was over, *Variety* on August 7, 1963 reported that "Contents of Hal Roach Studios—some 5,000 items with an estimated original value of $10,000,000—went on the auction block...

"First day's activity drew several thousand persons, who shelled out for over a 1,000 items. Carted home was everything from 22 moviolas to a variety of cameras, booms, dollies, animation and special effects equipment and theatre seats.

"Friday's session saw bidding on contents of the woodworking, machine, sheet metal, blacksmith, paint and wallpaper shops...Props, curtains, draperies, books, lamps and lighting fixtures highlighted the Saturday sale and office equipment of all descriptions, rifles, pianos and antiques topped offerings at Sunday's windup.

"Among the more bizarre artifacts which accumulated at the Roach studios during 50 years of filmmaking which the odd-item hunter was offered during auction were: A six foot pencil, three slot machines, license plates from every state, 20 tomahawks, hundreds of phones from every era, a wide selection of bearskins, a ten-foot beer bottle, and 10,000 stills heavy on the 'Our Gang'-sters and Cesar Romero."

That same August 1963 day *Variety* was reporting on the results of the Hal Roach Studios bankruptcy sale, the publication also reviewed Mr. Roach's appearance on NBC-TV's *The Today Show* which devoted its entire two hours ("minus the myriad interruptions for news, weather and blurbs") to the career of Hal Roach.

"Roach's interesting reflections and anecdotes were punctuated by a number of memorable clips from his classic comedies," stated *Variety*.

"The 71-year-old producer concluded with the opinion that, as long as there are children, visual comedy is going to be funny to an audience.

"'It's a shame that it has died out [said Roach]...there could be a lot more than there is today.'"

Following the four-day sale, Auctioneer Wershow (1910-1980) donated the business papers, correspondence and office files that were left at the Hal Roach Studios to the University of Southern California. Additional papers that were meant for a proposed Hollywood Museum were temporarily housed in an abandoned city jail, but as the Museum project never materialized, those documents were also entrusted to the USC Cinematic Arts Library. Long after the bankruptcy, material that had been acquired by the Earl Glick Canadian incarnation of the Hal Roach Studios were donated by Richard W. Bann to USC in the early 1980s.

As though the property literally did not want to "go gentle into that good night," "FIRE RAGES IN HAL ROACH FILM STUDIO" on September 28-29, 1963. "All available Culver City firemen and equipment early today were battling flames sweeping the old Hal Roach Studio...." reported the *Los Angeles Times*. "The blaze broke out shortly before midnight. It engulfed buildings currently being demolished to make way for a shopping center and industrial complex... Flames shot high into the air. Their glow could be seen for miles."

In October all the buildings had been razed. The former Fort Roach was demolished by an Army tank.

Author Goldstein wrote: "Torn down last year amidst the insults and tears of a public old enough to remember, the Studio has given way to an empty field. Later this year, businessmen plan to fill the space with light industry and used car lots."

By the fall of 2013, fifty years after the buildings were razed and new "modern" concerns had taken their place, even the light industry buildings and used car dealerships that had replaced the Lot of Fun had been abandoned. Twenty-first century gangs had claimed the property: graffiti art covered the walls. Worn sofas and piles of empty spray paint cans littered the ground. Our Gang had been replaced by Another Gang living out another destiny, 21st century style.

In the spring of 2014 new construction commenced at the site for an outdoor "fashion and foodie hub" along with office space to be known as The Platform and slated to open in 2015. Wouldn't it be wonderful if a Hal Roach Studios Museum could be created nearby?

Transformation, too, has taken place in the world known as "Hollywood." [The studios] "were now international corporate empires," wrote Edward Jay Epstein in *The Big Picture, The New Logic of Money and Power in Hollywood*, "with their shares traded on stock exchanges in New York, Tokyo and Sydney and their debt managed by global banking syndicates... By the dawn of the third millennium, six global entertainment companies—Time Warner, Viacom, Fox, Sony, NBC Universal and Disney... choose the images that constitute a large part of the world's popular culture and it is these six companies that will continue to shape the imagination of a universe of youth for generations to come." The names Fox (after founder William Fox) and Disney, after that shy Midwestern cartoonist Walt whose first invitation to a Hollywood party was to Hal Roach's 1933 event, are the only family names among that list of giant motion picture corporations to survive into the New Millennium.

All around the former Roach property Culver City has gone through a transformation. Buildings have been renovated and lovely new shops and beautifully decorated streets beckon just blocks away. Wouldn't it be wonderful if some creative investors and the Culver City Board of Directors could get together, buy that abandoned land at 8822 Washington Boulevard and if not build a film studio, at least erect a replica of the Hal Roach Studios' main building and open a museum dedicated to the works and career of Hal Roach?

The two signs which greet visitors who arrive in Elmira, New York honoring two of the city's hometown boys.

Dorothy "Echo" De Borba and Eugene Gordon "Porky" Lee, two Our Gang kids from the 1930s, at a celebrity event in Studio City, California in the year 2000.
Photo by author.

At a 2007 Sons of the Desert meeting in North Hollywood, California are left to right, Lois Laurel Hawes, Stan Laurel's daughter; Addison Randall, one of Hal Roach's grandsons, the son of Roach's eldest daughter Margaret and actor Robert Livingston; and the author. Photo by Richard W. Bann.

Three champions of the Hal Roach legacy on the hillside steps in the Silverlake neighborhood of Los Angeles made famous in Laurel & Hardy's 1932 Academy Award winning comedy classic *The Music Box*. Top to bottom: Randy Skretvedt, author of *Laurel & Hardy, The Magic Behind the Movies*; Richard W. Bann, film preservationist who wrote, along with Leonard Maltin (bottom) *Our Gang: The Life and Times of The Little Rascals*. Maltin is a well known film critic, historian and television personality.

The author spent much of 2013 doing research for this book at the University of Southern California's Cinematic Arts Library in Los Angeles. Here he examines a historic document under the watchful eye of Cecil B. DeMille.
Photo by Stephen Helstad.

Abandoned buildings at the site of the former Hal Roach Studios, Culver City, California in 2013. Gangs from a new generation were using the former comedy studio as their own playground until construction began for new businesses in the Spring of 2014. Photo by author.

Fifty years after the studio was demolished in 1963, the author visits the plaque which had been placed near the Lot of Fun in 1980, brainchild of Bob Satterfield of the Sons of the Desert, the international fraternal organization devoted to the memory of the persons and films of Stan Laurel and Oliver Hardy. Photo by author.

Ironically, this sign had been spray painted by some Gang member at the former site of the Hal Roach's studio 100 years after Roach became a movie producer. And Roach lived to be 100 years young. Let's see what the Second Hundred Years will bring. Photo by author.

10

Punch & Hoody
Beyond the Studio
1964-1992

IN 1964, two European retrospectives were presented of the movies of Hal Roach, at the Cinémathèque Française in Paris and London's National Film Theatre. On July 7th *Variety* reported, "Hal Roach was [in Paris] recently on sort of a pilgrimage to see if somewhere in Europe, and especially France, there still existed the seeds with which to continue the great comic tradition of the silent and early sound comedy screen. Roach insisted that great visual film comedy was not dead, but only dormant...

"Roach thought that oral comedy had replaced the slapstick and sight comedy of past years since it was cheaper to get laughs by talk.

"He pointed out that France had really created the gag comedy in the early days of film and produced one of the first great international comics in Max Linder. He tagged Jacques Tati a fitting successor of that sort of silent film know how...."

On November 22, 1964 Hal Roach's oldest daughter Margaret died at the age of forty-three from pneumonia, the condition that had taken her mother at forty-five and would later take her brother at the age of fifty-three and her father who lived to be nearly 101.

Three months after that, Stan Laurel died at the age of seventy-four. More than 300 mourners filled the Church of the Hills at Forest Lawn Memorial Park, Hollywood Hills that February day in 1965 for his funeral service. Among the mourners were Hal Roach Sr. and his son, Hal Roach Jr., and brother Jack Roach, Leo McCarey, Buster Keaton, Alan Mowbray, Babe London, Patsy Kelly, Andy Clyde, Clyde Cook and Joe Rock, who had produced a number of Stan's silents before his teaming with Oliver Hardy. Laurel's widow, Ida was accompanied by the comedian's daughter,

Mrs. Lois Brooks and her daughter, Laurel and grandson Randy Brooks Jr. Dick Van Dyke delivered the eulogy.

Goldstein wrote: "The death of Stan Laurel last week reminds us of the energy and skill which were the origins of an art form we appreciate from habit."

But Hal Roach kept going. In mid 1965 he was invited to the San Francisco Film Festival to screen the rough cut of his compilation film *The Crazy World of Laurel & Hardy* "which he is presently compiling with editor-writer William Scott," according to *Variety*. "Roach will attend the Frisco showing accompanied by Mrs. Stan Laurel and Mrs. Oliver Hardy...."

That summer he traveled to Berlin to receive a commemorative medal at the Berlin Film Festival for his contribution to the screen as well as to the Munich Stradtmuseum for a program in his honor set for July 8. *Variety* on June 30th reported that Roach "anticipates a return to film production, possibly within the next year."

"'The thing that they're losing is timing,' Roach commented last week in N.Y., speaking of the trend in comedy today. 'You have to anticipate when the laugh is going to come and build up to it. Both motion pictures and television are guilty of this.'

"'Visual comedy just can't be written on a piece of paper. You have to rehearse it carefully and then try it out. Sometimes what was hilarious on paper isn't even a chuckle when acted out. On the other hand, some of the funniest things are those that are spontaneous or improvised. This was the strength of the earlier film comedians.'"

Later in July of that year Roach was in New York City, where the Gallery of Modern Art presented a two-month retrospective program of his career.

"The 74-year-old [*sic*] film pioneer... a spry, erect man with shrewd, twinkling eyes" as Howard Thompson put it in his *New York Times* article "Hal Roach's Laugh Factory."

"Mr. Roach himself will supply a personal commentary during the program's first four days. He also will appear on screen as guide to a photographed tour of the Hal Roach Studios in Culver City, which he shot one month before its demolition last year [*sic*]."

"'The wheel turns, though... Public taste changes, true. But there's not a thing Harold Lloyd did back in the old days that Dick Van Dyke couldn't do today.'

"Today," continued Thompson, "ironically, Mr. Roach does not own the rights to a single one of his films, short or long, and the titles total almost 1,000."

"'But I hope to get 'em back. When I was on active duty in Europe during the war, the Air Force took over the studio, then it was sold to my son and it finally hit bottom, involving the studio itself and eleven other companies. Here's how stupid I am as a businessman.

"'Originally believing there'd be a big gap between television and movie houses—not realizing that pictures would fill so much of the home-screen—I sold one big batch of pictures, around 700 titles, to TV, specifying that my trademark, 'Hal Roach Presents,' be deleted. I didn't want to offend the *theater* people showing my pictures. So there are all those pictures showing around today, with no credit.' He laughed. 'And it's my fault. Most of the money made from my comedies today comes from repeat showings in the foreign market.'"

On the afternoon of July 17 the capacity audience at the Gallery of Modern Art had a surprise when Roach introduced—Harold Lloyd, who happened to be in New York City following a Shriner's national meeting in Washington. The two reminisced about the early days, and one would never have known watching them banter with one another that Hal Roach had sued Harold Lloyd three years earlier for $1 million "charging that his prestige and reputation as a film producer had suffered 'great and irreparable damage' through his name having been omitted as producer on films starring Harold Lloyd... in both theatres and on TV." [*Variety*, November 7, 1962]

In May of 1962 Harold Lloyd had released a compilation film, *World of Comedy*, and the lawsuit was obviously a symbolic gesture on Roach's part. *Variety* reported that the two had not seen one another until that day since the suit was filed three years earlier and that "it still hasn't come up in court due to neither side pushing the issue. In California the statute of limitations is five years before a suit is automatically dropped."

Richard Schickel had written in 1974 that Roach and Lloyd had "agreed to continue splitting future profits on the pictures they had made together on the basis of the contracts under which the films had originally been produced, and Lloyd would claim that as of 1928 his one-reel glasses [*sic*] character films—in which he had no percentage—had trebled their original grosses in re-release for Roach and Pathé. At some later date he bought up his short films, save the Lonesome Lukes, and the few he had made prior to them, and his estate now has full ownership of them all."

"Harold Lloyd & Hal Roach: Old Chums & Litigants" went the *Variety* headline describing their public appearance together that July day in 1965. There was comedy in that. What wasn't so funny were the final years of Harold Lloyd, at least according to Richard Schickel. In his biography of Lloyd, Schickel writes that by the 1960s his wife "Mildred (or 'Mid' or 'Molly' as Lloyd called her) was deeply troubled herself [like her son Harold Lloyd Jr., whose disturbed life deserves a book all its own]... In an unhappy family she was perhaps the most pathetic member. One thinks of her... wandering the hall of the great house, her husband either absent or preoccupied by one of his interests, her children all gone, and none of them bearing her any very kind feelings, caring mainly for her two companionable poodles and her booze, and one sees the end results of the flaws that almost from the first people had detected in Lloyd's art—its abstractness, its mechanical quality, its lack of real warmth [*sic*]. It is all dreadfully sad."

Is this Schickel waxing excessively gothic? Were Lloyd's comedies really so "abstract, mechanical and lacking real warmth?" In any event, Schickel goes on: "His friend [Richard] Simonton cannot believe Lloyd was entirely the author of his family's misery. He thinks the children were at least partly to blame for their own problems. They refused Lloyd's friendship, especially in the later years when he needed them most... Finally, we see, he slipped entirely away from the problem... focusing his concern on his granddaughter and her contemporaries...." Lloyd died in 1971, two years after his wife, in his great Beverly Hills estate Greenacres at the age of seventy-seven.

Meanwhile, in 1965, 73-year-old Hal Roach was ever-productive, presenting an elaborate plan that would bolster film-going attendance and profits while cutting film and television production costs by thirty percent. His plan also included providing technicians and creative talent with long term contracts and profit participation. This would all be done via the creation of what Roach called The Performing Arts League, a 4,800 theatre membership for movie patrons. As with many of his latter-day dreams, this one did not materialize.

In 1966 the unflagging Roach Sr. became the associate producer of a remake of his 1940 feature. *One Million Years, B.C.* remains memorable for the performance of Raquel Welch as Loana, daughter of the Chief of the Shell Tribe as well as for the visual effects of Ray Harryhausen. It was released in the United States by Twentieth Century-Fox in 1967.

In September 1964 Robert Youngson had released *The Big Parade of Comedy* which included clips from many of MGM's great movies of the 1930s including a scene from Laurel & Hardy's appearance in *Hollywood Party* (1934). Then in June 1965 Youngson released his fifth retrospective compilation feature starring The Boys, *Laurel & Hardy's Laughing 20s*. Shortly thereafter Hal Roach filed a breach of contract suit totaling $1,730,000 in

New York Supreme Court against Metro-Goldwyn-Mayer, Robert Young-son Productions and Robert Youngson charging that within the past two years, Metro and Youngson had, as reported by *Variety* on August 3, 1966, "wrongfully distributed and exhibited [*Laurel & Hardy's Laughing '20s*] as being produced by Youngson and that no credits are given to him (Roach) as creator and producer... For this he wants $500,000 and a second $500,000 for a film *The Big Parade of Comedy*... on which no credits were given Roach.

"He asks $250,000 each for two other causes of action; that defendants used his creations and exhibited and distributed them in a mutilated and abridged version, thereby destroying the artistic merit of his work; and a like amount for the same reason for *Big Parade of Comedy*.

"The last $280,000 is asked, Roach says, because Metro employed him to produce a film in England under an employment agreement. Metro, he states, represented that its British subsidiary would complete the terms of the contract in England. He traveled there, he says, entered his duties and was ready to perform, when they refused to complete the terms and prevented him from producing a film."

It seems that this lawsuit might have been abandoned, or allowed to lapse, just as Roach's symbolic complaint against Lloyd had been. In any event, Roach decided that it was indeed his turn to make a compilation film of his own. In 1967 the film he had been working on for two years, co-produced with Jay Ward Productions *The Crazy World of Laurel & Hardy*, which in 1965 received a commemorative medal at the Berlin Film Festival, was given an appreciative review in *Variety* on December 27, 1967: "... *Crazy World* permits the viewer new to the Laurel & Hardy scene to form an excellent impression of what made this dissimilar twosome click. For L&H addicts, of course, it's lagniappe... A delightful session with two of the screen's all-time great comics and a film that should never be allowed to go out of circulation."

Roach was still making plans to form a comedy unit to make one hour shows for television. He told *Variety* that his dream cast would include Dennis Day teamed with Frank Fontaine, Imogene Coca and Martha Raye, Wally Cox, Bob Newhart, Hans Conried and George Jessel.

"He said that he's talking to American Broadcasting while he's in New York," reported *Variety* on December 20, 1967. "'They'll probably say it's a lousy idea and I'll go back to playing bridge at the Bel Air Club.'"

The Further Perils of Laurel & Hardy was released in March 1968 by—yes—Robert Youngson, with Roach's own Herbert Gelbspan again the associate producer.

The next year Hal Roach Sr. was in London again announcing he was planning a movie comeback. He was there with Raymond Rohauer, former film curator of New York's Gallery of Modern Art, for a BBC-TV press unveiling of a 26-week fall series, *Golden Silents*, built around old time comedy films, with Roach to appear in the first four shows. The series, the result of two years of work by producer Richard Evans in liaison with Rohauer, plus acquisition of global rights, cost the BBC an estimated $500,000.

From February 12 to March 24, 1969 the Museum of Modern Art in New York City presented "A Tribute to Hal Roach: Four Decades of Distinguished Contribution to Comedy." Approximately 100 films were screened, shorts, features and streamliners, from *Just Nuts* (1915) to *Brooklyn Orchid* (1942).

Roach told *Variety* on May 21, 1969, "I get tired of sitting around doing nothing. But I won't do anything at all unless conditions are right." He stated he was in talks with NBC-TV to produce a show called *Young Stars*.

In August 1969 if one didn't feel like traveling to Woodstock for the big music festival there was the comedy show at the Carnegie Hall Cinema in Manhattan to enjoy. Held over for more than seven weeks, "Hal Roach's New *Crazy World of Laurel & Hardy*" played along with three of his "rival" Mack Sennett's best (and last) shorts, the W.C. Fields classics *The Barber Shop*, *The Pharmacy* and *The Fatal Glass of Beer* ('And it ain't a fit night out for man or beast...')" There was even an added treat, a featurette comprised of scenes from the television program *Fractured Flickers*.

On September 30, 1969 several features produced by Roach were screened in a New York City theater for the first time in nearly thirty-five years. They included *Our Relations*, *Way Out West*, *Block-Heads*, *A Chump at Oxford* and *Saps at Sea*. The program comprised of a feature and five two reel shorts "all in their original versions."

Mr. Roach attempted to reenter production by selling stock to the public, but this plan failed. In New York, the Museum of Modern Art held a six-week Hal Roach tribute showing many rare shorts as well as the well-known popular ones and national interest in the Roach productions increased: in 1970, more than 500 shorts and thirty features produced by Hal Roach from 1915-1942 were added to the American Film Institute Collection at the Library of Congress. Sixty-six Roach films had been there previously.

In September 1970 Robert Youngson and Herbert Gelbspan released their final Hal Roach Studios compilation feature, *4 Clowns*.

On January 31, 1971, Hal Roach Studios, Inc. announced it had entered into an agreement to sell substantially all of the film production, distribution, and licensing assets of the company to Portcomm Communications Corporation of Vancouver and Toronto, Canada. The rights to the use of the name 'Hal Roach Studios' would also be transferred to Portcomm. Earl and Norman Glick, who were involved in the gas and oil products business were the purchasers.

According to Richard W. Bann, "When Hal Roach Studios emerged from bankruptcy, the equity was split in 1971 as between the Eastern and Western Hemispheres. In the latter, rights passed from Hal E. Roach, Sr., Herb Gelbspan, and the trustee in bankruptcy, to, principally (to simplify a convoluted situation), Earl Glick's Portcomm Communications, Robert Halmi's RHI, Hallmark Entertainment, and back to RHI."

The newly-acquired studio co-produced a spy film with Universal, *The Groundstar Conspiracy* in 1972 directed by Lamont Johnson starring George Peppard and Michael Sarrazin. The following year, *Tom Sawyer* starring Josh Albee as Tom with Buddy Ebsen, Jane Wyatt and Vic Morrow was aired on television by CBS.

Hence, I did not know in October and November of 1973, when I first met Mr. Roach, that it had been a mere two years since he had officially ended his association with the Hal Roach Studios and was, much against his inclination, in retirement. I also later learned that two significant events had occurred the year before I met Mr. Roach: his daughter Maria married astronaut Scott Carpenter, and sadly, his son, Hal Roach Jr., died of pneumonia at the age of fifty-three on the tenth anniversary of filing his bankruptcy petition. He apparently had produced only one movie during that intervening decade, an exploitation semi-documentary entitled *Spree*, set in the nightclub world of Las Vegas. The movie received scant release and tepid reviews.

Nevertheless, in that autumn of 1973, Mr. Roach remained eager and interested in discussing the business of comedy. We talked about the state of comedy entertainment in the mid-1970s:

"A whole new style of comedy has to be created for television," said Mr. Roach. "A new art of intimacy. The impact in a theatre is much bigger than that of TV. When I saw *Bridge on the River Kwai*—one of the greatest of all films—I was so impressed by the size of it all, what with the men whistling that tune—when it came on TV I told all the family that they couldn't miss this great picture. But the impact was so completely reduced on that small screen, and with the interruption of so many commercials… it just didn't work. Television is for an intimate audience, for a very few people, and should have its own type of production. The same holds true for comedy.

"Canned laughter ruins the illusion of TV comedy. First of all, you are brought into a family's living room, like *All in the Family* and *Sanford and Son*. But hearing an audience laugh ruins the illusion that you are eavesdropping and actually seeing those things go on for yourself.

"Laurel and Hardy—who've been as funny on TV as any show before or since—had no laugh track. If they're funny, you laugh. If you don't think they're funny, you don't laugh. As soon as a hundred or two hundred people can be heard laughing at 'All in the Family,' then the whole thing stops; it's no longer intimate."

Mr. Roach then mentioned that he was busy on a project for "pay television"—this was years before the real advent of cable television—and he was full of plans and ideas. It was quite obvious that he knew how to take life easy and yet remain engaged and enthusiastic; in short, in spite of unexpected and often discouraging events, Hal Roach appeared to be supremely content.

The interview was drawing to a close. I had one last question: were there any other old-timers around who would enjoy talking with me about the Hal Roach era?

"Well, let's see," he thought aloud. "There's Billy Gilbert. I had dinner with him about a year ago. Oh, no—he's passed on."

Mr. Roach thought some more.

"Gee, I'm afraid they're all gone."

And on that sad note, we shook hands and I said goodbye to Hal Roach, the comedy maker. It would be nine years before I saw him again.

Laurel and Hardy remained entities to contend with. In August, 1975, Hal Roach and Richard Feiner lost a five-year legal battle against the widows of Laurel and Hardy and Larry Harmon Productions over the use of the names and likenesses of Laurel and Hardy for merchandising purposes.

In 1976, Roach was honored by USC as Film Pioneer of the Year.

In February of 1977, after a three-year hiatus in film production, the Toronto-based Hal Roach Studios completed a $2 million science-fiction film called *Alien Encounter* starring Robert Vaughn and Christopher Lee. Said Norman Glick, co-owner of the Hal Roach Studios: "We feel it's time to get back into film."

On April 6, 1977 Alexander L. Guterma, the man who had caused the bankruptcy of the Hal Roach Studios some eighteen years earlier, was back in the news again. As usual with Guterma, it wasn't good news. Certainly not for his family and friends. The day before, the private plane he was traveling in, along with the pilot, Guterma's wife and five of his six children, crashed in a Bronx, New York park while attempting to land at La Guardia Airport in the rain and fog. Guterma, the pilot, his wife, two daughters and three of his sons all died. His fourteen-year-old son Marc did recover, only to die several years later in another plane crash. His one remaining son, Robert, died in July 2013 at the age of sixty-one, like his father, a convicted felon. One may wonder if Mr. Roach read about the tragic 1977 accident. It was reported in the major newspapers.

"A Tribute to Hal Roach Sr." was held one Saturday in December 1979 at the Crown Theatre in Pasadena, California. Attending the screening were Hal Roach, two of his leading ladies Anita Garvin and Dorothy Granger, and Our Gang alumni Joe Cobb and Bob Davis and director Gordon Douglas. The host of the evening was Myron Meisel, film critic for the *L.A. Reader* weekly. (Meisel years later would co-direct and co-produce the 1993 documentary *It's All True*, about Orson Welles's unfinished South American film for RKO in the early 1940s.) Harold Lloyd, Laurel and Hardy and Our Gang comedies were screened at this one night event.

On July 31, 1980, Culver City mayor Ron Perkins unveiled a mini park at the corner of Washington and National Boulevards. At this tiny site of grass and some trees and a picnic table is a plaque placed on the ground which reads: "Site of the Hal Roach Studios, Laugh Factory of the World 1919-1963." Hal Roach was there for the unveiling, along with George "Spanky" McFarland, Tommy "Butch" Bond, and Dorothy "Echo" de Borba of the Our Gang kids, Stan Laurel's daughter Lois Laurel Hawes, and Ollie's widow, Lucille Hardy Price. It was a tiny park, because most of the studio grounds were now occupied by a car dealership and an antique warehouse.

In October, 1980, *Variety* announced that Alan Douglas of the Douglas Brothers Corporation purchased rights from Hal Roach Studios to transform black and white films into color by the use of a new electronic process known as colorization. The first films to undergo this subsequently controversial treatment were *Topper* and *Way Out* West. When asked by reporters what he thought of the colorizing of his old black and white films, Roach snapped "I don't think the pictures get any funnier because of the color."

By this time I was living in New York City, and when I read that on January 14, 1982, Hal Roach had celebrated his ninetieth birthday, I was as pleased as punch. Two months later I found myself in Los Angeles, so I phoned Mr. Roach and asked if I could visit.

His answer was "Sure! Just don't come on Monday. I go hunting on Mondays."

Was this ninety-year-old man pulling my leg, or did he really go hunting on Mondays?

In any event, this time my friends Rick and Linda Greene, prominent members of the "Sons of the Desert" Laurel & Hardy International Fan Club, accompanied me to Mr. Roach's home high up in the winding hills of Bel Air. His attractive housekeeper led us to his study, a sunny, pleasant room lined with photographs from the glamorous Hollywood years. The study faced the backyard with its obligatory swimming pool. An Irish setter ambled along the poolside tiles.

Hal Roach entered, looking as fit and feisty as he did nine years earlier. He was thinner, that's true: now he looked sixty-five.

We were late in arriving, and I apologized. Again, or perhaps, even more so, I was rather in awe of this great survivor. With the passage of every year, with the shifting tides of fortune, the wars, fads, movements, catastrophes, media events, collapsing governments, and faltering economies, the world of slapstick comedy-making of the 1920s seemed ever so remote. When will we again look so optimistically at the world? When will our laughter be as carefree?

Mr. Roach conceded that in his youth he had a much easier time than young people do today. Those were the pioneer days of movie making, before the major studios imposed the rigid divisions of labor over its employees that still exist today and which hamper individual creativity. Perhaps it was this flexibility in the work environment, coupled with Roach's own ebullient personality and his keen, intuitive eye for talent, that made the Hal Roach Studios such an enjoyable place in which to work, and which produced so much joy.

I lamented aloud the state of American comedy of the past ten years, its paucity, its poverty, especially on television. Mr. Roach agreed. And as regards to entertainment in the early 1980s, he had plenty to say.

"Amusement has gone haywire. Nobody wants to go to the theatre anymore. They're all staying home watching television. We used to have beautiful picture palaces where you could escape the hum-drum life for a while. Now they chop a theatre into little rooms to cram as many shows into a place as they can. And just look at television today—where's the progress?

"I still believe comedy should not exceed forty-five minutes. These new channels opening up should provide the opportunity for producing thirty-five, forty-minute comedies—*without* laugh tracks.

"My folks were very skeptical about my desire to go to California and make pictures. After all, I was only twenty years old. They planned to indulge me for a while, but I knew I'd never go back."

Anyone who cares about the art of film comedy is grateful that Hal Roach didn't go back to Elmira, New York in 1912. The very idea is inconceivable. Indeed, he lured his family out West and his father, Charles H. ("Dad") Roach, became Secretary and Treasurer of the Hal Roach Studios until his death in 1936. Roach's brother Jack was involved in casting and was an assistant cameraman, and Roach's parents and his brother lived in a house on studio property!

When it was time for me to take my leave, I again apologized for being late. And I *was* late—sixty years too late, for I wish I could have worked at that memorable Laugh Factory of the World during the golden age of slapstick comedy. I returned to New York and continued my own career as an actor and writer, but I always followed the continuing saga of the Hal Roach legacy.

On May 24, 1982 the Academy of Motion Pictures Arts and Sciences presented "Hal Roach: Master of Comedy," a program of discussion and film clips at their Samuel Goldwyn Theater in Beverly Hills. "Roach, a writer, director and producer for more than 50 years," stated the *Los Angeles Times*, "will be present to talk about his career. Clips from Roach films with Harold Lloyd, Will Rogers, Laurel and Hardy and Our Gang, are scheduled."

What a pleasurable surprise to turn on the television a few months later, on the night of November 9, 1982, and discover that Hal Roach would soon appear as a guest on *The David Letterman Show*! He was a most delightful entertainer, talking about his early days with Harold Lloyd and showing photographs of his all-animal series, *The Dippidy Doo Dads*.

He even demonstrated The Bashful Hula Dance. With the studio orchestra playing a dubious approximation of a Hula Dance, Mr. Roach rose from his seat, turned his back to the audience, put his hands on his head, and wriggled his rump.

When Letterman asked him his age, Roach gave an impish grin and boasted like a cocky boy, "a little over ninety."

Later on Letterman asked Roach who he considered the best comedian around today on television. Roach's comments were revealing:

"If he would just get above the belt, I like Benny Hill, the Englishman. I think that he would be funnier than Chaplin if he would stop doing all the dirty things that he does, but how is anybody with kids going to say 'watch *Benny Hill*?' As I say, the kids made Chaplin and the kids could make Benny Hill too if he'd just clean it up a little bit."

Letterman asked Roach about American comedians.

"[Carroll] O'Connor is very good and ... there's not, I mean, there's a lot of comedians but there's not a lot of very funny ones."

The most interesting aspect of the evening was Roach's story about his boyhood experience in the early part of the century seeing one of America's greatest humorists.

"I went to Sunday school at Park Church in Elmira, and... every once in a while they had guest speakers for the children. And believe me, they were lousy... and on this particular day, an elderly man with a grey moustache and raggely [a new word—and a good one!—coined by Mr. Roach] grey hair rode down and they announced that there would be a guest speaker.

"And the guest speaker got up on the rostrum and he looked the kids over and he said, 'This is not going to be a very long speech because I know you children don't want to hear a very long speech. In fact, I was in church a while back and there was a missionary talking about the poor heathen Chinee. And I was interested and I thought, 'Well, I will give a dollar for the poor heathen Chinee.' He says the man kept talking and talking and talking about the heathen Chinee, until finally I said 'Maybe fifty cents was enough for those heathen Chinee.' He said he kept on talking and talking, and finally they passed the plate. He said 'I reached into the plate and took out five cents for my car fare home.' That was the end of the story by Mark Twain."

After the laughter subsided, Letterman, with tactless bluntness, asked, "Have you had any recent offers to get back into producing anything for television?"

Roach answered, "Oh, nothing that was very financial...."

Letterman: "Do you remember the last time somebody brought a proposal to you and said, 'What about this, Hal?'"

Roach: "Well, I have written—and still have in my book, I mean—dozens of shows I think would be good on television, but I don't think anybody's very interested—and I'm getting a little bit too old to do it anyway."

Letterman: "So you're just going to take things easy pretty much from here on?"

Roach: "Yeah, I hope so."

On December 10, 1982, The *New York Post* reported that a four year search by the Hal Roach Studios "has turned up nearly 100 lost films of Laurel & Hardy...."

While this is an obvious exaggeration, a number of exciting events have occurred: A couple of once-lost Laurel & Hardy silents have been recovered, as well as the soundtrack to their first talkie, *Unaccustomed as We Are*. A three-minute segment from the long-lost *The Rogue Song* (1930) has been discovered, and a few of the foreign-language versions of Laurel and Hardy's talkie shorts were found, restored, and given a special screening by UCLA some years later. Amazingly, a locker full of nitrate films was discovered buried under a hockey rink in a Yukon mining town. Preserved under a thick layer of permafrost, 500 silent films dating from as early as 1903 were recovered; these included a number of Hal Roach one-reelers.

In June of 1983, I phoned Mr. Roach from New York to get his reaction to these reports of new discoveries that were continually popping up in the press. He suggested I take the reports of "lost" films discovered "with a grain of salt."

"Every film that I ever made, the Cinémathèque Française has a copy. I don't know what they mean by 'lost' films. I started out with Pathé [1915-27]—a French company—and the French government has a print of everything I made with them. When I released through MGM (1927-38), the French obtained a print of each picture. They have no negatives, but they have all the prints. About seven or eight years ago they gave me a champagne dinner and showed me their library. I saw pictures I had forgotten I had made."

In any event, the discovery of "lost" films had become all the rage: in the fall of 1983 the Hal Roach Studios toured several major cities in North America with a showing of six newly-restored 35mm prints of Laurel & Hardy silent shorts, including historically and happily, the very first film starring Laurel & Hardy working as a team under the auspices of Hal Roach, *Duck Soup* filmed in September 1926, it was released in March 1927. The film was a milestone in comedy history if ever there was one, and it was one that had long been thought to have disappeared.

Mark Lipson, film library curator of the Hal Roach Studios, acknowledged to me on a visit to New York in 1983 the studios' "grateful support of international archives, both public and private, in aiding in the discovery and restoration of the lost screen classics."

The restoration of Roach's films are progressing on the "Eastern Front" as well. In Munich, Leo Kirch bought exclusive rights to all 1,200 Hal Roach titles for theatrical, television, and video distribution in the Eastern Hemisphere sometime in the 1960s. According to a February 1992 article in *Variety*, Kirch's company BetaFilm has been borrowing

U.S. Library of Congress nitrate copies and converting the films to safety stock. Two Los Angeles labs handled the conversion. According to Beta-Film, of the total 1,200 Roach titles 400 have deteriorated or become lost.

Certainly Hal Roach, the only surviving pioneer of the earliest days of movie making, was not completely lost to modern-day Hollywood. On April 9, 1984, the Academy of Motion Pictures Arts and Sciences presented Hal Roach with an Honorary Academy Award "in recognition of his unparalleled record of distinguished contributions to the motion picture art form." Televised around the world, Hal Roach was presented the award by "Spanky" McFarland of the Our Gang comedies.

Mr. Roach was truly moved.

"This is the nicest thing that has ever happened to me."

Spanky replied, "Well, the nicest thing that ever happened to me, Mr. Roach, was when you hired me fifty-two years ago."

Spanky continued—"But there was something I never did ask you. What was Hollywood really like out here in 1912?"

Roach paused and pondered.

"1912." (He seemed to be savoring that year, bringing it back to life) "...the first day that I worked in motion pictures, I received a dollar a day for car fare and lunch. The car fare was two tokens from in front of the post office downtown to Hollywood—one to take you there and one to bring you back to Los Angeles. The lunch was two sandwiches and a banana. And that is a little start of the 1912 business.

"But I understand the thing has grown a little more expensive today, and people are trying a little harder to save money in making pictures and they're doing a lot of things to try to curtail the expense and the only thing I can add to that is my experience in those days as far as making pictures were concerned. For example... when a comedian for Mack Sennett did a Brodie or fell on his rear... he fell on a cake of soap or a pile of oil or something like that... but the Hal Roach Studios did it a different way. You remember I said two sandwiches and a banana. Well, the property man after lunch would pick up all the banana skins and put them away for safekeeping. Then, anytime that a Hal Roach comedian did a pratfall, he slipped on a banana peel. And they slipped many times and every time they did we used another skin. But the thing that was great about it was the fact that the bananas didn't cost me *anything*.

"Just one thing in conclusion, and that is this, that all these talented people that have been trying to and winning Oscars here tonight, they all make their money the old-fashioned way—they earn it!"

And a good imitation he did, indeed, of John Houseman in his television commercials.

In November 1984 KOMO-TV Seattle aired "an affectionate, informative look at the activities of Hal Roach Senior in early Hollywood days," according to Rex Reed in *Variety*.

"Program, enhanced by good research by David Blacker, lets Roach, now 92, and his stars and associates talk about those early achievements without getting too sentimental or defensive...."

"Good interviews include those with Jackie Cooper of 'Our Gang,' along with Ernie Morrison, who, he says, 'was the first black star, the first black millionaire.' The veterans talk nostalgically about the sense of freedom they felt at the Roach Studios, where there was no 'division of labor, no set budget or schedules' – and about why such freedom is absent these days; child labor laws, strength of unions, high cost of film, etc...."

"'What's wrong with pictures today,' says Roach, 'is that they're made entirely on a dollar basis. Properly handled, it is an art.'

"Overall it's a fine show," concluded Reed, "with all aspects first rate, and a credit to all concerned. One slight niggle: Viewing the subject and material, it would have been better as an hour-long show."

In the following year, 1985, Roach was feted twice: a Life Achievement Award was given by the Los Angeles Teachers Association and he received a life membership by the Motion Picture & Television Fund—he was the only surviving member of their first board of trustees, formed in 1924 by the likes of Mary Pickford, Douglas Fairbanks, Charles Chaplin, William S. Hart, and Cecil B. DeMille.

Nineteen eighty-six was quite a year of awards for the 94-year-old. Culver City civic officials declared April 4, 1986 as "Hal Roach Day" and honored him with a dinner. In August he was feted in his hometown of Elmira, New York at the Samuel Clemens Performing Arts Center. (Samuel Clemens, better known as Mark Twain, spent his summers in Elmira and is buried there.) In December, Roach was present at the Sixth Hawaiian International Film Festival in Waikiki. Leonard Maltin was the master of ceremonies, and the evening featured dancing, entertainment, and a video tribute to Mr. Roach. He again demonstrated his "Bashful Hula" to a delighted audience.

Variety of January 16, 1987, carried the headline "Hal Roach at 95: Man with a Dream"...."and at 95 he's a smooth dancer, too, as he demonstrated Wednesday night at the black tie birthday celebration given by Mr. and Mrs. James De Rosa in his home away from home, the Bel-Air Country Club."

On August 19, 1987, once more in California, I gave Hal Roach a call. He was now ninety-five years young. He told me he would like to meet with me, but he had been "laid up" due to what he called "an eye implant." He suggested I call him in a week or so to set up a time to meet.

Our meeting occurred at his home on August 31, 1987. It had been five years since we last met, thirteen years since we first met, sixty years since he teamed Laurel & Hardy, and seventy-five years since he first arrived in Hollywood. Perhaps Mr. Roach no longer went hunting on Mondays.

A little boy of about six was sitting on the steps of his house when I arrived. He was the housekeeper's son. He went to find Mr. Roach, whom he called "Grandpa." As I entered the house, Mr. Roach was yelling at one of his dogs for chewing up something in his bedroom. This was a fat black Labrador whom he banished to the backyard. The Irish setter, the housekeeper informed me, had passed away but, in addition to the Lab, he now had a prized cream Lab hunting dog which had been given to him on the occasion of his ninetieth birthday. I also discovered that Mr. Roach had been a widower since 1981. The housekeeper told me Mr. Roach was in excellent health.

Again I was escorted to the studio and admired the many photographs: he and Will Rogers playing golf, at his 20th anniversary party in 1933 with Laurel and Hardy and Walt Disney, autographed photos of old-time vaudeville performers, American humorist Irvin S. Cobb, John F. Kennedy, at the Hearst Castle with Chaplin and Garbo and Valentino, even a signed photograph of Benito Mussolini!

Mr. Roach entered looking, if anything, younger than he had in 1982. The only difference was that now he wore two hearing aids. In spite of what he said about an "eye implant," both of his shone with clarity and sprightly good humor.

On his coffee table where we sat was an issue of *Time* magazine with a photograph of comedian Steve Martin on the cover. I asked Roach what he thought of Mr. Martin.

"*Three Amigos* was a so-so comedy. He's made one good picture, in my opinion—*Roxanne*."

He thought the *Time* article was "much too long... it goes on and on about what a nice guy he is, after a while you start to wonder."

I didn't have to wonder about Hal Roach. I had brought along my portfolio of photographs from my own ventures into the world of comedy acting. I had been performing for years, primarily in comedy roles, and had collected a variety of photographs from my shows. Mr. Roach was impressed. I told him that I understood his style of comedy and had incorporated it into my own performances. Indeed, I had been smitten with the comedy bug ever since, as a young kid, I saw the early Roach comedies on television.

He pronounced my portfolio "excellent" and launched into a description of a feature comedy project he said he had been planning, entitled *Punch & Hoody*. He was convinced it would be a hit; he had even planned a sequel, and said he knew that the two leads, for whose roles he wanted to cast "unknowns," would become stars as a result of these films. He also discussed his plans to place about twenty actors under contract for five years and utilize them in both film *and* television projects.

Our 1987 meeting was not a nostalgic look to the glories of the past; it became a business meeting with a view to the future. Hal Roach said he would consider me for the part of Hoody. What a glorious dream come true that would be!

I showed Mr. Roach the recently published *Laurel & Hardy—The Magic Behind the Movies* by Randy Skretvedt—the most thoroughly researched study about the Hal Roach Studios and the making of Laurel and Hardy films yet written. Mr. Roach said that he was aware of the book and wondered if historian Richard Bann had been involved with this work. I noticed that Mr. Bann had been given thanks in the Preface for the use of photographs. I didn't know of Richard W. Bann at the time, who was not only a close friend of Hal Roach's but has done valiant work in film preservation. ("He saved the Hal Roach negatives from destruction, for crying out loud!" proclaimed Randy Skretvedt in 2013.) Bann's article "Film Preservation—Another Fine Mess" on the website www.laurel-hardy.com is a must read. Bann was also the first to identify many of the Laurel & Hardy supporting players for the first time in the 1970s as well as to escort Mr. Roach to various functions, events and parties during Roach's final years.

Still an unabashed fan, I asked Mr. Roach to autograph the book on the first page of the chapter called "Lot of Fun," which was the moniker given to the Hal Roach Studios by his employees. Mr. Roach graciously obliged.

He requested I leave my photo/resume with him and he said we'd be talking soon. I expressed my happiness at seeing him again and at his wonderful new prospect.

He walked me to the front door, which was a big double door with two large, round doorknobs in the middle.

"The left," he instructed, but I absent-mindedly pulled on the right door knob, and the door didn't budge.

"Left!" he bellowed, like a Laurel and Hardy heavy.

I did a Stan Laurel fumbled expression, pulled on the left door knob, the door opened, I lifted my arms in a Stan Laurel "there we go!" manner—and Hal Roach beamed.

I think I passed the audition.

On March 6, 1988, the UCLA Motion Picture/Television Department presented a showing of several newly restored 35mm prints of Laurel & Hardy's Spanish-language shorts. My former UCLA film professor from the '70s was there, Robert Rosen, renowned film critic, preservationist and later dean of the UCLA School of Theater, Film and Television, and he told me that Hal Roach was currently in need of a literary assistant! I immediately contacted Mr. Roach. He interviewed me and I submitted some of my own comedy scripts for his consideration. Some weeks later he informed me that I was the one, and he invited me to stay at his home and help him create a screenplay of his story *Punch & Hoody*.

I arrived at the Roach residence on Monday, April 4, 1988. I was given my choice of one of two bedrooms: one of them was rustic and masculine, with equestrian designs on the bedspread, a saddle on the floor, old bookcases of aged timber, and some rare photographs of Hal Roach as a young man taken during his Wild West days. But the room was covered in dust, as if it hadn't been touched in years. So for health reasons I opted—at least temporarily, I thought to myself—for the second bedroom. This room was painted pink, with 18th century courtly prints on the walls and delicate, lady-like knickknacks on the dresser. Not my ideal bedroom, but at least it was dust-free. It was the second Mrs. Roach's bedroom—the late Mrs. Roach—and that first night I had an eerie experience, though not an unpleasant one.

I sensed the sweet, loving presence of a feminine entity in that room. It enveloped the room, and I knew it was Mrs. Roach. The next morning I asked the housekeeper, Luz, a sweet lady from the Dominican Republic, about her employer's late wife.

"Oh, she was such a nice lady. So good for Mr. Roach. She loved to play the piano."

I asked her when Mrs. Roach passed away. Luz could not quite recall—she had written it down somewhere and went to find the information. When Luz returned, her eyes were wide with wonder: Mrs. Roach died on April 4, 1981—seven years ago TO THE DAY I moved in!

Hal Roach had written a twenty-page treatment of his story for *Punch & Hoody*. It was an old-fashioned, slapstick fantasy for children, though Mr. Roach resented my remark that the film as described by this treatment might appeal *only* to youngsters.

"I make pictures for all ages!" he bellowed.

The main characters in *Punch & Hoody* are two rival gangsters of the George Raft/Edward G. Robinson variety, who through a series of misadventures are given injections of a "youth" serum invented by a mad scientist. The serum changes these cold-blooded thugs not physically, but mentally—so that they think and act like innocent, clown-like children. Thus, their natural rivalry and hatred for one another vanishes and they become as close and friendly as—well, Laurel & Hardy?

While I was attempting to develop this treatment into a screenplay, I made a most unexpected discovery. In the closet of the pink bedroom I found a copy of a 1967 deposition pertaining to a lawsuit between Hal Roach and the MGM Studios. It involved the 1961 invitation by the MGM Studios in London for Hal Roach and his immediate family to come to England to develop and produce films there. According to this document, Mr. Roach and family *did* move to London. Mr. Roach presented a treatment—yes, it was *Punch & Hoody*—but this work was deemed "unacceptable," according to the deposition, to the executives of MGM London. Apparently, Mr. Roach was unable to show MGM *any* acceptable projects, and he and his family were forced to return to California empty-handed, hence the lawsuit. I now understood why Mr. Roach was so defensive and belligerent when I'd suggest changes to his story—changes I felt would be more appealing to a modern audience.

One member of the modern audience lived at Hal Roach's home, and he was quite a fan of the earlier Roach product. José was Luz's seven year old son, the boy I had met in front of Mr. Roach's house some eight months before. During my first evening at the Roach home José had proudly showed me the Oscar statuette his "grandpa" had received in 1984. The little boy climbed up to the top of a cabinet to retrieve the priceless trophy, nearly causing his mother a heart attack.

Little José also showed me the ONE Laurel & Hardy videotape in the house. It consisted of two 1931 shorts: *Chickens Come Home* and *Laughing Gravy*. These were full-length versions, including footage excised, for some reason, from all the American releases. [For Laurel & Hardy aficionados: this includes the flame throwing, water-guzzling magician scene in *Chickens Come Home* (which was seen in the restored Spanish version), and the extended farewell scene in *Laughing Gravy*—exactly as described by Randy Skretvedt in his Laurel & Hardy book.] José laughed uproariously at the screen antics, and Luz confided to me that her son watched that videotape over and over again, never tiring of it. To think that of the scores of films Laurel and Hardy made for Hal Roach, not to mention all the other films produced at the Lot of Fun Laugh Factory, only these two films existed in the house! And this videotape, as it turned out, was a gift.

At least Hal Roach took José to meet the little boy's idol, superstar Michael Jackson, who was a big fan of the "Our Gang" comedies. José proudly showed me the framed photographs of himself being held by Michael, with Hal Roach standing beside them, beaming. José also had a giant autographed poster of Michael Jackson on his bedroom wall.

All in all, I had a very enjoyable stay at the Roach home. Though Mr. Roach was ninety-six years old at the time, he was in fine health. His housekeeper Luz marveled at how well he was. All the more remarkable when one reflects upon the early demise of so many of his associates: all the young actresses who shuffled off this mortal coil in their twenties and thirties, including Clarine Seymour, Katherine Grant, Mabel Normand, Lyda Roberti, Thelma Todd and Jean Harlow; F. Richard Jones was only thirty-seven; James Parrott died at forty-one, his brother Charles at forty-six; Mae Busch was only fifty-four. H.M. Walker was fifty-eight; Roach's first partner Dan Linthicum lived to be seventy-four, but he had now been gone for some thirty-six years. So many of his writers and actors drank heavily and smoked constantly. Hal Roach certainly enjoyed his parties and smoked into his nineties. When I stayed at his home in 1988, however, I saw neither liquor nor cigarettes. Hal Roach, hale and hearty, had outlived them all, all except his secretary Ruth Burch, who would actually survive into the year 2000 and become a centenarian herself, or pert near.

Every day Mr. Roach would walk his tan, big-boned hunting dog—the one given to him on his ninetieth birthday. (The black Lab was nowhere to be seen.) Mrs. Frances Hilton (1915-2006), the widow of Conrad Hilton of the famous Hilton Hotel dynasty, whose great-granddaughter is celebrity Paris Hilton, would drive Mr. Roach to the Santa Anita horse races on a regular basis. Luz, a wonderful cook, always had hearty and delicious meals prepared for us, which we ate in the nicely appointed dining room with its gallery of celebrities up on the wall, near the ceiling. Those framed portraits varied through the years I noticed: early in the 1980s I remember seeing photos of Mussolini and John F. Kennedy. They were not there now. I think Ronald Reagan's portrait was. And Will Rogers, Irvin S. Cobb, Laurel & Hardy, those were still there of course, and many others that I can't even remember any longer. On one wall was a huge photograph of what looked like a 1926 party at Hearst Castle, or was it Marion Davies' beach house—with stars such as Norma Shearer and Buster Keaton dressed for *The General*, and John Gilbert and, was Garbo in that photo, too? Mr. Roach was certainly there, big and healthy with his warm and friendly good natured grin.

Why hadn't I thought of taking pictures of all of those photos? I remember a signed and framed 1930s photo of Bette Davis in the living room. "To Hal, With Love, Bette." I never asked him about her, and to think I was at that very same time working with Ms. Davis on another script! In hindsight, I certainly did not take full advantage of my historic opportunity. But then again, I wasn't staying at Mr. Roach's home as a historian or as a reporter, I was there to be his writing assistant. The man commanded respect and privacy.

At dinner Mr. Roach was most gregarious and talked about the days when Will Rogers taught him to play polo.

"I had a lot of fun," he said, "but I lost a few teeth in the process."

But Hal Roach at ninety-six could be cantankerous and downright ornery, as well as forgetful. One day, while I was working on the script while basking in the sun by the swimming pool, he demanded to know why I was home and not "in school."

"Mr. Roach, I've told you several times already—I have already graduated from UCLA."

"Well, I don't need an actor hanging around the house all day. I was hoping you'd be away working or in school during the day, and help me with the script at night."

Of course I had already explained to Mr. Roach that I was both an actor AND a writer and that I had graduated from UCLA some years before. And considering that he went to bed around seven o'clock each evening it would have been difficult, at best, to work with him "at night." It occurred to me that he was expressing frustration over the fact that he had been attempting to develop his *Punch & Hoody* project for nearly thirty years without success and that he might have been feeling, at that moment, the futility of this latest endeavor.

To be honest, I was worried that this project might be more reminiscent of an early 1940s streamliner than a classic from the glorious era when Laurel & Hardy ruled the roost. But Roach certainly flattered me when he announced that he wanted ME to play one of the leads. I don't recall whether I was to be Punch or Hoody. But I knew he was serious. After all, I had by then ten years of professional theatre credits mostly performing in leading comedy roles in theaters from coast to coast. I won a Best Actor in a Comedy Role at the Old Globe Theatre in San Diego back in 1978—in a George Bernard Shaw comedy starring an unknown but supremely talented Kelsey

Grammer. I certainly realized that much of the success of Mr. Roach's dream project would be dependent upon the casting. I thought about creating the role of "Doctor Finlayson," and wouldn't Steve Martin be marvelous in it?

And then there was the matter of the story. Roach was so vague about that. He wanted it to open in a prison. "Then they break out and get into all kinds of mischief." I remember trying to pin him down. Exactly what kind of mischief he was thinking of, what sort of settings would he like to see these characters in?

"Well, I want them to meet a mad scientist who gives them a truth serum. Give 'em a lot of variety," said Roach. "Know what I mean?" And he ambled off. Sitting there by the pool, with pad and pens and notes all around me, the sun glistening on the water, the air silky and quiet, I suddenly felt as though my firm confident grasp had slipped from the hands of a giant clock dial, and there was no safety platform below to catch my fall. Safety Last, indeed.

It was years later when I read Stan Laurel's 1955 letter to a friend wherein he discussed the anticipated return of Laurel & Hardy to the Roach lot to make television films with Hal Roach Jr. and Stan writing with relief, "Think it will work out this time as we don't have Roach Sr. to contend with & his 'you know what I mean' stories." And John McCabe, in his book *The Comedy World of Stan Laurel*, quotes director George Marshall as having said, in 1973, "Roach was rather deficient along this line [story construction]. He would suggest the vaguest outline of a story, say 'know what I mean?' and then walk away, leaving us to try and figure out what in the hell he did mean. So we just went ahead and did our stories. Stan was always very instrumental in getting these stories together...."

So that was it. I was getting the ole "know what I mean" treatment myself! Yet, alas, I had no George Marshall or Stan Laurel to turn to. Or any of the other happy gang of writers. As a matter of fact, I had NO ONE to turn to. It was an odd feeling, sitting there, that bright and sunny spring day in 1988, all alone, by the pool at the Hal Roach residence, wondering what in the hell to do about this script idea that had been kicking around for so many years. I was also working on a project of my own, a modern day comedy, my homage to the Hal Roach style of the early '30s called *Skidoo Ruins*. Mr. Roach read the first draft and bellowed, "This is Rip Van Winkle profanity!" I beamed, knowing I was on the right track.

Then out of the blue, I received an offer to work at MGM/UA of all places. And virtually at the same time the possibility of working for Orion Pictures Corporation materialized. On top of that, for the previous six months I had been working with 80-year-old Bette Davis on a screenplay based on my stage play *The Turn of the Century*. This mystery-comedy revolved around a series of murders that occur at the mansion of a 100-year-old Shakespearean actress. The play was a hit at all the staged readings it had received; I was complimented by none other than Audrey Wood, the literary agent who had discovered Tennessee Williams; and the play had been represented by ICM in New York. Many of the older stars read the play for an anticipated Broadway production and I had the supreme pleasure of showing the play to Estelle Winwood when she was 100 in 1983. Ms. Winwood had a photograph of Bette Davis on her mantelpiece, so I eventually got the script to her. Bette was recovering from a stroke but she phoned me, quite out of the blue, months after I had sent her the play script: "I am THROUGH with the theatre. But I LOVE this play. "When it is made into a movie, I want to play the lead." I showed the draft I was working on to Mr. Roach, who liked it, but he cautioned me that it would be extremely expensive to produce. But all that, as they say, is the subject for another book.

As much as I relished the experience of living in the peaceful home of Mr. Roach, I did need to earn a salary. I was more than grateful for the room and board, the fantastic company and the chance to work with this legendary pioneer. But I wasn't being paid. I had taken the opportunity of this once-in-a-lifetime invitation to attempt to complete a satisfactory and fully developed treatment of Mr. Roach's project, make sure it would appeal to a modern audience, and receive his blessing. It would be at that point that I would be prepared to talk business before plunging into writing a feature length screenplay. But the reality of the situation as well as these new job offers forced me to change my plans. I didn't have time now to complete the treatment. I certainly wasn't going to abandon *Punch & Hoody*, but I certainly needed more time to figure it all out. And I couldn't do that by lounging around the pool daydreaming. Mr. Roach concurred.

My last dinner with Mr. Roach we were served duck soup prepared by Luz, who was an excellent cook. Ironic in that this was the title of the very first film, made in 1926, in which Stan and Ollie first appeared as a team. The duck, I was informed, was shot (with a gun) by Mr. Roach himself, and indeed, I found little leaden pellets in the soup. I wish I had kept those little bee-bees. And how amusing to consider how many of Mr. Roach's personal interests could be discovered in the films he produced— for example, in Laurel & Hardy's *Sons of the Desert* (1933), Mrs. Laurel's hobby is duck hunting. Also consider that the clothing worn by Laurel & Hardy throughout their career, as well as the many songs Ollie would sing, and the jalopies they would drive—are all from the 1912 era—when Hal Roach was a young man newly arrived in Hollywood.

In any event, sixty-two years after *Duck Soup* launched Laurel & Hardy on their successful careers, I was partaking of my last supper with their venerable comic benefactor. Mr. Roach assured me that he would be contacting me soon—he still wanted me to play one of the comic leads in *Punch & Hoody*. How realistic was the possibility of this movie being realized? By that time I had the distinct feeling that Hal Roach was happy just to have some companionship and a sense that he was still viably involved in the creative process. He certainly strongly believed in this old, old project that stubbornly refused to get produced. I know that feeling well.

I was to learn later that I was not the first, nor the only film enthusiast to have been invited to stay at the Roach home to develop the script, and then after a time, to depart without completing the task. As charming and privileged as my time with him was, nevertheless I felt sad to think that this still-vibrant producer, ever filled with vivid dreams and plans, did not have an opportunity to put any of those dreams or plans into action. But that is an old Hollywood story, and one need only think of D.W. Griffith, Rouben Mamoulian, Preston Sturges, or Frank Capra living out their final years in creative inactivity. The film *Sunset Boulevard* for all its grotesquery and exaggeration touched on this "glass ceiling" that separates Hollywood's past from its present.

There was no sentimental parting. We'd be in touch. See how things developed. Mr. Roach found it ironic that I would be working for companies that he had been so completely involved with so many decades ago, MGM and United Artists, and how that now in the late 1980s they had merged as one. He had a great sense of the ironic—and always responded with good-natured humor. He wished me well the next morning and was off to the races. "Leave your key on the table. And don't take the television. Bye bye."

As I was leaving the house with packed bags, his prize hunting dog bolted out the front door and ran off. I spent the afternoon driving up and around the hills of Bel Air searching for the wayward beast. On top of everything else, I didn't want to be held responsible for the loss of Hal Roach's pet dog!

I finally found the wayward mutt loping along a hillside. I managed to lure the four-footed delinquent into my car, drove him back to the Roach house, pulled the reluctant creature out of the car, and hauled him into the house. I locked the door behind me, and off I trundled.

Well, the Hal Roach story goes on, of course. On May 14, 1988, shortly after I had left his residence, Mr. Roach received an honorary Doctorate in Humane Letters from Loyola Marymount University at a black tie dinner held at the Bel Air Country Club. The dinner was to benefit the newly established Hal Roach Fund to purchase state-of-the-art film and video equipment for Loyola Marymount's Department of Communications. James and Ninon DeRosa were honorary co-chairs of the $250-per-plate dinner and $60,000 was raised at the event. Coinciding with The Fund, announced Arthur W. Bloom, LMU Dean of Communications and Fine Arts, is the new Hal Roach Entertainment Award for deserving film students, to be given.

A couple of weeks later Mr. Roach traveled to Washington, D.C. with his friend Richard W. Bann "in town for a recent tribute" according the *Washington Post* of May 22, 1988. Hal Hinson, a *Post* staff writer, interviewed Roach for his article entitled "Funny Man Emeritus, Film Director Hal Roach at Age 96," quoted him as stating, "I'm 96 years old, you know... so I think I'll have another cigarette. To celebrate." Hinston wrote, "This comes from a man who was given a medical deferment during World War II because he had 'an 80-year-old heart.'" Well, that's news to ME. Wasn't he sent off to war for four years? Well, no one could say the old man didn't have anything new to share. He even elaborated on the first screening of Our Gang in 1922.

"He sent the first of the Hal Roach Rascals films to his friend Sid Grauman," writes Hinton, " who then ran the biggest theater in Los Angeles [the Egyptian had opened in 1922], and didn't hear back from him. But at the end of the week—they ran comedy shorts for a week then—he saw an ad in the paper advertising, as Roach remembers it, 'One of the funniest comedies ever made. You can't miss it, Our Gang.'

"'I called Grauman and said, 'What's going on? You can't keep this thing. It's the only copy I got!'

"And he [Grauman] said, 'I don't care. I've already advertised it. Don't give me any talk.'

"'Well, the thing ran a week,' [said Roach] 'and it went so big that we changed its name from Hal Roach Rascals to Our Gang. From there it just took off and went on for years.'"

"Now he spends most of his time either traveling, pursuing his many hobbies, or at the Santa Anita race track, which he founded." wrote Hinton. Also, the movies still occupy a lot of his thinking, and he still has ideas, plenty of ideas, 'but who wants to listen to what an old man has to say?'

"Then too, of course, there is the job of attending the tributes and collecting the honors.

"'I'm being given an honorary something by Loyola University,' he says proudly, taking another pull on his long brown cigarette. 'A doctorate or something.'

"'A PhD of humane letters, Hal,' says Richard Bann, Roach's biographer, from his station at the far end of the sofa.

"'Huh?'

"'A PhD of humane letters.'

"'Whatever.'

"One of the young men stationed at Fort Roach back in the 1940s was Ronald Reagan, who, in fact, is to be Roach's host later in the day.

"'This afternoon we are going to see the president,' Roach interjects abruptly. He's serious now. 'And I have one thing to say about the president. Will Rogers made the statement that he'd never met a man he didn't like. And I say of Ronald Reagan: He never met a man who didn't like him.'

"The car to take Roach and his party to his old friend's house is coming soon, so the attention shifts to preparations to leave… Amazingly, his energy seems as high and strong as it was at the start of the conversation. The search is on, though, for the words that might sum things up. But what, after all, can you say?

"Then finally. 'I couldn't have been luckier.'"

In October "Legendary producer/director Hal Roach toddled into town last week to visit pals and play the ponies at Hawthorne Race Course," reported the *Chicago Tribune* on October 16, 1988.

"Looking dapper in a navy blazer and puffing on pencil-thin cigarillos, Roach, 96, was wearing the title of 'legend' quite well, thank you, relating Hollywood-sparkled memories with as much enthusiasm as he does his plans for films.

"'I hope to make a dozen more pictures, all comedies,' he said. 'I've got an idea for a feature called *Punch and Hoody*. And I'd like to create another Laurel and Hardy—wait a minute, I'm not going to give that away.'"

Teacher Linda Carpenter had been teaching a cinema course under the auspices of Coastline Community College for high school age and older held evenings at Edison High School in Huntington Beach, California. Back in 1976 Ms. Carpenter asked her students to write to a film personality. One student wrote to Roach, who agreed to come and speak to the class. When he arrived at the school, he was greeted with posters, balloons, flowers, a cake and a plaque from the students.

Afterwards, Mrs. Roach wrote to Ms. Carpenter to tell her that her husband had felt quite honored by the reception, and would be happy to come to the school again. Since then, he has never turned her down. He had spoken there nine times in the past thirteen years, the string broken only in years when the class was not offered. In May of 1989 Mr. Roach arrived twenty-five minutes late—because he had accidentally slammed his thumb in the car door. He had to be taken to an emergency room for several stitches. He arrived at the classroom nevertheless, his hand was heavily bandaged.

"…but the 97-year-old film pioneer seemed unconcerned," reported Rick Vanderknyff of the *Los Angeles Times*, "as he answered questions about his work as producer of comedies starring such famous names as Laurel and Hardy, Harold Lloyd and the 'Our Gang' kids."

"'Yesterday, it was amazing to me that he was still insisting on coming,' even after the hand injury, Carpenter said. 'I can't tell you, honestly, why he's done this all these years… I think he does it for the kids.'

"Roach, looking fit, walked unassisted down a series of steps to a chair at the front of the room. In a still-strong voice aided by a microphone, he gave the young crowd a few general words of wisdom (such as 'don't do anything… if you don't want to do it') before the questions started.

Hal Roach was interviewed for the Kevin Brownlow documentary *Harold Lloyd: The Third Genius* which aired in England on Thames Television in November 1989. This superb documentary was broadcast in the United States in February 1992 as part of *The American Masters* series.

On January 14, 1990, Mr. Roach celebrated his ninety-eighth birthday. I saw his picture in the papers—he was looking quite dapper, standing erect in formal attire, attending a Santa Anita racetrack party with Frances Hilton.

From February 9th through the 11th, 1990, a special "Birthday Tribute to Hal Roach" was presented by the American Cinematheque in Hollywood, showing a variety of his shorts and feature length films at the newly-opened Directors Guild building on Sunset Boulevard. Included in the program were *Dogs of War* (1923), an early Our Gang short which gives an informal tour of the Hal Roach Studios, several of the Laurel & Hardy Spanish-language shorts, some Harold Lloyd comedies, a Will Rogers silent from 1918, and the features *One Million B.C.*, *Sons of the Desert*, and *Topper*.

In March of 1990, Hal Roach was awarded the Producer's Guild of America David O. Selznick Life Achievement Award in Theatrical Motion Pictures. That year he was interviewed for England's television documentary *The South Bank Show Stan Laurel—The Last Laugh*.

Daily Variety on January 11, 1991, noted that "Hal Roach, celebrating his (ninety-ninth!) birthday, will be toasted at a dinner party given by Ninon and James DeRosa at Bellagio Place."

At around this time I discovered that the Silent Movie Theatre, founded in 1942 by Dorothy Hampton and her husband, and which had existed for some thirty-five years on Fairfax Avenue, had been refurbished and reopened after having been dark and abandoned for some twelve years. I spoke with Mrs. Hampton, who was so very happy that the Silent Theatre was once again open to the public. They were showing Harold Lloyd's *Dr. Jack* that weekend. I told her that Hal Roach would be interested to learn about the resurrection of the Silent Movie Theatre and the showing of one of his first features.

"How marvelous Mr. Roach is still alive!" exclaimed Mrs. Hampton. Tell him he is welcome as a guest of honor."

I phoned the Roach residency. Mr. Roach couldn't attend as he was completely absorbed in the latest developments of the Gulf War. "But," he said brightly, "I have six or seven projects I'd like to discuss with you some day...."

A dear friend sadly commented that early 1990s Hollywood power brokers no longer cared about ancient Hal Roach, living or not, and whatever projects he may still be clinging to with the hopes of seeing them produced in the 100th year of his life. To a television interviewer in 1990 he stated emphatically, "The one thing that I am certain about is that people's ability to laugh and wanting to laugh is not a bit different today than it was 100 years ago—and they laugh at the same things."

It was that year that I finally starred in my first comedy role for television. My director declared, "The future is now!" And I must, indeed, face this future. I've learned much from the past, but I must not remain there. After all, it *is* a new world, a new world in the making... a world which will need pure comedies more than ever.

On Sunday, May 4, 1991, NBC television's *Sunday Night at the Movies* presented *White Hot: The Mysterious Murder of Thelma Todd*, a dramatization of the mysterious 1935 death of one of Hal Roach's leading comediennes. This rather superficial affair starring television actress Loni Anderson was directed by Paul Wendkos.

Hal Roach was played by character actor Paul Dooley. In the first "Hal Roach scene," Dooley is discussing business with Thelma and her mother. Ostensibly, the time is 1931 and Roach is proposing creating "a female Laurel & Hardy" team starring Thelma and Patsy Kelly, though never in the film is the name ZaSu Pitts mentioned. Pitts was the comedienne first teamed with Thelma in 1931; Patsy Kelly was her replacement in 1933, seventeen shorts later.

The second and last scene in which "Hal Roach" appears is when he comes to the girls' dressing room to find out why they are not on the set. (Thelma is hiding in the dressing room because she sports a black eye, courtesy of her abusive husband.) Patsy gallantly saves Thelma's face by telling Roach that she (Patsy) has "female trouble" and can't film that day. Roach is embarrassed and allows them the day off. Dooley plays Roach as a firm, though benevolent producer with an easy-going manner and generous, sure-of-himself air. At least that part sounds about right.

Naturally, I called Mr. Roach himself the next day, and naturally, he had seen the television movie.

"It's 100% cockeyed," he told me. "The thing they ran last night about gangsters and stuff—it's just a lot of crap."

Mr. Roach said Thelma had returned home "quite a little intoxicated, went up a long bunch of stairs to where her car was… probably to get her car or nobody knows what. The guy she was living with [director Roland West] got dressed quickly and ran after her and once she got in the garage he locked her in the garage so she couldn't get out. And she apparently turned the engine on, maybe to keep warm at night, and she died of monoxide poisoning. That's the true story.

"She [Thelma Todd] was not at all like the girl [Loni Anderson]. She was not sexy, she was not chasing men, she was quite the reverse. She was a lady. She did love parties, and there wasn't one on Saturday night—we worked six days a week in those days, she had one herself, and as I say, she went out the night before… The people who wrote this thing, they knew damn well, they knew exactly what this story was."

I asked Mr. Roach about the portrayal of Thelma Todd's mother, presented in the film as a totally domineering "stage mother" who helped negotiate contracts, and screamed to the police, upon seeing the body of her daughter, "Don't you know murder when you see it?" Though later the mother supposedly denies having made that scandalous statement and ultimately states that she believes her daughter died an accidental death.

"The mother—absolutely not. When she [Thelma] passed away her mother was in Boston and we sent her money and a ticket to come out and take over things. She arrived the day after she [Thelma] was found in her car."

What about the controlling influence Thelma's mother had on her daughter's career?

"Her mother was never any influence with her out here whatsoever."

He also noted the erroneousness of the film showing Thelma teaming up with Patsy Kelly only, rather than with ZaSu Pitts.

"It was first ZaSu Pitts. After her contract expired, because we were making the pictures in four weeks, we started making them in two." Apparently ZaSu felt she deserved twice the salary as she was now to make twice as many shorts in a four week period. "ZaSu wanted too much money and that's when the other gal [Patsy Kelly] took her place."

"Did Thelma's mother sit in on these negotiations with you?"

"Never. I never had any dealings with the mother any way at all."

"Did Thelma have an agent handling her career, or did she handle it herself?"

"I don't think she ever had an agent... I saw a picture of her, I sent for her, she photographed well, I put her under salary, not under contract. Then when she played the lead, played in the pictures with Charley Chase and a couple with Laurel & Hardy, [I teamed her] with ZaSu and then with Patsy Kelly."

"Was she better with Patsy or with ZaSu?"

"Oh, I think that ZaSu was a little better than Patsy. But as far as dollars were concerned, we got about the same for the one as we did for the other."

Mr. Roach again insisted that Roland West locked Thelma in the garage that fateful night. As far as Lucky Luciano doing her in, "It never happened in any way. That's all the imagination of the people that wrote the book [*Hot Toddy*]. All that stuff about him opening a gambling joint— it never happened... I'm going to sue them for using my name. They never had any permission from me whatever."

"They didn't consult you at all?"

"Not at all. They came to me years ago on the story and I told them exactly what happened and how... this idea that she was beat up to death— she was not beat up in any way. When the detectives found her dead in the car, she was dressed exactly as she was on Saturday night, even to the little bouquet which the colored girl had put on her, and there wasn't a scratch on her in any way. And she definitely died because she turned the engine on, presumably to get warm, and [it was] a small garage and so she died of breathing the air. And the police said it was accidental death."

"Do you think she possibly did that on purpose?"

"You mean, that she committed suicide?"

"Yeah."

"Definitely not. No, no. She was not that kind at all. But she always went to parties and did quite a bit of drinking and there was no question but that she was intoxicated when this happened Saturday night. And so she probably turned [the engine] on and probably went to sleep and never woke up."

In July of 1991, comedian/producer Rob Reiner presented to the television viewing world a new show: *Morton & Hayes*, a fictitious comedy team from the thirties and forties who look like an amalgam of Abbott and Costello and Laurel & Hardy. An industry screening was held at the Goldwyn Theatre in Hollywood and Rob Reiner's guest of honor was Hal Roach himself. According to *The Hollywood Reporter* of July 24, 1991, he "received a standing ovation." I learned later that Mr. Roach did not like *Morton & Hayes* at all.

In November of that year, Roach traveled to London and the same month was also honored by Loyola Marymount University at a dinner and given the Hal Roach Entertainment Award "for excellence in family entertainment."

In January of 1991 Mr. Roach had proudly proclaimed to me, "On my next birthday, I will be 100 years old." "Congratulations, Mr. Roach," said I, "I'm looking forward to it." And indeed, he made it. The festivities began early. On January 11, 1992, about 200 well-wishers gathered on the steps of the Irving Thalberg Building on the old MGM Studio lot (now Sony Pictures Studios) to greet the almost-centenarian. An Amsterdam television crew filmed the ceremony as Roach was made the Honorary Chairman of the 75th Anniversary Steering Committee—Culver City's seventy-five years as an incorporated city. Mr. Roach was given the key to the city, naturally, as well as a badge—for he was now the honorary Culver City Police Chief as well. A hearty lunch was served in the commissary.

On the following day, January 12, a party was held at the Motion Picture & Television Fund's retirement home in Woodland Hills, California. MCA Universal Chairman Lew Wasserman, Charlton Heston, Virginia Mayo, Robert Blake, Burgess Meredith, Dan Aykroyd, Jackie Cooper, and Jay Leno were among the guests. Anita Garvin, one-time Roach comedienne, was now a resident of the retirement home and gave her former boss a big, lipsticky kiss. Roach passed out mechanical pencils with "Hal Roach 100th Birthday" embossed on them, and donated a $1,000 check to the home he helped establish.

On January 14, 1992, Hal Roach indeed celebrated his 100th birthday. The following week he traveled to the East Coast. On January 23, following a screening of Charley Chase and Laurel & Hardy shorts at the Smithsonian's National Museum of Natural History in Washington, D.C., Roach was presented, along with birthday cake and champagne, the James Smithson Medal—the Smithsonian's highest award—"in recognition of exceptional contributions to art, science, history, education, and technology." A *New York Times* article covering the event noted that he was still talking about his *Punch & Hoody* idea.

"Mr. Roach, who lives in Bel Air, Calif." continued the article, "relies on a hearing aid these days, and getting out of a chair is a minor event. But his vision is sharp, his memory runneth over, and he has some decided opinions on Hollywood comedies.

"'They don't make the right kind of thing,' he said in an interview at his hotel here today. 'You can't make people laugh for more than half an hour and be consistent...'

"One idea for a feature comedy is *Punch and Hudy* [*sic*] about the two toughest convicts in a prison who, inexplicably, get along with no one but each other. Mr. Roach admitted that the idea is 'Laurel and Hardy Go to Jail,' more or less.

Roach reiterated once again the origins of Harold Lloyd's glasses as being inspired by comic Earl Mohan coming on the set with horn-rimmed glasses.

"'As soon as we put the glasses on [Lloyd] he became a profitable comedian,' he said. 'I made enough money off him to build the Hal Roach Studios.'

"...Money comes up a lot when Mr. Roach talks about film. Names may occasionally escape him, but never a salary or a box office figure. And a clever bit of improvising that paid off put him in seventh heaven. He recounted the tale of a panic meeting of the film producers' association after a rash of bank closings in 1924.

"'Everybody was scared they couldn't pay their stars,' Mr. Roach recalled. 'I got up and said: 'To hell with the stars. You're the guys that make the pictures. If you can't do anything else, star a horse.' And I walked out and made *King of the Wild Horses*, one of the top ten films that year.'

"Here came the beauty part. 'I made five pictures with the horse,' he said, 'and then sold them for $10,000 to Fox.'"

Roach then traveled to his hometown of Elmira, New York. When asked by reporters, he said the place hadn't changed much. "The people who have money have money and the people who don't have money don't."

Back in Los Angeles Mr. Roach was a guest on *The Tonight Show*, hosted by Jay Leno. During the January 28 telecast he revealed that he still had his driver's license, saying "That lasts me till I'm 102."

He talked about how he came up with the idea for "Our Gang" and reiterated that his favorite of all his films was when his leading lady was free (Jean Harlow's photo used in Laurel & Hardy's *Beau Hunks*). It was a polite way of saying "How can you choose a favorite out of thousands?" He mentioned how he signed the first African-American to a seven-year movie contract ("Sunshine Sammy" Morrison). He culminated his appearance with his Old Man's Hula Dance, a dance that had been seen ten years earlier on *The David Letterman show.*

In February of 1992, against doctors' orders, Roach traveled to Germany to attend the 42nd Berlin International Film Festival, which presented a tribute consisting of sixty Roach films and awarded him the Berlinale Kamera.

On March 27, back at the Universal Sheraton Hotel in California, he was given a Special Award of Merit by the Publicists Guild.

Hal Roach attended the 64th Academy Award ceremonies on March 30, 1992. Host Billy Crystal introduced the centenarian, who rose and began to address the audience. Alas, his words were inaudible as there was no microphone picking up his speech. Nonplussed, Billy Crystal quipped, "What do you expect? He started in the silent days!"

For months I had wanted to visit Mr. Roach and show him the Laurel & Hardy style silent comedy I had appeared in (as James Finlayson) in an industrial film made for General Motors. The two actors who played Stan and Ollie, Jeffrey Weissman and Bevis Faversham, were the Laurel & Hardy impersonators who greeted Mr. Roach at his 100th Birthday party. They have been a featured attraction at the Universal Studio Tours for several years now. I also wanted to show Mr. Roach the video demo tape I had recently completed, highlighting scenes from my own budding Hollywood acting career. And had Mr. Roach seen the nine-minute tribute to him aired on the "American Movie Classics" cable TV channel? No, he hadn't. When I talked to him on April 29, he told me he had just returned from a trip to Texas and needed to rest up. "Call me next Tuesday for an appointment." Finally, our schedules matched, and a date was set.

May 8, 1992 was a rather drab, overcast day. I drove those familiar curves up the hillsides of Bel Air to Roach's modest house. Everything looked the same as it did when I was there four years prior. Everything, that is, except for the large mansion that was being erected across the street from Chez Roach. A crew of workmen was busy erecting the edifice. The once-quiet street was bustling with activity.

Luz answered the door. She was as sweet as always, and showed me in. I immediately heard Mr. Roach bellowing at his fat black Labrador, Tripper.

Luz smiled. "He's in his bedroom, feisty as ever. Go right in."

I walked down the familiar corridor and into the bedroom. Mr. Roach was seated in a chair, putting on a shoe. Several canes and walking sticks were propped against the wall. Otherwise, the room looked exactly the same as it did four years ago.

"Hello, Mr. Roach, I'm here!"

He gave me that wonderfully crinkly grin, eyes shining. Tripper the dog gave me a sloppy wet greeting.

"Dick Bann is supposed to be here." Mr. Roach was suddenly serious, even angry. I was a bit taken aback at his demeanor.

"I want him to be here when you show this thing."

"We can wait a few minutes, Mr. Roach. How have you been?

"I've had some trouble with this arm."

He held out his left forearm on which was a large bandage. He didn't elaborate further, and I didn't inquire.

"Did you bring a VCR?"

"Yes. It's in my car."

"Go get it and bring it in here. We'll watch it in the bedroom."

"Okay, Mr. Roach."

I went to the car, brought out the VCR and the videotapes and brought them into the bedroom.

"I'm going to lay down while we watch."

He stood up and, moving not as easily as he did four years ago, walked across the room and clambered onto his bed.

"Get me some newspapers for my feet. I don't want to get the bedspread dirty."

I dutifully laid a bunch of newspapers at the centenarian's feet. He propped his head on some pillows and lay down.

I busied myself connecting the VCR to his color television set, which was resting on a stand at the foot of the bed.

"Where is Dick Bann? I don't have all day. Go ahead and show it."

Once all the connections were made, I popped the first video tape in.

"This first video I'm going to show you is the tribute American Movie Classics TV made for your 100th birthday. You haven't seen it, have you?

"No, I haven't."

I played the nine-minute documentary for him, which chronicled in still photos, film clips, and a recent interview his first years in Hollywood as an extra at Universal Studios, meeting Harold Lloyd and creating the Hal Roach Studios, etc. I watched his expression while he watched the screen. I could tell he was scrutinizing every word just waiting for some gaffe or error. There was none. At one point the host, Peter Jones, asked Mr. Roach the secret to his longevity.

"There is no secret," Hal responded. "I haven't the least idea why I've lived so long. I did everything you shouldn't do as far as I can understand. I ate everything I wanted to eat, I drank everything I wanted to drink. I smoked up 'til a year ago and I quit that 'cuz the doctor told me to quit."

Peter Jones: "Hal Roach told me he'd still be working if Hollywood weren't so prejudiced against 100 year old producers. Still the promoter, though, he presented me after the interview with this mechanical pencil inscribed "Compliments of Hal Roach, 100th Birthday.""

When the documentary was over, Mr. Roach seemed very pleased.

"Very good, wasn't it?" I ventured.

"Yes it was. Where's Dick Bann?"

As he hadn't yet arrived, we proceeded with the show. I put in General Motors' industrial *Teamwork* film, starring those Laurel & Hardy impersonators Jeffrey Weissman and Bevis Faversham. I played their arch nemesis, James Finlayson. The moment "Laurel & Hardy" appeared, Roach shouted "I thought that *was* Laurel & Hardy!" Of course, upon closer scrutiny he realized they were impostors, but it was quite a compliment to two talented contemporary comedians.

After *Teamwork* was over, Roach said of Faversham (Hardy) "He sure knows how to take plenty of punishment to get laughs."

I then showed Mr. Roach my 20-minute video demo. During the showing, Richard Bann finally showed up. He had been delayed due to traffic. He sat on the other side of the bed and watched the rest of my video.

Once the screening ended, I turned to Mr. Roach.

Out of the blue he said to me, "Do you know I was the first producer to hire Groucho Marx for television?"

"No. I didn't know that."

"He would always corner me in the hall with a joke. You couldn't pass him with a simple 'good morning,' but he'd corner you and tell you a lousy joke. It got to the point where I couldn't stand it anymore and I had him fired."

I can just imagine what that joke might have been. There's one attributed to Groucho that appears in Leslie Halliwell's *Filmgoer's Companion:*

"I find television very educational. Every time someone switches it on, I go into another room and read a book."

"Well, my friend," said Roach as he rose from the bed and plopped himself into an easy chair, "God made you in a certain special way. But I don't have any more time for this. Mr. Bann and I have important business to discuss. So if you'll excuse us...."

We took photos together and he kindly autographed an 8x10 glossy I had purchased at Larry Edmund's Cinema Bookstore—a head shot of a smiling young Roach taken around 1920 when he was already conquering Hollywood.

I then disconnected the cables from the VCR and his TV.

"I must say, Mr. Roach," I ventured, realizing this was goodbye, "You look great. You don't look a day over seventy."

He beamed and said, "I've got to use the little boys' room."

He did a funny little dance with his feet, hoisted himself up from the chair, and shuffled across the room to his bathroom.

"Goodbye, if I don't see you before you return from your trip," I said. As I packed up the VCR and the tapes I asked Dick Bann when the biography he was writing on Hal Roach would be published. I knew he had been working on it for a very long time.

"I have no idea," he replied.

I went to the kitchen, said "adios" to Luz, took a last look in the Hal Roach study at the signed photos of Will Rogers, Bette Davis, Harold Lloyd, Walt Disney, Ed Sullivan, Robert Benchley, the group photo taken at a Malibu beach house with a galaxy of Hollywood stars of the 1920s. May 8, 1992 was mere days after the end of the L.A. Riots in which I, living not in the safety and seclusion of Bel Air but in a vulnerable area of Hollywood, was engulfed and affected. These harsh urban realities never touched the moneyed hills, of course, and as I descended to the "flatlands" of Los Angeles I had a feeling that Mr. Roach had already put me, and the rest of the teeming masses down below, out of mind.

In early June, Mr. Roach received yet another award. This time it was the Rose Media Achievement Award of the Jewish Home for the Aging. A banquet was given at the famous Four Seasons Restaurant in Los Angeles. Charles "Buddy" Rogers and Statesman's Club official Monty Hall wheeled a beaming, tuxedoed Roach to the spotlight to accept his award.

In July, Roach attended the annual Sons of the Desert convention in Las Vegas. To the amusement of his hosts, he insisted on visiting a strip show during his stay and was given special attention from the star stripper. It turned out to be his last public hurrah.

Variety on August 7, 1992 noted "Hal Roach gets another chance to be heard. You recall the 100-years-young Roach's words weren't picked up by mikes at the Oscars this year. He'll speak at the 50th anniversary of the First Motion Picture Unit Army Air Force, which was stationed at his studios, nicknamed Fort Roach, during World War II. Invaluable training films came out of there. The group reunions September 26 at Sportsman's

Lodge with alumnus Bill Orr mc'ing the program… Gene Autry will also attend. Reagan will, too, if he's not on the campaign trail."

On September 3, 1992, I ran into Dick Bann at the Hollywood Roosevelt Hotel (the Cinecon Society was about to hold their convention). I asked him how Mr. Roach was. "Not well," was his grave reply, and he did not elaborate.

On October 2, 1992, a new film version of *Of Mice and Men* starring Gary Sinise and John Malkovich was released. I was curious to know if Mr. Roach had any interest in seeing the remake of his 1939 movie. Alas, I did not have the opportunity to find out.

On November 2, 1992, at approximately 2:00 p.m., Hal Roach died at his home. He was a little more than two months shy of his 101st birthday. Luz told me, "He is at peace with the Lord." Incredibly strong Santa Ana winds whipped through the Los Angeles area that night.

Many have commented on Mr. Roach's greatest gift: perfect timing. And what better timing for this long-time friend of Ronald Reagan than to leave the scene the day before the U.S. Presidential Election in which the Republican party was finally defeated after twelve years in the White House?

The announcement of Mr. Roach's passing was front page news the following day, November 3rd. That day Jack Davis, the younger brother of Mildred Davis and the brother-in-law of Harold Lloyd and who had appeared as a child in the very first Our Gang shorts of 1922-24 passed away at the age of seventy-eight.

The funeral mass was held at the St. Paul Apostle Church in Westwood on Thursday evening, November 5, 1992. Gaylord Carter, the old time silent movie organist, played the church organ. The large church was filled with about 200 friends and family. "Our Gang" veterans George "Spanky" McFarland, Eugene "Pineapple" Jackson, Dorothy "Echo" de Borba, Darwood "Waldo" Kaye, Tommy "Butch" Bond, and Buckwheat's son William V. Thomas were there. Ironically, and another proof of Hal Roach's timing, is that it was seventy years ago to the day—November 5, 1922—that the very first "Our Gang" comedy was released. Stan Laurel's daughter Lois Laurel Hawes and her husband Tony were there, and a dark, turbaned Indian sat in the pew behind me. He told me and the little pixie-like lady who takes care of "Our Gang" vet Joe Cobb who was sitting next to him, that he was "the last person to see Hal Roach alive." He was Hal's next door neighbor. Sons of the Desert aficionados were there, including my old friend Rick Greene, with whom I had visited Mr. Roach ten years previously. As I was leaving the church, none other than Anita Garvin, eighty-five at the time, gave me a look with her sharp eagle-eyes and for a moment I thought she suspected that I might be about to lob a custard pie in her direction!

Hal Roach's body was flown to his home town of Elmira, New York. He was buried alongside his mother, father, brother Jack, and near that other great American humorist he once met as a boy, Mark Twain.

"It was just me and his three daughters, along with Frances Hilton," wrote Roach's friend and associate Richard W. Bann in January 2014, "who attended the internment in Elmira. As a result of my bringing him an offer to visit his hometown in the the mid-'80s, he rekindled his love of the place and changed his mind about where he would be buried."

Charles Champlin wrote an admiring "appreciation" that appeared in the *Los Angeles Times* on November 4, 1992. Champlin concluded: "In lamenting Hal Roach, we lament as well the passing of that glorious era of those majestic and irreplaceable clowns—Laurel and Hardy high among them—who with and without words made us laugh and cry and recognize our own foolish frailties."

An era had ended, yet I knew the spirit would endure, that spirit reflected in all the films that remained and those that were still to be rediscovered, and in the videos and digital files that would be made from them and screened on computers and mobile devices and in theaters and classrooms and meeting places around the world. Yes, these moving images would continue to delight audiences in the coming generations.

— THE END

Epilogue
The Second Hundred Years
Preserving and Sharing the Legacy
1993-2093

THE LEGACY DOES INDEED LIVE ON as the decade of the 1990s saw the birth of the Internet, the arrival of DVDs, the steady improvement in digital technologies including big screen television, Blu-ray HD etc., and the consolidation of global communication. Indeed, in the more than twenty years since his passing, Hal Roach's gifts to the world have multiplied and expanded. In the early days, a movie disappeared into the vaults once it had run its course. Now, even the oldest of films are available to the public 24/7 and the continual discoveries of lost films as well as the great restoration projects yet underway ensure the public will have added cinematic treasures to enjoy as the future unfolds.

Richard W. Bann, a tireless defender of the Roach legacy and a valiant force behind film restoration and preservation who had worked for Blackhawk Films, the Hal Roach Studios' principal non-theatrical licensee, in the 1970s, was personally offered original Hal Roach Studios film material by Hallmark, "which at the time was paying to store the nitrate in Los Angeles... As much as I felt a proprietary interest in the Hal Roach library, as a moral imperative I easily reasoned that a far more worthy custodian would obviously be the UCLA Film & Television Archive, and with the aid of associate curator Rob Stone (then at UCLA, now with the Library of Congress), we steered the collection there, where it resides now."

"So UCLA now has the best surviving nitrate," writes Bann, "and is soliciting tax-deductible donations large and small from anyone and everyone all over the world. If devotees wish to give something back and to feel as though they have made a contribution to propagating the spirit and genius of Laurel & Hardy insofar as insuring the films will survive in as many archives as possible and continue to entertain as many future generations as possible, here is the opportunity they have been waiting for. The films *are* already beautifully preserved and stored in Munich, but corporate interests serve a different purpose than an institutional film archive at a leading American university which is perhaps more interested in the cultural value of classic comedies."

As an homage to the Our Gang comedies, Universal Pictures and Amblin Entertainment released *The Little Rascals* in August 1994 directed by Penelope Spheeris. The new kids' comedy received decidedly mixed reviews. Leonard Maltin gave it two stars. "Aimed squarely at young children, who will probably enjoy it," he wrote in his *Movie Guide*, "though it's no match for the original 1930s Hal Roach comedy shorts."

In the Spring of 2014 Capital Arts Entertainment and Universal Pictures released a new direct to DVD feature *The Little Rascals Save the Day* directed by Alex Zamm with Doris Roberts as Grandma. The verdict from dvdverdict.com: "...very young children will probably enjoy the mayhem, but adults will tune out quickly." *Influx Magazine*, on the other hand, called it "A surprisingly pleasant family film and a nice homage to the original Little Rascals."

Hal Roach's original movies have been available to the home market on VHS cassette since the late 1970s. The first Roach product on DVD to be made available to the public came with the release of *The Lost Films of Laurel & Hardy*, a collection of silents in several volumes, in December 1998. These quickly went out of print and now command premium collectors' prices.

In June of 2003, DVD overtook VHS as the dominant home video format. A year later, from the United Kingdom, came a 21-disc set of Laurel & Hardy silents, talkie shorts, and several features. In the U.S., 2004 saw the release by Kino Video (now Kino Lorber) of many of Harold Lloyd's 1918-1922 shorts as well as *The Stan Laurel Collection* followed by *The Oliver Hardy Collection*. Beginning in 2004 Nostalgia Merchant has released multiple disc DVD sets of restored Hal Roach Studios television series, including *Trouble With Father*, *The Life of Riley*, *Blondie*, *Topper*, and *The Gale Storm Show: O! Susanna*.

In 1998 a Charley Chase biography was published, *Smile When the Raindrops Fall*, by Brian Anthony and Andy Edmonds. A number of Charley Chase shorts have became available on DVD and in 2007 Chase's 1926 short, *Mighty Like A Moose*, became a selection by the National Film Registry of the Library of Congress to be one of twenty-five U.S. films "with cultural or historical significance" to be preserved that year. In November 2012 Milestone Cinemateque released a two-disc collection of sixteen Chase silents from 1924-26 providing over five hours of entertainment.

In 2008 *The Little Rascals Complete Collection* was released on DVD and comprised eighty restored and uncut talkie shorts from 1929-1938. This eight-disc anthology includes commentaries by historians as well as interviews with surviving Our Gang members. In 2009 more Charley Chase shorts were released on DVD and in 2010, Germany's Filmmuseum released "(Hal Roach) *Female Comedy Teams*," a two-disc, 12-short collection of Thelma Todd/ZaSu Pitts/Patsy Kelly comedies and *A Pair of Tights*, the 1928 silent classic starring Anita Garvin and Marion Byron. *Harold Lloyd the Definitive Collection* a nine-DVD Box set was released by Optimum Studios in the United Kingdom. And a Max Davidson two-set DVD from Germany includes eighteen shorts as well as Roach's first talkie release *Hurdy Gurdy* in English with German subtitles. In June 2009 two of Roach's silent Westerns *Thundering Hoofs* and *King of the Wild Horses* were released on DVD. In 2010 Synergy Entertainment released a two volume DVD set of *My Little Margie* episodes. Along with this TV series, *The Veil* and *The Public Defender* are also available via Amazon Instant Video.

From January 4th to 25th, 2011, Turner Classic Movies presented a mammoth Hal Roach Tribute, a once-a-week, 24-hour marathon which included fifty-three Our Gang shorts, the forty Laurel & Hardy talkie shorts, and three of their features, seventeen other Roach features including such rarities as *Nobody's Baby* (1937), *There Goes My Heart* (1938), *Merrily We Live* (1938), *Captain Fury* (1939), and *Turnabout* (1940). Also aired for the first time in over fifty years were ten *Screen Directors Playhouse* television episodes from the series that was filmed at the Roach Studios and which aired on NBC-TV in 1955-56. The episodes of this prestigious program, made from new digital video transfers, were directed by the likes of John Ford, Alan Dwan, Fred Zinnemann, Frank Tuttle, Ida Lupino, and Hal Roach veterans Leo McCarey and George Marshall. Even his 1914 extra pal Frank Borzage directed three episodes. Great actors in these casts include John Wayne and Erroll Flynn (in their television debuts), Buster Keaton, Rod Steiger, Ray Milland, Robert Ryan, Angela Lansbury, Jeanette McDonald, William Bendix, a young Dennis Hopper, and more! If this weren't enough, more Hal Roach shorts were aired on TCM that glorious month, including rarities with Harry Langdon, Charley Chase, *The Taxi Boys* and *Boy Friends*, Todd/ZaSu Pitts/Patsy Kelly and Lyda Roberti. More rare Hal Roach shorts have been restored and aired on TCM during the ensuing years, films that have been virtually unseen by the public since their initial release eighty and ninety years ago.

In 2011, UCLA's Film and Television Archive announced their years-long project to restore all of the Hal Roach films in their collection. In October of that year the long-anticipated ten disc box set, *Laurel & Hardy: The Essential Collection*, was released. Produced by RHI Entertainment (which became Sonar Entertainment in March 2012), this magnificent product has more than thirty-two hours of meticulously restored material including all forty of Laurel & Hardy's talkie shorts, Spanish and French foreign language versions of several shorts, and ten features, along with commentaries and many bonus materials. The digital audio and video restoration process was immaculate and impressive and has been universally praised.

In 2011-2012 several Roach features and streamliners of the late '30s and early '40s became available on DVD including *Vagabond Lady*, *Mr. Cinderella*, *Pick A Star*, *Nobody's Baby*, *Road Show* and *Miss Polly*.

In 2012, Laurel & Hardy's 1933 feature *Sons of the Desert* was selected by the National Film Registry as one of their twenty-five films to be preserved that year. 2012 also saw the appreciation society known as Hollywood Party, founded in 2000 by archivist Stan Taffel and a group of enthusiasts dedicated to the preservation and exhibition of motion pictures made by Hal Roach Studios, begin their regular monthly meetings and screenings at the Hollywood Heritage Museum located in the historic Lasky-DeMille Barn.

In 2012 a biography of Charlie Hall appeared, *This Is More Than I Can Stand*, by fellow Brit from Birmingham, United Kingdom Sons of the Desert Sheik John Ullah.

As a testament to the continued improvement and development of digital technology, in October of 2012 Laurel & Hardy's 1934 feature, *Babes in Toyland*, (released as *March of the Wooden Soldiers*) was presented in a newly restored 3D, Blu-ray DVD. In 2013, for the ninetieth anniversary of the release of Harold Lloyd's *Safety Last*, Janus Films created a new digital restoration of the feature released on Blu Ray by The Criterion Collection. It was a 2K transfer of an original nitrate print. Over 300 hours of digital work went into cleaning the image. Composer Carl Davis then re-synced his original 1989 score to the restored master to create the best possible match for theatrical presentation. Gaylord Carter's traditional organ score can be heard on an alternate soundtrack. Three Lloyd shorts have also been restored and included with this DVD, *Take A Chance* (1918), *Young Mr. Jazz* (1919) and *His Royal Slyness* (1920).

In March 2014 Janus and the Criterion Collection restored Harold Lloyd's feature *The Freshman* in a new 4K digital transfer. *The Freshman* was produced by Lloyd after he left Roach, but along with this restored feature are included with this DVD three newly restored Roach-produced Lloyd shorts *The Marathon* (1919), *An Eastern Westerner* (1920) and *High and Dizzy* (1920).

Also in 2014 two of Roach's silent features became available on DVD, Glenn Tryon's *The Battling Orioles* and the Western *No Man's Law* starring Rex the Wonder Horse, Oliver Hardy, James Finlayson, Barbara Kent and Theodore von Eltz, which was restored to its full 76 minute length. Barbara Kent, by the way, lived to the venerable age of 103. She passed away in 2011.

Many of Hal Roach's films and clips, as well as interviews and documentaries, can all be viewed for free on the Internet. There are Facebook pages devoted to his works, including the fabulous 'Laurel Hardy Archive' created by Harry Hoppe of Dusseldorf that shares hundreds of rare photographs and stills culled from the earliest days of Hal Roach's career. And there is the website Another Nice Mess created by Dave 'Lord' Heath in 2011 devoted to the films of Laurel & Hardy which is filled with fascinating facts, photos and endless delightful trivia about the boys, their films (both as a team and when they were solo), their supporting players, their directors, etc. The website continues to expand; it now includes the other major Hal Roach stars and series from the teens through the '30s.

In Spring 2013 a hefty 522-page tome with the equally lengthy title *Smileage Guaranteed: Past Humor, Present Laughter. Musings on the Comedy Film Industry 1910-1945 Volume One: Hal Roach* was published. It is unusual in that it focuses on Roach's lesser known comedians, such as Charley Chase, Snub Pollard, Glenn Tryon, Max Davidson, Eddie Boland, Clyde Cook, Toto and The Spat Family. Although Roach's prolific talkie period is provided a mere twenty-five pages, *Smileage Guaranteed* contains a profusion of extremely entertaining and very rare photographs, and possibly the most complete Roach filmography yet published.

There are even museums dedicated to the life and works of Stan Laurel and Oliver Hardy. The Laurel & Hardy Museum in Harlem, Georgia presented its first annual Oliver Hardy Festival in 1989 and it continues strong, the first Saturday in October. The museum itself opened in 2002. Across the pond in Ulverston, England a little room was dedicated as The Laurel & Hardy Museum in 1983. Twenty-six years later, on April 19, 2009 a newly expanded museum opened in the Roxy Cinema Complex complete with a statue of Stan Laurel.

In July 2014 The Sons of the Desert held their international convention in Hollywood; yours truly introduced this very book to the fans and conventioneers at the Loew's Hotel. A selection of rare Roach comedies was screened at the historic Egyptian Theatre, and at the Hollywood Museum located in the Max Factor Building, a wonderful exhibit "100 Years of Hal Roach Studios: Laurel & Hardy, Our Gang and Harold Lloyd" delighted the public.

Many of the rare items in the exhibit including stills, movie posters, Roach's 1984 honorary Oscar, a menu from the studio's Our Gang Cafe, a blueprint of the entire layout of the studio, original scripts, a collar worn by Our Gang's Pete the Dog, Laurel & Hardy's suits, as well as the plaque that was presented to The Boys on the television show *This Is Your Life* in 1954, rescued from storage after sixty years – were all donated by collectors, particularly members of the Sons of the Desert, which co-sponsored the show in conjunction with their convention.

The Hal Roach Studios Exhibit was so popular it was extended through October 2014.

Despite all these developments, there is still the desire for *more* Hal Roach comedies. One example is the Hal Roach DVD Petition Drive, wherein fans are urged to contact Sonar Entertainment so that the public can enjoy on DVD all forty-one Todd/Pitts/Kelly shorts, ten *Taxi Boys* shorts, 104 Charley Chase shorts, fifteen *Boy Friends* shorts, and three from the *Dippy Doo Dads* series. (While we're at it, what about the Max Davidson series, the Will Rogers silents and the 1929-1930 Harry Langdon talkie shorts?)

Even one of the Our Gang kids is still active. Jean Darling, born in 1922 returned to the screen for the first time in sixty years to play Lady Cavendish in a fifteen minute short entitled *The Butler's Tale* directed by René Riva. Jean had appeared in some thirty-four Our Gang shorts from 1927 to 1929 (including the Gang's first five talkies). She returned in 1934 for an uncredited appearance as Curly Locks in Laurel & Hardy's *Babes In Toyland* and then moved Back East to work on the stage. Jean made just one more movie, the 1953 musical *The I Don't Care Girl*, and didn't return to acting in front of the camera until sixty years later, when in 2013 at the age of ninety-one she appeared in *The Butler's Tale*. That must be some sort of record, and I am so happy Jean Darling has provided me with some of her memories for this book.

In May 2014 a German video documentary *Hollywood's Fun Factory*, all about Hal Roach's career, by Andreas Baum, was released. The documentary has some great rare photos, there is excellent interview footage of Hal Roach from the later years and the present day interviewees, including two of his daughters, his grandson Addison Randall, Lois Laurel Hawes and Richard W. Bann, all well chosen and well photographed—but the fact that all these American voices were DUBBED—as were Stan and Ollie's voices—horribly so—in random oddly inserted clips (many badly colorized), merely makes one think of all the trouble Mr. Roach went through in the early talkie days to create his foreign language versions. The producers of this documentary should have allowed us to hear the voices in their original languages, to honor the spirit of international courtesy.

And why did they spend so much time rehashing the Fatty Arbuckle scandal and Buster Keaton's career, even if Buster did appear in one Roach-produced TV show in the '50s? The documentary was about Hal Roach and his studio and should have stayed completely focused on the Roach cast of characters, many of whom were not even mentioned. The often portentous, solemn and deeply serious tone of the narration also belied the Hal Roach experience. Still, and despite all, it's nice to know that in this day and age at least Mr. Roach, Stan and Ollie, Harold Lloyd and the Gang are still so fondly remembered.

The future is sure to bring even more surprises as well as technological developments and improvements. Hal Roach was a visionary; he was always forward thinking and forward moving, and his remarkably fertile and vibrant legacy is sure to live on and on.

Richard W. Bann, Hal Roach's long-time business associate, friend and companion during the latter years, should have the last word. Mr. Bann has worked tirelessly for decades in the fields of film scholarship and restoration to keep the Hal Roach legacy alive and here are some insightful comments Mr. Bann made on Facebook in 2013:

"Hal was always a gentleman, a dignified gentleman... But no one could ever take advantage of him, and he commanded, deserved and received great respect, always. The better he knew you, however, the tougher he could be... Being such an original thinker, with such a great sense of humor, he could effortlessly see things in a fresh, new way, and fast, like no one else could. And best of all would be to see him interact with Hal Roach Studios alumni; you'd see the enormous respect they held him in, and how he'd tell them what they should do, or what he wanted them to do, giving orders and sizing up a situation with clear thinking and brainpower that amazed me. I'd be a witness to these events and think WOW this is the man I would have seen running Hal Roach Studios in 1920, or 1930, or 1940, or 1950.

"Those were treasured glimpses into the past when I'd see things like that taking place. At every age, even 100, he was still Hal Roach. Everything he'd been and done, it was still all there, even if stratified beneath the layers. Once in a while you'd see the man Will Rogers knew, or Thelma Todd knew. Like the time he threw that book about her [*Hot Toddy*] across his living room at the fireplace because he wanted SO MUCH to protect the reputation of his defenseless friend, long dead.

"'No one was ever better liked at the studio than she was,' he said on her behalf.

"It was easy to see why the people who worked there showed him such fierce loyalty, and I mean everyone I ever met who worked there. But he didn't live in the past, nor did he feel any need to prove anything to anyone. What a great man."

Bibliography

BOOKS:

Anthony, Brian and Edmonds, Andy, *Smile While The Raindrops Fall* (Lantham, MD: Scarecrow Press, 1998)

Barr, Charles, *Laurel & Hardy* (Berkeley, CA: University of California Press 1968)

Barrios, Richard, *Screened Out: Playing Gay in Hollywood from Edison to Stonewall* (New York: Routledge, 2003)

Bennett, Joan and Kibbee, Lois, *The Joan Bennett Playbill* (New York: Holt, Rinehart & Winston, New York: 1970)

Bogdanovich, Peter, *Who The Devil Made It?* (New York: Alfred A. Knopf, Inc., 1997)

Bond, Tommy "Butch" with Ron Genni, *Darn Right It's Butch* (Wayne, PA: Morgan Press, Inc. 1994)

Brooks, Tim and Marsh, Earle, *The Complete Directory to Prime Time Network and Cable TV Shows 1946-Present* (New York: Random House, 2003)

Crafton, Donald, and Koszarski, Richard, *History of American Cinema: The Talkies: U.S. Cinema's Transition to Sound, 1926-31* (New York: Charles Scribner's Sons, 1997)

Donati, William, *The Life and Death of Thelma Todd* (Jefferson, NC: McFarland & Company, 2011)

Durgnat, Raymond, *The Crazy Mirror, Hollywood Comedy and the American Image* (London: Faber and Faber Limited, 1969)

Eliot, Marc, *Cary Grant* (New York: Harmony Books, 2004)

Epstein, Edward Jay, *The Big Picture, The New Logic of Money and Power in Hollywood* (New York: Random House, 2005)

Everson, William K., *The Films of Hal Roach* (New York: Museum of Modern Art, 1971)

Everson, William K., *The Films of Laurel & Hardy* (New York: The Citadel Press, 1967)

Eyman, Scott, *Lion of Hollywood: The Life and Legend of Louis B. Mayer* (New York: Simon & Schuster, 2012)

Gans, Eric, *Carole Landis A Most Beautiful Girl* (Jackson, MS: University of Mississippi Press, 2008)

Hake, Sabine, *Screen Nazis: Cinema, History and Democracy* (Madison, WI: The University of Wisconsin Press, 2012)

Lloyd, Annette D'Agostino, *Harold Lloyd, Magic in a Pair of Horn-Rimmed Glasses* (Albany, GA: BearManor Media, 2009)

Louvish, Simon, *Stan and Ollie* (New York: St. Martin's Press, 2002)

Magill, Frank N., *Magill's Survey of Cinema* (Englewood Cliffs, NJ: Salem Press, 1982)

Maltin, Leonard, *Leonard Maltin's 2007 Movie Guide* (New York: Penguin Group, 2006)

Maltin, Leonard and Bann, Richard W., *The Little Rascals: The Life and Times of Our Gang* (Crown Publishers, Inc., 1977, 1992)

McCabe, John, *The Comedy World of Stan Laurel* (Beverly Hills: Moonstone Press, 1974, 1990)

McCabe, John, *Mr. Laurel & Mr. Hardy* (New York: Grosset & Dunlap, 1961, 1966)

McCabe, John and Kilgore, Al, *Laurel & Hardy* (New York: E.P. Dutton, 1975)

McKay, James, *The Films of Victor Mature* (Jefferson, NC: McFarland & Company, 2013)

Okuda, Ted and Neibaur, James L., *Stan Without Ollie: The Stan Laurel Solo Films, 1917-1927* (Jefferson, NC and London: McFarland and Company, Inc., 2012)

Roberts, Richard M., *et al.*, *Smileage Guaranteed Past Humor, Present Laughter: Musings on the Comedy Film Industry 1910-1945 Volume One: Hal Roach* (Phoenix: Practical Press, 2013)

Rosenberg, Bernard and Silverstein, Harry, *The Real Tinsel* (London: The MacMillan Company, 1970)

Schickel, Richard, *D.W. Griffith, An American Life* (New York: Proscenium Publishers, 1984)

Schickel, Richard, *Harold Lloyd, The Shape of Laughter* (Boston: New York Graphic Society, 1974)

Shipman, David, *The Great Movie Stars* (New York: Little, Brown and Company, 1970, 1995)

Skretvedt, Randy, *Laurel and Hardy, The Magic Behind the Movies* (Beverly Hills: Moonstone Press, 1987, 1994)

Smith, Don G., *Lon Chaney Jr. Horror Film Star 1906-1973* (Jefferson, NC: McFarland & Co., Inc., 1996)

Sperber, A.M. & Lax, Eric, *Bogart* (New York: William Morrow and Company, Inc. 1997)

Steen, Mike, *Hollywood Speaks! An Oral History* (New York: G.P. Putnam's Sons, 1974)

Stone, Rob, *Laurel Or Hardy, The Solo Films of Stan Laurel and Oliver "Babe" Hardy* (Temecula, CA: Split Reel Books, 1996)

Thrasher, Frederick, editor, *Okay For Sound How The Screen Found Its Voice* (New York: Duell, Sloan & Pearce, Inc, 1946)

Vance, Jeffrey and Lloyd, Suzanne, *Harold Lloyd: Master Comedian* (Harry N. Abrahams, 2002)

Walker, John, Editor, *Halliwell's Filmgoer's Companion,* 12th Edition (New York: HarperCollins, 1997)

Wansell, Geoffrey, Cary Grant, *Dark Angel* (New York: Arcade Publishing, 1996, 2011)

Ward, Richard Lewis, *A History of the Hal Roach Studios* (Southern Illinois University Press, 2005)

ARCHIVES:

Hal Roach Collection and Hollywood Museum Collection, USC Cinematic Arts Library (Los Angeles, California)

National Archives at Riverside (Perris, California)

NEWSPAPERS:

Atlanta Constitution
Baltimore Sun
Boston Globe
Chicago Daily Tribune
The Chicago Defender
Evening Independent (St. Petersburg, Florida)
Hartford Courant
International News Service
Los Angeles Examiner
Los Angeles Herald & Express

Los Angeles Mirror News
Los Angeles Times
The Memphis Flyer
The Morning Oregonian (Portland)
New York Amsterdam News
The New York Sun
New York Times
New York World-Telegram
Palm Beach (Florida) *Daily News*
Reading (Pennsylvania) *Eagle*
Wall Street Journal
Washington Post
Watertown (New York) *Herald*

MAGAZINES:

Box Office
The Film Daily
The Film Daily & Weekly Film Digest
Films and Filming
Harrison's Reports
Hollywood
The Hollywood Reporter
Interview
Liberty
Motion Picture
Motion Picture Classic
Motion Picture Exhibitors Herald-World
Motion Picture Herald
Motion Picture News
Moving Picture World
New Movie
Photoplay
Picture-Play
The Silent Picture
Vanity Fair
Variety
Village Voice

Websites:

Another Nice Mess
Brittanica.com
Charley-Chase.com
Death in Toyland
Hollywood Renegades Archive
Internet Movie Database
Laurel Hardy Archive
Laurel-and-Hardy.com
Letters From Stan
The Lucky Corner
Wikipedia, etc.

Television Documentary:

Hollywood, Thames Television, 1980

About the Author

CRAIG CALMAN is an actor, writer and director, a native of California. He studied at Pacific University, Forest Grove, Oregon; traveled and studied in Mexico at the Universidad de Querétaro and made a 45 minute film documentary about Mexico at the age of 20. Accepted to the UCLA Motion Picture/Television Department, he graduated in 1975.

Craig then became a professional stage actor and performed in classical and repertory theatres as well as in summer stock from California to New York to Boston. Winner of the Old Globe Theatre [San Diego, California] Atlas Award 1977-78 for his portrayal of Private Meek in George Bernard Shaw's "Too True To Be Good." Other roles: The Vagabond in "The Tavern," Rosencrantz in both "Hamlet" and "Rosencrantz & Guildenstern Are Dead" [Boston Shakespeare Company], leading roles in "The Firebugs," "Madame De" "The Good Doctor" and "Charley's Aunt."

Following his travels around the United States as an actor he settled in New York City where he lived for most of the '80s. He then returned to Los Angeles where he worked behind the scenes as an executive assistant at many of the major motion picture studios including Walt Disney, MGM/UA, Twentieth-Century Fox and Orion Pictures Corporation.

Craig is the author of numerous plays and screenplays. For five years he was a member of the Actors Studio West Playwright/Director Unit. As an actor, his television, video and film roles include *Flesteron In Amazonia, Teamwork* and *Commercial Break*. He appeared as the memorable Anthony Zipper on both the radio and television versions of *The Howard Stern Show* in the year 2000 which inspired the production of his first digital video feature some years later, *The Calistra Zipper Story* which he filmed, directed and edited and which was a se-

355

lection of the first annual Zero Film Festival in 2008 where it won the Purple Heart Award; the video also received an Award of Merit from The Indie Fest in 2009.

From 2010-14 Craig worked as an office employee for the fictitious New York City ad agency Sterling Cooper Draper Pryce (later Sterling Cooper & Partners) on the acclaimed Emmy-award winning television series *Mad Men* from Seasons 4 to 7 where he can be glimpsed walking the corridors, chatting with secretaries and going up and down stairs whilst the stars emote.

In December 2014 Craig worked as an actor on the Coen Brothers newest movie *Hail, Caesar!* a comedy set in Hollywood in 1950.

His website is www.craigcalman.com.

Index

357